The English Rebel

The English Rebel

One Thousand Years of Troublemaking,
from the Normans to the Nineties

DAVID HORSPOOL

VIKING
an imprint of
PENGUIN BOOKS

VIKING

Published by the Penguin Group

Penguin Books Ltd, 80 Strand, London WC2R ORL, England
Penguin Group (USA) Inc., 375 Hudson Street, New York, New York 10014, USA
Penguin Group (Canada), 90 Eglinton Avenue East, Suite 700, Toronto, Ontario, Canada M4P 2Y3
(a division of Pearson Penguin Canada Inc.)
Penguin Ireland, 25 St Stephen's Green, Dublin 2, Ireland (a division of Penguin Books Ltd)
Penguin Group (Australia), 250 Camberwell Road, Camberwell, Victoria 3124, Australia
(a division of Pearson Australia Group Pty Ltd)
Penguin Books India Pvt Ltd, 11 Community Centre, Panchsheel Park, New Delhi – 110 017, India
Penguin Group (NZ), 67 Apollo Drive, Rosedale, North Shore 0632, New Zealand
(a division of Pearson New Zealand Ltd)
Penguin Books (South Africa) (Pty) Ltd, 24 Sturdee Avenue, Rosebank, Johannesburg 2196, South Africa

Penguin Books Ltd, Registered Offices: 80 Strand, London WC2R ORL, England

www.penguin.com

First published in 2009
1

Set in 12/14.75pt Monotype Bembo
Typeset by Rowland Phototypesetting Ltd, Bury St Edmunds, Suffolk
Printed in Great Britain by Clays Ltd, St Ives plc

A CIP catalogue record for this book is available from the British Library

ISBN: 978–0–670–91619–1

www.greenpenguin.co.uk

For Jules

Men would be angels, angels would be gods.
Aspiring to be gods, if angels fell,
Aspiring to be angels, men rebel.

Alexander Pope, *An Essay on Man* (1733–4)

Contents

Illustrations *page 232*

Acknowledgements

Rebels in English history have been on my mind at least since I was given a copy of R. J. Unstead's book *Princes and Rebels* by my parents. I don't suppose they would have expected it to take more than thirty years for the gift to bear fruit, but it is thanks to them, first of all, that it has. My mother knows how much effort goes into writing a book and preparing it for publication, and has been a reassuring comparer of notes. My father has read this book chapter by chapter as it was being written, and has proved an ideal constructive critic, as well as a generous lender of Oxford Histories. My much-missed uncle Lodewijk Blok, who died just as I was coming to the end of writing this, was a historian of the Netherlands who was always encouraging of his nephew's ideas about English history. My family debts extend to my brother, and to my mother- and father-in-law, who provided in Dorset one of the many different homes in which the book took shape. My second home has been the London Library, where all things – books, reading room and staff – are congenial to reading, writing and thinking.

At the *Times Literary Supplement*, my editor, Peter Stothard, was uncomplainingly accommodating, while my colleagues – particularly Robert Potts and Adrian Tahourdin – were always supportive. Rupert Shortt has not only been a wonderful sounding-board, but also an example of authorial professionalism. Martin Smith's help with picture research was invaluable. Outside the office, both Harry Mount and Mark Bostridge have repeatedly bolstered my confidence, and shown how friendship and authorship needn't be mutually exclusive. To Harry I owe also the recommendation of the peerless Douglas Matthews to index the book. Katie Bond's shared experience of the publishing process has kept me sane.

Peter Straus was the first person to convince me that this book was one worth writing. In finding a home for it at Viking, he also introduced me to the ideal editor in Kate Barker, who constantly realigned my thinking, and patiently helped me turn a series of chapters into a book. Will Hammond, Sarah Hulbert and Mark Handsley have all carried through the good work.

Several wiser heads have kindly agreed to read the book and share their thoughts before publication, including Professors Diane Purkiss, Peter Hennessy, David Kynaston and Linda Colley, as well as Ferdinand Mount. Professor Nicholas Vincent of the University of East Anglia did even more, combing through the text and giving me the benefit of his extraordinary erudition and insight. With such formidable help, errors shouldn't remain, but those that do are most certainly my own fault.

My greatest thanks go to the two people who have had to put up with this book pretty much all the time for about three years. My son Jude has lived cheerfully with English rebels in term time and on holiday. To say that the book couldn't have been written without my wife, Jules, would miss the point. Nothing in my life would work without her, but she has constantly spurred me on – reading, helping to correct, typing up new text, gently suggesting ways of improving what was already there – and carved out time from her own much busier schedule to enable me to work. All that should have received far more recognition than it did. Dedicating this book to her doesn't begin to cover the thanks I owe her, or the love.

Introduction

For we are the people of England, that never have spoken yet.

G. K. Chesterton, 'The Secret People' (1915)

Rebels, unlike rulers, don't often get the chance to build things. The easiest bits of our heritage to remember are those we can see, the castles, palaces and country houses that still survive all around us. But rebellion is part of England's heritage too. If I were asked to take someone on a rebels' tour of London, I might start in Stoke Newington in north London, say Walford Road, where one of the Angry Brigade was picked up in 1972, and a stone's throw from the flat on Amhurst Road that four Angries turned into a bomb factory. Then we could head for Church Street, past Defoe Road, where Daniel Defoe, who fought with the rebel Duke of Monmouth in the last pitched battle on English soil, once lived. Somewhere on Church Street itself stood Wallingford House, where a clique of New Model Army officers led by Charles Fleetwood gathered to plan the overthrow of Richard Cromwell, the unlucky heir to the reluctant revolutionary Oliver, who was flunking the Army's idea of how the country should be run. From Stoke Newington, we could start to travel into central London, going past Highbury, where the medieval manor was 'consigned to destruction in the ravening flames' by Essex rebels in the Peasants' Revolt of 1381. As we reached Clerkenwell, we would pass Spa Fields, where a meeting of parliamentary reformers turned into an insurrectionary riot in 1816; and Cold Bath Square, once Cold Bath Fields, where a policeman was killed in a rebellious demonstration after the 'betrayal' of the Great Reform Act in 1833. We could pause for a moment at Gray's Inn, where Thomas Percy, one of the Gunpowder Plotters of 1605, stayed in a local pub on the night before Guy Fawkes was discovered.

Actually, what I've described isn't a special tour of London designed to take in historical associations with rebellion. It's my school run and journey to work. Most journeys in London could be rebel tours. The journey to my old office used to take me past Hoxton, where Lord Mounteagle received the letter that revealed the Gunpowder Plot, and past the Tower, which rebels attacked, were imprisoned in, escaped from or were executed at, for about 800 years. If I came in from south London, I could stop at London Bridge, where (in the bridge's earlier incarnation) rebels resisted William the Conqueror, where the Kent contingent of the Peasants' Revolt crossed into the City and where Jack Cade's rebels fought a bloody battle in 1450. Rebels, like rulers, tended to aim for the capital, but from Cornwall to Norfolk, from Sussex to Northumbria, England is crisscrossed with the ghosts of rebels marching, meeting and fighting.

So perhaps the first thing to say about English rebels is that G. K. Chesterton was wrong: the people of England have spoken repeatedly. The idea that English history is one of peaceful evolution or a 'silent' populace, dominated by solid uncomplaining yeomen or loyal public servants, is a fantasy. It is, admittedly, one with a long pedigree, visible in Edmund Burke's self-satisfied trust in the 'simplicity of our national character and . . . a sort of native plainness' as a safeguard for a conservative constitution, or Wyndham Lewis's ideal Englishman: 'straightforward, tolerant, peaceable, humane, unassuming, patient'. But to accept that these are the principal characteristics of English history or English people is to ignore those times when tolerance, peaceability and patience were cast aside. Nor is rebellion confined to 'the people'. English rebellion has permeated English society, from top to bottom.

It is worth trying to outline, if only loosely, what I mean by a rebel. Perhaps the easiest way to define the term is negatively, by what isn't required. Rebels don't have to have tried to overthrow the government, let alone the state. They don't have to have been violent. They don't have to have been 'left-wing'. I have mostly confined myself to overtly political rebellion, as cultural rebellion would require another book. But rebels are more than straightforward political opponents. They are opponents who take serious risks, of losing life, limb or liberty. So most peaceful demonstrations, MPs not toeing the party line, or strikes after striking was legalized don't count. Although some, which went beyond expressions of dissatisfaction or simple trade disputes into challenges on the status quo or to the government, do.

The concentration on 'English' rebels is deliberate, more than an expression of a geographical limit (or a lazy shorthand for 'British'). England's history as a colonizer, first of its own island, then of its archipelago, sporadically of parts of the Continent of Europe, and eventually of a third of the world, can be an obstacle to seeing the importance of the rebel tradition at home. A country that spends so much time putting down external rebellion seems less likely to contain a rebellious nature itself. In a British context, let alone an imperial one, rebellion usually had different objectives. A book about the Irish, Scottish or Indian rebel would tap into a well-recognized tradition. The search for English identity, for what makes the English different, has been addressed with increasing urgency as Scottish, Welsh and Irish identity becomes ever more confidently defined. Historians of England often point to 'continuity in the institutions of government', the fact that 'in no other [country] has there been such continuity in the exercise of effective authority over so wide an area for so long', as the feature that marks England out. But English 'individualism' has also been a constant, and that has more to do with the numbers of Englishmen and women who were rebels rather than conservatives by instinct. As for those institutions, many of them, from Parliament to the police, have their origins tied up with the history of rebellion.

The English have proved remarkably tenacious rebels, but rather less effective revolutionaries. One of the features of rebellions is that they are likely to end as failures, particularly in the short term. This is partly because if they succeed, they aren't called rebellions any more. Or as Sir John Harington put it rather more eloquently in 1618: 'Treason doth never prosper, what's the reason? / For if it prosper none dare call it treason'. The result is it's easy to think of most (failed) rebellions as insignificant, mere interruptions to the steady flow of the mainstream. Of course, that assumes that we know where the mainstream is going, and that rebels haven't caused an interruption or diversion, however imperceptible at the time. Concentrating on rebels, the ways they tried to interfere with the flow, is a useful corrective to reading the present back into the past, one result of the tendency known as the 'Whig Interpretation' of history. It can cast even the most familiar parts of English history in a different light. So the Norman Conquest is shadowed by the English resistance, the Tudor Reformation by the risings that challenged it, the top-down reform of Parliament by the drawn-out struggle for voting rights. Some rebels can seem 'before their time', introducing democratic or socially levelling ideas that are universally accepted now but were once dismissed. The important thing about these rebels, however, as well as the ones who promoted causes that seem less palatable to us (the xenophobes, religious bigots and megalomaniacs whom we will also encounter), is that they were *of* their time. It is important that they had their ideas and promoted them when they did, and in the circumstances they did.

The fates of most English rebels will explain why the rebel tradition is not a continuous one. The luckier ones survived their rebellions, like the Anglo-Saxon rebels Edgar the Aetheling or Hereward the Wake, defeated and pensioned off to obscurity. Some early rebels even made it back into their master's affections, like Ranulf Flambard, William II's calculating bishop, whom the King couldn't do without. Later rebels were less fortunate, even when their rebellions were less overt. Thomas Becket was murdered and martyred in his own cathedral; Simon de Montfort, butchered, dismembered, his head paraded on a spear just as his son arrived on the battlefield; the popular rebels Wat Tyler and Jack Cade, stabbed in the heat of their uprisings; the 'student revolutionary' William 'Longbeard' fitz Osbert in Richard the Lionheart's reign, dragged like so many others to his place of execution and lingeringly, ritualistically put to death. Even a quiet death couldn't spare some rebels. Oliver Cromwell died in his bed, but his corpse was disinterred after the Restoration, decapitated and the head impaled outside Westminster Hall as a grim warning for almost twenty years. After England's only genuine revolution, rebellion still continued, and rebels were still executed, transported or imprisoned for centuries to come.

But a history of failure is not a history of insignificance. Rebellions reveal the alternative histories contemporaries wanted to write. Different rebels imagined a world where England was still ruled by Anglo-Saxons, where the king couldn't dispense justice on a whim, where a different king, or none at all, might be in charge. Others conceived of England as a 'common property', as a country where every man and (later) every woman had the vote. Some rebels imagined England as a Protestant land, some dreamt of returning it to Catholicism. Some thought that if you just got rid of the Flemings, or the Nonconformists, or the Irish, or the Catholics, or the Jews, England's problems would be solved. Others thought that if you got rid of industrial machinery, or private industry, or capitalism in general, or the banking system, a golden age might return. The least well supported really do seem to have been 'doomed' to failure, and, looking at the list, we can be thankful that some of them were. But, sometimes, the bigots got further than the freedom-fighters with their rebellions. Being a rebel sounds like a badge of honour to many modern ears, but some rebels incline one to more old-fashioned judgements that equate rebellion with wrongdoing. So this book is not about heroes. Some rebels were heroic and public-spirited, but others were self-seeking, manipulative, vicious and venal. Most were a mixture, which is to say that rebels are no different from anyone else.

What succeeds or fails in a rebellion can look predictable, but most things can with hindsight. Recent experience has taught us to be aware of how powerful 'asymmetric' challenges can be, when apparently all-powerful societies can be deeply wounded by under-resourced opponents. Technology may have a lot to do with that today, but even medieval rebels could have a disproportionate influence. Often, rebellions that seemed to have failed could live on. Magna Carta was cast aside before the wax had dried on King John's seal, and if he had survived a bout of overeating a year later, it might have stayed that way. It was only the need to legitimize an embattled minority government that led to the rebels' charter being reissued, with all its consequences for English freedoms, American independence and 'why, oh why' journalism. That rebellion 'succeeded' in the long run, and it forces us to think how others, from Jack Cade to the Jacobites, from the Fifth Monarchists to the miners, might have turned out differently.

I have mentioned a rebel 'tradition', but is there more to English rebellions than a sequence of unrelated reactions to events? Well, it would be absurd to pretend that rebellion runs like an unbroken 'golden thread' through English history. There are (though surprisingly rarely) times without rebellion or the threat of it, and one rebellion does not necessarily draw on its predecessor. Often, rebels stand for the very opposite of what their predecessors fought for, as in the convoluted, serve-and-return history of the English Reformation, which modern historians are surely right to describe in the plural: England didn't have one Reformation; it had several. If we are looking for an analogy for the English rebel tradition, then perhaps it is closer to a scent that goes cold and is picked up again. Nonetheless, some English rebels were inspired by their forebears. Rebels in the seventeenth century looked back to the eleventh. Rebels in the nineteenth century looked back to the thirteenth. And rebels in the twentieth century looked back to the fourteenth. Sometimes the models could be more recent. It seems unlikely that Perkin Warbeck would have been taken to Ireland and set up as a Yorkist pretender if the same thing hadn't been tried for Lambert Simnel a few years earlier. William of Orange learnt from the mistakes of the Duke of Monmouth three years before. The suffragettes examined the example of the Chartists. In 1984, Arthur Scargill tried to re-create the miners' triumph of 1972, which in turn he had seen as laying the ghost of the General Strike of 1926. Many of the examples rebels took from their forebears were mythical versions of what really happened, but myths can have a powerful influence on people, and the myth of the rebel is one of the most powerful. It survives any number of doses of reality. Rebels' myths can also help to challenge more-cherished historical myths, such as the myth of the Tudors ushering in an era of calm after the storms of the Wars of the Roses, or the 'Whig' myth of England's steady march to democracy.

The ways in which the English rebel also link up unexpectedly. Some set up camps, like the 'woodsmen' who joined the English resistance to the Normans, various medieval outlaws, the sixteenth-century followers of the Kett brothers or the women of Greenham Common. Others march, often congregating in the same places, especially if they are marching on the capital: Blackheath and Kennington Common hosted musters of rebels centuries apart. Others conspire, often over a drink. The Gunpowder plotters sealed their conspiracy at the Duck and Drake, the 'ulterior' Chartists in the Orange Tree, the Angry Brigade at the Walford. Dis-agreements over how to rebel also recur. Some rebels draw up programmes of reform, others want a change of personnel. Some believe that only force will get their way, others that violence loses the argument. Most seem agreed, however, that gesture politics are important. That is why 'demonstrating', whether armed or not, is often a synonym for rebelling. Rebels have had to show what they wanted, when asking politely for it was too ineffective and fighting for it was too dangerous. Their ways of doing so – from the medieval baron's *diffidatio* (a formal rebellious ritual), through the blunt language of the eighteenth-century riot, right up to the twentieth-century protestor's targeting of the evening news – have rules as formal as the most venerable of English institutions. Some, like the barons who rebelled against King John in 1215, or the 'Immortal Seven' who invited in the Prince of Orange in 1688, looked for foreign help. Others, like those who rebelled against John's son, Henry III, or Oswald Mosley's Black-shirts, who took to the streets of the East End, thought 'foreigners' were the problem.

We will also encounter more cerebral rebels, like Algernon Sidney or John Locke, though English rebels habitually conform to one stereotype by being stronger on practice than theory.

Rebellion had a lot to do with the development of political thought in England. Theories of the legitimacy of resistance were hugely influenced by the great rebellions. But it is easier to see how the Magna Carta barons, or Simon de Montfort, or the English republicans, or the Glorious Revolutionaries influenced political thought than how political thought influenced them. Thinkers tended to follow on the heels of rebellions, not lead them. Where rebellion can be seen to have been inspired by theories, they tend to be imported ones, like syndicalism or situationism. That is not to play down their significance; English rebellion, like the rest of English history, does not happen in isolation from the wider world.

Finally, the story of the English rebel is a personal story. For the medieval period, which can often seem so remote from our own, we find the origins of rebellion in personal relations again and again. Medieval rebels were sons-, brothers-, fathers-in-law, first and second cousins, uncles, not to mention sons and daughters, of those they rebelled against, as well as of those they rebelled with. The ones who weren't blood-related had very often worked together, either in the royal household or administration, or in military service. When men (and the occasional woman) like these didn't get what they felt was fair treatment, or when others with less conspicuous connections or achievements were favoured instead of them, the reaction could be extreme. Of course, principles lay beneath some of these rebels' actions, and public events – wars, taxes, famines, legal and administrative reforms – had their part to play. Indeed, it is sometimes remarkable how far rebels were willing to curb or adapt their own personal agendas to others' concerns. But very often the nature of the conflict became a matter of personal, frequently wounded, pride: Thomas Becket and Henry II unable to seal their peace agreement with the traditional kiss of peace, Simon de Montfort enraged by Henry III's broken promises, the earls around Edward II goaded to action at the name-calling and baiting by Edward's favourite, Piers Gaveston. Perhaps less unexpectedly, personality carried on fashioning rebels and rebellions in later centuries, from Oliver Cromwell's providential zeal to the Duke of Monmouth's dysfunctional upbringing, through Lord George Gordon's 'twist in his head', right up to the Pankhursts' weakness for melodrama or Mosley's monstrous egotism.

The English rebel may only rarely be a triumphant or even a particularly likeable character. But he and she are as much a part of the fabric of English history as the monarchs, law-makers and political leaders they defied. They serve as inspiration, as warning, and sometimes simply as example. They may not always be visible, but they, too, are all around us.

1. Resistance

The Norman Occupation 1066–86

We have had one king made for us in the last forty years, and we
intend to make the next ourselves.

Charles Kingsley, *Hereward the Wake* (Ch. XXIII)

The story of English rebellion begins with a famous defeat. The
scene, on a ridge a few miles outside a small Sussex town on the
morning of 15 October 1066, is one of the most revisited in English
history. The 'bloodstained battleground was covered with the
flower of the youth and nobility of England'. Only sixty years
later, the familiar verdict on the Battle of Hastings was already in.
This was England's 'fatal day', when the English 'doomed themselves and their country to slavery by giving [William the Con-
queror] an easy victory in a single battle'. At Hastings, the last
Anglo-Saxon king, Harold II, his two loyal brothers, and many of
his greatest lords were wiped out.

When Duke William of Normandy landed unopposed in
Pevensey Bay at the end of September, Anglo-Saxons had been
living and governing in England for roughly 600 years. By comparison, William's own duchy was an upstart domain, a consequence of Viking invasion only 150 years earlier. The English, too,
had suffered numerous invasions, and had survived the imposition
of foreign kings before, but their kingdom had been forged, not
consumed, in those fires. William, the bastard son who had inherited a dukedom, extinguished Anglo-Saxon England for ever.
Yet the Norman Conquest was not the work of a single, bloody
day. The Battle of Hastings is so indelible a moment in English
history, resulting in such an apparently complete break with what
had gone before, that it can seem as if it alone transformed one

nation into another. One reason for that abiding impression may
be that the most famous and memorable account of the Conquest,
the Bayeux Tapestry, ends with William's triumph on the field of
battle: *Et fuga verterunt Angli* – 'And the English turned to flight.'
(In fact, this is only how the embroidery has survived to modern
times; it is incomplete, and could well have covered later events
in its original condition.) But what became known to generations
of rebels as the 'Norman yoke' was fitted onto English shoulders
in a matter of years, not hours. Hastings accounted for the last
Anglo-Saxon king and much of his nobility, but it did not suppress
English resistance to William from every quarter. The first English
rebels took on a role that is familiar to us throughout later history,
and across the world. They were resisters against a colonial
oppressor. That original sense of grievance proved a powerful
source of inspiration centuries after the Conquest itself was complete. There were English earls after Hastings, English claimants to
the throne, and English people of all ranks who refused to stomach
the changes that William brought with him. Although this resistance, like so many rebellions that followed, failed in its primary
objectives, it still succeeded in changing the course of English
history.

William's conquest of England was variously shaped by the
rebels he faced in his new kingdom, particularly in the first five
years of his rule. In the longer term, the way that English society
came to be governed under the Normans and some of the conquest's most lasting legacies were also affected fundamentally by
the early opposition to it. To take the most conspicuous example,
Domesday Book, the great survey of William's holdings – testimony to his determination to know his kingdom intimately and
to the residual efficiency of the Anglo-Saxon institutions he had
taken over, in being capable of delivering so thorough an inqui-
sition – can be seen in part as a final reckoning of a now subdued
realm. Yet twenty years had passed after William's first victory
before he felt secure enough to count his chickens (or as the
Anglo-Saxon Chronicle put it, to leave out from the count 'not one
ox nor one cow nor one pig'). Similarly, the castles with Norman

origins that now seem such an integral, domesticated part of the English landscape, from Dover to Durham, were another tool of occupation, put up first in wood, later in stone, as the most effective method of dealing with violent uprisings. These buildings permanently changed the fabric of England, and the way it was ruled. A castle didn't just impose a military garrison on a community, leaving locals in no uncertainty about being under occupation. The construction of the fortification itself stripped the country bare for miles around, changing the landscape itself as a direct result of conquest and resistance. Right at the beginning of our story, rebellion is not marginal, but central.

In 1066 William's own decision to invade was presented as a response to rebellion. Harold Godwineson succeeded Edward the Confessor when the latter, on his deathbed, apparently reversed his previous inclination towards William as his heir, and designated Harold. But the new King Harold had previously sworn allegiance to William when, as Earl of Wessex, he had found himself at the Duke's court during Edward's reign, a scene evoked in the Tapestry. So Harold was technically William's man, as far as the Duke was concerned, and William could legitimately (or at least, legalistically) argue that in invading England he was merely punishing a rebellious vassal. Like all such rebels, Harold had forfeited his right to his land (in Harold's case, the kingdom that William claimed as his). The ultimatum sent by the Duke to the new king emphasized the fact that the latter had 'made himself my vassal'.

It was this version of events that William is also likely to have presented to Pope Alexander II, to secure divine backing for a politically motivated project. Alexander gave William his blessing, and the Norman army claimed to have fought under a papal banner. William arrived in England on 28 September, the eve of the feast of St Michael, the archangel who had defeated the arch-rebel, Satan, whose disobedience hung over all medieval rebellion. William's victory at Hastings could be presented as the righteous victory of true believers. Harold became 'the execrable tyrant who was forcing you into a servitude that was both disastrous and shameful'. Killing him was 'held by all peoples to be a famous and praiseworthy deed'. The note of special pleading evident there also betrays William's understanding that triumph at Hastings guaranteed nothing. It had to be followed up by a systematic occupation, which would be enforced in the teeth of real and prolonged resistance.

How did the English deal with William? How, and why, did some of them resist him? Why is simple. The Conquest killed and dispossessed thousands. It would have been extraordinary if there *hadn't* been a resistance. The victory at Hastings was the result of a very large slice of luck, dependent in part on the simultaneous invasion by a Norwegian army that looked on paper to be at least as threatening, if not more so, than the Norman duke. Defeating that force in the North and then marching to face William had depleted Harold's strength, and his decision to fight William straight away before replenishing his army has often been questioned. Even so, Hastings was a close-run thing. Victory had increased the odds in William's favour, but it was by no means certain that his luck would hold. Resisting the Normans was not only justified: it had a fair chance of succeeding.

In later years, the imposition of the 'Norman yoke' became shorthand for anything that rebels wished to present as unjust and contrary to 'traditional freedoms', however contrived, or frankly imaginary, those might be. But the *way* that many of the first English rebels fought – attacking and then melting into the forests and marshes, which was why the Normans referred to them as *silvatici* ('woodsmen') – would become part of a tradition, which can be traced through the myth of Robin Hood and right up to the 'eco-warriors' of our own time. This legacy was practical, as others copied the first rebels' methods, and rhetorical, as the life of the outlaw in the greenwood steadily became a central part of English folklore. 'To the greenwood gone, to be a bold outlaw; and not only an outlaw to himself, but the father of all outlaws', as Charles Kingsley put it in his novel about the best-remembered rebel against the Norman Conquest, Hereward 'the Wake'. Yet, in the first instance, guerrilla tactics were simply the best way of challenging a conventional military force.

Some of the resistance to Norman occupation drew on an already existing tradition. Rebellion was hardly unknown in pre-Conquest England. According to one twelfth-century historian, the English of the far West and North were 'still barbarous, and had only obeyed the English king in the time of King Edward and his predecessors when it suited them'. That may be something of an exaggeration, but only a year before William arrived, when Edward the Confessor was still king, the people of Northumbria, where William too would encounter the strongest resistance, had successfully rid themselves of their earl, Harold's brother, and replaced him with Morcar, the brother of Edwin, Earl of Mercia. The earliest English rebels were inspired as much by traditions of regional autonomy as by nascent thoughts of national identity.

The resistance begins

Neither Edwin nor Morcar fought at the Battle of Hastings. But the two earls did join a resistance party that backed an English pretender against William straight afterwards. Their champion was Edgar 'the Aetheling' (princeling), nephew of Edward the Confessor and grandson of King Edmund Ironside, who is likely to have been passed over at Edward's death because he was not yet of age (he lived until 1125). In the absence of a mature champion of royal blood, however, Edgar became the focus of English resistance after William's victory at Hastings, though later Harold's sons also returned from exile to try their luck. Morcar, himself the beneficiary of a rebellion, and his brother were joined after Hastings by the archbishops of York and Canterbury and 'the citizens of London'. 'At that time, indeed, a crowd of warriors from elsewhere had flocked thither, and the city, in spite of its great size, could scarcely accommodate them all.'

They awaited William's arrival, and fought him off as he approached London Bridge, the only way across the Thames into the City, and the crucible of rebellions in centuries to come. William set the area around Southwark, south of the river, alight,

and withdrew. Then, taking a slow, relentless approach that became characteristic of his dealings with his uncooperative new
subjects, he embarked on a steady encirclement of London, isolat-
ing his enemies, and leaving them with no option but to give up.
The first to cave in was the Archbishop of Canterbury, Stigand,
who approached William at Wallingford to swear fealty. William's
advance continued, along the Chilterns, and soon afterwards the
remaining English resistance knew the game was up, for the time
being, at least. Anglo-Saxon England conceded defeat not on the
battlefield at Hastings, but at Berkhamsted two months later, where
Edgar the Aetheling, Edwin, Morcar and the remaining archbishop
and bishops submitted. The Anglo-Saxon chronicler thought they
were merely facing up to what had long been inevitable: 'it was a
piece of great folly that they had not done it earlier.'

It looked like the resistance to William had fizzled out as soon
as it had begun. But the Normans were still jumpy. On Christmas
Day 1066, just over two months after Hastings, William was
crowned king, but the event was not exactly a demonstration of a
conqueror's self-confidence. The coronation – on the first day of
the New Year (as Christmas was at this time), in the new abbey of
Westminster, built in Edward the Confessor's reign, probably
under Norman influence – was the first manoeuvre in what today's
military occupiers invariably call the 'battle for hearts and minds'.
But it did not go entirely to plan. In a (possible) break with
tradition, the ceremony included a formal request for acknowl-
edgement by the people of William's right to be king. The question
was asked in English by the Archbishop of York, who had performed the coronation, and in French by the Bishop of Coutances.
Although those inside the abbey duly obliged by shouting their
acclamation, the noise was taken by the mounted men outside as
a sign of rebellion. They set fire to the surrounding buildings.

The fire spread rapidly from house to house; the crowd who had been
rejoicing in the church took fright and throngs of men and women of
every rank and condition rushed out of the church in frantic haste. Only
the bishops and a few clergy and monks remained, terrified, in the

sanctuary, and with difficulty completed the consecration of the king, who was trembling from head to foot . . . The English . . . never again trusted the Normans who seemed to have betrayed them, but nursed their anger and bided their time to take revenge.

The proud victor of Hastings seems to have been a nervous wreck, and his men, feeling unwelcome in a hostile foreign country, were clearly on edge.

As this rebellion was only in their minds, nothing came of it, but it wasn't only in hindsight that the occupation seemed perilous. William knew that there was a propaganda battle to be won, if he was to set himself up as the legitimate king. The coronation was a part of that battle. The most obvious and sustained way in which he pursued it was to portray himself as the direct heir of Edward the Confessor. Harold II's nine-month reign was expunged from the official record. The shorthand *TRE* (*Tempore Regis Edwardi* – 'in the time of King Edward'), appears throughout the most famous written legacy of William's reign, Domesday Book, with no mention of Harold. William was not a mere conqueror but a rightful successor, able to endorse the holdings of the 'previous' king, Edward.

Initially, it seemed that the remaining English magnates who had submitted to William would find roles in the new regime, but as William's reign wore on, so the influence of his own men increased. Whether this would have happened in any case, we can't be sure, but what sealed the fate of most of the English was that they rebelled. Of the men who submitted to William at Berkhamsted, only Ealdred, Archbishop of York, remained on the new king's side. When William returned to Normandy, early in the New Year, 1067, he took the principals of the early resistance party (Stigand, Edgar the Aetheling, Edwin and Morcar, and Earl Waltheof of Northampton) with him, keeping his enemies close. But all these men joined or initiated the various rebellions that would dog William for five years. Even as late as 1075, a major rebellion, encompassing Normans as well as Englishmen, resulted in the only execution of a senior rebel.

The annals of the *Anglo-Saxon Chronicle* for these years, especially the first five after William's arrival, reflect an almost unbroken sequence of rebellion, in Dover, Exeter, Hereford, Nottingham, Durham, York and Peterborough. William's reaction to them could be merciless, but one abiding mystery is why he persistently let off Edgar the Aetheling. Edgar may have been under age but he remained the primary focus for these rebellions, whenever the rebels sought to replace William on the throne with a 'native', although some were equally happy to press the claims of Danish royals. Notions of English 'patriotism' at this time are probably premature; when the people of Kent invited Eustace of Boulogne to be their saviour from William in 1067, 'It was because they hated the Normans that they reached an agreement with Eustace, formerly their bitter enemy. . . . They thought that if they were not to serve one of their own countrymen, they would rather serve a neighbour they knew.'

William's initial occupation has been compared to the German occupation of France in the Second World War, with the country divided into two zones – the 'occupied', south of the Humber, and the 'unoccupied', to the north. One difference was that, in Anglo-Norman England, the unoccupied zone was not allowed a measure of self-government because it collaborated with the new regime. On the contrary, northern England hadn't been conquered yet. Outlying parts of England could not be relied upon to collaborate or even co-operate, although, in the beginning, William did attempt to make use of native English appointees to govern on his behalf. But violent resistance meant that this policy would change: the Norman Conquest became more Norman with each passing month.

At Dover, Eustace's venture was easily suppressed by the garrison and the mere threat of the arrival of William's half-brother, the formidably ruthless Odo, Bishop of Bayeux. On the Welsh Marches, in Herefordshire, there was also unrest in the same year, where Eadric 'the Wild', a local landholder, allied with a Welsh prince and attacked the garrison at Hereford. Eadric's resistance did not occasion the King's intervention either, but, like other rebels who were not severely dealt with at the beginning, Eadric would feature later in more serious disturbances.

The West was next to rise, with Exeter defying the King rather more resolutely. At the beginning of 1068, the townsmen attempted to become the focus of a general resistance, sending 'envoys to other cities to combine with them in similar measures . . . to fight with all their strength against the foreign king'. The foreign king arrived in person, perhaps stirred into direct action by the presence of Harold's mother, Gytha, whose plea to give up her son's body after Hastings William had refused. But William's reputation for invincibility initially made little impact. The rebels of Exeter first offered to submit to him on their own terms, and, when this was rejected, retired behind their walls to await a siege. They held out as William displayed his whole army, including a force of 500 knights, before the city walls, publicly blinded a hostage, and began to set siege. The siege lasted eighteen days, with William launching 'unremitting attacks' on the walls. Eventually, the town gave in, and William, possibly conscious that he had to rely on the co-operation of even the most awkward subjects if his conquest was to last, contented himself with building a castle to ensure the rebels' good behaviour.

The disturbance at Exeter turned out to be the prelude to a more widespread challenge to William's authority throughout 1068 and beyond. Edwin and Morcar were next to turn defiant. Edwin had reportedly been given authority over 'his brother and almost a third of England', but he had also been promised a marriage to William's daughter, which did not materialize. Perhaps William was toying with the idea of forming an Anglo-Norman senior aristocracy by intermarriage. If so, it was a notion he didn't pursue. Yet the impression that much of the rebellion against the Normans stemmed more from private than from patriotic reasons seems to apply again here. If some individuals felt they had nothing to lose by attempting to overthrow the King, and took a chance on another candidate, however unlikely, most of those who joined rebellions simply wanted to improve their own situation. William's indulgence, as displayed at Exeter, seemed to offer a way of leaning on the new king to do this, but it was a risky game, and one that, for some, less privileged rebels, would backfire spectacularly in the end. In fact, Edwin and Morcar once again lost their nerve, and obtained William's pardon. Further north, however, the country was still 'seething with discontent'.

The northern rebellion would continue to reignite and damp down for some years, but it was obvious from the beginning that Northumbria would provide William with his most serious challenge. Initially, a succession of Anglo-Saxon noblemen was tried out to govern the territory and raise taxes on William's behalf, but after two murders and one change of sides the King was persuaded of the need to intervene personally. He marched northwards in the summer of 1068, building castles as he went in Warwick and Nottingham, before arriving at York, where the resistance party melted away before him. Some of the rebel leaders fled to the court of the Scottish king, Malcolm, while others made a formal submission. Once again, William was remarkably unvengeful, making 'peace' with those who submitted, and negotiating a settlement with Malcolm. He marched away leaving a castellan and a guardian in charge of the castle at York.

When William attempted once again to reinforce his newly established northern authority, however, it became clear that the resistance had only been dispersed, not destroyed. In January 1069, Robert de Comines marched into Durham as the latest Earl of Northumbria. Unlike William's previous choices, Robert was a Norman. William's experiment with 'native' lords was coming to an end, though he persisted in some areas, with very limited success. But Robert's term was as disastrous as those of his English predecessors. On his first night in Durham, he was surrounded by the citizens and killed, along with his retinue of, according to varying reports, between 500 and 900 men. Even at the smaller estimate, this was by far the most bloody and serious blow to William's rule. The rebels next killed the guardian of the Norman castle at York, again with 'many of his men', and besieged the castle itself. Their party was led by a group including the Aetheling. 'Fealty, oaths, and the safety of hostages were forgotten in their anger at the loss of their patrimonies and the deaths of their kinsmen and fellow countrymen.'

The rebels had at last made William angry. He returned in full force, and in an account of his intervention there seems an almost biblical tone to the inevitability of the outcome. 'Swift was the king's coming; he fell on the besiegers and spared no man. Many were captured, more killed, and the remainder put to flight. The king remained a further eight days in the city, built a second castle, and left Earl William fitzOsbern as castellan there.' FitzOsbern, the new man, was able to deal with a couple more attacks without having to resort to royal assistance, but this was still by no means the end of the English resistance to William; 'storms of war . . . rose on every side.' And once again, the King had not dealt with the leaders of the rebellion. For the first time, as the unrest spread, it can be said that the resistance took on a more patriotic character, even if the failure to unite efforts from different sources ultimately cost the rebels any prospect of success.

While the North continued to simmer, an attack from the West arrived, led by two of Harold's sons, who had fled to Ireland. They had made one attempt in 1068, and the following summer they landed in Exeter with a force of sixty-six ships and men. William's lieutenants did not let him down, but they had to fight two battles in a day to drive off the sons' threat. Their mother, who had remained after Exeter's first defiance, seems to have given up on any prospect of her family being re-established after this latest setback. 'She secretly gathered together a great store of treasure and, through fear of King William, fled to France, never to return.'

The outside help that the northern rebels had sought eventually arrived in the form of a Danish force, sent by the King of Denmark under the leadership of his sons. Their 'great fleet' was manned not only by Danes and English, but by troops from Poland, Frisia, Saxony and Lithuania. This multicultural force followed a traditional Viking route, starting on the south coast and working their way up the eastern coastline of England, making occasional forays inland, from Dover to Sandwich, then Ipswich, Norwich, the Humber and eventually York. Along the way, they made

contact with the English party, including the Aetheling and Earl
Waltheof. Again, however, an initial success against William's garrison in September 1069 did not embolden the rebels to face the
King himself. When William mustered and arrived in person, the
rebels 'fearing the conqueror, had fled across the Humber and
landed on the Lindsey side'. William left his brother, Robert of
Mortain, and another Robert, Count of Eu, to watch for a breakout. These early English rebels, like many of their successors, were
confident when facing royal representatives, but they balked at the
prospect of attacking an anointed king in person.

Perhaps inspired by the scale of events in the North, other areas
began to rise. In the West, there were attacks in Dorset and
Somerset, and Eadric the Wild took his opportunity to try again,
this time attacking Shrewsbury, while 'the men of Devon were
attacking Exeter in the same way, allied with hordes from Cornwall.' William sent two earls to deal with these disturbances, and
himself tackled 'large forces of rebels' in the Midlands, at Stafford.

The Harrying of the North

Meanwhile, the northern uprising had still not been quashed in
any meaningful way, with the Danes awaiting their opportunity
on the Humber, and their English allies likewise biding their time.
After a breakout was only partially contained, York once again
seemed to be in rebel hands. William marched north from Nottingham in the winter of 1069, but was delayed for three weeks at
Pontefract by a rebel force. By the time the Normans reached
York, the Danes had fled again. At last, William's patience appears
to have snapped. Realizing that the rebels had decided not to meet
him in a pitched battle, he conducted a devastating campaign to
root out his enemies and destroy their means of support. The
Anglo-Saxon Chronicle records that William 'utterly ravaged and laid
waste the shire'. Orderic Vitalis, a monk of mixed Anglo-Norman
parentage writing at the beginning of the twelfth century, is more
graphic:

Nowhere else had William showed such cruelty. Shamefully he suc-
cumbed to this vice, for he made no effort to restrain his fury and
punished the innocent with the guilty. In his anger he commanded that
all crops and herds, chattels and food of every kind should be brought
together and burned to ashes with consuming fire, so that the whole
region north of the Humber might be stripped of all means of sustenance.

Another chronicler describes the effects of the depredations: 'so
great a famine prevailed that men, compelled by hunger, devoured
human flesh, that of horses, dogs, and cats, and whatever custom
abhors; others sold themselves into perpetual slavery, so that they
might in any way preserve their wretched existence.'

William's punishment became known as the Harrying of the
North. References to refugees fleeing as far as Evesham in Worcestershire (in the Chronicle of the abbey there) seem to back up
the impression that William's actions starved people off their land.
Orderic writes that 'more than 100,000 Christian folk of both
sexes, young and old alike, perished of hunger', which is certainly
an exaggeration, as the population of the whole of England is only
estimated at its highest at around 2 million for this period. Perhaps
less of the region was devastated than was once thought (Domesday
Book's references to 'waste' land may not mean exactly that), but
the trauma of the Harrying of the North was remembered with
something like shock for centuries afterwards. Where the more
prominent rebels were concerned, however, William could still be
remarkably merciful. Despite their repeated defiance of William,
some of the leading rebels were still able to secure his pardon, even
in the midst of the King's scorched-earth campaign.

Edgar and Hereward: the wages of rebellion

Other rebel leaders, implicated in the northern uprising to varying
degrees, went several ways. The nuisance-making of Edgar the
Aetheling is particularly impressive. He first fled to Scotland, where
he had previously been welcomed at the court of Malcolm III.

Although he would rebel against the Conqueror one more time, when the Danes returned the following year, the failure of that rebellion forced him to flee to Scotland once more. He stayed for a time in Flanders, and was only prevented by shipwreck from taking up an offer of a castle from the King of France. However, Edgar ended up reconciled to William, in 1074, and was received by the King in Normandy 'with great honour and he stayed there at court and received such dues as were appointed him'. Edgar's career as consummate survivor was not over, even then. He seems to have spent his time at William's court getting friendly with the King's eldest son, Robert, and was probably inspired by Robert's example to break with William at the end of his reign, in 1086. On this occasion, without a rebellion to lead, Edgar travelled to Apulia, where he disappears temporarily from view. He had returned by 1091, when he continued to support Robert, this time against his brother, William's successor, William Rufus.

After Robert's bid for the throne failed, Edgar joined him on crusade to the Holy Land. He would have a chance to fight one more Norman king, however, when his continued support for Robert led him to take part at the Battle of Tinchebrai in 1106, when Rufus's successor and the youngest of the Conqueror's sons, Henry I, defeated Robert, and took Normandy. Henry was married to Edgar's niece, Edith (known to Normans as Matilda), and seems to have felt that his own English credentials were strong enough for Edgar not to pose any further 'native' threat. So, although Henry's brother Robert would end his days imprisoned, Edgar lived out his on a modest holding in Herefordshire. Edgar outlasted two Norman kings, but by his death he had long since ceased to be a pretender to the throne: a retired rebel with a cause, but no one left to fight it. Perhaps it was some consolation that his family, in the shape of his niece, had managed to reinsert themselves in the royal bloodline.

The treatment of the senior rebels seems to show that William could combine extraordinary ruthlessness with almost exaggerated clemency. The last purely native rebellion against his rule, one which would take on a mythical life out of proportion to its historical effects, involved two rebels who had already tested the King, and been the beneficiaries of his mercy, if not his favour: the brothers Edwin and Morcar. The rebellion they joined was that of Hereward, in Ely in East Anglia. Hereward (his nickname 'the Wake' was a posthumous one) was a Lincolnshire thegn, a minor lord whose name has endured as the emblem of the last, doomed stand of Anglo-Saxon England against the Norman Conquest. If we compare his short-lived rebellion with Edgar's far longer record of resistance, it might seem strange that one has become legendary while the other is barely remembered. But the story of Hereward's brief, heroic failure fits much better with the traditional picture of the Norman Conquest as a clean break with the past.

The historical Hereward's decision to take up arms against William looks more like a local power game than anything to do with noble ideals of English independence. It came at a time, around Easter, 1071, when William was carrying out a sustained policy of replacing English senior churchmen with Normans. But the fact that the man who was chosen to replace the abbot of Peterborough arrived with an armed retinue of 160 is an indication that trouble wasn't sparked by the change: trouble was already expected. The abbey at Peterborough had already been plundered, according to the *Anglo-Saxon Chronicle*, and probably by Hereward's men. The *Chronicle* doesn't make much of the subsequent rebellion, and the moment when the brothers Edwin and Morcar joined it: 'In this year Earl Edwin and Earl Morcar fled away and travelled aimlessly in the woods and moors until Edwin was killed by his own men and Morcar went to Ely by ship.' But in another account the earls become heroes, one fighting to the last against the treachery of his own men, the other unjustly being tricked into captivity 'for the rest of his days'. Although the rebels tried to link up with the reinforced Danish fleet, William separated the allies by paying off the Danes, and surrounded and flushed out the native rebels, although Hereward got away, ensuring his place in legend. Again, the rebellion failed because the combination of forces was too shaky, but, at last, by imprisoning Morcar for life,

William seems to have acknowledged that he had to take the initiators as well as the consequences of the English resistance seriously.

The Revolt of the Earls and the first rebel martyr

The relentless cycle of rebellion and repression was almost over. William's readiness to allow English magnates to stay in their positions may have been questionable from the beginning, but the fact that those he trusted – and repeatedly forgave – persisted in their rebellion left him with little choice. Earl Waltheof, for example, seems to have been incapable of cleaving to the King for long. In 1075, having twice submitted to and twice rebelled against William, he joined another rebellion, led not by English but by Frenchmen. The Revolt of the Earls, as it was known, in part followed a pattern that would become a familiar ritual of rebellion in the years to come, whenever disaffected barons, often feeling that they had split loyalties, rose up against the English king. The two 'French' ringleaders of the rebellion, Roger of Hereford (a Norman) and Ralph 'the Gael' of East Anglia (a Breton), attempted to overthrow William using their own castles as bases from which to carry on the rebellion. They questioned William's royal legiti-macy (by questioning his parental legitimacy), and, unusually, they proposed to put one of their own number in his place (declaring that 'One of us shall be king and the other two dukes', though who was to get what was never clear), instead of sponsoring a more 'royal' candidate, such as an aetheling or, more likely, a foreign king. But, failing to secure enough backing, the rebellion was quickly quashed.

Waltheof became the only leading Anglo-Saxon to be executed for treason, in 1076. Perhaps William had been trying to avoid creating martyrs by not executing rebel leaders. Sure enough, there was an account of a miracle at Waltheof's death, the first of many such in the chronicles of English rebels. The executioner, impatient as the Earl struggled to finish the Lord's Prayer, struck off his head

as he stumbled over 'And lead us not into temptation . . .'. 'Then
the severed head was heard by all present to say in a clear voice "But
deliver us from evil. Amen".' Despite this miracle, the apparent
popularity of the Earl, and the burial of the decapitated body at
Crowland Abbey, where it might have become a site of pilgrimage,
Waltheof never seems to have become more than a local hero,
unlike Hereward.

One reason that the punishment meted out to the three earls
was so harsh – Roger was imprisoned for life, Ralph dispossessed
and banished – may have been that the earls had not relied on
even a spurious justification for their break with William. Theirs
was neither a purely native resistance, nor, as would later be the
case, when rebels backed the King's brothers or sons against him,
the favouring of one lord over another, nor again an attempt to
'guide' the King by force to be a better or more sympathetic
ruler. It was a simple conspiracy, apparently motivated by anger at
William's 'ingratitude' in rewarding his supporters. Normans and
English shared an aversion to simple treachery, but until the reign
of Henry III rebels were rarely defined as plain traitors. The
punishment for betraying your lord in Anglo-Saxon law was death,
and in Norman it could be life imprisonment, but Orderic seems
to be speaking for both cultures when he has a reluctant Waltheof
say that 'No good song is ever sung of a traitor. All peoples brand
apostates and traitors as wolves.'

The afterlife of the resistance

The rebellions in the early years of William's reign were frequent,
persistent and serious. Historians who prefer to concentrate on
organizations rather than people, and who emphasize the institutional continuity between pre- and post-Conquest England, risk
making the transition sound altogether too smooth. In fact, so
many rebels refused to honour the trust placed in them by their
new king, even when it was re-offered after being rejected, that
the resistance looks like the principal factor in ensuring that the

top of England's post-Conquest society, both lay and ecclesiastical,
became almost entirely Norman. Only thirteen tenants-in-chief of
English origin are recorded in Domesday Book, and only four of
these had anything approaching a substantial holding. By the end
of William's reign the facts on the ground were simple: rebellion
had broken any trust in the English aristocracy that William might
have had.

The resistance had other consequences, over the next few years,
over decades, and even over centuries. In the short term, we have
already seen how Domesday Book, the greatest legacy of the
reign, could have been inspired by a wish to know the achieved
settlement of William's kingdom once his hold on it was secure.
The last serious rebellion, in 1075, and the Domesday survey, in
1086, look too far apart for domestic unrest to be a serious factor
in the making of Domesday. But the more immediate occasion for
the survey might well be linked to the threat of resistance. As the
Anglo-Saxon Chronicle records, 1085 was the year when the most
serious Danish force yet was assembled by the new Danish king,
Cnut, a threat which William countered by importing the 'largest
force of mounted men and infantry from France and Brittany that
had ever come to this country'. Clearly, he wasn't yet ready to
trust the native levies to fight off a foreign invader, whom they
might see as a deliverer. Though some of these hired men returned
when the threat passed, the requirements for billeting the extra
troops could have persuaded William, at a council in Gloucester
at the end of the year, to send 'his men all over England into every
shire and [have] them find out how many hundred hides there
were in the shire, or what land and cattle the king himself had in
the country, or what dues he ought to have in twelve months from
the shire'. A survey on the unprecedented scale of Domesday was
most likely commissioned for a host of different reasons: as a tax
assessment; as a reckoning of the new 'feudal' arrangements of
society; as a way of recording the settlement of land disputes. But
the threat of rebellion also played its part.

If the legacy of English resistance in the medium term was to
exclude natives from a part in running their own country, in the

longer term the rebels' actions, and what they were perceived as fighting against, would become part of the foundation story of English rebellion, and ultimately of Englishness. Two elements of this myth stand out: the personal myth of Hereward, and the national myth of the 'Norman yoke'. Hereward became the representative rebel of the period, even if, as we have seen, he was hardly William's most troublesome opponent. Hereward begins as an essentially local hero, whose connection to a national myth of resistance would have to wait for several revivals. The first of these centres on the composition of a heroic Life of Hereward, the *Gesta Herewardi*, probably written in the 1150s. Hereward, a bear-wrestling superman, is shown there to be moved to resistance by a combination of the personal and the political. According to the *Gesta*, Hereward was away from England at the time of the Conquest, and on his return the country is 'now subject to the rule of foreigners and almost ruined by many'. Hereward's dealings with the Danes, to whom he passes the treasure he acquires from the sack of the abbey (an episode confirmed by other sources) does not seem to detract from his status as a national talisman. Other revivals of Hereward's story in the Middle Ages include an account in Gaimar's *Estoire des Engleis* (*c.*1136–7). The fact that this work was composed for a Lincolnshire landlord may account for the inclusion of Hereward, but it is still curious that a Norman audience would not mind hearing about a noble Englishman struggling against 'dishonourable and cowardly' Normans.

Hereward's nickname 'the Wake' appears to derive from the prolonged effort of a Lincolnshire family of that name to link themselves to him, based on a single use of the epithet in a thirteenth-century chronicle. The publication in the nineteenth century of an edition of the *Gesta Herewardi* among other materials, was the inspiration for the novel that has ensured the continuation of Hereward's legend: Charles Kingsley's *Hereward the Wake* (1865), with its subtitle that leaves nothing to the patriotic imagination, *Last of the English*. Kingsley was Regius Professor of History at Oxford, and pitches his novel as a fenland counterblast to tales of the 'heroic deeds of Highlanders' (actually, Scott's first 'purely

English subject', *Ivanhoe*, with its own version of the eternal
struggle between honest Saxon and oppressive Norman, had been
published forty-six years earlier, so the reference seems a little
tenuous). *Hereward* is also presented as based on the most relevant
evidence – quoting Thomas Wright's recent edition of the relevant
manuscript sources in the preface. Kingsley even dedicated the
novel to Wright, who had enabled him to make 'Hereward, the
hero of your youth, reappear at last in a guise fitted for a modern
drawing-room. To you is due whatever new renown he may win
for himself in that new field. You first disinterred him, long ago,
when scarcely a hand or foot of him was left standing out from
beneath the dust of ages.'

The result of all this scrupulous sourcing was a thoroughly
anachronistic hero. Kingsley's Hereward is not just the quintessen-
tially independent Anglo-Saxon, 'free as long as the wind blows
in the clouds', but a colonizer whose proto-imperialism has a
distinctly contemporary ring: 'If men had invaded his land, he
would have . . . died where he stood. But that was not the least
reason why he should not invade any other man's land. . . . To
him these Frieslanders were simply savages, probably heathens,
who would not obey their lawful lord, a gentleman and a Christian;
besides, renown, and possibly a little plunder, might be got by
beating them into obedience.' As the English Rebel mutates into
the English Imperialist, we strain to detect a note of irony in
Kingsley's portrayal. Is it wishful thinking to see the professor using
heavy-handed historical expediency to make a point about freedom
being universal, not confined to the 'civilized'?

Kingsley's Hereward can be accommodated into the other
legacy of the English resistance to the Norman Conquest, the idea
of the 'Norman yoke'. This concept was taken up in the sixteenth
and seventeenth centuries and expanded upon into the twentieth.
In the Civil War era, radicals like the Levellers promoted the idea
of the Conquest as the moment of deprivation of 'true English
liberty'. But these mythological interpretations of later centuries
were not based on pure invention. Certainly, the idea that Anglo-
Saxon England was constitutionally far more 'free and equal' than

what followed it would be pretty difficult to substantiate. But the idea that the Norman occupation was actively resented, and that assimilation took centuries, is less easily dismissed. We need only look at the origins of the phrase 'Norman yoke' itself. This was not a seventeenth-century invention. The Anglo-Norman Orderic Vitalis used it, though he exempted William from its effects: 'But meanwhile the English were groaning under the Norman yoke, and suffering oppressions from the proud lords who ignored the king's injunctions.' At an institutional level, the Norman yoke is a fantasy, predicated on a non-existent wholesale abolition of English customs and their replacement with Norman ones. But both as a focus for a sense of injustice and as a rhetorical device with the power to inspire action, the idea of the Norman yoke can be connected back to the Conquest itself. In the twelfth century it was taken up by Geoffrey of Monmouth, who has Merlin prophesy the 'yoke of perpetual slavery' for the Saxons at the hands of 'a people dressed in wood and iron corselets'.

The Norman Conquest was not a historical inevitability. Rebels ensured that it was much more than the product of an 'easy victory in a single battle'. Even though they failed to overthrow William, they changed the way he approached the government of the country. Their guerrilla tactics inspired both practical and poetic imitators, making the woodland English outlaw the symbol of national identity. And the oppression they fought against, part invention, part reality, would inspire later generations of rebellious followers. More immediately, however, the division of spoils between powerful landholders on both sides of the Channel, a state of affairs in part dictated by the rebellions of native magnates, would create the circumstances for a series of aristocratic uprisings that form a distinct phase of English rebellion, lasting through six reigns, from the death of the Conqueror to the sealing of Magna Carta.

2. A Kingdom Divided

Odo of Bayeux to Geoffrey de Mandeville 1087–1144

Until it was resurrected in the seventeenth century, the idea of English rebellion as 'native' resistance was over. For 300 years after the death of William I, most English rebels came from the assimilated landed nobility. Usually these aristocrats' causes were entirely opportunistic, the muscle-flexing of already powerful men thwarted in their wider ambitions. Medieval society was traditionally divided into three classes: those who worked, those who fought, and those who prayed. The workers were not among the leaders of major rebellions until the fourteenth century. But not all English rebels of this period came from the second category either. Some were men of the cloth.

There are two kinds of medieval bishop: the pious, introverted churchman, and the magnate in a mitre. There was very little pious or introverted about Odo, Bishop of Bayeux and Earl of Kent. The half-brother of William the Conqueror (they had the same mother), Odo is one of the first figures in English history who did not let a lifetime of serial rebellion prevent him from achieving high office, great wealth and an imperishable cultural legacy. In fact, the most resourceful of the rebels who challenged William's two younger sons when they succeeded him on the English throne were clergymen: Odo in William II's reign, and Ranulf Flambard in Henry I's. These two bishops, for whom the religious life was more of a career move than a vocation, are representative of a type that would become familiar more generally in medieval England: the rebel on the make. Rebellions in the English Middle Ages contain the origins of some of the most lasting and admired legacies in the nation's history, from Magna Carta to Parliament. But these years were also dominated by rebels for whom the greater good only meant more for themselves. To understand how later rebels managed to impose controls on otherwise ever more powerful monarchs, from some of which we still benefit today, you also have to see how the likes of Odo or Ranulf – and their counterparts among the laity – set out the path for rebellion as a natural challenge to England's rulers, a way of keeping them in check and, in the last resort, of replacing them altogether. There was no such thing as a loyal opposition in the Middle Ages. But medieval rebellion set the pattern of opposition to authority for hundreds of years to come, long after the Middle Ages had passed. Medieval rebels were not always reformers, but medieval reformers had to be rebels. On a path that would be trodden, often more honourably, for centuries, Odo and co. showed the way.

Odo was five years into an open-ended term of imprisonment at Rouen as his brother, King William I, lay dying in 1087. The fading King was persuaded to forgive the Bishop, releasing him to create the upset that Orderic Vitalis, writing thirty or so years after the event, has William predict: 'You are ill-advised to free this traitor, and you are asking for serious trouble for yourselves.' William was right, but he only had himself to blame. The conditions inherited by his successors virtually ensured that his prediction came true. The Norman Conquest had linked England to Continental Europe, and had begun a dysfunctional relationship that would last for hundreds of years. William's own solution to the problem was to attempt a trial separation after his death. He split his inheritance between his two elder sons – bequeathing Normandy to the oldest, Robert (whom William apparently nicknamed 'Curthose' because he was so short), and England (and the Crown) to his middle son, William 'Rufus' (after his red hair). This wasn't a recipe for peace. It divided the loyalties of many powerful men who held land on both sides of the Channel, and created a ready source of support for any moves to unite Normandy and England under one man again. That meant rebellion.

As for the beneficiaries of William's will, it was likely that neither Curthose nor Rufus would feel they had inherited as much as they might have (to say nothing of the youngest son, the future Henry I, who had been left vast wealth, but no land at all, and supported one brother or another as the balance of power shifted).

So each might be willing to put himself at the head of rebellions in duchy or kingdom. Lastly, the method their father had used to bring the newly conquered kingdom under control – building castles and deputing landed barons to hold them – had created the conditions under which aristocratic rebellion could prosper. In March 1088, only five months after Rufus inherited, he faced a challenge from a group of barons led in England by Odo, who supported his brother Robert's cause. The rebels burnt the King's and his loyal supporters' land, and then 'each of them went to his castle and manned and provisioned it as best he could'. The men who led this serious threat to the new king were some of the most powerful in England, including six of the ten greatest baronial landholders recorded in Domesday.

The failure of Odo's alternative candidate for the Crown, Robert Curthose, to arrive in England allowed Rufus to deal with this challenge efficiently. Odo was captured for the second time in the rebellion after a siege of Rochester Castle. Despite a 'crowd of Englishmen' baying for his blood ('Halters, bring halters, and hang this traitor bishop and his accomplices from the gallows'), he was merely banished from England for life. His restless journey ended nine years later in Sicily, where he was struck down by illness on his way to participate in the First Crusade. Odo's ambitions were too large to be accommodated by the opportunities open to him. The offence that had first landed him in gaol appears to have been an attempt to become pope – which Odo had proposed to achieve by mounting a military expedition, 'borrowing' his brother's troops. It would be difficult to conceive of a man less suited to the life of religious contemplation. And it seems as true for Odo's time as our own that the psychology of the rebel, in so far as we can speculate about it at such a distance, is often that of the individual unwilling to accept the role assigned to him by social convention. Naturally, only very few men had at that time much opportunity to do anything about it. Odo was a man of action as well as ambition (appearing in the Bayeux Tapestry, which he almost certainly commissioned, wielding a mace or club at Hastings). He holds the unique distinction of intriguing for the thrones of St Peter and of England.

The reaction to the rebellion Odo led, or at least the way that reaction has been presented to us, hints at another, wider and perhaps unexpected consequence of baronial rebellion for Odo's own time. It united the English behind their Norman king. Most of the chroniclers emphasize that Rufus was able to call on native assistance to put down the 'foreign' insurgency of his brother and uncle. His English subjects stiffened their king's resolve, declaiming a loyal manifesto based on specious historical precedent, and one that would be severely tested in the coming centuries:

We will fight for you to the death, and will never support another against you. It is both foolish and wicked to prefer a foreign enemy to a known king. A people who betrays its prince is utterly despicable. An army that welcomes the ruin of its lord is ripe for destruction. Study the pages of English history: you will find that the English are always loyal to their princes

– even if those princes had been foreign enemies a generation before.

Actually, another chronicler does have Englishmen fighting on the other side, for Odo. Loyalty to princes could be complicated when there was more than one to choose from. And this episode hardly marks the uncomplicated intermingling of Norman and English. Later, when those around Henry I wished to insult the new king, who had married Edgar the Aetheling's niece, they called him Godric and his wife Godiva. Nonetheless, Rufus does seem to have been able to rely on native English manpower to an extent that his father, who at the end of his reign had drafted in mercenaries to England to deal with a threatened attack, had never managed. When Rufus wished to turn the tables on his brother in 1094, leading an expedition into Normandy, he was able to summon the English fyrd, the traditional levy of Anglo-Saxon kings, to accompany him. According to the *Chronicle*'s (surely exaggerated) estimate, this force amounted to 20,000 men. It turned out that the summons was a ruse to extract money to hire more-professional soldiers, as the force was dismissed after being fleeced of 10 shillings per man, but it is significant that these loyal Englishmen turned out at all.

William Rufus spent much of his reign intriguing against his elder brother in Normandy, with Robert's sponsorship of the unsuccessful rebellion in 1088 giving him the perfect justification. Back in England, Northumbria twice necessitated an armed intervention – in 1092, and then in 1095, to quash the defiance of the Earl of Northumbria, Robert de Mowbray. The second of those rebellions, which involved some of the same leaders as Odo's, and conspired to replace Rufus with a cousin, was put down more harshly than any other. De Mowbray was imprisoned indefinitely, another ringleader was blinded and castrated, and a third was whipped in every church in Salisbury, and then hanged.

No wonder that Rufus faced no more rebellions in his reign, though the King's unexpected death, shot by an arrow in the New Forest while hunting in 1100, may not have been accidental. Whether by chance or by a conspiracy too distant to disentangle, it was Rufus's younger brother, Henry, who managed to gather support for his succession with lightning speed, ensuring that, once again, Robert Curthose missed out. Rufus's part in the story of English rebellion is not that of a victim but of a beneficiary, who capitalized on the threat posed by apparently unscrupulous rebels to strengthen his subjects' commitment to an alien monarchy.

Henry I acquired a reputation as 'the Lion of Justice', praised by a contemporary for taking 'special care of England so that none dared rebel'. But before he could settle down to the legal and administrative reforms that made his name, Henry did have his own rebels to deal with. Initially, his difficulties were almost a carbon copy of his brother's. Like Rufus, Henry had to contend with a threat from Robert Curthose, still Duke of Normandy and no happier at being passed over a second time. And for Odo of Bayeux, the powerful churchman who didn't allow clerical scruples to obstruct a bid for power, read Ranulf Flambard, Bishop of Durham. Like Odo, in whose circle he may have begun his career, Ranulf was an able administrator, though one from much humbler origins, who had risen to occupy a position as the King's right-hand man, a trusted and exacting minister, 'above all the magnates of the realm'. Like Odo, too, Ranulf found himself in prison, though

his confinement was one of the first acts of the new m͏͏
hoped to gain popularity by imprisoning one of the lea
men in the country. It was Ranulf who had mastermi͏
sting on the summoned fyrd in 1094. He was reputed to ͏
double the amount of any tax he was instructed to collect. W͏
ten days of Henry's coronation, Ranulf became the first recorded
state prisoner in the Tower of London.

About four months later, he also became its first escapee. Flambard's getaway reads like a mixture of undergraduate high jinks
and medieval derring-do. The Bishop had a rope smuggled into
his cell in a flagon of wine, waiting till his gaolers had downed the
drink before shinning inexpertly down the wall, equipped with his
pastoral staff. Ranulf's hands were 'torn to the bone', but he made
good his escape across the Channel, and met up with Robert
Curthose. This time, Robert did persist, at least to the extent of
actually making the voyage to England, where Ranulf paid off
the coastal defenders, who instead of resisting the rebels led the
invasion party to harbour in Portsmouth. Again, 'all the English'
rallied to the crowned King's side, but Robert had some powerful
men in his camp. As well as the resourceful Ranulf, the rebels also
included Robert de Bellême, who had major holdings on both
sides of the Channel, and William de Warenne, Earl of Surrey. In
August 1101, the two forces drew up against each other at Alton
in Hampshire, and exchanged challenges, Duke Robert answering
his brother's demand as to why he had 'presumed to enter English
territory with an armed force': 'I have entered the kingdom of my
father with my magnates, and I demand the right due to me as the
eldest son.'

What might have been the prelude to battle, however, turned
out to be mere bellicose posturing. Either through their advisers
or face to face, the two brothers decided to negotiate. Robert gave
up his claim to England, and Henry almost all his interests in
Normandy, while agreeing to pay the Duke a large annual stipend
of either 2,000 or 3,000 pounds sterling. Later, in 1106, when
Henry, like Rufus, led the attack to Normandy and managed to
dispossess his brother after the Battle of Tinchebrai, the Treaty of

Alton might have seemed an opportunity missed for Robert and his followers. At the time, however, the apparently genuine promise of good relations and a regular income to a man who all the sources agree was perennially short of cash might have seemed a far safer bet than the risk of a battle. Henry was the first post-Conquest English king, but certainly not the last, to realize that promises made to rebels did not have to be kept. The money was never paid, and Robert Curthose's position only grew weaker in the succeeding years. The fates of his three most eminent followers, however, show that rebellion at this time was not an unmitigated risk. Ranulf Flambard, William de Warenne and Robert de Bellême were rehabilitated at different rates, with Ranulf, the most able if the least trustworthy, forgiven fastest. But Robert de Bellême rebelled once too often. After his third open defiance of the King, he was imprisoned for life.

As the various fates of the rebels of 1101 show, the inevitable sequence of failed rebellion leading to disgrace, dispossession and even death had not yet been established. Medieval justice was not always as bloody as its reputation. Though Henry could be savage in his reprisals, particularly to more humble opponents (he notoriously threw a rebel burgess, Conan, from a high tower in Rouen, before he became king), he also seems to have been content to overlook treachery if its perpetrator might prove useful, even if only temporarily. Like his father, Henry sometimes saw the merit of keeping his enemies close. So rebellion was not yet the all-or-nothing gamble it would later become. It was a strategy, almost expected at times of disputed succession, from which rebels might hope to gain even if their original project failed.

Lost at sea

Henry's less than secure hold on Normandy after Tinchebrai meant that he was often in his duchy rather than his kingdom. The English 'resistance' was well and truly dead by now, and England stayed calm during these absences. As both kingdom and duchy knuckled under his rule, Henry seemed to be paving the way for the first unchallenged succession of an Anglo-Norman king. But in 1120 the sea that both joined and separated the two halves of Henry's dominion took a more direct part in their destiny, and rebellion was part of the flotsam. The King's only legitimate male heir, William, drowned when the *White Ship* sank off Barfleur. It was a personal tragedy for Henry (who also lost two daughters and many close associates in a death toll of 300), but it was also a political disaster, which would be played out after Henry's death, in the long years of the 'anarchy' of King Stephen's reign. (Stephen himself, Henry's nephew and one of his courtiers, had almost boarded the doomed vessel, but turned back at the last minute when he realized how drunk the crew were.) The *White Ship* was lost just at the moment when Henry had achieved a long-sought-for settlement in Normandy. But 'the calm of this brilliant and carefully arranged peace, this anxious and universal hope, was destroyed in an instant by human fate.' A drunken crew, high on the glory of securing an appointment as royal transport, rowed the ship onto one of the many rocks that lie outside Barfleur harbour, and all hands, except a butcher from Rouen, went down. Henry's wife Matilda, William's mother, had died two years before. Though the King now remarried, no more children, and crucially no more boys, arrived.

Henry tried to preserve his inheritance by taking the radical step of persuading his magnates that his daughter Matilda would be able to rule. When the King first formally introduced this idea, Matilda had recently been widowed. Since her husband had been the Holy Roman Emperor, Henry V, this may have made matters slightly easier: the barons would not have been keen to see their lands subsumed into the Empire. But the question of another marriage was bound to come up. The King required his magnates to swear two oaths in which they promised their allegiance to his daughter, once before Matilda remarried, and once afterwards, in 1127. Her new husband was Geoffrey, son of the Count of Anjou, to whose daughter Henry's only son, William, had been married. Two years later, Geoffrey became count in his own right.

From one point of view, the marriage was a success. It provided three sons, though the eldest, named Henry after his grandfather, was still a child when the old king died. But at a time when sole rule by a woman was practically unheard of (Urraca of Castile is the usually quoted exception), it was as important that Matilda's husband be acceptable to Henry's senior subjects as the Empress herself (she retained the title, and seems to have insisted on it). In this, despite his demands for allegiance to his daughter, Henry was less helpful. He refused to ratify Geoffrey's part in the succession, and at his death, which was unexpected despite the King's great age (for the time) of sixty-six, the position of the couple was not as clear as it could have been. Anjou was a traditional enemy of Normandy, which of course was part of the reason for the marriage alliance, but that made its count an unpopular prospect for those whose holdings were mainly or exclusively in the duchy.

Civil war

Even if the succession had been better choreographed, these were the seeds of potential rebellion. Despite Henry's best efforts, Matilda didn't succeed when he died. Henry was a fatal victim of food poisoning (the famous 'surfeit of lampreys'), on a hunting trip in Normandy in 1135, and it was his nephew Stephen of Blois (the younger of Henry's sister Adela's two sons) who best emulated his uncle in the swiftness of his reaction. Stephen crossed quickly from Boulogne, rode to Winchester to secure the all-important treasury, and had himself crowned on 2 December, only three weeks after the King died. This efficiency was not a sign of things to come. Stephen's reign saw the first genuine civil war in English history.

There are more literary accounts of Stephen's reign than of his predecessors', but the judgement of one, the *Anglo-Saxon Chronicle*, has traditionally been taken as definitive:

There had never been till then greater misery in the country, nor had heathens ever done worse than they [the treacherous barons] did. . . .

Whatever cultivation was done, the ground produced no corn, because the land was all ruined by such doings, and they said openly that Christ and his saints were asleep. Such things, too much for us to describe, we suffered nineteen years for our sins.

Modern historians argue that the 'anarchy' of Stephen's reign is exaggerated by local witnesses (like the Anglo-Saxon Chronicler) letting their own experience speak for the whole nation. But the reign still tends to be seen as a hiatus in the story of the monarchy's ever-growing strength.

There are more constructive ways of looking at this period. It was a time when, as the often unintended side-effect of rebellion, important influences beyond the court began to emerge. As well as magnate power, which is to be expected when most of the challenges to authority came from those with land and armed men at their disposal, there was a first outing for urban power, from the commune of London. Perhaps surprisingly, the power of the Church to influence lay affairs, and govern its own, rose. There were innovations, too, in the more practical aspects of rebellion. The military lessons of the importance of castles and the destructiveness of guerrilla warfare may be familiar ones, but Stephen's reign also set precedents for negotiation, conferences, treaties and councils. And in the example of Robert of Gloucester, Matilda's half-brother and the man who became the leading rebel against Stephen, there was a crucial wider development in the history of English rebellion. Through Robert's careful recasting of his break with the King as an honourable course of action, the idea of rebellion as a formal, legitimate move was strengthened. As early as the twelfth century, rebellion is about more than a power struggle. Here – paradoxically, in an era meant to be the classic one of the unscrupulous 'robber baron' – are the origins of the notion of the ideologically justified rebel. For all these reasons, Stephen's reign is a pivotal time in English history, not an inconvenient pause.

Stephen ruled for nineteen years, in the face of sustained opposition – from Matilda, the previously accepted rightful heir, from her husband in Normandy, Geoffrey of Anjou, from her principal supporter and half-brother, Robert of Gloucester, and latterly from her son Henry, together with an ever-changing constellation of more or less powerful supporters. The politics of the time might have been designed to illustrate the medieval figure of the Wheel of Fortune, which raised and dashed men's hopes with every turn. It was also a reign in which almost every action, episode, or influence was reciprocated. It seems appropriate that two of the most influential figures of the time were twins, Waleran of Meulan and Robert of Leicester, who, naturally, shifted their allegiances during its course, and ended up on opposite sides, though subtly in equilibrium.

This seesaw pattern of events did not emerge immediately, however. At first, after Stephen's smart snapping-up of the Crown, he seemed to face a similar set of challenges to previous kings, and went about dealing with them in the same way. As individual rebellions and threats arose, he responded to them swiftly. A Scottish invasion, for example, was so comprehensively repulsed that the Scots king, David, though he was Matilda's uncle, played relatively little part in the English civil war that followed (though he did make territorial gains in the North). Other early threats to Stephen might later have been interpreted as a warning of what was to come. But the rebellions of Baldwin de Redvers in Devon, or Robert of Bampton in Somerset, seem to have been isolated cases, and although Baldwin later joined Matilda's party, there is no reason to see his initial rebellion as anything more than a testing of the waters by a powerful baron who wanted to extend his influence. Baldwin was forgiven after that rebellion. Does that make Stephen 'half-hearted'? Not necessarily. In earlier reigns, rebels did not automatically face severe punishment if they submitted. In fact, if we compare Stephen's early experiences with rebels to those of his two predecessors, Henry and William Rufus, let alone to those of his grandfather, Stephen's situation looks rather more secure. Matilda's claim, as a woman, and more importantly her support were much weaker than the early declarations for Robert Curthose at the beginning of both previous kings' reigns.

We need look no further than Matilda's half-brother, Henry I's illegitimate son, Robert of Gloucester, one of the most powerful men on both sides of the Channel, and, it might be expected, a natural supporter of his sister. In fact, Robert joined Stephen's court in 1136, pledging his allegiance, and even accompanied the King on an expedition to Normandy against the encroachments of Matilda's husband, Geoffrey of Anjou. There may from the beginning have been a ready-made alternative to Stephen as monarch, but early signs were that it wasn't a very popular alternative; to that extent at least, there was no 'inevitability' about the civil war.

So what went wrong? Historians have, over the centuries, found the answer in Stephen's character, in the 'system', and in the barons' disloyalty. Stephen has been blamed for being over-generous to his supporters, and conversely for being over-strict; for neglecting parts of his appropriated inheritance, particularly Normandy, where opposition was allowed to coalesce. Powerful men in his court, including the Beaumont twins Waleran and Robert, have also been blamed for influencing the King to divisive favouritism. There seems to be some truth in all these explanations, but other kings might have got away with it. Even the existence of Matilda as a rival might not have ensured civil war if she had been unable to gather real support. The key to that, and Stephen's biggest blunder, was the treatment of Robert of Gloucester, whose qualified support the new king somehow managed to transform into open rebellion.

We cannot know what might have guaranteed Robert's con-tinuing loyalty, but what happened practically guaranteed the opposite. During the campaign to eject Geoffrey of Anjou from Normandy in 1137, in which Robert lined up alongside his king, a fight broke out in the royal army. Stephen's Norman barons were offended en masse, but it was one baron in particular that Stephen could not afford to alienate, and Robert of Gloucester announced that he had uncovered a plot to ambush him, ordered by Stephen. The campaign was called off, and a treaty negotiated with Geoffrey, so that Stephen had achieved the triple feat of not dealing with his chief opponent, offending that opponent's potentially most powerful ally in his own camp, and not even exposing the potential rebel by having him go into battle against Geoffrey. There was little to stop Robert changing sides, but, even so, he took his time about breaking with Stephen. It was a whole year before he came out explicitly against his king, but it seems that this episode had decided the matter.

Robert declared his rebellion formally, remaining in Normandy and sending envoys in June 1138 to announce his *diffidatio*, or defiance, transferring his allegiance from one lord to another. There was no real precedent for such a formal declaration (Robert's chief historical spin doctor, William of Malmesbury, said it was 'according to custom', but that is because custom always sounded safer than new ideas to a medieval audience), so this looks like an innovation in the history of rebellion. To Robert, unlike, say, Baldwin de Redvers, the act of rebellion was more than a personal response to unfavourable treatment (though his Norman experience suggests that came into it). It was the result of a genuine deliberation over the ideological justifications for giving or withholding fealty to a king. Surviving correspondence from among Robert's circle even suggests the biblical text the Earl discovered to justify his support for a female descendant. Robert was a formidable opponent, who gave Matilda's party the powerbase they lacked, but it is important too that he felt it necessary to 'occupy the moral high ground'.

Robert's soul-searching suggests that he had the sort of intellectual complexity not readily associated with his class, or his time. It shows too the power of religious thinking to influence what laymen did. Such considerations would emerge ever more strongly in subsequent rebellions. It is from Robert's agonized break with his lord that we can trace the beginnings of more considered disavowals of the 'rebel' label. Religion might not yet have become the reason for rebellion, but Christian faith was the reason why so many rebels went out of their way to describe themselves as anything but rebels. Those who took up arms against Stephen's successors called themselves the 'Army of God', the 'community of the realm', 'Ordainers', 'true commons' or 'Appellants'. 'Rebel' was a dirty word. It is difficult to reclaim how threatening the notion of rebellion once was from a present-day perspective, when it has become mostly a fashion statement. But there is a vestige even today, if you know where to look. Perhaps the last place in English culture where the idea of rebellion is not embraced or accommodated is in the Anglican order of service. At a baptism, godparents are still asked, 'Do you reject the devil and all rebellion against God?' For centuries, rebellion against the king *was* rebellion against God. To be a rebel was to take on the role of Satan, to be a traitor was to betray your lord like Judas Iscariot. The only way rebellion could be justified was by showing it wasn't rebellion at all.

Stephen's mistakes had given Matilda a viable position from which to claim the throne, but it was England's misfortune that neither side was competent, or incompetent, enough to ensure total victory or total defeat. The result was a messy, confusing and extended civil war. Its two most significant engagements, the Battle of Lincoln in February 1141 and the siege and rout of Winchester seven months later, ended in the capture first of Stephen, secondly of Robert of Gloucester. As they were exchanged for each other, it seemed that even apparently decisive victories could not end the conflict.

Following her side's triumph at Lincoln, Matilda blew her chance of securing the throne by her treatment of her subjects, specifically of the 'commune' of London. Londoners had already played a part in deciding the fate of the kingdom, when at the beginning of his reign they had agreed to support Stephen. They did this not just as the representatives of a powerful city but while claiming a specific electoral right: 'it was their own right and a peculiar privilege that if their king died from any cause a successor should immediately be appointed by their own choice'. One may assume that, even if such a custom had not been invented on the spot to suit Stephen's case, it was in general manifested in acclamation (as at William the Conqueror's coronation) rather than by formal election. Whatever the reality of the tradition, Londoners clearly felt that, in the peculiar circumstances of Stephen's reign, they had a significant say in the fate of the Crown. The events of Matilda's brief 'queenship' tended to bear them out.

From the beginning, London was a doubtful adherent to the new queen, but the increase of grants to the custodian of the Tower of London, Geoffrey de Mandeville, had secured his (temporary) allegiance, and he seems to have been able (temporarily) to deliver London's support as well, though the custodian and the citizens were not natural allies. But it was a fragile support. The Empress was alleged to have made unreasonable tax demands from the capital's citizens, and dismissed their entreaties for a relaxation of terms. The appearance of Stephen's queen (also called Matilda) outside the city walls, with an armed force laying waste to the area across the river within sight of the Londoners, persuaded them to rebellion against the Empress: 'with the bells ringing everywhere as a signal for battle', the citizens 'flew to arms, and all, with the common purpose of making a most savage attack on the countess [Empress Matilda] and her men, unbarred the gates and came out in a body, like thronging swarms from beehives'. The Empress, caught unawares, took flight. This was the moment at which her hopes of installing herself as a legitimate replacement for Stephen were dashed.

How much had 'the people' to do with it? It is an important question for a history of English rebellion, because this is the first time that a popular revolt appears to have played a leading role in the fate of the Crown. In 1141, the Londoners' actions in ousting Matilda went beyond the 'consultative' role they had played in endorsing Stephen. A delegation had already been summoned to deliver its verdict on Matilda's pretensions to the throne at a conference in Winchester, shortly after the King had been captured at Lincoln. When this party, purporting to speak for the 'commune' of London (a municipal body not officially recognized until fifty years later), instead pleaded for Stephen's liberty and submitted a statement from his queen, they were dismissed. So Matilda would have known how difficult it would be to secure London's support, yet still believed that she needed to establish herself there. This congruence of opinion about the importance of London and its 'representatives' allowed the Londoners to flex their muscles. Matilda may have been in a weak position, and it is inconceivable that a more powerfully placed monarch would have stood for it, but in 1141, the people of London decided who was to rule the country.

Although Matilda attempted to re-establish herself at Oxford, holding court and making various grants there, the tide was turning again around the kingdom. The siege of Winchester followed, in which Stephen's brother Henry, Bishop of Winchester and papal legate, twice swapped sides. Winchester was the dramatic counter-point to Lincoln. Robert of Gloucester was taken prisoner, and both sides were left back where they started, neither of them powerful enough to force a result, but with enmities too well-entrenched to allow a negotiated settlement. The talks which led to the exchange of the two illustrious prisoners, King Stephen and Earl Robert, might have been the occasion for a more lasting peace. A proposed deal would have reinstated Stephen, with Robert as his second-in-command, as justiciar (an office that in the event had to wait for Stephen's successor to be tried out, when the deputy appointed to the role would stand in for the King during his many absences). The general willingness to change sides may not have extended to Robert, however, and in any case the pro-posal left no place for Matilda's claims, so could hardly have been acceptable.

The rebel as robber baron

The continuing hostilities have often, following the evidence of various chroniclers, been blamed in part on the willingness of great men in the kingdom to prolong war while it suited them. The quintessential rebel-for-hire in this scenario was Geoffrey de Mandeville, who certainly changed sides on three occasions, and possibly more. The *Anglo-Saxon Chronicle* gives such an extreme picture of anarchy in Stephen's reign because it was written by a monk of Peterborough, reflecting the experiences of an area devastated by Geoffrey. A classic biography written towards the end of the nineteenth century by one of the modern pioneers of English medieval history, J. H. Round, built up a picture of an 'unscrupulous magnate' to whom loyalty meant nothing, who sold his support to the highest bidder, and whose last, ruthless personal rebellion epitomized the 'anarchy' of Stephen's reign.

If we examine Geoffrey's actions in greater detail, however, they seem less arbitrary, though no less cynical. When Stephen was in the ascendant, Geoffrey stayed loyal. But when Stephen marched on Lincoln, and his future was in doubt, Geoffrey, as custodian of the Tower of London, refused to let Stephen's queen take her daughter-in-law, Constance of France, with her when she wished to retreat to safety in Kent. That was a riskily offensive move, but it might have seemed sensible for Geoffrey to have something to bargain with if the Empress Matilda's party succeeded, as indeed they did. As the Empress entered London, she rewarded Geoffrey with various additional grants in his earldom of Essex. When the Londoners rose up against her, Geoffrey fled at her side. Although Matilda continued to reward Geoffrey after the London debacle, her grip on the kingdom was so insecure that she was offering him land over which she had no power. Following his instinct of trimming to the prevailing wind, Geoffrey managed to reingratiate himself with Stephen's queen, despite the fact that he had imprisoned her daughter-in-law. When Stephen himself was reinstated, Geoffrey's rehabilitation seemed to be complete, with the King entrusting him with ever more power, so that over the next two years 'everywhere in the kingdom he took the King's place, his advice being sought more eagerly than that of the King, and his orders more strictly obeyed.'

Geoffrey's final break with Stephen condemned him in the eyes of the *Anglo-Saxon Chronicle*, and has sealed his reputation as a ruthless, unprincipled operator. But the cause was treachery, not on Geoffrey's side but on the King's. Two years after Geoffrey's offence of imprisoning the King's daughter-in-law, Stephen finally decided to punish him for it. He suddenly arrested him at court and demanded that the Earl surrender his castles. Stephen had behaved like this before; it was exactly what he had done earlier in his reign to a group of self-aggrandizing bishops. Though he had made his case then, Stephen had forfeited the trust of his senior subjects. His treatment of Geoffrey, and in particular his misguided belief that the removal of castles would render the Earl powerless, resulted in a savage reaction. Geoffrey, allowed to go free, took advantage of a disputed election at the abbey of Ramsey to take control there himself, turning it into a fortress, and initiating what seems to have been a reign of terror, seizing men and women at random to get money, torturing them and attacking their land. Geoffrey's behaviour was shocking to contemporaries, as it is to us, but it was not motiveless. And it has to be admitted that it was the King, by removing his sources of wealth and power, without confining him entirely, who cornered Geoffrey into such activity. Geoffrey de Mandeville was an insulted and wounded magnate, not the natural product of a flawed system. He died, excommunicated, during an attack on a castle in Cambridgeshire, and the revolt he spearheaded died with him.

Geoffrey's posthumous reputation bears comparison with that of an earlier East Anglian rebel whose legend fared better, but who on the surface had much in common with him: Hereward 'the Wake'. Both Hereward and Geoffrey seized abbeys (Peterborough and Ramsey) from which to wage their campaigns. Both used guerrilla tactics and the natural defences of the fens around Ely to make themselves difficult to pin down. And both have depended on a nineteenth-century historical rediscovery to recast their reputations. But where Hereward became the subject of a romantic historical novel, albeit one written by a Regius Professor, Geoffrey was pinned, mounted and displayed as a specimen of feudal aberrance, by a thoroughly 'modern' nineteenth-century historian, J. H. Round. And while Hereward's legend was burnished by a single family, the Wakes, who spuriously gave him their name, Geoffrey cropped up as a local folk tale, the village bogeyman rather than the local hero. One such story has to square the fact that Geoffrey was known to have founded Walden Priory, hardly the act of an unmitigated villain. But a tradition of Geoffrey's curse

on the land grew up after it passed, on the dissolution of the
monasteries, into lay hands. In armour and cloaked in red, with a
ghostly dog at his side, evil Geoffrey haunts these lands every six
years around Christmas time. The identification of an effigy in
Temple church, London, as Geoffrey's reminds us that his reputation was not so heinous a few years after his death as to stop him
eventually receiving Christian burial.

Was Geoffrey's revolt symptomatic of a more general breakdown
in order across the kingdom? Chroniclers' descriptions of lawlessness aren't restricted to the area around Peterborough. But the
complaints of a pro-Stephen chronicler about the West Country,
for example, which remained mostly under the control of Robert
of Gloucester, were more a reflection of the fact that Robert was
compelled to institute his own methods of governance to substitute
for the King's (including, apparently, the issue of coinage), which,
to a royalist, looked like anarchy. The fact that a powerful opposition party remained at large throughout the reign obviously
meant that Stephen's grip on his kingdom was nothing like as
complete as that of his predecessors. But that is very different from
a total breakdown in law and order.

In some instances, the diffusion of power to the magnates
resulted in less violence, not more. Although Stephen, Robert of
Gloucester, and later Matilda's son Henry, the future Henry II, all
hoped for a final triumph and complete defeat for their opponents,
those who followed them were more circumspect. Two of the
most powerful, earls Robert of Leicester (one of the Beaumont
twins) and Ranulf of Chester, drew up a limited-aggression pact,
around 1149, which acknowledged that the liege lords of the two
men (Stephen and Henry) might force them to fight each other,
and confined the retinues on either side to twenty knights. It was
hardly a robust guarantor of peace, but it demonstrates that the
magnates were less committed to all-out war than were their
masters.

After the death of Robert of Gloucester in 1147, and the emergence of Henry as an active leader, only such private arrangements
could contain the harm civil war inflicted, in the absence of a

deciding battle between the two principals. Henry was able to take control of Normandy, but couldn't press his advantage in England. Only when Stephen's elder son Eustace died in 1153, thus removing a potential heir (another son, William, survived until 1159, but Stephen had not nursed the same ambitions for him), was there a prospect of a negotiated peace. This was largely drafted by the two leading churchmen in either party, Theobald, Archbishop of Canterbury, and Stephen's brother Henry, Bishop of Winchester, where the negotiations were held and the Treaty signed. Stephen was to remain on the throne until his death, but he was to be succeeded by Henry. Less than a year later, in November 1154, Stephen died and Henry succeeded. The Treaty of Winchester acknowledged that both Stephen and Henry's followers might suffer, and made provision that the 'disinherited should be restored'. As land had changed hands more than once, and different families could have legitimate claims, this was not a straightforward matter in practice. Restitution did lead to rebellion on occasion (for example at Drax in Yorkshire). But such reaction was remarkably limited. In general, the barons are more noteworthy for their restraint than their licence.

The picture that emerges from Stephen's reign is of a more responsible, and practical, baronage than received opinion, and some of the more lurid chronicles, would have us believe. Stephen's became a divided kingdom, and allegiances certainly shifted during the nineteen years of conflict. But to portray all rebellious subjects as unprincipled grabbers of the main chance is to caricature them. Rebellion did not automatically mean chaos.

3. Rebels with a Cause

Thomas Becket to Magna Carta 1154–1215

. . . we have granted all the aforesaid things for God, for the reform of
our realm and the better settling of the quarrel which has arisen
between us and our barons . . .

Magna Carta (cap. 61)

English rebellion didn't die with King Stephen in 1154. True,
the man who succeeded him was an infinitely more impressive,
and substantially more powerful, monarch. Matilda's son, King
Henry II, made England part of a bigger empire than anything it
had known since Rome, and introduced a programme of legal and
administrative reforms to help him govern a territory stretching
from southern France to the Scottish borders. Yet even this mighty
medieval prince was challenged. In fact, those who confronted
Henry and his successors left some of the most lasting of any
rebels' legacies. Among these opponents was an archbishop whose
resistance and martyrdom made him one of the most frequently
invoked names in English history. Less than fifty years after the
Archbishop's murder, a successor inspired by his example was
instrumental in making Henry's younger son, King John, put his
name to a document that still resonates today: Magna Carta. The
rebels who imposed this great contract on their king were mostly
practical men, and their rebellion originated from conditions on
the ground, not lofty ideals. Yet Magna Carta crystallized the idea
that rebels could act from principle, and sought to establish
rebellion as an English subject's right.

Together, the rebels who opposed Henry and his sons began to
set the limits on the power that even undisputed kings of England
could expect to wield. In some of the appeals they made to a

community beyond their own interests, they also began to enshrine the idea of national rather than merely sectional rights and liberties. The dramatic ways in which their conflicts played out – the murder in the cathedral in 1170, and the King at the public mercy of his subjects at Runnymede in 1215 – were equally vital in ensuring that their defiance was imprinted on the national memory. The rebels who succeeded them, right up to the Civil Wars of the 1640s, took the lesson of these indelible confrontations to be this: that resisting a king did not have to mean backing an alternative. It could also mean presenting a case to compel your rulers to do their job better. The twelfth- and thirteenth-century rebels had built on the foundations laid by Robert of Gloucester in setting out a moral case for rebellion. We don't have to swallow their professions of sincerity whole to recognize the importance of the insight they had stumbled upon: a justified rebel is far more difficult to deal with than one who only sees the main chance.

None of this righteously rebellious future would have seemed very likely in 1154. Henry's first task was to mop up the remaining mess of the civil war – which included a few diehards who were prepared to test out the new king – and he did so with little fuss. His opponents were not initially willing to concede the influence they had secured in the previous reign. Barons as powerful as William le Gros, Earl of York, 'more truly a king than his master' in his region, and Roger, Earl of Hereford, the son of one of Matilda's staunchest allies in the civil war, took up arms against him. But Henry's response was swift and strong enough – marching up to York in person to confront William, for example – to bring these early rebels to heel. Henry's no-nonsense reaction has been favourably compared with Stephen's less resolute approach, but that ignores the facts. In both cases, these early rebellions might be seen as testing the waters, but the difference in Henry's was that there was no prospect of local defiance developing into a more widespread opposition, because there was no alternative candidate for the Crown. These early tests were, in truth, nothing like as severe as those Stephen faced (and initially dealt with). Unlike Stephen (and, for that matter, any of Henry's Anglo-Norman

predecessors), Henry II was an undisputed heir, and that counted
for more even than his own unswerving approach to business.
While rebels could only present themselves as engaged in a power
struggle, the most powerful man in the land had little to fear from
them. Only when they added a moral dimension to their armoury
could they hope to threaten a securely enthroned sovereign.

Henry's choices of senior figures to help him administer his new
realm show that rebels could still expect to be readmitted to royal
favour. Of the three most senior men appointed to the offices of
co-justiciars and of Chancellor, the first two were Stephen's men,
and recent enemies: Richard de Lucy (who had inherited most of
Geoffrey de Mandeville's lands) and Robert of Leicester (the canny
Beaumont twin who had waited until the final turn of the wheel
to place his bets with Henry, in 1153). These former opponents
were to prove trustworthy servants of a more authoritative king.
Henry's third choice, whom he made chancellor, eventually
became a more wounding opponent than any baronial rebel. He
was a capable archdeacon from Archbishop Theobald's staff,
Thomas Becket.

Becket was not a rebel in the sense that we have been using
the word up to now, but he became the exemplar of principled
opposition (or, some would argue, of personal animosity and obsession disguised as principled opposition). He resisted Henry not
with arms, but with all the force of organized religion, and the
backing of the only man who could legitimately claim in some
spheres to be the King's master, the Pope. The 'low-born clerk'
whom Henry plucked from obscurity to occupy two of the highest
offices in the land, as Chancellor and then as Archbishop of Canterbury, showed how even the most powerful of kings could be
resisted by intransigent self-belief. His break with Henry, a dispute
apparently about legal jurisdiction that somehow led to martyrdom,
cast a shadow over the reign and the King's legacy. Becket's tragic
life is a drama often revived, but his significance in the history of
rebellion cannot be ignored.

The dispute between Becket and the King emerged from the
climate of rebellion in Stephen's reign, though the way it escalated

owed more to the personalities of the two antagonists. Church affairs as much as state politics had been shaken up by the civil war. While it would be simplistic to say that Church authority filled the vacuum left by lay incapacity (churchmen had often found themselves at the mercy of rebellious barons), some of the assumptions of Stephen's predecessors – that the island of Britain was a special case as regards papal relations, that the king could assume a natural pre-eminence in the appointment of bishops and archbishops – had been allowed to wither.

The Archbishop of Canterbury when Henry came to the throne, Theobald, had been instrumental in securing the King's succession. So, although Thomas would later claim that, from the beginning, Henry had attacked the privileges of the Church, the circumstances of the King and his first archbishop favoured a mutual respect. It was only on Theobald's death and the appointment of Thomas, Henry's man, that the King began a more thoroughgoing pro-gramme of reform, intended to bring the Church, like the rest of his domain, to a state of efficient compliance. For Thomas, how-ever, the freedoms of the Church, partially acquired in Stephen's time, and theoretically developed in the burgeoning study of canon law that was happening simultaneously, could not be relinquished. Their dispute was just as much a power struggle as any between barons and king, but in the Church, and the papacy, Becket had the advantage of institutional backing. Henry's dispute with Becket was not the first time an English king had lost out to a rebel (Stephen and Matilda could attest to that). But it was the first time a king had lost the argument, and that counted for even more.

The souring of Henry's friendship with Becket and its deadly conclusion were first and foremost a great personal tragedy. The depth of animosity between the two former friends is illustrated by one of the sticking-points in an attempted settlement. Thomas insisted that their rapprochement be sealed by the traditional kiss of peace. Henry refused. As Thomas's actions became increasingly provocative, it can appear as if he actively sought martyrdom. But it is difficult to believe that Henry wanted to fulfil that destiny when he blurted out, on Christmas Day, 1170 (in the most reliable

if not the best-known version), 'what miserable drones and traitors
have I nourished and promoted in my household, who let their
lord be treated with such shameful contempt by a low-born clerk.'
There was already supposed to be an 'official' party gathering to
arrest Becket for his latest defiance, but this remark seems to have
inspired more drastic action. Four knights took it upon themselves
to dispense with the niceties. Four days later, on 29 December,
William de Tracy, Reginald Fitzurse, Hugh de Morville and
Richard Brito pursued Becket into Canterbury Cathedral. When
the Archbishop, having refused to run away, resisted their attempts
to carry him off, they fell on him with their swords. They sliced
off the top of his head, and then took it in turns to slash him
with their swords. Henry's most vociferous opponent had been
murdered in his own church. The personal drama of Henry and
Thomas had come to an abrupt end, but the political fallout was
about to begin.

As a Christian, and soon to be canonized, rebel, Thomas – or
more specifically his violent death – had two principal legacies, one
short- and one long-term. First, Henry reacted to the widespread
outrage that greeted the murder, and the suspicion of the King's
part in it, by conceding some of the central points on which the
dispute had turned. The issues of the trial of 'criminous clerks' in
lay courts and the free elections of bishops without royal interference were both conceded by Henry in the Church's favour. In
1175, Henry received the first papal legate to England (excluding
those resident bishops who had been appointed to the role) since
1138. To us, death might seem a pretty high price to pay for what
sounds like a technical knockout, but Thomas, who had become
(or been revealed as) something of a fanatic during the dispute,
might have disagreed. It also made him a rare instance of a successful
English rebel, even if he did not live to see his triumph.

Thomas's second, and greater, legacy was as a sainted example
to his successors. Because his name lived on after death, because
his shrine became the most popular destination of pilgrimage in
England for hundreds of years, Thomas's principled stand against
the King could be fearlessly invoked by other rebels. Later arch-

bishops, from Stephen Langton to John Stratford, were among those who explicitly followed Becket's example. But because he was a universally popular saint, he could also be co-opted by rebels outside the Church, to such a degree that, more than 350 years after his murder, Henry VIII came to see him as the symbol of rebellion – 'really a rebel who fled to France and to the bishop of Rome to procure the abrogation of wholesome laws'. Until that withdrawal of official backing in the larger break with Rome, Thomas's martyrdom made it impossible to dismiss all rebels as traitors. The first person to realize this was Henry II himself, and the circumstance that forced him to make public penance for his part in Thomas's death was the only major conventional rebellion of his reign.

A family affair

Becket's stand had demonstrated that a challenge to the King's authority didn't need the backing of an army to make it effective. The rebels who defied Henry in 1173 were more reminiscent of those who had confronted his predecessors. They were gilded aristocrats, and they originated from very close to home, in fact from Henry's home itself. The leaders were his eldest son, Henry 'the Young King', and his own wife, Eleanor of Aquitaine. Their bid for power had none of the moral force or resonance either of Thomas's defiance or of the Magna Carta resistance in the following century, but their rebellion did have wider significances. Not only did it expedite official recognition of the Becket cult, with all the implications for English religious and political life that entailed; it also saw the first leading role taken by a woman in an English rebellion (a forerunner to another unhappy queen consort, Edward II's wife, Isabella of France). And over the long term, in the concessions the rebels made to the French Crown, it stored up profound consequences for the English monarchy in decades to come.

Henry II had worked hard to ensure that his eldest son would be recognized as his sole successor. In fact, a dispute over the Young King's coronation while the current incumbent was still alive had been a point at issue between Henry and Becket. Henry junior was indeed crowned (though not by Thomas), but, to him, the honour and the part in government that followed were no compensation for his father's refusal to grant him any significant lands of his own. Even his youngest brother, John, despite being known as 'Lackland', had fared better on this score. By 1173, the Young King had decided that the old one needed to step aside. In this rebellion to enforce early retirement, young Henry drew the support first of his father-in-law, Louis VII of France, and then of his own family – brothers Richard and Geoffrey and their mother, Eleanor of Aquitaine.

Eleanor, whose reputation has tended to be bound up with doubtful stories of courts for lovers, of troubadours and romance, would perhaps be more fittingly remembered for being the first female rebel in British history after Boudicca. Women are usually consigned to supporting roles in medieval history, though already we have seen some exceptions to this in the lives of Harold's wife Gytha and those of the two Matildas. But Eleanor's part in her sons' rebellion against Henry II, actively encouraging Geoffrey and Richard to side with their elder brother, and summoning her own vassals to arms (and, it should be added, throwing in her lot with her ex-husband, Louis VII), was unprecedented. Henry was caught unawares, but was fortunate to capture his wife as she made her escape in male disguise when his forces drew close to her Poitiers stronghold; he was sufficiently disquieted to imprison her indefinitely. It would be fairer to her memory to recall Eleanor not as the leisured overseer of an indolent court, but as a woman who was prepared to risk everything in pioneering pursuit of her own and her sons' interests. She would be rewarded by Richard at his succession, becoming a trusted adviser and fixer.

The support of the King of France made the Young King's rebellion a serious one. As well as a dynastic jockeying for position, the rebellion represented an outlet for powerful barons who thought that Henry II's interference in their affairs was too much to bear. As one chronicler put it, 'the father, with a view to increasing the royal dignity, was trampling on the necks of the proud and haughty.' Though Henry could rely on some powerful allies, the defectors to his son included the earls of Norfolk, Leicester, Chester and Derby. Even almost twenty years after the end of the civil war, the reverberations from Stephen's reign can still be sensed in these defections. All four came from families who had been affected by Henry's shakedown on coming to the throne, losing land and honours which had been fought over in the previous reign.

Henry initially concentrated his own efforts on Normandy, but from the beginning parts of England were in rebel hands. The centre of rebellion was Leicester, but when the rebels started to lose ground in Normandy, they reimported their defiance, landing in East Anglia, hoping to link up with the rebels in Leicester. At Fornham in Suffolk, the Earl of Leicester, with a large force of Flemish mercenaries, was confronted by the King's constable, Humphrey de Bohun, and was defeated. In 1826, a mound on the site was found to contain forty skeletons, neatly arranged, feet facing inwards, faces out. But Fornham was not the end of the rebellion, despite the capture of Leicester and the woman usually described as his 'amazon wife', and the surrender of the Earl of Norfolk. Rebels in the North joined forces with the King of Scots, William, who had been promised the earldom of Northumberland by the Young King. Another party of Flemings landed in East Anglia, where the Earl of Norfolk renewed his rebellion and captured Norwich.

Only at this point was Henry persuaded to abandon Normandy, where he rightly feared the King of France and his own son would make inroads in his absence. And it was now that he grasped the importance of the murdered Archbishop as a symbol of rebellion. On his return to England in 1174, Henry followed in the footsteps of a growing number of his subjects and made a pilgrimage to the shrine of the man who had defied him to the death. Within sight of Canterbury Cathedral, where Thomas had been struck down, Henry dismounted and began to walk; with half a mile to go, he removed his boots. When he got to the shrine, he prostrated himself and confessed his sins, including his unintentional part in the murder. The timing, four years after the event, can only lead us to one conclusion: Henry did not want the new rebels to be legitimized by association with Thomas. But it was Thomas's own less warlike rebellion that had driven the King to such a public humiliation. One of Thomas's contemporaries later told the King about a dream that Becket had described, in which Henry was attacked by a flock of birds. In the dream, Thomas helped to drive the birds off, and in reality the rebels were tamed. The King of Scots was captured at Alnwick, apparently on the day of Henry's penitence, and Henry's own intervention at Huntingdon and Northampton drew the surrender of the remaining English rebels. Returning to Normandy, Henry saw off Louis, and the Young King's rebellion collapsed.

By the time of Henry's act of contrition, Thomas had already become an object of veneration, and a worker of miracles. His popularity continued up to (and beyond) the Reformation. In 1341, when one of Thomas's successors who also defied his sovereign, Archbishop Stratford, complained about the decline of gifts to the shrine, popular donations were still running at an impressive £400 a year. Back in 1174, King Henry's endorsement removed the symbolic connection to rebels in his own day. Becket's memory continued to be contested, invoked by rulers and ordinary pilgrims alike, as well as by other defiers of royal authority. Visitors to his shrine included most of Henry's successors, up to and including Henry VIII, before the Tudor attack on Rome led him to change his view of Thomas and order the shrine's destruction.

Perhaps Thomas's most striking reappearance as a symbol of rebellion, however, was in the reign of Henry's youngest son, John, who faced rebellion on a scale not seen since the time of Stephen. The rebels' spiritual leader was another archbishop, Stephen Langton, this time imposed on rather than handpicked by the King. Thomas's example was on contemporaries' lips from the moment that the Pope, whose choice Stephen was, tactlessly warned the King in his letter of commendation that John should not 'fight against God and the Church in this cause for which St Thomas, that glorious martyr and archbishop, recently shed his blood'. Langton himself seemed to take his predecessor as his defining example, from his first open letter to the people of England, in which Langton mentioned Thomas's struggle, his taking up residence (while waiting to be allowed into England) in Pontigny, where Becket too had spent his exile, through his choice of seal showing the martyrdom, to his presiding over the jubilee translation of Becket's relics in 1220 (at which he emphasized the rebel-archbishop's essential Englishness). As an English rebel, if not an English icon, Langton has even more claim to fame than Thomas; because he is credited as one of the main authors of the most influential rebels' statement in English history: Magna Carta. Yet Langton certainly saw Thomas as his chief inspiration.

After the defeat of the Young King's rebellion, Henry II was able to reign relatively undisturbed, until another outbreak of filial revolt seemed to hasten him to his grave in 1189. The so-called Angevin system of government, a combination of efficient administration and quasi-federal control that was suited to his widely scattered domain, is usually seen as Henry's greatest achievement, though it was adapted to rule an empire that didn't survive his youngest son's reign. A less well-recognized but perhaps more lasting legacy was the one left by his sons' rebellions. Both Henry the Young King, and Henry II's younger sons Richard, Geoffrey and John in their later rebellion, had turned to the King of France, Louis VII, and his son and successor, Philip, for support against their father. John would do so again in his brief uprising against his brother, Richard. The concessions made on each occasion to the French Crown meant that the French kings' authority over their Angevin vassals, which as far as Henry II had been concerned was fairly nominal, began to bite. When John eventually succeeded to the throne, he would suffer the consequences. Philip first tried to support John's nephew, Arthur of Brittany, against him. When that failed, he formalized (with a payment from John of 20,000 marks) John's subordinate relationship for his French possessions, and, when the time came, was able to eject him from most of them. It was John and his elder brothers' rebellions that had set the French king's juggernaut rolling, but it was John alone who was crushed by it.

Robin Hood and the bearded revolutionary

Henry II's system of government allowed a degree of administrative autonomy, so that the system kept running whether the king was there or not. The same might not be true of maintaining order: the best guarantee of keeping the peace was the king himself. Defying your anointed sovereign face to face was always a bigger deal than defying his representatives. So, while Henry's successor Richard I was away on crusade, his administration was able to function in his absence (despite the unpopularity of William Longchamp, the man who had assumed responsibility for it as justiciar). But when Richard was taken prisoner on his way home, things changed. Although the ability of England's bureaucracy to raise cash for Richard's astronomical ransom demonstrated its unparalleled efficiency, the possibility of his permanent absence prompted a challenge from his younger brother, John. Despite the support of the King of France, Philip, and the threat of an invasion, however, John's rebellion was swiftly snuffed out. The principal reason was the release of King Richard. Once it was known that the King was returning, enthusiasm for the rebellion melted away – in some cases rather rapidly: the rebel castellan of St Michael's Mount in Cornwall died of fright on hearing the news of Richard's landing.

Perhaps it is the rare lack of sustained rebellion during Richard's reign that accounts for the placing in it of a fictional one, led by the most famous, if non-existent, rebel in English history. The first mention of Robin Hood in literature comes in the fourteenth century (in *Piers Plowman*, where it is joked that he is already better known than the Lord's Prayer), but it was not until 1521 that a Scottish writer, John Major, dated him (on no particular authority) to Richard's reign, and his activities specifically to the time when

Richard was on crusade and then in captivity. It was another Scottish writer, Sir Walter Scott, who in *Ivanhoe* (1819) crystallized the modern version of the legend and its chronology, setting it at a time when 'four generations had not sufficed to blend the hostile blood of the Normans and Anglo-Saxons, or to unite, by common language and mutual interests, two hostile races, one of which still felt the elation of triumph, while the other groaned under all the consequences of defeat.' Shortly after the Conquest, as we have seen, England was an occupied, deeply divided realm. But if there is any truth to the legend of Robin (and various candidates for the 'real' outlaw have been offered), it would be very difficult to find its origins in the continuation of this resentment between Normans and Englishmen.

Robin is more important as a rebellious archetype, whose example could be enlisted in any number of causes. He was invoked by Royalists and Republicans, one side emphasizing his support for the true King, the other his policy of redistributing wealth. In the latest version of the legend, a BBC children's television drama serial, Robin deals with some very contemporary problems, including multiculturalism (Saracen knights as asylum seekers), a 'weapon of mass destruction' (Greek fire, which was indeed used in the siege of Nottingham on Richard's return in 1194) and a case of 'Crusader sickness' that sounds very much like Gulf War Syndrome. One notion pressed into service for its up-to-date resonances has a longer pedigree – that of the criminal rebel as misunderstood outcast: Robin is pictured with his hood up, glowering at the camera with all the implied menace of a teenage thug. For Robin of Locksley's confiscated land, forcing him into the forest, read closed down youth club, forcing our hooded heroes onto street corners.

There was, however, a real rebel in Richard's reign who, like the fictional Robin, had been on crusade with the King, and seems even to have established some sort of personal relationship with him. William fitz Osbert, the son of a London clerk, went to the Holy Land at Easter, 1190, and returned later that year. His story gives an insight into the political atmosphere of London and the pressures of raising the King's ransom. It also shows how, even at this early date, a commoner, albeit one of higher social standing than the people he led, could strike fear into the rich and powerful. William, a charismatic figure who cultivated a long beard so as, it was said, to stand out in a crowd, became a spokesman for poorer Londoners, who he argued were bearing the burden of the ransom unequally, especially when compared to those richer citizens like the mayor and the powerful members of the London commune (including twenty-four councillors), which had been formally granted in 1191 by Prince John during his brief ascendancy. William made it clear that his opposition was directed against these men, and presented himself as strongly loyal to the King.

William became a public risk when he started formally gathering support for a sworn association to get justice for ordinary Londoners in 1195, after the King's release, but while the remainder of his ransom was still being collected. Speaking outside St Paul's Cathedral, where the ransom was stockpiled, William recruited in 1195–6 – with the usual proviso about medieval witnesses when it comes to numbers – 52,000 citizens to his cause (as estimates of the city's population at this time hover around 100,000, even a quarter of this figure would give a huge proportion of Londoners). The London councillors complained about William to Hubert Walter, the King's justiciar, who was also the Archbishop of Canterbury. Fitz Osbert responded by taking a boat across the Channel to present himself at Richard's court in Normandy, where he appears to have been allowed to make his case and to return home. It may be that the King, who had been faced with the fait accompli of the London commune on his release, was happy that someone was making trouble for these self-appointed governors of the first city of his realm.

In 1196, however, as the threat to security grew (William had taken premises in Guildhall, where he was gathering crowbars to break into the houses of the rich), Hubert Walter took action. First, he undermined William's support, summoning a crowd of the rebel's supporters on whom he urged restraint, and to whom he promised a fair assessment of taxes. More to the point, Hubert obtained hostages from these followers as security for their good behaviour. Next, he tried to get hold of William himself. Hubert's first summoner was too frightened of the crowd around the rebel to deliver his instructions. So Hubert sent an armed posse to bring William back. Fitz Osbert resisted arrest violently, killing one man himself, while another was killed by a follower. With a small retinue, including his lover, he took refuge in the church of St Mary Le Bow. When the expected crowd of supporters did not materialize to rescue him (probably because Hubert had those hostages), the justiciar was able to close in. In an act for which he would be censured at his death, Hubert violated the sanctuary of William's refuge (which happened to belong to the monks of Canterbury Cathedral) by setting fires at each of the exits, smoking out the rebel and his nine followers. William was stabbed by the son of the man he had killed, but he was still alive as he was taken to the Tower and tried for treason. Along with his fellow rebels, William was found guilty and condemned to death. Tied to horses' tails, they were dragged through the City, to Smithfield Elms. On 6 April 1196, William fitz Osbert and his followers, leaders of the first recorded popular uprising in English history, were hanged in chains.

The story of William fitz Osbert, of his brief political moment and summary dispatch, has some of the constant themes of popular English rebellion. First, there is the avowed adherence and appeal to the monarch, over the heads of an oligarchy, which would be seen again in, for example, the Peasants' Revolt of 1381 and in the rebellion of Jack Cade in 1450. Secondly, the authorities' ruthless reaction, left to the King's representative rather than enforced in person, would become characteristic. Thirdly, William, like Wat Tyler, was used as a morality tale by those who wrote up his life. Most disapproved of his attempt to challenge the natural order of society. For a brief time, however, a popular cult threatened to take hold around him. The chain he was hanged in was used to cure fever, and the earth around the place of execution was dug up and taken away as a relic. But the idea of William as martyr was quickly suppressed, and it was pointed out that a man who could sleep with his girlfriend in a holy place was no saint. William's hairiness is intriguing too. It might be evidence of that Anglo-Norman enmity which Walter Scott took as the defining cause of the twelfth-century outlaw. Normans, as the Bayeux Tapestry shows, were short-haired and clean-shaven, while Anglo-Saxons had long locks, moustaches and beards. William had a Norman name, but he seemed to have adopted a 'native' look. Perhaps long hair is an older signifier of rebellion than we realize.

We have seen before how the fictional rebel has tended to overtake the genuine one in English historical memory, as in the case of Hereward 'the Wake', whose (initially historical) story as it was adapted over centuries shares many elements with Robin Hood's. William fitz Osbert, unlike Hereward or Robin, is re-membered by almost no one. In the reign that followed Richard's, real rebels came to the fore again, and once again they were barons, not champions of the people. The names of the individuals who defied King John may not be known outside the households of medieval historians, but the document they produced, Magna Carta, has proved immortal, despite the King's attempts to smother it at birth.

Magna Carta: the rebel as reformer

Before John, English rebellions usually fell into one of two cate-gories. They were either expressions of individual disaffection, like those of Robert de Bellême in William Rufus's reign, or of William le Gros in Henry II's. Or they were started to support a rival candidate for the throne, from Edgar the Aetheling to Henry the Young King. The barons who rebelled against John in 1214 eventually followed the latter path, too, when they adopted Philip of France's son Louis as their champion in 1216. But Magna Carta was the outcome of an alternative third strategy, dictated by the initial absence of a pretender. It was a programme of reform, the first in English history. And the rebels who produced it were the bearers of the first English 'party-political label': not the 'Army of God', as they styled themselves, but 'the Northerners', a description that expanded from the geographical to encompass all who rose against King John.

Why did they do it? The 'party-political label' doesn't help us with the answer to that question; though some found common cause against the King and managed to couch their grievances in the extended form of the great charter, they were not initially signed up to a manifesto, and their grouping did not long outlive the King, who died only a year after the charter was sealed. One answer to the question of why the barons rebelled is 'because they could'. As we have seen, armed rebellion, though not exactly routine, was hardly a last resort. Every king from William I onwards had faced one or more. But no other rebellion produced an expression of grievances quite like Magna Carta. The examples of Robert of Gloucester in Stephen's reign and, much more dramatically, of Thomas Becket in Henry II's had demonstrated the appeal of the justified rebel. They laid some of the groundwork for the Northerners' self-presentation. But the reasons John's rebels first came together, and came together around a document as unprecedented as Magna Carta, lie in the peculiar circumstances of John's reign, and of John's personality.

The big political fact of John's time was his loss of Normandy to Philip Augustus, the French king, in 1204 – a partial consequence of those dynastic rebellions of Henry II's sons. This resulted not just in a fall in prestige, and revenue, but in a reopening of the question of divided loyalties. Men like William Marshal, who held land in both territories, tried various contortions to retain them, which John did not appreciate. But the barons' great rebellion did not break out for a decade after the loss of Normandy. What exhausted the barons' patience was not losing Normandy, but trying to get it back. To do so, John needed the military support of his chief subjects, who held their land in return for the provision of military service. More than that, he needed money. The first requirement became hotly disputed, especially when John tried to raise forces to fight in his other French possessions, which were also slipping from his grasp. On two occasions, in 1205 and 1213,

John was unable to command expeditions, which had in fact mustered, to cross the Channel. Both times, the royal ship, known as the *Esnecca* (meaning 'snake', an appropriate flagship for this slipperiest of kings), even put to sea, perhaps in the hope of embarrassing his barons into following, but after sailing aimlessly off the south coast for a time John realized that nobody was coming with him, and returned, humiliated. Unable to rely on direct military support, John became adept at squeezing money out of his subjects to pay for the hire of mercenaries (who, because of inflation, cost three times as much in John's day as in his father's), using and 'improving on' the methods of his father and brother with unprecedented zeal. The ways he went about this were a fundamental cause of the great rebellion, and of the form it took.

One way John raised money to pay for his campaigns was scutage, 'shield money' levied in lieu of military service. Scutage wasn't new. Henry II and Richard I had used it, but they had done so a combined total of eleven times in forty-four years. John equalled that number in his sixteen-year reign and demanded more than twice the rate of his predecessors. Towards the end of his reign, when he tried to push the rate even higher, the barons refused to pay. Other general taxes proved extremely unpopular, and since the barons' consent (and, to some degree, their co-operation) was needed to levy them, John was only able to use them twice. His revenue streams thus relied on more sporadic and often arbitrary methods, taking advantage of duties on inheritance and thinking up infringements for which he could impose fines.

In these more arbitrary money-raising techniques, the King's personality had a large part to play. Later chroniclers would emphasize John's cruelty, accusing him of murdering his nephew Arthur with his own hands, or encasing a wayward exchequer clerk in a 'lead cloak' before starving him to death. But the clauses of Magna Carta make it clear that the King's personal vices were not as important to those who defied him as the sense that he could not be trusted to be fair in the way he extracted money from his subjects, however eminent they might be. The second clause of the charter, for example, after the confirmation of the freedoms of the English Church, is not some general expression of rights, but a swift getting down to brass tacks; it fixes the amount payable to the royal coffers as a 'relief' on inheritances: '£100 for a whole barony; . . . 100s., at most, for a whole knight's fee'. The next eleven clauses all seek to rein in the King's uses of subjects' inheritance, debts and borrowing to raise cash.

John's personal involvement in English government was not new but, again, he increased it, partly as a result of being in England more than his predecessors. There are records, for example, of very large sums demanded simply to 'obtain the king's good will': in other words, John had indicated that he was displeased with a subject, and fined him for it. In 1211, for instance, Robert de Vaux was fined 2,000 marks 'for the king's benevolence'. Again, such fines had been levied before, but never so often, nor so swingeingly. In Magna Carta, a clause specifically abrogated the practice: 'All fines made with us unjustly and against the law of the land and all amercements imposed unjustly and against the law of the land, shall be entirely remitted.'

There was one serious challenge to John from his barons before the uprising that led to Magna Carta. Some of the same rebel leaders were involved, but this first time they took the low road. In August 1212, as John was preparing a major expedition against the Welsh, a conspiracy was uncovered of barons who planned to murder the King and replace him, apparently with a French noble, Simon de Montfort. Simon was the father of the more famous rebel and political reformer namesake who came to dominate the reign of John's son, Henry III. Two men were implicated deeply enough in the plot to take flight: Eustace de Vesci and Robert Fitzwalter. Both later took leading roles in the Magna Carta rebellion. Though John seized the lands of the two men whose flight confirmed their involvement, he was inclined for once not to force his advantage. The Welsh expedition was cancelled, and the King issued orders to relax some of his harsher financial impositions.

John might have decided to react leniently because Eustace and Robert were almost certainly not acting alone; it was just that they were too obviously implicated to brazen it out. Those who remained at John's side could well have been involved, and John wanted to regain their loyalty. In fact, he needed to, because the rebellion came during a major dispute between the King and the papacy. John had refused Pope Innocent III's choice of Archbishop of Canterbury, Stephen Langton, and the Pope had responded by placing the kingdom under an interdict, suspending all church services, and then excommunicating the King. Formal deposition was the next step. Robert Fitzwalter even managed to persuade the papal legate in France that the King's excommunicate status was the reason for their conspiracy. If John were to remove a source of, or at least a pretext for, rebellion, he needed to resolve this dispute with the Pope, and retake the moral high ground from those who made their defiance an act of piety. When at last John did re-enter the Pope's favour, it was at the price of some pretty stiff concessions. Stephen was accepted as archbishop, John offered the realm of England in vassalage to the Pope, and Eustace de Vesci and Robert Fitzwalter, who had plotted against his life, were restored to their lands. It is perhaps no surprise that two rebels who had so thoroughly humiliated their king when apparently guilty of plotting to murder him should have had the confidence to defy him again, becoming leading players in the more nuanced rebellion that followed.

From Bouvines to Runnymede

Another compelling reason for John's forgiving attitude was that he was still planning a campaign in France. Despite the clear opposition of some of his barons, he managed to mount one. By the time this eventually sailed in 1214, forming an alliance with, among others, the Holy Roman Emperor, Otto of Brunswick, John had already made promises of general reform in order to persuade his barons to follow him, or pay not to. If his expedition had been as successful as an earlier naval sally to destroy a French invasion fleet, John would have been in a good position to resist baronial demands in his kingdom. But the campaign ended in disaster. First, John was deserted by his Poitevin soldiers just as he was about to face Philip's son Louis in battle in Poitou. Then, while he decided on his next move, the other part of his force, under the Earl of Salisbury, which had linked up with the Emperor, was defeated by the French army under Philip at Bouvines in Flanders. The two kings made a truce, but John's hopes of winning back his French possessions had gone. With them went any remaining leverage he had over his barons back in England.

Exactly how the growing discontent among the barons tipped into open and widespread rebellion, and the reasons for the form that rebellion took, are not at all clear. The initial occasion for defiance was another demand for money, another scutage, which had been issued while John was still in France in May 1214. Apparently sensing that the King was on shaky political ground (for there was no real legal justification), numerous barons, especially in the North (and including Eustace de Vesci), refused to pay, saying that the terms of their tenure didn't require them to fight, or finance, overseas campaigns. This argument was a fiction, but the Northerners' reliance on it shows that, at the beginning, their rebellion was a simple trial of strength with a king who had placed them under heavy burdens, and now didn't appear to have the muscle to enforce his will.

John had been expecting trouble. After Bouvines, while he was still in France, he sent orders to his justiciar, Peter des Roches, that the royal castles should be put in readiness. The defiance was by no means universal, but as the barons' opposition became more explicit and more widespread on John's return, he accelerated these preparations, ordering his mercenary captains to strengthen defences and prepare engines of war. Yet what ensued was not war but negotiation. The barons had stumbled on a new rallying point for their cause: a charter. Not yet the great charter of Runnymede, but one which dated back to the coronation of John's great-grandfather, Henry I, in 1100. Stephen Langton's role in reminding the barons of this charter isn't quite clear, but it seems likely that the Archbishop, who from the time of his arrival in England had

tried to restrain the King, and who later became involved with the
rebellion, might have tried to direct it along reformist, as against
simply destructive, lines.

Given something concrete to decide on, John procrastinated.
He promised to consider regranting Henry's charter and to give
an answer on the Sunday after Easter, 1215. He used the time to
send envoys to the Pope, take vows as a crusader (which released
him from secular obligations for three years), and gather more
reinforcements. Though John missed his first deadline, he carried
on negotiations with the rebel barons, with Stephen Langton acting
as intermediary (a role for which the Archbishop was upbraided
by the Pope). But these talks came to nothing, and it must have
been in the hope of forcing a reaction that, on 3 May, the rebels
at last formally announced their defiance, withdrawing their fealty
just as Robert of Gloucester had done from King Stephen in 1138.
The military leader of the newly formed 'Army of God' was
Robert Fitzwalter, the man who had been embroiled in the less
godly conspiracy to murder John three years before. The glimpses
we are afforded of Fitzwalter's personality do not flatter him. A
turncoat as early as 1203, when he had surrendered the Norman
castle of Vaudreuil to Philip Augustus without a fight, Fitzwalter
also appears as a bully who was allegedly prepared to turn up at
court with a large armed retinue in order to show support for a
murderer (who happened to be his son-in-law). His appearance at
the head of the rebel forces, and as a prominent witness to Magna
Carta, is a demonstration that the Charter's enshrinement of
liberties was a by-product of a more venal agenda, controlled for
the most part by men who put their own welfare some way ahead
of abstract principle.

In fact, Magna Carta's long afterlife as an embodiment of English
freedom can obscure the fact that it was the result of a peculiar set
of circumstances which came about in June 1215. It was not the
culmination of decades of struggle and debate: the earliest that any
chronicler dates a discussion of any sort of charter is 1213. It was
also the product of a sort of stalemate. At first, it looked as if the
rebels, who numbered about forty at the beginning (to which we

must add their sons, vassals and knights), would be outflanked by the King and those who remained loyal to him. But, on 17 May 1215, they turned the tables on John, by beating the loyal Earl of Salisbury in a dash to take London. This created an impasse. John could not risk trying to dislodge the rebels, and the barons would not want to stay in London indefinitely. The city's growing influence in the kingdom is shown by the importance that could be attached to holding it, but it was a tactical advantage, not a *coup de grâce*.

Some kind of formal concession from the King had been on the cards from the beginning of the year. Even after the rebels had defied him, John had made a short public declaration of his intention to treat even the rebellious barons in accordance with the law. The first result of the negotiations between the barons in London and the King in Windsor was an expansion of this promise into the 'Articles of the Barons'. Five days later, on 15 June, after further discussions, the document we know as Magna Carta was drawn up, and sealed by the King.

We have already seen how much of the Charter consisted of hard-nosed financial measures, the sounds of baronial pips squeaking. It has been described as having 'all the glamour of an appeal against an assessment by the Inland Revenue', and although the clause in which the King promises 'to no one will we sell, to no one will we deny or delay right or justice' has a universal ring, the references to scutages, aids, amercements, socage, bridges and fish-weirs are more representative of the whole. Magna Carta is still invoked today by politicians and leader writers, but it is usually with some wishful thinking – whether Gordon Brown is talking up the 'Britishness' of a document that makes special reference to the Welsh and Scots as completely separate cases; or editorials about unlawful detention appearing to confuse the Charter with habeas corpus. Nevertheless, Magna Carta's famous references to 'free men', rather than restricting itself to the barons' own class, indicate that there was more than naked self-interest at work. The phrase already appears in the Articles of the Barons presented to John earlier that June, from which, in part, Magna Carta grew. It is not even quite true to say, as has often been argued, that the earlier but undated Unknown Charter of Liberties (a much shorter document which seems to belong to the time of negotiation before John's last French expedition) refers only to barons. There, too, 'my man' and 'men' are discussed.

So the idea that someone, perhaps Archbishop Stephen Langton, persuaded the selfish rebel barons to expand their horizons and reach out to the community of the realm in an unprecedented gesture cannot stand up. The rebels seem to have been aware of these other interests almost from the start. But this awareness was not the barons' unique insight. It was a growing feature of Angevin government to address itself to 'barons, knights *and free tenants of the shire*'. John had twice prepared to muster the free men of the realm, and had required men over the age of twelve to swear an oath of communal loyalty in 1205, after the loss of Normandy. In referring to free men, the rebels weren't posing as revolutionaries: they were reflecting the status quo. If we are looking for glimmers of altruism in Magna Carta, the best candidate is the clause about the levying of fines ('amercements'). Here, the unfree 'villein', whose support can have meant little or nothing to the rebels (indeed, it is difficult to imagine that villeins themselves would have been aware of their inclusion), also finds protection from arbitrary government. There were other seeds of more progressive politics in the Charter. Rebels in the reign of John's son Henry built on the idea of the kingdom as a commune in a radically new way after 1258. The constitutional implications of the community of the realm imagined by Magna Carta's references to free men rather than noble ones also became a cause célèbre over four centuries later. But Magna Carta had to wait a long time to assume its more familiar role as an icon (what the Victorians called the 'palladium') of liberty.

A more immediately explosive clause was the last one, the so-called 'security clause', which appointed a council of twenty-five barons who would 'with all their might observe, hold and cause to be observed, the liberties which we have granted and confirmed to them by this present charter of ours'. The remedy available to the twenty-five if the King failed to keep his side of the bargain was more than recourse to a court of law. They 'together with the community of the whole land shall distrain and distress us in every way they can, namely by seizing castles, lands, possessions, and in such other ways as they can, saving our person and the persons of our queen and our children, until, in their opinion, amends have been made': in other words, a licence to rebel, though one which, again, expressly included reference to the wider 'community of the whole land' rather than the barons alone. The mechanics of this measure were made even more explicit in a separate list of the twenty-five, together with their quotas of knightly followers, which ends: 'All these barons with their full complement of knights and with the commune of the whole of England must rise up against the king if by chance the king turns against his own charter.'

With provisions like these elevating the King's subjects to a position of authority over him, it is hardly surprising that Magna Carta's immediate fate was to be rejected. John appealed to the Pope, who duly condemned this 'agreement which is not only shameful and base but also illegal and unjust . . . extorted from a great prince who had taken the Cross'. Innocent III declared it to be 'null and void of all validity for ever'. It seemed that the months of negotiation had come to nothing, as the country plunged back into civil war, with the Charter merely providing a justification for the 'distraint' of a recalcitrant king.

At the time, it is likely that the drama of the sealing of the Charter made a greater impact than the text itself. The prelude and moment of concession of Magna Carta were seen as great theatre very early on. The Charter itself declares picturesquely that it was 'given by our hand in the meadow that is called Runnymede between Windsor and Staines', even though the details of text were in fact hammered out over several days by Chancery clerks. The confrontations that led to the production of Magna Carta, on 15 June, were conducted in public. At some point, the rebels publicly renewed their allegiance, so that the Charter could be granted to a conspicuously loyal rather than a rebellious barony. It seems likely that all parties – baronial rebels, mediating churchmen, and royal entourage – who lived their lives in daily rehearsal of public rituals and ceremonies, were well aware of the importance of such an overt act. The rebels' achievement lay as much in forcing John to display himself so openly as in their power, as in making him set his seal on their words. The King and his successors could repeal or reject the parts of Magna Carta that challenged their authority, but they could never erase the picture of a king being dictated to by his rebellious subjects.

Magna Carta began its life as prop in a performance, an early instance of the importance of 'gesture politics' in the story of English rebellion, and this dramatic legacy lasted. During its long afterlife, the Charter was taken up by the Founding Fathers of the United States in the eighteenth century, and at Runnymede the memorial to Magna Carta was paid for by the American Bar Association in 1957. In return, an acre of the meadow was later donated to the United States in memory of one of the greatest of all exponents of political theatre, John F. Kennedy.

Magna Carta's survival, however, and its illustrious future, depended on a bout of overeating. King John died unexpectedly at Newark Castle in October 1216, in the middle of a civil war against the rebels. Their rival candidate for the throne, Prince Louis of France, had already been in the country for five months, gaining support all the time, apparently on the point of delivering the killer blow. If John had not contracted dysentery, reputedly after a gluttonous feast, it is quite possible that a second defeat for him at French hands, but this time on English soil, would have extinguished the Angevin line and given the rebels their triumph. But a victory for the French prince wouldn't have revived Magna Carta. A triumphant Louis was no more likely to countenance the concessions of the Charter than a triumphant John. Only John's death gave the Charter a chance of survival, because his successor, the nine-year-old Henry III, and his supporters, needed all the legitimacy they could get. So it was that in the fight to secure his throne, the rebels' manifesto, Magna Carta, was adopted by royalists.

4. The False Dawn of Reform

Simon de Montfort to Roger Bigod 1216–1307

> . . . in tears was made the song of our gentle baronage, who . . .
> let themselves be torn asunder, their bodies hacked and
> dismembered to save England.

Lament for Simon de Montfort (1267–8)

Magna Carta was the last thing on rebels' minds when King John died suddenly in 1216. The Charter, and the righteous resistance it represented, had been overtaken by events. Instead the rebels were fighting an old-fashioned civil war, in which one party backed their candidate for the throne, Prince Louis of France, against the other, John's nine-year-old son, Henry III. Later in the thirteenth century, rebels revived the notion of rebellion as a way of forcing the king's government to reform. Simon de Montfort was the most memorable, though not the only leader of that type. Over the very long term, Montfort's rebellion, like that of the Magna Carta barons, would come to stand for something much more fundamental to English conceptions of freedom than a dispute over medieval governance. But, at the time, Montfort and his rebellion, committed to a published political programme and a new arrangement of government to deliver it, turned out to be the exception, not the rule. More often in the two centuries after John's death, English rebellion moved in a different direction, and the high-stakes, low-ideals rivalry of the beginning of Henry's reign turned out to be more of a foretaste of those years than the reforming impulse behind Magna Carta or Montfort.

Over the next hundred years, English high politics narrowed to a test of strength. The result for a time was a stronger monarchy. The thirteenth century in England emerges as a drawn-out experiment in the possibility of containing and directing the monarchy by the threat of rebellion. But from the rebels' point of view the experiment was a failure, and the only conclusion a negative one: that rebels' ultimate fortunes depended on the all-or-nothing risk of replacing one king with another. Rebels did carry on dressing up their opposition in reformist clothes. They persisted up to the Wars of the Roses, and some of them meant it. But the fit became less comfortable each time, as rebellion was increasingly exposed on both sides as a fight to the death between competing factions, a battle to run the country, not remake it. So in 1216 the new reign began, with appropriate inauspiciousness, in the midst of a full-scale civil war – the outcome of a rebellion from which principle had been thoroughly drained.

Henry III, whose greatest legacy would be a rebuilt Westminster Abbey, where later monarchs were crowned with increasing ritual splendour, had to make do himself with a gold circlet provided by his mother, and without the Archbishop of Canterbury to place it on his head, as Stephen Langton was away in Rome. 'Dressed in royal robes made to his size', the 'fine little knight' was anointed and crowned at the abbey church of Gloucester, and then, tired out by the occasion, he was carried back to his chamber, 'where he was dressed in other, less heavy clothes'. The papal legate, Guala, presided, and the loyalist circle was headed by William Marshal, who took on the role of regent. Although the Marshal, as he was known (his surname came from the hereditary office he held as Marshal of the Army), had once made himself unpopular with John by retaining his dual allegiance in Normandy and England, he was recognized as a paragon of chivalry, celebrated in a verse biography written by his entourage. He had remained utterly loyal to Henry's father, despite provocation. Now approaching his eightieth year, he tried to pass the burden of responsibility for the son on to another. Eventually persuaded that he was the only man for the job, the aged knight promised to carry the boy king on his shoulders from island to island, if England would not have him.

The reason for the Marshal's gloomy pledge was that the rebels appeared to be wholly in charge. In 1216, more and more powerful men had gone over to the rebels' side since Prince Louis had landed in May. Now, although Henry's party included useful allies like Peter des Roches, the Bishop of Winchester, the justiciar Hubert de Burgh (holding out in Dover Castle against all odds) and the mercenary captain Falkes de Bréauté, the rebels could count among their number, as well as their royal leader and his followers, six earls, and others whose loyalty alternated with the fortunes of war. In the resources of the French Crown, the rebels also seemed to have far better financial backing.

This was not how their rebellion had first presented itself, as a confederation of faithful servants regretfully forcing themselves to bring their ruler to his senses. But when John died in 1216 the movement against him was stripped of its pretensions. If it had only been about the misrule of one man, then his son, nine-year-old Henry III, could hardly be expected to bear the sins of the father. If, on the other hand, the point at issue was the reforms embodied in Magna Carta, then the new regency government in Henry's name called the rebels' bluff, by reissuing the Charter (minus the 'security clause' which had given the barons *carte blanche* to rebel) only a month after John's death. Only a handful of rebels were persuaded by that to make their peace. The truth was, the rebellion was no longer about the Charter. It was, once again, about who should rule. By inviting a rival, a prince of France, to seize the English Crown with their help, the rebels had discarded the question of reform. The rebellion had come down to a straight fight between the supporters of two rival claimants. Prince Louis was hardly likely to go home because the wearer of the crown had changed, especially as John's heir looked so vulnerable. Faced with a choice between carrying their reform programme and putting their own man on the throne, most rebels chose the latter.

Lincoln Fair

Battles in the Middle Ages were not very often decisive; Bouvines, in 1214, had been one, guaranteeing the French monarchy's supremacy on French soil for the foreseeable future. Now, only three years later, there were two more, at Lincoln and off the coast of Sandwich, which ensured that England did not become part of Greater France. The loyalist victories against rebel forces on land and sea bolstered Henry's tottering government and put paid to the rebels and their Continental allies. Lincoln is a forgotten victory, but this street fight was, in its way, as important as the great set-piece encounters of English military history, like Bosworth Field or Marston Moor. If the rebels had triumphed, the next king of England would surely have been Louis I. But the barons and their French allies, who had occupied the city but were still laying siege to the castle, were surprised by a loyalist relief party, many of whom had forced a gate in the castle wall. Some rebels were killed, many more were taken prisoner: 300 knights, about half the mounted men in the whole rebel army. Caught unawares, the rebels put up so unimpressive a fight that the battle was known as 'Lincoln Fair'. As usual, the victors had God on their side. At the rout of Lincoln, the 'hives of Christ sent forth the iron-girt bees of war'. The loyalists, granted crusaders' absolution by the papal legate Guala, acted with the sort of murderous zeal only holy warriors can summon up. They pillaged the city and cathedral, accusing the inhabitants of collaborating with the enemy.

After passions cooled, however, no rebels were executed. The idea that rebellion meant treason, and failure meant death, was not yet a self-evident truth. In this, as in much else, twelfth- and thirteenth-century England looks more 'enlightened' to our eyes than the darker age that followed it. In 1217, there was an attempt to recast the rebellion as a straightforward invasion: 'England hath grasped her conquering swords by impulse of God.' In reality, both sides were an assortment of English, Normans, Poitevins and others. Louis sued for peace and returned home, while his English allies were offered reasonably generous terms, in recognition that their initial argument with King John had some justification. The treaty with Louis proclaimed a general amnesty and restoration of lands. Magna Carta, the rebels' abandoned manifesto, was then freely reissued under the seals of the new king's guardians.

On the face of it, the rebellion was a complete failure, from which the perpetrators were lucky to escape with their lives and possessions, while the Crown was reinforced. But for the time being, the balance of English political society had changed. Despite the rebels' earlier attempts to shrug it off, Magna Carta began to be established as a guarantee against arbitrary government. Accompanied by a Charter of the Forest (the smaller charter from which the Great one now had to be distinguished), Magna Carta was reissued for a third time in 1225 (in its final form), then again in 1234, 1237, 1253 and in the 1260s, and in Henry's son's reign in 1297 and 1300, very often as a concession when the king wanted to raise taxes. The rebels had, quite by chance, achieved something more permanent than the replacement of one crowned head with another by force. Eventually, Magna Carta lost its power as a rallying point for medieval rebellion, when more calculating and violent methods prevailed. But its revival in Henry's reign gave the rebels' charter its place on the statute books, and made possible its reincarnation in such different circumstances so many hundreds of years later.

During Henry's minority, a succession of wise older hands ran the government on his behalf. After the death of the regent William Marshal in 1219, a triumvirate took over, consisting of the new papal legate Pandulf, the justiciar Hubert de Burgh, and the Bishop of Winchester, Peter des Roches. Henry's minority, lasting nearly a decade, might have been expected to produce a more consultative kingship when Henry assumed authority at his coming of age. In fact, the mature Henry (though frequently this was the last adjective one could apply to him) relied on various closed circles of advisers, and attempted an increasingly personal and arbitrary style of government. Henry could be impulsive, provocative and pig-headed. He surrounded himself with favourites, who were often blamed for policies that were unpopular with those outside the charmed circle.

The occasional reissue of Magna Carta did not 'cure' the problem of baronial rebellion, especially with such a whimsical man on the throne. The troubles Henry faced were another part of the legacy of the Magna Carta revolt, which had demonstrated that rebels who justified their actions could expect more support than those who simply took up arms. In 1233, for example, William Marshal's younger son, Richard, Earl of Pembroke, reacted to the dispossession of one of his allies by the 'Poitevin' circle around the King (headed by Peter des Roches, who was actually from the Touraine, and his nephew, Peter des Rivaux) by withdrawing from court and leading attacks on royal supporters. Eventually, the revolt escalated and Henry responded by leading a force against Richard to the Welsh Marches. The two sides never actually came to battle, but because of the stalemate a group of leading churchmen was able to persuade Henry to dismiss the 'Poitevins' from his inner circle, removing the *casus belli*. Richard Marshal did not live to experience the fruits of his (partially) successful rebellion. He crossed the Irish Sea to support his brothers, who were now being attacked by royalists as the conflict spread to Ireland. At a skirmish near Kildare, he was wounded, and later died of his injuries.

The dismissal of Peter des Roches and his cronies ushered in a period of relative calm, in which Henry took advice from a wider circle, and kept the loyalty of his subjects. It was in 1235, for example, that the first mention of a 'parliament' in English history crops up in official records. For the time being, parliaments were fairly literal embodiments of what the French origin of the word, 'parlement', implies: they were conversations between the king and his very senior subjects. The transformation of that closed shop into the institution we know today originated as a by-product of the next challenge to Henry, which became the most serious rebellion yet seen in England.

The model of a medieval rebel

Richard Marshal's rebellion was part principled reaction against arbitrary government, part spat over who should have access to the King's patronage. A far better-remembered rebel, Simon de Montfort came to be associated with some of the most principled, and revolutionary, opposition to royal government of the Middle Ages. But he was also on an ego trip. For all his standing as a proto-republican, or, more dubiously, as 'father of the House of Commons', much of Montfort's historical resonance is purely personal, the effect of a powerful character still reverberating through the record of his own words and actions. He is the first English rebel with a visible hinterland – though in fact he was as English as St George. Simon's father was a northern French nobleman who devoted himself to fighting the Albigensian heresy in the Languedoc, an occupation that apparently made him famous enough to be offered the English Crown by early conspirators against King John. Simon himself did not even set foot in England until he was about twenty-two years old, in 1230. When, thirty years later, the expulsion of foreigners came to form a central plank in the reform movement he led, the irony was not lost on contemporaries, one of whom remarked that it was 'ridiculous that this alien should presume to subjugate the whole kingdom'.

It was a claim to the earldom of Leicester that first brought Simon to England, but this was not the limit of his ambition. The history of what became the first English revolution is in part the story of a close personal relationship between king and favoured courtier that went wrong, with echoes of Henry II and Thomas Becket. It was a relationship in which the normal dynamic between king and subject was oddly reversed. Matthew Paris, monk and court chronicler, tells a story of Henry III taking refuge from a storm in the palace of the Bishop of Durham, where Simon too happened to be staying. The King still seemed to be disturbed by the weather when the Earl went to greet him. ' "What is it you fear? The storm has now passed over" ', Simon asked. 'To which the king replied, not jestingly but seriously and with a severe look, "I fear thunder and lightning beyond measure; but, by God's head, I fear you more than all the thunder and lightning in the world.'" By the time of this encounter, Henry seems to have realized on which side the real power lay. Simon's motives, and the overlapping of private and public grievance in his opposition to Henry, have long been the subject of debate. What has never been in question is the unshakeable self-belief and sense of entitlement he brought to pursuing his cause.

Simon seemed to have sealed his place in Henry's inner circle by his marriage to the King's sister Eleanor, eight years after his arrival in England, but a shadow hung over the betrothal almost from the beginning. The marriage was hastily completed in partial secrecy, and Henry later complained, 'you seduced my sister before her marriage. . . . When I discovered this I gave her to you, though unwillingly, to avoid scandal.' Whatever the truth of the accusation, it was certainly the case that Eleanor was a widow who had pledged her life to chastity after her husband's death in 1231. Her taking up with a man who would still have been regarded as a parvenu must have been a surprise, even if it was not a full-blown scandal. The marriage continued to be significant in English politics because of the financial and territorial claims that attended it and which Henry was never able to settle. In time, Simon de Montfort seems to have become a genuinely (and religiously) committed reformer, but he fell out first with his brother-in-law over matters as close to the hearts of medieval barons as to our own: money and status.

Simon was too capable and too charming to be out of the King's confidence for long. The first split over money and the marriage was patched up, and in 1248 Simon was prevented from going on a (second) crusade by Henry's insistence that he take on a major task, the stewardship of Gascony, the remaining rump of French possessions still under the overlordship of the English Crown. But the uncompromising way Simon went about mastering this difficult territory made him unpopular, and Henry failed to give his full support, either financially or morally. When a Gascon rebel complained of his treatment by Simon, the King took the rebel's part instead of his lieutenant's. Further appeals from Gascony to Henry resulted in Simon's 'trial' in 1252 in front of his peers, a month-long ordeal conducted in the refectory of Westminster Abbey. In his defence, Simon was typically aggressive. As with the episode of the Durham storm, he reversed the usual balance of power, accusing his accuser. Henry was the guilty one, having promised so much and hung his loyal servant out to dry. 'Who can believe that you are a Christian?' the Earl demanded: 'Have you ever been to confession?' When Henry replied that he had, Simon asked, 'What use is confession without penance and satisfaction?' Henry was a Christian in name only; Simon, pious to the point of fanaticism, took his obligations seriously. If the King promised something, as he had in 1248, Simon expected him to deliver. When, a decade later, Simon took a solemn oath to uphold a plan of reform, he stuck to it longer and more faithfully than any of his confederates. It was this refusal to break his word that put Simon at the head of the rebellious party, and led him unyielding to his death.

Simon emerged as leader of the reform party, but he did not initiate the final break with the King, with whom he came to terms after he was exonerated at his 'trial'. Proposals for radical reform had been made as early as 1244, the date for which Matthew Paris gives an outline of baronial proposals known (because they were never acted upon) as the 'paper constitution'. But the real split between the great barons and the King came at least fourteen years later. In 1258, when the confrontation occurred, the earlier reconciliation between Henry and Simon had apparently broken down, although for the time being the Earl was only a leading member of the opposition party, not its head. The outcome of the Gascon affair earlier in the decade had been that Henry in effect bought his lieutenant out of the post, for a large lump sum and a later agreed annual fee. Unfortunately, if not unpredictably, given what had gone before, Henry was unable to keep up the payments to his subject, so personal financial demands formed one element of Simon's opposition, along with an unassuaged sense of grievance at the way he had been treated over Gascony. But the barons' reform movement was not a one-man show, and Simon was not alone in feeling that the King was not giving him what he had been promised. The 'confederation' of seven that came together to enforce their will on the King in April 1258 was headed not by Simon but by Roger Bigod, Earl of Norfolk, and included Richard de Clare, Earl of Gloucester, Simon himself, Peter of Savoy, Hugh Bigod (Roger's brother), John fitzGeoffrey and Peter de Montfort (no relation to Simon).

As well as various personal grievances, the rebels shared two broader complaints. One was that, in 1254, Henry had taken up the offer from the Pope of the Crown of Sicily, to pass to his younger son, Edmund. Henry and his advisers seem to have been in a very small minority of people who thought this was a good deal. Any strategic advantage was more than outweighed by the breathtaking cost of the venture. Henry agreed to pay the Pope the oddly precise figure of 135,541 marks, roughly £90,000 – a reimbursement, the Pope claimed, of the money he had already spent on winning the kingdom back from the deposed king, Frederick II. A rough estimate makes that the equivalent of around £4.7 billion today. At a time when Henry was short of cash, and seemed unable to persuade his barons to agree to extra taxes, the 'Sicilian business', as it came to be known, was as provocative as it was ill-conceived.

The final factor in bringing the barons into rebellious harmony against their king was the one on which contemporary commentators concentrate most: the influence of 'aliens' on the government. Here was an issue that had already supplied the fuel for risings in the earlier Angevin period, and would play a part in English rebellion for centuries to come. If Matthew Paris is to be believed, 'foreigners' were not merely planning a takeover of government, but the wholesale slaughter of those in positions of power. 'Many of the nobles of England were treacherously poisoned' by the outsiders, and there are even details of the special jars 'commonly called "costrells"', which were discovered to contain poison. Historians who usually speak of Matthew Paris as a reliable chronicler pass over this more lurid accusation in silence, but it is at least an indication of the strength of feeling against 'foreigners' in English politics. 'Poitevin' monopoly on government, as personified by Peter des Roches and Peter des Rivaux, had already provoked one rebellion. By 1258, a second wave of Poitevins was the target of the barons' (and chroniclers') anger. From 1247 onwards, Henry had introduced his half-brothers, the offspring of his mother's second marriage, to Hugh de Lusignan, to positions of favour, granting pensions to two, marrying another into high aristocratic English circles, and making a fourth Bishop of Winchester. The Lusignans were suspected of excessive influence at court, particularly on the all-important heir to the throne, Henry's son Edward.

The member of this hated family who had been raised to the Winchester bishopric, Aymer de Lusignan, was an immediate trigger of the confrontation with the King in 1258 that eventually led to a much wider plan for reform, to civil war, and to a short-lived experiment with something like a constitutional monarchy. A dispute between Aymer and a leading English baron, John fitzGeoffrey, brother-in-law to one of Henry's magnates, Roger Bigod, Earl of Norfolk, had been unfairly decided by the King in his half-brother's favour, and the grievance was aired at a parliament of the King and his barons in London in April 1258. The latest financially disastrous ramifications of the Sicilian business were also part of their agenda. Henry had been threatened by the Pope with excommunication if he did not pay up and send an unrealistically large force to Sicily. The 'confederation' headed by Bigod appeared armed, ostensibly because the King wished to lead an expedition against the Welsh. They marched into Westminster Hall to face down Henry. It took three weeks to come to some agreement in London, and the language of the resulting document shows how low Henry had been brought. In return for the concession of a committee of twenty-four (twelve chosen by the barons, twelve by the King) to decide how to 'reform the state of our realm', the barons agreed not to provide any money as such, but 'loyally [to] use their influence with the community of the realm so that a common aid [levy of money] should be granted to us'. Both parties also agreed to meet again at Oxford just over a month later, 'and whatever shall be ordained on this matter by the twenty-four . . . we shall observe inviolably'. There, Henry found that the barons had decided to take matters permanently into their own hands.

The Provisions of Oxford

What was set in motion at Oxford in 1258 would in retrospect look like the high-water mark of the notion of rebellion as reform. In Simon, who increasingly came to the fore, the rebels turned out to have a leader who was more sincere about the letter of their programme than any of the Magna Carta barons had been. Eventually, the legacy of this rebellion was polished up to represent the first stirrings of wider participation in government, the forerunner of democracy. But the more immediate lessons taken from the seven years between Oxford and Simon's eventual defeat and death in 1265 were that a rebel who wanted to control the king had better depose him, not reform him.

When the parties reconvened at Oxford, the confederation had drawn up a comprehensive programme. Part of that was the uncomplicated matter of expelling the Lusignans; whatever its later reputation, this rebellion continued to be suspicious of 'alien influence'. Beyond this, the rebels' proposals, the Provisions of Oxford, were meant to be the 'knot to bind their Proteus', the shape-shifting King who had resisted all previous efforts to make him govern by consent. The Provisions went way beyond the remedy of individual grievances, or even of the general reform laid down in Magna Carta. They were a wholesale redrawing of the constitution. Various overlapping groups of overseers were mentioned, but the most significant was the body of fifteen men, to be nominated by four individuals (not including the King, or, indeed, Simon de Montfort), as the king's council. Their remit was to 'advise the king in good faith on the government of the kingdom and on all things touching the king and the kingdom; to amend and redress everything that they shall consider to need redress and amendment; and over the chief justiciar and all other persons'. This formalized the work of the king's council, but it also made its sphere of activity far greater than anything that had previously been accepted. The king could stay, but he would be rubber-stamping the work of the fifteen. Where Magna Carta had contained a single, 'security' clause to attempt to enforce co-operation if the king reneged, the whole tenor of the Provisions was to change the decision-making process into one initiated and enforced by the council of fifteen.

Perhaps even more remarkable than this baronial *coup d'état* were the various proposals contained in the Provisions to expand the share in government of other classes. The reference in the first negotiations at Westminster to the 'community of the realm' was more than a delaying tactic. At that first meeting, seven barons, including Simon, had formed a confederacy, swearing to support each other, and had then forced Henry and his son, the Lord Edward, to swear to it too. At Oxford, they expanded this oath, to encompass the whole kingdom, the *commun de Engleterre* (the Lusignans weren't the only ones for whom French was the native tongue). The idea of the commune was familiar from towns and cities, where, as in London in 1191, a common oath of mutual support was taken by citizens to strengthen their hand. King John had made use of it in 1205, when men over the age of twelve had been made to swear an oath of loyalty. In 1258, the barons seem to have regarded the commune of the realm as one way of binding Henry to a new form of government, one in which his people had an active interest. At least one of the rebel leaders also had a genuine concern for the plight of less fortunate subjects. Simon de Montfort's piety brought him into contact with Robert Grosseteste, the uncompromisingly outspoken Bishop of Lincoln, and with Franciscans including Adam Marsh, whose view of the importance of caring for the (Christian) poor would certainly have rubbed off on the Earl.

The events of 1258 took place against a backdrop of terrible hardship, as England endured the second consecutive year of famine. Matthew Paris described its horrendous effects, and leaves the reader in no doubt as to who suffered most: '. . . numberless dead bodies were lying about the streets. . . . No one, indeed, could remember ever having before beheld such misery and such a famine, . . . And if corn had not been brought over for sale from the Continent, the rich would scarcely have been able to escape death.' The barons used the levelling device of the commune to bridge this divide. In Simon's mind, the fact that it required an oath made it powerful. His refusal to compromise on this oath eventually brought him to the head of the reformers' party.

At Oxford, Henry had no choice but to cave in. He conceded the Provisions, but, like his father after Magna Carta, wrote to the Pope to ask for support. The hated Lusignans were expelled, and a justiciar, Hugh Bigod, the Earl of Norfolk's brother, was appointed, with undefined powers but with a fixed annual term of office. The King agreed to thrice-yearly parliaments, with representatives to be summoned from 'le commun' as well as the fifteen. The barons began the work of active reform envisaged in the Provisions, with four knights appointed in each county to gather complaints, which were in turn brought before the next meeting of Parliament. Bound by their oaths, in which they promised to 'do justice and take nothing that we cannot take without doing wrong', the barons seemed genuinely prepared to make positive use of their new powers. The Ordinance of Sheriffs, issued in the King's name in late October 1258, shows the progress of reform at local level, and the government's response to delay in redressing it. This measure shows that the rebels' commitment to reform was genuine, not a cloak for a power grab. It was to be read at every county court in England, and reassured the people that 'if we cannot accomplish this [reform] as fast as we would like . . . you must not be surprised, for these things have gone amiss for so long . . . that it can by no means be so speedily put right.'

Documents like that may have been sealed by Henry, but they represent his voice as mediated through the barons. The reforming impetus continued in the King's name with the Provisions of

Westminster, addressing local government more generally, the following year. Henry's real reaction became clearer in the ensuing months, as he showed himself determined, once again, to wriggle free. While the barons stayed united, the King had little room for manoeuvre. But soon the rebels began to show that their political success had not changed a mental world in which they still expected to look to the king for leadership. In 1260, Henry made his first attempt to sow discord among those who presumed to order his affairs. Away in France negotiating a peace with King Louis, Henry sent word that the Candlemas parliament, one of the regular meetings agreed to in the Provisions, should be postponed. The justiciar, Hugh Bigod, agreed with him; Simon did not. Simon had been personally disadvantaged by the King's negotiations in France, but his case for holding the parliament was, characteristically, presented on principled grounds: it was what had been sworn to in the Provisions of Oxford. Some of the councillors closest to Simon agreed with him, others preferred to wait for Henry's return. One of the fundamental principles of the Provisions, that the council and Parliament could govern in the king's absence, had been compromised.

The return of the King once again put the baronial confederates on the back foot. Henry ensured that divisions deepened, and recovered more of the authority lost two years before. He summoned a parliament to London in July, and put Simon on trial. Though he was acquitted again, the division between loyalists and Montfortians widened. In April 1261, Henry struck another blow when he secured a papal bull absolving him 'from this moment, from any oath . . . to observe certain statutes, ordinances, and undertakings which they [the barons] are said to have made in your name'. Like the rebels against Henry's father before him, Montfort and his followers had their moral authority trumped by the King's appeal to a higher one. By the following year, the royal position seemed completely reinstated when the King announced that the Provisions of Oxford were cancelled. Only Simon disputed this, but he was away in France. Unlike John, Henry seemed to have faced down a concerted rebellion while avoiding civil war.

The Magna Carta barons, however, hadn't had a leader as unwavering as Simon de Montfort.

Simon didn't have to wait long for the scales to tip back towards him. In 1262, while Henry was in France, his government back in England succeeded in alienating key supporters. While Henry travelled to Burgundy on a pilgrimage to give thanks for his recovery from an epidemic that had killed sixty of his retinue, Simon de Montfort reappeared in London, and produced a bull from the new pope, Urban IV, cancelling the previous papal support for the King and upholding the Provisions of Oxford. The document, unlike those issued in support of Henry, hasn't survived, so we can't be sure if it was genuine, though Simon's religious devotion makes it unlikely that he would have fabricated it. Though Simon departed again for France shortly afterwards, he ensured that Henry arrived back in an England once again divided between rebels and royalists.

Over the following year, there was a gradual descent towards civil war, but neither side seemed to have the will, or perhaps the resources, to commit to one. In September 1263, they took their dispute before Louis IX, the universally admired King of France, and Henry's feudal overlord for his French possessions. This was the first of two appeals to King Louis, and the course of the second, which was far more protracted, has tended to distract attention from the first. At Boulogne, meeting both Henry and Simon in person, Louis came down on the side of the barons, agreeing that he had no jurisdiction over complaints about English matters, and that every country should be governed by natives, not aliens. He also approved the barons' *acta*, which has been taken to mean the Provisions of Oxford.

Once again, however, neither side was able to keep the upper hand. By the end of the year, they had agreed to return to France to get a more comprehensive judgment from Louis, both parties accepting that they 'will in good faith observe whatever the Lord king of France orders or decrees on these matters'. On his way to sail to France, Simon had an accident, falling from his horse and breaking his leg, and so was unable to attend the arbitration.

But the documents in which the arguments were presented have survived, and eloquently sum up the ideals of government by consent on one side, and sacred kingship on the other. What we cannot know is the influence on Louis of any personal representations. When Simon had been present at Boulogne, his party had carried the argument. In his absence, they lost. This moment brings home acutely how important chance and personality could be. Another judgment in the barons' favour could have defused the rebellion. But the Mise of Amiens, as Louis's opinion is known, vindicated Henry completely, and seemed almost contemptuous of the barons' pretensions to any principle: 'we quash and invalidate all these provisions, ordinances, and obligations, or whatever else they may be called . . .'. Here is the traditional, Continental view of kingship, uncomprehending of the sort of measured but aggressive challenge that was becoming an English habit. Simon and his supporters in crucial areas such as London and the Cinque Ports rejected the verdict, and this time civil war could not be avoided.

The first encounter of the war was a victory for Henry, who in April 1264 captured the town of Northampton and its garrison, which was loyal to Simon. The Earl still had control of London, however, so all was not lost. His followers needed money to continue their campaign, and their brutal solution to the problem was to massacre and rob the city's Jewish population, a crime with which Simon was complicit if not actively involved. He certainly had a record of such behaviour: his first act on taking control of Leicester more than thirty years before had been to expel the Jews from the city. It should come as no surprise to us that his religious conviction could take such rebarbative form, as it was entirely typical of the age. Massacres of 'foreign' elements in London are a recurring feature of subsequent rebellions. The moral stock of medieval and later rebellions rose and fell, but vulnerable 'outsiders' were always likely victims of a more general sense of disgruntlement, whether its source was religious bigotry, covetousness, or plain xenophobia. Throughout the Middle Ages, when rebels marched on London, they were also entering the place with the largest immigrant population. Simon de Montfort may have been remarkably forward-looking in some ways, but he and his followers also lived according to the values of their own times, however abhorrent those values can occasionally be to ours.

From Lewes to Evesham

The next confrontation took place in May 1264, on the chalk downs outside the Sussex town of Lewes. Though Simon's side offered the royal party £30,000 in return for a watered-down version of the Provisions, Henry, on the advice of his brother and his son (Edward, whose support for the reformers had waned), rejected the proposal, and trusted to his superior numbers, estimated at three times greater than his opponent's. The Montfortians formally withdrew their fealty, the same process of *diffidatio* that Robert of Gloucester had enacted against King Stephen. The following day, 14 May, the rebels managed to seize the high ground outside the town as dawn broke. Their army wore the crosses of crusaders, a role reversal from Lincoln fifty years before, when the loyalists had been the holy warriors. Simon, his leg still healing, was unable to take an active part in the battle. But his speech to his followers inspired them to a pitch of religious and patriotic fervour. The battle was bitterly fought, over more than five hours. Mass graves discovered in the nineteenth century contained around 2,000 bodies. By the end of the day, Henry and Edward had been forced to take refuge in the priory of Lewes. Although incendiary arrows had set the town on fire, the rebels were unwilling to assault the priory. The victorious Montfortians agreed a settlement, known as the Mise of Lewes, which (though it has not survived) appears to have included concessions on both sides, including a promise of yet more arbitration on the Provisions.

To any observer, the niceties of negotiations couldn't hide the fact that the King and his son were in the Earl of Leicester's power. Simon may have had to sit out his greatest victory in a cart, but the composer of the 'Song of Lewes', shortly after the battle, was in no doubt as to who had triumphed, and why:

May the Lord bless Simon de Montfort and also his sons and his army who, exposing themselves to death, fought bravely for the English people . . . Simon de Montfort had few men used to arms; the royal party was large, having assembled the greatest warriors in England . . . but God provided . . . since God is a help for those who are on the side of justice.

The rebels counted their blessings for a little over a year, during which time Simon strove to extinguish the pockets of resistance that remained, particularly in the Welsh Marches, and to find a form of government under which he could enforce the Provisions. This involved keeping Henry and Edward under close supervision, while parliaments were summoned at which Simon issued new directives for the government of England. The council of fifteen, which had long since gone into abeyance, was replaced by an inner circle of three – composed of Simon, the Earl of Gloucester and the Bishop of Chichester – who in turn were to nominate a council of nine, who would choose all officials and 'advise' the King.

The constitutional implications of these measures, dictated by the circumstances in which they were issued, didn't survive Simon. The mechanism under which they operated, however, set a precedent for the wider consultative parliaments of Edward I's reign, and, ultimately, for parliamentary representation as we know it. For the first time, as well as 'county' representatives (the knights of the shire), representatives from every borough were summoned. Boroughs were those settlements, larger than villages, that had been granted privileges and exemptions by the issue of formal charters. These 'burgesses of parliament' gave England's growing mercantile, town and urban population a say in their government for the first time. But Simon was not a conscious 'founder' of our House of Commons. To him, the expansion of representation was a characteristic case of principle and necessity coinciding. As many of the more powerful barons had gone over to the royalist side, he looked for affirmation to the knightly class, and beyond. It just so happened that these classes also made a more convincing case as the 'commune of England', and that, once their opinion had been canvassed, they would expect to be heard again.

More important to Simon than any prototype for the House of Commons was wider participation in the rebellion itself. Traditionally, the rebellion and the reform movement which preceded it from 1258 to 1265 have been described as 'baronial'. But there are scraps of evidence that the barons' cause had wider support in the country. The villagers of Peatling Magna, in Leicestershire, for example, confiscated a royal party's horses in 1265 because the royalists were 'acting against the utility of the community of the realm and against the barons'. Isolated instances like this show that both the barons' programme and their slogans were more broadly known. Recently, statistical analyses of the various proceedings issued against the rebels after their defeat have shown that in both town and countryside, and, crucially, across the lines of lordship, participation in this first English revolution was not confined to the top of society. It is estimated that while 35–40 per cent of barons took part, they were joined by as many as 60 per cent of knights in the country as a whole. Participation was much lower among the less well-off (though at the lowest level they might well have escaped legal pursuit), but as many as half the total number of rebels are reckoned to have been freeholders and villeins. These numbers do not include those who successfully pleaded that they were constrained by their lords to rebel, as some accused did. The barons' cause was genuinely popular. Popular enough that playing at Simon de Montfort could become a children's game – though, typically for the times, one with extreme consequences. In a village in Kent, a boy's father killed the prior of a local hospital for punishing his son, who had been playing at a game of Simon and the Lord Edward.

The outcome of Lewes made Simon the real leader of England. He used his title as Steward of England, a ceremonial function traditionally given to the Earl of Leicester, as a way of formalizing his pre-eminence. But he wasn't above more straightforward power-grabbing. Simon's commitment to the reforms he rebelled for was genuine, but so was his desire to enrich himself and his entourage. With the kingdom largely at his mercy, and with land in the hands of men he could not trust, Simon transferred large portions in his own direction. Nonetheless, he continued to command widespread loyalty. The force he mustered to resist a possible French invasion at Barham Down in Kent was 'one of the largest armies seen in England since the Conquest', and it included men from villages across the country, as well as the more conventional feudal levy. So the most impressive demonstration of English national unity in the Middle Ages was not orchestrated by a king, but by a rebel.

Simon looked after his own, but he was also able to project a sense of communal identity that his royal predecessors had frequently found impossible. He was the first in a line of glamorous aristocratic rebels with a common touch, would-be captains of the people like the Earl of Essex in Elizabeth I's reign, or the Duke of Monmouth in James II's, right down to less salubrious examples like Lord George Gordon in the eighteenth century and Sir Oswald Mosley in the twentieth. In some respects, Simon combined all the qualities and qualifications that these others possessed in part. He had a good military reputation, like Essex and Mosley; he was a religious fanatic, like Lord George (and, to some extent, Essex again); and, like Monmouth – though in Simon's case by marriage rather than blood – he was connected to the ruling dynasty. These rebels' causes might have been entirely different, but such advantages meant they all shared a self-belief that, for a time at least, they were able to project onto a wider public.

We cannot say how long Simon might have held on to power, or what he would have made of it, since one mistake set in train a series of events that led directly to his downfall. A riding accident had helped to set the rebellion on its course. In May 1265, a cross-country hack led to its end, when the Lord Edward, permitted to exercise his horse under supervision, slipped his leash. He quickly made an agreement with Gilbert de Clare, Earl of Gloucester, a former ally of Simon's who had been alienated by the actions of the Earl's sons. Together, they gathered an army and conducted a campaign which succeeded in cutting off Simon in Wales. Outside Evesham in Worcestershire, on 4 August 1265, Edward and Gloucester defeated Montfort and his sons in another bloody battle. Simon and his younger son Henry were killed, as were thirty of their leading followers. Simon's body was hacked up, and his eldest son arrived too late at the battlefield, in time only to see his father's head paraded on the end of a spear. The first English revolution was over.

King Henry, who had been held captive in Simon's army and had had to make himself known to avoid being caught up in the slaughter, was back in power. Rebels in other areas of the country still held out, on the Isle of Ely, where Hereward and Geoffrey de Mandeville had made their stands in previous centuries, and in Kenilworth Castle. The latter resistance prompted a deal from the King, who wanted to end the rebellion for good. The *Dictum* of Kenilworth, which made only practical, rather than political, concessions to Henry's opponents, showed how far their cause had fallen. Those most deeply implicated in the rebellion were dispossessed. But, like the defeated Magna Carta rebels, those who had fought for the Provisions of Oxford still had something to show. In the Statute of Marlborough in 1267, Henry not only reaffirmed that Magna Carta must be observed, but that the authority for doing so 'has been provided by the joint counsel of ourselves and the magnates of our realm'. This was a formulation first adopted by Simon's ill-fated administration, revealing its rather less 'democratic' tendencies, in 1265. But the real legacy of the rebellion was shown in the reigns of those who followed Henry on the throne. Under Edward I, governing, and raising money for war, through parliamentary consultation became commonplace. When he and his successors tried to bypass this accepted process, the leading men of the realm were prepared, like their predecessors, to threaten (and use) violence.

Simon's personal cult briefly resembled Thomas Becket's – just as his dispute with the King had echoes of the Archbishop's. Simon, like Thomas, was found to have worn a hair shirt as a daily penance. Songs of praise and lament honoured him as one who 'loves right and hates wrong', and is trusted by the 'common folk of the land'. Another song compared him directly to 'the martyr of Canterbury. . . . The good Thomas did not want holy church to be destroyed; the earl also fought and died without flinching.' Miracles were reported from Evesham Abbey, where Simon's mutilated body was taken (only the body: the head, gruesomely adorned with his severed testicles, had been sent to the wife of a royalist – and grandmother of a future rebel – Roger Mortimer; the hands and feet to 'divers places to enemies of his'). But, in time, he came to be remembered less as a personal martyr than as an inspiration to future rebels. Simon had made the strongest possible case that, on occasion, it was not only a subject's right but his duty to rebel. In the final lines of the 'Song of Lewes':

But if he [the king] have sought to degrade his own men, have overturned their rank, it is vain that he will ask, why when so deranged they do not obey him; nay they would be mad if they were to do so.

The Hammer and the blow that didn't fall

The new king, Edward I, succeeded while he was on crusade in 1272, but it is a measure of the extent to which the country had been pacified, or perhaps exhausted, that the succession was a smooth one. Edward was able to take almost two years to return to assume his Crown, but did so unopposed. Henry's son is remembered for his bristling projection of English power, and his violently uncompromising dealings with Welsh and Scottish 'rebels'. In Wales, Edward made his mark in stone, in the ring of castles that still encloses the north of the principality. In Scotland his intervention was less definitive, stirring up a resentment that would shape the fortunes of his successors. In England, it looked at first as if this vigorous soldier had learnt how to avoid the armed conflict with his own subjects that had dominated his father's reign. He had to be 'in all things his predecessor's opposite', as one historian has put it. The way he went about that was to draw on the example of the rebels who had opposed his father. His coronation in 1274 was quickly followed by a thorough overhaul of local government and justice that closely mirrored the Montfortian reforms stemming from the Provisions of Westminster (1259). Though Edward began energetically by bringing in new legislation, he framed these statutes in regular parliaments, attended not only by the great barons and churchmen, but also by knights and burgesses chosen from counties and towns across the country. These were the legacies of rebellion, not only from those who stood against his father but against his grandfather too. No longer could the king enact legislation through a small clique of followers. Edward's success early on could be measured not only by the support he gathered to expand his rule into Wales, but also in the decline of the cult of his father's greatest adversary. By the late 1270s, the miracles that had been regularly reported from Evesham Abbey had dried up. When the king could be trusted to deliver the justice his subjects clamoured for, no one needed the rebel-saint any more.

But Edward did not always trouble to appease his internal critics. A more direct echo of earlier rebellions was sounded by the events of 1297–1301, in which a baronage squeezed by the demands of royal military efforts on three fronts (Wales, Scotland and France) made their own show of strength to bring the King back into line. While this opposition never escalated into an all-out military revolt, Edward's rebels were still prepared to combine their deference to an impressive and generally trustworthy King with the threat of violence.

In February 1297, at a parliament in Salisbury, Edward asked for his barons' service in an expedition to reclaim Gascony, which had been confiscated by King Philip IV of France. They refused. When Edward tried to bully one of their number, the Earl Marshal Roger Bigod, of Norfolk, with the words, 'By God, O earl, either you go or hang', the Earl was not exactly chastened: 'By the same oath, o King, I shall neither go nor hang.' This exchange with Bigod and the way the confrontation developed in the following months reveal the 'Hammer of the Scots' in less familiar guise, unable to nail down his English subjects with the same certainty. Edward's success on the battlefield had earnt him the respect of the military classes who served him, but even he could run up against the limits of his power.

The dispute continued when Edward attempted to press ahead with a muster of troops to accompany him to Flanders, where he planned to join his allies in an attack on the French king. At London, Roger Bigod and Humphrey de Bohun, Earl of Hereford, refused to record the numbers and strength of the gathered forces, which Edward ordered them to do in their respective capacities as Marshal and Constable of the Army. In a proclamation issued in August, Edward put his side of the argument, and in a move that smacks of protesting too much he tried to make clear that at no point had he refused any programme of reform proposed by the two earls, a matter 'of which the king knows nothing, for they neither showed him anything nor caused anything to be shown to him'. For their part, the earls issued a petition in the name of the 'community of the land' – smoothly picking up the baton left by the Magna Carta barons and Simon de Montfort – in which they made it clear that the summons to fight in Flanders exceeded any normal feudal duties. Edward only made matters worse by imposing a further tax on movable property without proper consultation. The allegation that he agreed it with 'those standing about in his chamber' conveys the fear of a return to the clique-ridden government of Henry III.

The confrontation of 1297 had many of the elements of previous clashes and it foreshadowed future ones. Arbitrary taxation and extraordinary military service outside accepted bounds were the two main points of dispute, set out in the petition known as the '*monstraunces*' or 'remonstrances' issued in the barons' (and the senior churchmen's) names in 1297. This would find a direct echo in the beginnings of a rebellion 350 years later, when Parliament issued its 'Grand Remonstrance' against Charles I. The barons' proposed remedy was a tried and tested one: they requested a reconfirmation of Magna Carta and the Charter of the Forest, and they added specific clauses to remedy their own complaints. They were also careful to couch their demands not in purely personal terms, but invoking the 'preservation of the people' and the 'community of the land'. The leading personalities in the rebellion, Bohun and Bigod, did not have to look far for personal inspiration to oppose the King. Bohun's father had been wounded and captured fighting on Simon de Montfort's side at Evesham in 1265, and had died in captivity, condemning his son to a long struggle to regain his inheritance. Bigod's father and uncle, too, had been part of the baronial opposition in 1258, although both went over to Henry's side during the course of the rebellion.

Initially, Edward's response to the rebellion was also reminiscent of his father in its dismissiveness. He would not be put off his plan to cross to Flanders, hiring troops when his attempt to levy them failed. But the government he left in charge during his absence, with his son as regent, was cornered into offering the rebels some consolation. What hastened a settlement was a more pressing crisis on the northern border. On 11 September 1297, William Wallace's army routed an English force at Stirling Bridge. It is intriguing that the result was not what we might expect – internal dissent collapsing in the face of external threat and the pressure to show loyalty. In fact, though the English rebels were concerned about the Scottish situation (and had made Edward's neglect of it to pursue Continental interests part of their complaint), they clearly saw the crisis as an opportunity to wring concessions from the government. In October, the regency that Edward had left behind issued a Confirmation of the Charters, which included a reissue of Magna Carta and the Charter of the Forest and, in a separate document, a series of additional clauses. Part of this Confirmation, which forbade the arbitrary levying of tallages (*de tallagio non concedendo*), would again be revived in very different circumstances at the beginning of Charles I's reign, when the concession the rebel barons had wrung from the King was given the status of a statute. Although in the next three years the barons had cause to make further complaints against Edward, who, like his father, did his best to wriggle out of any commitments, they were not compelled to revolt.

In substance, although in 1297 there was nothing quite as provocative as the Sicilian business or the nepotism of Henry III's reign to fuel the rebels' anger, their grievances were broadly similar. The most crucial difference between 1258 and 1297, however, was in the characters of the opposing leaders. Edward could be like his father in combining stubbornness and unreliability, but he had worked hard to throw off the accusation levelled at him in his youth that he was as untrustworthy as a 'pard' – a leopard. He eventually saw the value, after melodramatic confrontation had obviously not worked, of listening to his subjects' complaints and acting on them. On the rebels' side, the strong wills of Bigod and Bohun cannot be compared with the fanatical *amour propre* and acute sense of honour (and sensitivity to dishonour) of Simon de Montfort. When it came to it, both sides blinked.

One way in which the heat was taken out of the dispute was in the central role played by Parliament, as the space where king and subjects met, if not as equals then at least with some mutual understanding. The history of rebellion is one of institutions adapting as well as individuals clashing. While violence was threatened, and the two leading rebels even barged into the exchequer with an armed retinue to stop the collection of one of the King's unpopular taxes, the two sides never came to blows. It is probable, too, that Edward's formative experiences, first as part of a rebellion against his father and then as the main instrument of its destruction, had better prepared him to deal with his own rebels. For their part, the leading rebels also knew from the experiences of their families where rebellion could lead. These personal factors, as much as political circumstance, meant that the confrontation of 1297 turned out to be an unusually successful rebellion, which achieved its aims without a blow struck or a drop of blood shed. The combination of a strong king and a cautious baronage could make the threat of rebellion constructive.

Neither strength nor restraint, however, would be in great supply in the next century. The more positive lessons of the resistance of Montfort or Bigod and Bohun came to be resolutely ignored. The failures of rebels to make a lasting difference in the thirteenth century owed much to luck, most of it bad. A poorly guarded gate or a fall from a horse had affected the fate of the nation as decisively as the higher ambitions of barons and kings. There was nothing inevitable about the rebels' failure. The aborted attempts, particularly the one around the middle of the thirteenth century, to restrain royalty rather than simply repackage it are a prime example of the way that rebels frustrate posterity's notion that English history is a progressive story. We can't know what England would have looked like if Montfort's revolutionary constitution had survived more than a year. But by the first decade of the fourteenth century conflict at the top of society had become more personal and more violent, and the consequences were deposition, reprisal and bloody retribution. Rebellion was stripped down to its essentials. It became a contest for control, in which the punishment for losing on either side was death.

5. Revenge

Roger Mortimer and the fate of Edward II 1307–77

The last ten years of Edward I's reign were hardly tranquil. He pursued his campaign of subjugation in Scotland, and when he died in 1307 it was on his way to put down another bid for independence, led by the new self-appointed king Robert Bruce, who had murdered his rival to the throne John Comyn, in cold blood and on hallowed ground, the year before. But on English soil at least, after the events of 1297–1301, the English king and his subjects had achieved a modus vivendi. If there were lessons to be learnt on both sides from this outcome, they were emphatically disregarded in the reign of his son, Edward II. The twenty years of Edward II's rule witnessed a dramatic slide into rebellion, violent factionalism, civil war, and finally regicide, which had no precedent in post-Conquest England. Edward was the first English king to be murdered since his namesake, Edward the Martyr, was stabbed to death at Corfe in 978. The Anglo-Saxon Edward had also been heir to a powerful father, Edgar the Peacemaker. But while Edward the Martyr was only a boy, Edward II merely behaved like one. Nobody deserves Edward II's fate, but he must have seen it coming from a very long way away. Certainly, other witnesses did. The best literary source for most of the reign, the *Vita Edwardi Secundi*, completed before the King's deposition and death, nonetheless predicts his downfall repeatedly. Like the Old Testament King Rehoboam, 'who rejected the counsel of the elders and followed the advice of the young, he might perhaps through imprudence be deprived of his throne and his kingdom'. Edward appears to have walked towards the abyss with his eyes open.

There were seven months between Edward I's death and the coronation at Westminster Abbey of Edward II, in February 1308. By April of the same year, the country appeared to be on the brink of civil war. How did the situation deteriorate so rapidly?

Historians used to argue that the seeds of destruction were sowed in Edward I's reign, and it's certainly true that the father's methods of raising money, the parlous state of royal finances, and his confrontational ways with difficult subjects could all be seen as background factors. Yet Edward I's rule had not deteriorated into civil war, or even led to a particularly restricted royal sphere of action. The father's legacy left potential for opposition, or confrontation, but the much greater disasters of Edward II's reign were not structural in origin: they were personal. While rebels under successive kings had varying degrees of investment in programmes of reform, their strength and commitment often boiled down to a clash of personalities. Never was this truer than in the case of Edward II. The consequences of the very individual hatreds of his reign changed the character of all the rebellions that followed. After Edward, rebellion became a deadly business not just for rebels but potentially for monarchs as well.

The first stirrings of trouble came as early as January 1308. During negotiations in Boulogne for the new king's marriage to the daughter of Philip IV of France, a group of magnates made a written pact to assist each other in defending the Crown, but also in putting right 'the things that are still being done day after day to his people'. The vagueness of the formulation shows that a rebellion was some way off. But the detail that the barons sealed it so solemnly, requesting the Bishop of Durham to promise to excommunicate anyone who broke the agreement, has overtones of the rigid oath of the followers of the Provisions of Oxford fifty years before.

The royal favourite versus the royal cousin

The real focus of the barons' vague complaints was made clear by the events of the coronation at the end of the next month, and the parliament that followed it. By this time, the political weather of the reign had already set in – characterized by inaction in Scotland (where Edward I's successes were being conceded to Robert

Bruce) and a sense of grievance over arbitrary royal attempts to improve the King's finances. The storms that broke around Edward II had their direct origins in a third source of trouble, his 'unswerving love' for his favourite, Piers Gaveston. Edward's relationship with this Gascon household knight (whether they were lovers or not is less agreed upon now than it once was) had infuriated his father, who not only exiled Gaveston, but physically attacked his son, tearing out handfuls of the Prince's hair. With his father dead, Edward seemed determined to do as he pleased with his friend. Some disapproved of the relationship, but that only strengthened the resolve of the new king, whom it is difficult not to imagine as a permanently moody adolescent ('There is not one that pitieth my case: none who fights for my rights against them,' he moaned, when encouraged to stop antagonizing his magnates).

Initially, the barons supported Gaveston's return, and even nodded through his elevation to the earldom of Cornwall, which had been a royal title. A tournament in 1307, in which Gaveston appeared to cheat powerful opponents, was the first tweaking of baronial pride, including that of three earls who became confirmed enemies from then on. Edward's decision to leave Gaveston as custodian of the realm during his absence in France was the next. But the behaviour of the King and his favourite around the royal marriage and coronation was more provocative, to say the least. First, Edward ostentatiously sent all his wedding gifts, including those personally bestowed by the King and Queen of France, to Gaveston. Then at the coronation ceremony, he appointed the upstart Earl to the plum role of crown bearer, the last man to enter the abbey before the king himself. At the coronation and wedding feast, Gaveston wore imperial purple, as if he too had been anointed, and Edward ignored his new bride (and the eminent French guests who accompanied her), sitting next to and talking only to his favourite. The Queen's relatives were so insulted that they left the feast, and until Gaveston's death opposition barons could count Philip IV of France among their supporters.

The man who took the leading part in the marriage negotiations,

Henry de Lacy, Earl of Lincoln, had also signed the Boulogne pact. In the months that followed, he emerged as the first leader of real opposition to Edward, which stopped just short of outright rebellion. At fifty-five, Lincoln was the oldest of the King's senior subjects, and had a record of unblemished loyalty, having served Edward's father in Wales, Aquitaine and Scotland. The King had promised to hear the magnates' grievances in a parliament, but when they met shortly after the coronation, and Earl Henry attempted to pin him down, Edward put them off till Easter. By the time the magnates reassembled for a parliament at the end of April 1308, the country was on the verge of civil war. A group of earls had mustered at Lincoln's residence at Pontefract Castle, while for his part Edward busily replaced any suspect custodians of royal castles with more trustworthy ones. Gaveston made his own arrangements, discreetly lining up armed support, doubtless in the knowledge that he could well be the direct object of any deferred anti-royalist military move. '[I]t was thought most certain that the quarrel once begun could not be settled without great destruction,' writes the *Vita* author, but at the Easter parliament the King apparently bowed to the opposition wishes, and exiled Piers, though his appointment as royal lieutenant in Ireland was not the casting into outer darkness the barons had in mind.

The Earl of Lincoln showed himself to be a sophisticated and principled opponent. The 'articles against Gaveston' issued by him at this time need not be dismissed as self-serving or merely exculpatory, and because they took such a considered approach, they were to have a profound effect on the way rebellion and royalty were conceived of in times to come. In the articles, the Earl wrestled with the problem of how to force a king to act against his will, when recourse to the law was not an option, because 'there would be no other judges than royal judges, in which case, if the king's will was not accordant with right reason, the only result would be that error would be maintained and confirmed.' He answered by returning to and elucidating a concept – the separation between the office of the Crown and the person who held it – that had been broached by the signatories to the

Boulogne declaration the year before. Now, Lincoln's articles stated unequivocally that 'Homage and the oath of allegiance are more in respect of the crown than in respect of the king's person.' Gaveston 'disinherits the crown and, as far as he is able, impoverishes it', so even if the king disagrees, it 'behoves that the evil must be removed by constraint, for the king is bound by his oath to govern his people, and his lieges are bound to govern with him and in support of him'. Lincoln would most likely have been horrified by the deadly course that the application of the logic of separate Crown and person, the so-called 'doctrine of capacities', would take, not only for Edward but for numerous successors in the centuries up to and including the Civil Wars. The Earl did not live to see the downfall of the man whom he had tried to 'reinstate . . . in the dignity of the crown', and made a far less dramatic impact on his time than rebellious successors such as Thomas, Earl of Lancaster, or Roger Mortimer, Earl of March. Yet his contribution to the ideology of rebellion was a profound and lasting one – and it came, paradoxically, from an instinct for loyal service.

In the event, Piers's absence was short-lived, and a year later the magnates decided to try another approach to the King's undimmed insistence on the return of his favourite. At Stamford in Lincolnshire, they extracted a statute from Edward restricting one of the greatest abuses of his and his father's reign – prise and purveyance, which meant the enforced sale, and seizure, of goods to provide for the king's military expenses – in return for accepting back the Earl of Cornwall. The abuse of this royal prerogative was widespread and systematic. The fact that it affected the poorest subjects more directly than the richest might be taken as evidence of the magnates' more altruistic side. But there were two more selfish reasons why they made it the central plank of their reform platform. The first is that they were worried: if the peasants who were feeling the squeeze found a leader, they might rise up against their masters. It was not until more than seventy years later that England witnessed its great peasant uprising, but as a popular poem of this period made clear, the spectre of popular revolt was raised earlier in the fourteenth century: 'I fear that if they [the poor] had a leader they would rise in rebellion. Loss of property often makes people fools.' Later, the barons' reform programme, the Ordinances, issued in 1311, referred specifically to the fear that 'the people of the land will rise on account of the prises and divers oppressions inflicted before this time.'

The second reason the barons took a stand on prises was that their abuse eroded the long-fought-for principle of taxation by parliamentary consent. It was a variation on the theme practised by the Angevins, and particularly by King John, of making money out of arbitrary use of feudal dues, such as those on inheriting a knight's fee, another customary levy that the King started to take to unreasonable lengths. Edward I, at least, had put his prises to good use in his successful Welsh and Scottish campaigns. His son, on the other hand, took possession of cartloads of wheat and oats, of hundreds of pigs, but then cancelled his campaigns. As in John's reign, the combination of rapacity and conspicuous military failure was intolerable.

The granting of the statute at Stamford and the return of Piers did not solve the King's problems. Edward continued to abuse the system of prise, again demanding food supplies in November 1309, barely three months after the statute, although (again) no expedition to Scotland resulted. Then there was Gaveston. Edward carried on showering him with lordships, lucrative rights and money, and Piers carried on taunting the earls. He coined nicknames for them: 'Burst-Belly' for Lincoln, 'Horessone' for Gloucester, and 'Dog' for Warwick. The man whom Gaveston christened 'the Churl' or 'the Fiddler' now emerged as the King's chief antagonist and, ultimately, as Piers's nemesis. Thomas, Earl of Lancaster, was Edward II's first cousin. Like rebels before him, such as Odo of Bayeux, Thomas Becket or Simon de Montfort, Lancaster had once been the King's friend. Six years older than Edward, Thomas had corresponded warmly with him before Edward came to the throne, and their letters show that the two men did small favours for each other. Thomas and Edward were never as close as the King's inner circle, which, as well as Piers, included a number of younger men of differing degrees of nobility and one, Hugh Despenser the younger, who was to prove even more disastrous an influence than Gaveston. But the King's and the Earl's privileged backgrounds (Thomas was Edward I's nephew and heir to by far the greatest estates in England, many of them first confiscated from rebels against his grandfather Henry III) and their shared experiences could have made for a fruitful partnership. Although Lancaster had not been among those who called for Gaveston's exile at the beginning of the reign, he would not consent to his return after Stamford in 1309. Nobody knows for sure why Lancaster went from mild support, or at the very least neutrality towards Gaveston, to being one of his bitterest enemies. But, from that moment onwards, Lancaster was the focus of opposition and, ultimately, of outright rebellion.

There was little hint of the violence to come in Lancaster's first opposition moves. As the situation deteriorated after Piers's re-establishment in 1309, Lancaster and other earls only agreed to meet the King in a parliament in February 1310 when their safety was guaranteed. They arrived armed to submit a petition (probably Lancaster himself handed it over) which put their complaints in greater detail and suggested a mechanism for solving them. This petition led directly to the so-called Ordinances, and the appointment of a number of Lords Ordainer, with Lancaster at their head, to administer them. For fifteen months, while Edward and Gaveston engaged in another half-hearted and fruitless Scottish campaign, the Lords Ordainer consulted and modified their plans. They finally presented them in October 1311, to a reluctant King who had no real choice but to bow before an almost unanimous opposition. The Ordinances are divided by modern editors into forty-one clauses, many of which attempted to deal with the problems of prise, bad counsel and favouritism that had bedevilled the reign for all its five years. The longest clause was the one that called for the exile of the 'evident enemy of the king and his people'. Before, Edward had softened the blow of banishment by appointing Piers to command in Ireland. The Ordinances now specified that he was to leave 'England, Scotland, Ireland and Wales', and to do so 'forever without ever returning'. If he did

return, 'let there be done with him as would be done with the
enemy of the king and of the kingdom and of his people.'

'Enemies of the kingdom' had previously suffered confiscation
of lands, exile, imprisonment: death was an option, but it wasn't
the only one. Perhaps Piers wasn't inviting his eventual fate by
coming back, but he was certainly risking it. Edward II's reign
became very bloody, but up to this moment the opposition had
acted much as previous rebels had. They were prepared to use
force, but genuinely wanted to avoid it. Like Magna Carta or
the Provisions of Oxford, the Ordinances were a rebel manifesto
imposed on a king with little room for manoeuvre. And like his
great-grandfather and grandfather, Edward II lost little time in
declaring them void (because agreed under duress), and in securing
papal support for saying so. This time, Piers was barely out of the
country for two months before he returned, and his besotted king
reinstated him in the lands and titles of which he had been deprived
weeks before. But Edward was in no position to dictate terms,
conducting the business of government from York as Thomas of
Lancaster and the other four most powerful earls – Warenne (Earl
of Surrey), Arundel, Hereford and Warwick – decided how to deal
with the problem of the favourite who wouldn't go away. Had
Edward enforced Gaveston's exile, it is perfectly possible that
the Ordainers would have continued a programme of reform in
eventual co-operation with their king. Of course, there was more
to the breakdown in Edward's rule than the widespread hatred of
one man. But in his refusal to give up that man Edward distilled
the opposition to its essence. Piers was besieged at Scarborough
Castle by Lancaster, Warenne and Pembroke (though Lancaster
withdrew to save resources) while Edward attempted to draw off
the opposition by carrying on to Knaresborough. After ten days,
Piers surrendered to the Earl of Pembroke, a relatively moderate
opponent who kept him prisoner under agreed conditions as he
travelled south, and while it was decided how to proceed.

Whether by accident or design, however, Gaveston was left by
Pembroke in an unfortified manor in Oxfordshire, where he was
snatched by the Earl of Warwick, the man whom Piers called 'the

Dog' and his most entrenched foe. Pembroke was horrified and withdrew his support from the Ordainers. Even now, it was not automatically decided that Piers should die. A debate among the remaining earls concluded that he should be 'tried' under the letter of the Ordinances. They even took trouble to conduct proceedings in Warwick, where, it was later alleged, news of the revocation of the Ordinances ordered by Edward had not yet arrived. If there is any doubt about who was behind these actions, or who was prepared to take the blame for them, Piers's next, and final, journey settled it. He was taken towards Kenilworth, where the last of the Montfort rebels had surrendered to Henry III's forces, and handed over to the Earl of Lancaster. Lancaster ignored his pleas for mercy: 'Lift him up, lift him up. In God's name, let him be taken away.' At Blacklow Hill, two Welshmen carried out the earls' wishes, one running Gaveston through, the other cutting off his head. The head was brought to Lancaster, who, 'being of higher birth than the others and so more powerful than all the rest, took upon himself the risk of this business'. 'The land rejoices, the inhabitants rejoice that they have found peace in Piers's death,' Edward's biographer wrote. Neither the joy nor the peace lasted very long.

Blood will have blood

The quasi-judicial murder of Gaveston destroyed the rebels' unity. While Lancaster and Warwick remained as staunch upholders of the Ordinances and opponents of the King, their former allies, such as the Earl Warenne, the Earl of Pembroke and the Earl of Arundel, swapped sides and returned to Edward's favour. The growth of violence in the reign was not a steady progression, and the welcoming back of three of the most prominent opposition earls shows that Edward had not broken entirely with tradition in the way he treated reformed rebels. But if Lancaster did not achieve an ascendancy over the kingdom by killing off the hated favourite, nor did Edward manage to tighten his own grip. Two years later, the military disaster at Bannockburn – when Edward's army, without the assistance of Lancaster or Warwick, was defeated by Robert Bruce's – allowed Lancaster to press his case that the Ordinances must be observed, partly on the grounds that they had not been before the battle and the outcome had been utter failure. But Lancaster's own administration fared little better. A famine as a result of heavy rains lasted from 1315 to the following year. Renewed attempts to campaign in Scotland came to nothing. And Lancaster the rebel had himself to deal with a rebellion, as a former retainer, Adam Banaster, took up arms against him in Lancashire in 1315. For a month, Banaster evaded capture, before he and his confederates were taken and executed, though it is unclear if on the King's authority or merely on Lancaster's.

By this time, Lancaster's influence was waning as Edward built up another court clique, dominated by the two Hugh Despensers, father and son, and very clearly positioned against Lancaster. The most obvious manifestation of this new split came when the Earl Warenne, who had returned to the court party, ordered the abduction of Lancaster's wife. As before in Edward's reign, disputes over state policy were diverted into vicious personal vendettas. Although Lancaster justified his withdrawal from the King's councils and parliaments, a private war with Warenne demonstrated that his objections were as much focused on individuals as they were on 'constitutional' concerns. But Lancaster was not set on war, and in 1318 the Treaty of Leake was drawn up, in which the detail of the Ordinances, which Edward found intolerable, was sacrificed in exchange for a more official role in government for Lancaster himself.

It was a fragile truce: again, the combination of yet another failure in Scotland (a siege of Berwick came to nothing) and the rise of divisive favourites (principally the two Despensers) set the scene for another bloodletting, and thus for the long-drawn-out final act of the reign. As the Despensers acquired more and more land and influence in the Welsh Marches, so their rise was disputed. A group of Marcher barons, led by Roger Mortimer, Lord of Wigmore, with the support of Lancaster, attacked Despenser acquisitions in south Wales, and even marched on London. With an army encamped in Clerkenwell, and the whole country apparently united against him, Edward conceded again, exiling the Despensers, father and son. The elder went to Bordeaux, while Hugh the younger lived as a pirate, marauding off the English and French coasts.

The exile of the Despensers brought more neutral support back into Edward's camp. He was able to carry out a systematic attempt to reverse his fortunes, and to revenge himself on those who had once again humiliated his favourites and set limits to his rule. His choice of initial target was cunning. Bartholomew Badlesmere was a former favourite of the King who had become an ally of the Marcher lords against the Despensers. Crucially, he was a personal enemy of Thomas of Lancaster (a man who seemed to find it almost as easy as his cousin to lose friends and influence). So when Edward required Badlesmere to hand over Leeds Castle in Kent, and Badlesmere refused, the King had ample support in pressing his case. Although the Marchers, again with Mortimer in the lead, came to Badlesmere's aid, the Earl of Lancaster refused. It was the most effective and decisive display of Edward's entire reign. He moved steadily against his opponents, first capturing Leeds, and then turning towards the Marches. There, those who remained, such as the Mortimers, surrendered to their king (showing that defying him in person was still seen as a far more serious proposition than attacking his favourites), while others, such as the Earl of Hereford and two more disaffected favourites, Roger Damory and Hugh Audley, travelled north to link up with the Earl of Lancaster. Hugh Despenser the younger returned during the campaign, and, having once again split his opponents, Edward was able to isolate his cousin.

Edward and Lancaster did face each other on a battlefield in Burton-on-Trent that year, 1322, but it was perhaps symptomatic of the inconclusiveness of the dispute that it was not resolved in a straightforward fight between the principals. Lancaster avoided a full-scale battle and hurried north, but he was cut off by another loyalist force, led by Andrew Harclay, at Boroughbridge. At the last, Lancaster's failure to cement an opposition party, and to put personal enmity to one side in a greater cause, told against him. The first day of fighting was inconclusive, though one of Lancaster's principal allies, the Earl of Hereford, was killed, and another senior Lancastrian deserted. Overnight, another substantial chunk of Lancaster's support melted away, and in the morning, he and his remaining allies had little option but to surrender to the royalists. Lancaster was taken to his own castle of Pontefract, where the King at last confronted his rebellious cousin face to face. Edward recited a list of Lancaster's manifest treasons and rebellions, and the seven earls present, including two from Scotland, duly condemned him to death. Like Gaveston, over whose execution Lancaster had presided, he was shown only the mercy of being beheaded as a noble, rather than being drawn and hanged as a common traitor.

Thomas of Lancaster has been charged by historians with a lack of imagination and a want of charisma in leading his opposition to the King. Certainly, his vacillations show a man more committed to the main chance and personal advantage than to principle. A comparison with Simon de Montfort and his rebellion against Edward's (and Thomas's own) grandfather is instructive. Unlike Simon, Thomas never attempted to establish a wider power base among the 'community of the realm'. But equally well, Simon had been forced into such moves by a lack of options. He and Lancaster were both naturally inclined to seek support first among their own class. In fact, their strategies show similarities, both in their dogged adherence to a set of paper reforms (the Provisions of Oxford and the Ordinances) and their opportunist use of the office of Steward of England (which Lancaster had inherited) as a way of claiming a special role in government policy. Thomas made symbolic as well as practical efforts to connect himself to Simon, a rebel who had become a martyr for some. He supported the canonization of Thomas of Cantilupe, the late Bishop of Hereford, who had been Simon's chancellor (though he didn't go so far as pushing Simon's own claims to sanctity: the Earl of Leicester had, after all, died excommunicate). Simon bore some of the hallmarks of the fanatic, and drew the adulation such types can inspire, whereas Thomas appears a far more arid, and at times indecisive, man. Both men were concerned first with their own family interest, but Simon saw that this could be combined with an appeal to the public good, while Thomas used his vast resources as a way of protecting himself from attack. In the end, of course, neither approach succeeded, but it is understandable that Simon de Montfort's revolutionary energy has left a more definite impression on posterity than Thomas of Lancaster's calculating iciness. At the time, however, their legacies would have been seen as far more comparable. Thomas, too, became the centre of a cult, at Pontefract where he died (the Archbishop of York tried twice in 1323 to put a stop to the veneration). In London, a tablet at St Paul's commemorating the Ordinances became a shrine to 'St Thomas'. At the end of Edward's reign, or shortly afterwards, an 'Office of St Thomas of Lancaster' was composed, which traced a rebel lineage for Thomas back to his namesake Thomas Becket (just as popular tradition had done for Simon de Montfort).

There is one more aspect of Thomas of Lancaster's legacy that shows how rebellion could weave itself into the fabric of English history, albeit in a way that would only become apparent after the passing of many decades. Thomas's inheritance was not forfeit, passing instead to his brother Henry, and eventually, by marriage, to Edward III's son, John of Gaunt, father of Henry Bolingbroke, the future rebel-king Henry IV. Bolingbroke's usurpation began as a rebellion to recover his Lancastrian inheritance, which Richard II withdrew on John of Gaunt's death. Richard deprived Boling-broke of it for many reasons, but one was that it had come by a tainted route, via the rebel Thomas, whose family should never have profited from his treason, at least in Richard's very exacting interpretation of the inviolability of the Crown. None of this could have been known, or even predicted, in 1322, but it shows how a rebellion could continue to have an impact far beyond its own time, and in ways that had nothing to do with the original dispute.

Roger Mortimer and the road to Berkeley

The echoes between the rebellions of Simon de Montfort and Thomas of Lancaster, and the similar fates shared by the leaders, should not obscure the fact that, more broadly, the reactions to them were very different. The Montfortians, who had, after all, continued their defiance after Evesham, and had been responsible for a far more thoroughgoing suppression of royal power, were punished with imprisonment, exile, or confiscation. Lancaster and his allies were killed. Edward had already shown that he was in no mood for clemency at Leeds Castle, where twelve men had been seized and hanged at its surrender. After the Marchers surrendered, Roger Mortimer and his uncle were imprisoned in the Tower of London, but other lords, including Badlesmere, were executed, as were fifteen knights who had supported the uprising. For his cousin and supporters, Edward again turned away from the traditional policy of punish but forgive.

The steady increase in violence is a demonstration of the way rebellion could reflect wider changes, but also of how it could play its own part in fundamentally altering the character of society. It can be put down to three overlapping developments – one political, one personal and one that might be called cultural. First, the political: by this time, Edward had decided to rule with the advice only of his inner circle, so the king's traditional reliance on a wider class of magnate and baronial support was seen as unnecessary. To Edward, those around him were either friends or enemies. Enemies would only stop obstructing the king and his friends by being removed permanently from the scene. In this sense, Edward was more realistic in his dealings with rebels than many predecessors, from the Conqueror to Henry II, who have traditionally been presented as far more ruthless.

Next, the personal: the killing of Gaveston, Edward's adopted brother, more than likely his lover, was in part an act of personal spite, and it required a very personal revenge on those who had ordered it. On the rebels' side, the jealousy and loathing that had grown up around the King's favourite, which was reanimated when the Despensers took Gaveston's place in Edward's affections, drove them to extremes which thoroughly mixed up personal and political grievances. Gaveston's name-calling or Thomas of Lancaster's sense of wounded aristocratic pride took on a dangerous significance in this context.

Finally, the cultural explanation takes into account the more general rise in violence and ill treatment over the two Edwards' reigns, as well as more formal legal developments. Weak royal government made private feuding more likely, but even when the king was strong, if his strength was demonstrated in shows of military force and judicial revenge, then the resort to violence became ever more precedented. A powerful influence was the savagery of the Welsh and Scottish campaigns, which saw men who would once have been welcomed at the English court treated like traitors. The hanging, drawing and quartering to which William Wallace was condemned – a fate also suffered by Prince Llywelyn ap Gruffudd's brother, while Robert Bruce's brother was post-humously decapitated and his sister was imprisoned in a cage in Roxburgh Castle – became the sort of treatment that those who defied the king could expect wherever they were. And, of course, both sides used the semi-fiction of due process – for this age of political breakdown was, paradoxically, also one of legislative sophistication – to eliminate their opponents. Edward's father had defined rebellion, levying war against the king, as treason, punishable by a horrendous execution. This was a major change, which made rebellion a matter of life and death in a way that had almost never been the case over the previous 200 years. Edward II put the new legal sanctions into practice against English rebels. All these factors combined in a gruesome and lethal logic: if Gaveston must die, Lancaster must die, Badlesmere must die. Roger Mortimer, too, was apparently to be next to face the executioner, but, like Ranulf Flambard before him, this rebel managed to get out of the Tower. His flight to France, and the unlikely ally (and lover) he made in Edward's queen, Isabella, led directly to the final high-profile deaths of the reign: those of the Despensers and Edward.

Mortimer's escape from the Tower – drugging his guards, shinning over walls and getting to the river with the help of two
accomplices – might seem romantic, as would his liaison with
Isabella, had the whole reign not become so steeped in slaughter
that it brings to mind instead the denouement to a revenge tragedy.
Having let his enemy slip through his fingers, Edward now made
two ostensibly crass errors. He allowed first his disaffected queen
and then his son and heir (and so an alternative candidate for the
throne) to travel to France too – where, eventually, they teamed
up with Roger Mortimer to launch an attack in 1326. This would
be the first successful invasion of England since the Norman Conquest. At the time, however, Edward was persuaded that sending
Isabella and Prince Edward was the only chance he had of holding
on to Gascony, which had been declared forfeit by his brother-in-
law, Charles IV, because Edward refused to travel to France to do
homage for it. Edward and Despenser's rule was so unpopular by
this time that it would certainly have been suicidal for the King
to make the trip himself. Perhaps he couldn't conceive that his
queen and his son would make common cause with a traitor like
Mortimer. If so, he was wrong.

Isabella was the official leader of the expedition, and there is no
doubt that she took a personal role in directing it. She had risked
everything in very publicly renouncing her husband the King on
the grounds that Despenser had come between them. She was
much more than a figurehead for the designs of Roger Mortimer,
even though Mortimer was her military commander and her political adviser, as well as her lover. The relatively small army that they
raised from Hainault in Flanders should have been no match for a
well-organized and far bigger defensive force. But although
Edward summoned the largest army in English history, it failed
to materialize. In London, the citizens reprised their role as
kingmakers from Stephen's reign, rejecting Edward's pleas for
support and publicly throwing in their lot with the Queen. The
mood of the city turned ugly, and in a foreshadowing of the events
of the Peasants' Revolt fifty-five years later, a senior bishop, Walter
Stapledon, of Exeter, was accused of treason and summarily

beheaded. But Londoners also demonstrated that this was more than a riotous show of strength when they made the calculated political statement of insisting that the tablet inscribed with the Ordinances of 1311 be reinstated at St Paul's, where the cult of 'St' Thomas of Lancaster briefly flourished. Faced with the outbreak of mob violence in London, and the steady advance of an ever-increasing invasion force, Edward and Despenser fled westwards. Their attempts to get away from England altogether were frustrated by adverse winds, and it was Thomas of Lancaster's brother Henry who finally caught up with them near Neath. Despenser's father had already been executed, as had the Earl of Arundel. Now the younger Despenser was arraigned before a tribunal including Mortimer and the earls of Lancaster, Kent and Norfolk. Needless to say, he was found guilty of murder (of the Earl of Hereford, who had, of course, died in battle) as well as of various forms of treason and theft. At Hereford, Despenser and two followers were hanged, beheaded and disembowelled.

After the reckoning of the invaders' greatest enemies, there remained the question of the King himself. Edward had been sent to Kenilworth Castle, where he was held in fairly comfortable captivity. There was no chance now, after such a violent turn of events, that he would be allowed to retain the throne, even as a figurehead for Mortimer, Isabella and Henry of Lancaster. In the young Prince Edward, only fourteen, Isabella and Mortimer had the ideal, malleable substitute. But deposing the King while he was still alive was not a simple matter, and away from the battlefield was unprecedented. Parliament had played little role in recent events, bypassed by Edward and superfluous to requirements as the invading army advanced. Now, when the King was formally requested to attend Parliament, he refused. Nonetheless, on 13 January 1327, a parliamentary session at Westminster was summoned, including burgesses and knights as well as magnates, in other words, the 'community of the realm' on which Simon de Montfort had based his mastery of a captive king. Londoners had already made their support for deposition clear, taking a direct hand in the fate of the Crown just as they had done in Stephen and Matilda's time. In a highly stage-managed scene in Westminster Hall (which had been attempted without the requisite popular support the previous day), Roger Mortimer, his cousin, Thomas Wake, and then the Bishop of Hereford argued that the King must be deposed and replaced by his son. 'An unwise king destroyeth his people,' the Bishop preached. They were followed by others, including the Archbishop of Canterbury, Walter Reynolds. By popular acclamation and with the support of a large enough proportion of magnates, bishops and knights to give the impression of unanimity, Edward was deposed. A new scene had been played in the theatre of rebellion, one which went beyond even the forced public submission to Magna Carta or the armed confrontation with Henry III. The fact that Mortimer and his followers manipulated this episode does not detract from its unique quality. For the first time, the community of the realm had formally 'deprived' their anointed king of his office. From now on, rebellion would always raise this spectre, of the 'people' coming together to topple their king. It had very little to do with representation and even less with modern democracy, but Parliament had been given teeth in 1327. Although monarchy in time became more absolute, and the nobility more detached and self-interested, the record of an active Parliament could not be expunged.

Of course, the deposition, which was conveyed to the King in Kenilworth (in fact, he was allowed to abdicate, though he had no real choice), was not the last indignity forced on him. Mortimer and Isabella found just as many difficulties in ruling in Edward III's name as Edward II had done in his own. The presence of Edward II was a potential focus for renewed rebellion. The distinction between the person of the king and office of the Crown made by Edward II's first opponent, the Earl of Lincoln, could not yet pass the test of a king surviving his successor. The lurid story of Edward II's murder at Berkeley Castle, to which he had been taken not long after the deposition, was most elaborately told in a chronicle written some thirty years after the event. The disembowelling by red-hot poker is an embarrassingly popular staple of English history. If that was really the method of killing, it is difficult to believe that it was employed only to leave no trace on Edward's visible body. The personal viciousness of the reign provides a more convincing explanation of its horrific culmination. If, indeed, it really occurred: it was suggested shortly after Edward's supposed burial that he had in fact escaped, and Edward III was once introduced in Koblenz years later to a man claiming to be his father. The same had once been rumoured of Harold after Hastings, and would be of Richard II and the 'Princes in the Tower'. Whether Edward II died at the hands of his captors or escaped, however, the result was the same: Mortimer the rebel and Isabella the queen mother remained in charge of the kingdom.

In the event, the rebels' rule lasted just three years, an episode that only continued the bloody record of the previous reign, as more and more 'traitors' were exposed and executed. Mortimer, who had begun his administration in the shadows, was created Earl of March and raised huge sums of money in taxes granted by Parliament. The final conspiracy of the period was the one that removed Mortimer and replaced him properly with Edward III. Henry of Lancaster, who had fallen out with the Earl of March, was instrumental in planning it. An indication of how low royal fortunes had sunk is given by an oddity from this time. Edward III is the first English king whose handwriting is preserved, but not in any official document. Instead, a sample of Edward's autograph was sent to the Pope to give him something to check against when deciding if communications purporting to come from the King were genuine. The Pope was sympathetic to the cause of the puppet king, and by 1330 Edward was able to break free. At Nottingham Castle in October of that year, Edward III directed a conspiracy to seize Mortimer, and return him to the Tower. There was to be no duplication of the escape of three years before. Mortimer, condemned on fourteen charges of usurping royal power and murdering his opponents, was hanged, drawn and quartered at Tyburn.

The rebels who opposed Edward II almost unceasingly through his reign inspire little sympathy and less admiration. Thomas of Lancaster was a vastly privileged noble who let slip his opportunity to reform the kingdom or the King. Mortimer was the product of Edward's misrule. A loyal servant from a line of loyalists (the Mortimers were proud of their role in defeating Simon de Montfort's rebellion), his trust had been broken by the raising of the Despensers in the very areas where he and his fellow Marcher barons had fought hard to carve out their lordships. Violence and personal enmity formed the links in the chain of Edward II's reign, and Mortimer's contribution was only in keeping with what had gone before. But it is perhaps unsurprising that the result was the end for many years of the idea of rebellion as a method of reforming the kingdom. Edward III's reign benefited from an unprecedented period of domestic peace. But when aristocratic rebellion returned, the experience of Edward II's time seemed to guarantee that the stakes would be much higher, and the game much bloodier.

Edward III's long reign offered the governing classes of England what they had so singularly lacked in his father's time: a share in decision-making, positive leadership and, through the war with France, successful military adventure. By the end of the reign, however, Edward had become an old man, and the war effort had begun to falter in less capable hands during the 1370s. While violence receded at home, the practice of violence was kept up by Englishmen abroad, from the Black Prince to Sir John Hawkwood. In France, the consequence was a breakdown in public order, and once the grip of a powerful king on the English throne had begun to weaken, there was a growing expectation that the same would happen in England, too. The reign had also seen the terrible depredations of the Black Death, beginning in 1348, returning three times over the next three decades. The pandemic of bubonic plague was, in terms of the proportion of people it killed, simply the worst event in European history: up to half the population died.

This visitation of the wrath of God added to the apocalyptic mood and gave rise to penitential agonies, but it also called for practical responses. The government's reaction to the labour short-age caused by the Black Death, enacting through Parliament a Statute of Labourers that attempted to keep peasants' and other labourers' wages at pre-plague levels, germinated the discontent that was harvested in the reign of Edward's grandson, Richard II. Richard succeeded in 1377 as a ten-year-old boy, after the death of his own father, the Black Prince, the year before. His time on the throne ended in a similar way to his great-grandfather Edward II's, in deposition and death after an aristocratic rebellion. But it began with a different kind of disturbance, one that had no real English precedent, and for which the ruling classes were almost entirely unprepared: the Peasants' Revolt.

6. A Rebel People

The Peasants' Revolt 1381

. . . this impatient nettle
Will very suddenly sting us, . . .

There are three things of such a sort
That they produce merciless destruction
When they get the upper hand:
One is a flood of water,
Another is a raging fire,
And the third is the lesser people,
The common multitude;
For they will not be stopped
By either reason or by discipline

From John Gower, *Mirour de l'omme*
(1376–8) 26,496–26,506

For now is tyme to be war

From the 'Letter of Jakke Carter',
ascribed to John Ball, in the
Chronicon Henrici Knighton

In 2008, the Mayor of London promised that 'tackling the horrific spate of knife crime' was his 'top priority'. Six hundred years ago, a predecessor in the office was the one wielding the knife, in the most notorious stabbing ever to take place in the capital. The perpetrator, William Walworth, was in his second term as Mayor, and was later knighted for his services, while the victim was a Kentish labourer, an unknown who seemed to threaten the foundations of the state. The dagger featured in the coat of arms of the City may not commemorate the episode, as was once popularly believed (the dates don't quite fit), but the murder weapon is proudly preserved at the Hall of the Fishmongers' Guild, along with a statue of Walworth, cast in the role of hero rather than thug.

It is understandable that the City's rulers would want to remember Walworth. His intervention turned the tables on the rebellion that, more than any other before or since, struck fear into the ruling classes. What happened in the first two weeks of June 1381 was unique in English medieval history, perhaps in English history as a whole. A protest that began as a local tax dispute turned into an all-out popular assault on the government. Several thousand armed men – many of them from the bottom of a rigidly segregated society – managed to organize themselves into a force capable of capturing well-defended military installations, of storming gaols, of entering the capital and then confronting the monarch with their demands, on two separate occasions. The fact that, in the short term at least, the Peasants' Revolt was an unmitigated failure, and that it is so often seen in isolation, can make it seem more than an anomaly. To many observers both at the time and since, 1381 was a freak event, a 'great and unexpected calamity not experienced by previous ages', a warning to the ruling classes, but apparently not much of an inspiration to the 'multitude', who returned home to condemnation or pardon, without having achieved any concessions.

Popular insurrections before democracy can seem to emerge out of the blue. There isn't the same kind of pattern of deterioration in normal political relations as with rebellions from higher up, since normal political relations, especially in the fourteenth century, were a question of coercion, not discussion. When the rebels come from a class as little understood by their rulers as the peasants of 1381, it is hard to predict their actions. As Charles Canning prophetically observed immediately before the Indian Sepoy Mutiny of 1857, 'in the sky of India, serene as it is, a small cloud may arise, no larger than a man's hand, but which, growing larger and larger, may at last threaten to burst and overwhelm us with ruin.' Yet some contemporaries were observant enough to forecast the Peasants' Revolt, even if they couldn't have predicted the precise moment of the storm breaking.

The great catastrophe of the fourteenth century, the Black Death, had created a labour shortage. This attacked the roots of society, by threatening the tied status of agricultural workers, who began to leave their lords' land in search of better-paid work. The contemporary reaction to that development, the Statute of Labourers enacted in Edward III's reign (1351) and enforced for the next thirty years, attempted to obstruct the law of supply and demand, by freezing wages. It also restricted the movement of labourers (male and female), with harsh punishments for contravention. This repressive measure, which fell hard not only on farm labourers, but also on artisans and unbeneficed priests (two classes who would be strongly represented in the events of 1381), was followed by the introduction of a Poll Tax, to be taken from 'each person of the kingdom, both male and female' in 1377, repeated in 1379 and 1380. It was an attempt to enforce the final levy that triggered the revolt in Essex.

There were other reasons to be angry. In Kent, the revolt was sparked by a dispute about one man: was he free or 'bonded'? Most people in medieval England lived under a form of slavery. It is easy to overlook that fact, because these people left so little impression on the historical record, but it makes the past a very foreign country. Villeins were bonded to their lord, who had the right to decide on what services he required from them, to levy fines on them, and to restrict their movements. But bondmen had begun to challenge their status in the years before the revolt. Most of these challengers restricted themselves to their own cases, arguing that an individual or group categorized as unfree should be reclassified, but without challenging the status quo. They brought legal precedents, such as Domesday Book, to prove their case. They did not discuss whether it was right or wrong that anyone should be, in effect, another's property. At first, the principle of bondage didn't seem to be an issue in 1381 either. By the time the rebels got to London, however, they had adopted a far more radical position: that 'all men in the realm of England should be free and of free condition.' Once the idea of seeking justice had taken hold, the most unjust thing about so many rebels' lives could finally be called into question.

The most deprived in English society were not the only ones with grievances against the government. In the years running up to the revolt, England as a whole was feeling the strain of decades of war with France, always expensive but now also unsuccessful, as prosecuted by those around the ailing King Edward III and his underage successor, Richard II. Renewed (and futile) French expeditions over the last years of the old reign and the first of the new were the reason for the poll taxes. And the English were beginning to get a dose of their own medicine. The southern counties, where the revolt first broke, had been threatened with invasion by French forces in alliance with Castile. At the beginning of the new king's reign in 1377, French raiders captured and burnt Rye in Sussex, and later the Isle of Wight was briefly invaded; the following year the town of Fowey in Cornwall was burnt by a Castilian fleet. England was wounded, weakened and divided.

In previous decades, such widespread dissatisfaction might have led to threats of rebellion higher up in society, expediently incorporating the grievances of the poor. Rebels like Simon de Montfort had co-opted the unrepresented commons, or, in the case of Thomas of Lancaster and the Ordainers, tried to head off insurrection by demanding reforms to alleviate the plight of the poor. But by 1381 there was no one to speak for the peasants but themselves. The circumstances after the Black Death, as well as an expanded role in national political life for some below the very top rank, conspired to separate the lower levels of society still further from the rest. The achievements of previous rebellions, including the part played by burgesses and gentry in Parliament, fell hard on others, as the represented 'Commons' protected their own interests while piling greater demands on those – whom the rebels would christen the 'true commons' – who had no say in decision-making.

The essential features of this division of society, between the represented and the unrepresented, persisted right up to the twentieth century. The 'community of the realm', in part the invention of earlier rebellions, was a concept with universal and long-lasting appeal. The fight to expand it would go by different names, from 'native rights' to plain 'liberty', and was eventually subsumed in the modern panacea, the vote. But the desire to increase the number of people who had a say in the government of the kingdom was the source of rebellion for another 550 years. The birth pangs of this mass political consciousness took place in the fourteenth century.

At the end of Edward III's reign, the county knights and burgesses demonstrated their clout in the so-called 'Good Parliament' of April–July 1376. At this Westminster assembly, the first summoned for three years, with royal finances in a precarious state, the Commons appointed a speaker, put forward their demands for a new council, and drove through the impeachment of several royal officials. The fuel of so many previous rebellions, a resentment of poor counsel and a belief that evil advisers were corrupting the king and his government, was thus addressed in a formal, open (and non-violent) way. The first of the Poll Taxes that was conceded in the following year was part of an aristocratic reaction, led by Edward's son (and the future Richard II's uncle), John of Gaunt. But if the Commons in Parliament would not exactly welcome the tax, its flat rate fell hardest on those who had no say at all in its imposition.

As other groups reaped the rewards of earlier rebellions, so they exposed those beneath them to greater depredations. At the same time, they passed on the example of violent resistance. The hostile chroniclers of the Peasants' Revolt only grudgingly concede that the rebels had any sort of plan, preferring to paint them as a rabble who merely 'hoped to subject all things to their own stupidity'. But, just as much as rebels before them, those of 1381 had a programme, and adopted stratagems to enforce it. There is no evidence that these so-called 'rustic' rebels explicitly based their actions on their aristocratic forebears, and many aristocrats were the target of their anger. But in their methods, in appreciating the importance of London for example, or presenting the king in person with a programme of demands, they were (however unconsciously) emulating their predecessors. And in their often-repeated loyalty to the king and desire to replace his bad councillors, they were even more plainly (though perhaps more ingenuously) following earlier rebels, from the Magna Carta barons to Thomas of Lancaster.

Of course, the rebels of 1381 were also very different from those who had gone before them. Even the names of Wat Tyler, Jack Straw and John Ball, all credited with the leadership of the revolt, seem to emphasize the unprecedentedly humble origins of men who shook the established order to its core. This was not the first time that 'ordinary' men had attempted to take a direct, violent part in national politics. Londoners in Stephen's reign had ejected Matilda; and again in Richard I's reign, the followers of William fitz Osbert, the long-bearded clerk's son, had reacted to the way the toll of the King's ransom seemed to be falling unfairly on those least able to pay. But both these revolts found leadership higher up the social scale. Matilda had been resisted by a delegation of powerful Londoners before she was forced out by popular condemnation. As for fitz Osbert, he may have been a clerk's son, but his Norman name, and apparent ability to arrange a personal audience with King Richard, suggest that his championing of the poor was an early case of middle-class radical empathy. The leaders of 1381 weren't slumming. These were desperate men, driven to desperate measures.

Outside London, the lowest classes of English society had not been wholly passive before 1381. They had taken part in nation-wide rebellions led by aristocratic rebels. At a local level, as well as outbreaks of urban violence, there are much earlier instances of organized resistance to the established rural order, often on grounds that would be rehearsed in the great rising of 1381. In Harmonds-worth, Middlesex, in 1278, a dispute between a prior and his tenants turned violent. The tenants broke into the manor house and 'carried away charters and other writings and goods', and 'threaten[ed] the prior and his household as to their bodies and the burning of their houses'. This is a remarkable microcosm of the events of more than a century later, from the targeting of the landed clergy, to the dispute over tenant status and the payment of 'arbitrary' tallages, right down to the focus on written records, which the oppressed peasants correctly saw as the basis for what they regarded as their unjust treatment. Without these records to go on, the prior and those like him had no legal justification for their demands, though why the rebels held on to them in this case rather than destroying them is difficult to say. The naming of one John le Clerk as the ringleader also provides a rare sight of a named precursor to the men who emerged from obscurity in 1381 (his surname might be a clue to his apparent reverence for the written word).

There were other precursors nearer the time of the kind of resistance that exploded in 1381. In 1336, the villeins of Darnall and Over in Cheshire had their case for freedom turned down. At first, they made personal representations to King Edward III, but when these were brushed off, they became bandits, possibly in that classic place of outlawry, Sherwood Forest (they were certainly taken to Nottingham gaol on their arrest). There were also outbreaks of collective violent resistance to authority in Norfolk, Wiltshire, Hampshire, Worcestershire, Northumberland and Cambridgeshire in the fourteenth century. All involved more than a spontaneous upsurge of 'lawlessness', and the authorities' recorded reactions to them show concerns about conspiracies and confederations. Clandestine organizations were bad enough when barons and magnates formed them. The spectre of the great majority of the population arranging themselves formally to resist injustice must have been terrifying.

In the late fourteenth century, the mythical 'Merry England', a social order balanced between the rights and duties of the high- and low-born, was sunk in misery. In the years after the Black Death, we find instead a growing mutual hatred between the lowest in society and the rest. The plague itself – from which the ruling classes had been unable to protect the common people, and the social effects of which the rulers seemed determined to shift onto the ruled – was one reason for the increased antipathy. Perhaps this lordly behaviour only confirmed what the political struggles of the past three centuries had repeatedly suggested: that the 'community of the realm' was in practice a club with restricted membership. If the outbreaks of collective violence before the Peasants' Revolt show this breakdown from the side of the unfree, then the Statute of Labourers, with its penalties of being put in the stocks, is an example from the other side. By 1377, a petition *against* the villeins was presented by the Commons in Parliament (and given a sympathetic reception). The Commons complained about villeins who had the temerity to invoke Domesday Book (as the villagers of Harmondsworth had done a century before) to dispute their status, before sliding into more violent 'rebellion and resistance'. The anxiety of the time is nicely evoked by this petition, with its fears of 'counsellors, procurers, maintainers and abettors' leading the villeins astray. There is a specific reference to the example of the 'jacquerie' in France, a peasant rebellion of 1358 that the Commons feared might be replicated at home. The threat of a French invasion was also keenly felt, along with the possibility that rebels would 'adhere to foreign enemies', or follow the example across the Channel of a 'similar rebellion and confederation of villeins against their lords'. Here is the familiar tactic of painting potential rebels as traitors, an 'enemy within', as Margaret Thatcher famously christened the miners. In fact, when the revolt did come, the southern rebels were careful to 'ordain that no one who lived at any place within twelve leagues of the sea should come with them but should keep the sea-coasts free from enemies'.

Some contemporaries, then, could see that the country was ripe for revolt before 1381. It is clear, too, that ordinary men had some of the skills and resources needed to organize rebellion. There were precedents for acting together. Enforced poverty and bondage gave them reasons to do so. And these men, despite what may be assumed about the ignorance of the medieval peasant, were perfectly capable of using legal methods to advance their case, and of recognizing the importance of documents. In the course of the revolt, objectionable classes such as oppressive landlords, lawyers and sheriffs were targeted, but the rebels also demonstrated their awareness of national politics, with their deliberate focus on the power behind the young King's throne, his uncle, John of Gaunt. Before it took on its ambitious, revolutionary goals, however, the trigger for the revolt was very specific, and its origins very local.

The revolt begins

The men who wrote up the events of early June 1381 were invariably hostile witnesses. But there is no reason to disbelieve the connection the chroniclers make between the Poll Taxes and the revolt. In 1380, the third such tax in four years demanded a flat rate (increased threefold from the first levy) of a shilling from every adult above the age of fifteen. This tax was levied after a request was made to the Lords and Commons for £150,000, to support the Earl of Buckingham's French expedition, as well as other military ventures. Not only did the tax come hard on the heels of the two previous ones, but by trebling the flat rate demanded it naturally fell heaviest on those least able to bear it. There was mass evasion, with up to 450,000 people disappearing from the register. By the time the government-appointed commissions of inquiry to enforce payment started their work, in May and June of 1381, Buckingham's expedition, supposedly the reason for the levy, had returned home empty-handed after the Earl's Continental allies had agreed a separate peace with the King of France. How would news of that debacle have struck those faced with the commissions demanding their money? An unjust tax targeted at every adult in the land had given every adult in the land a reason to become a rebel.

In Brentwood, Essex, the royal commissioner, John of Bampton, summoned representatives from the nearby villages of Fobbing and Cottingham to render their payments on 1 June 1381. Instead, the people of both villages, together with those of a third, Stanford-le-Hope, 'gathered to the number of a hundred or more and with one assent went to the said [John] de Bamptoun and told him outright that they would not deal with him or give him any money'. The man who led the first rebels of 1381 was not a peasant. He was Thomas Baker of Fobbing, 'so called because of his trade [who] took courage and began to exhort and ally himself with the men of his village'. When Bampton ordered the rebels' arrest, they resisted, threatening him and his men. Bampton 'fled towards London and the king's council while the commons went into the woods for fear of his malice'. Like the people of Darnall and Over, these Essex rebels retreated to the forest, the traditional place for the outlaw, 'where there's no treachery or twisting of the laws', as a song from the first decade of the century described it for aristocratic consumption. But this was just the beginning. By the time another commission arrived to arrest the rebels, they had gathered support, going 'from town to town inciting other people to rise against the great lords and good men of the country'. Although some men were prepared to go on oath accusing the rebels, these jurors were rounded up and killed, and their houses destroyed. Sir Robert Bealknap, the Chief Justice who had been sent on the arrest-ing commission, bolted for home. The rebels were now in control of the county. The rising was in the process of becoming a mass revolt: 'fifty thousand of the commons gathered, going to the various manors and townships of those who would not rise with them, throwing their buildings to the ground and setting them ablaze.' We do not need to forego the usual pinch of salt when it comes to medieval chroniclers' numbers to believe that the scale of the rising was beyond anything anyone had seen before.

And it was to get much bigger. 'The commons sent several letters to Kent, Suffolk and Norfolk, asking them to rise with them.' It seems likely that these letters were more straightforward than the apocalyptic ones preserved in the chronicles. Supposedly written by the man who became a kind of spiritual leader to the rebels, an itinerant preacher called John Ball, the letters that we can still read are accurately described as 'full of obscurities'. They employ some of the language and imagery of Langland's *Piers Plowman*, written only a decade before. Where Langland's vision was of an ordered medieval world, however, Ball's is a mystical call to arms, to 'chastise wel Hobbe the Robbere' (who has been identified as Robert Hales, the King's Treasurer, though it is more likely to refer to a more familiar medieval robber figure). The preservation of these seditious letters, though it does nothing to help the modern reader understand exactly how the revolt was directed and organized, certainly allows us to see that the rebels had a sense of mission, and on a universal scale: 'Iohan the Mullere hath ygrounde smal, smal, smal; / The Kynges sone of heuene schal paye for al.' ('John the Miller hath ground small, small, small / The King's son of heaven shall pay for all.') The letters also suggest that the rebel leadership, at least, was literate.

In Kent, a different local dispute was the catalyst. It was the familiar one of a contested serfdom, in this case when the retainers of a local lord, Sir Simon Burley, claimed that a Gravesend man called Robert Belling was his serf. When supporters of Belling attempted to settle the claim, Burley's men demanded the unpayable sum of £300 in silver, 'a sum which would have ruined the said man'. The money was refused, and Belling imprisoned at Rochester Castle on 3 June. This was provocation enough for an attack on the castle, which took place three days later. In those three days, support for the rising had not only spread across Kent, with an attack on the town of Maidstone, but links had been made with the Essex rebels. Consequently, the Kentish rebels 'arrived in Rochester and there met a great number of Essex commons'. After a half-day siege, the constable of the castle handed it over to the rebels. Those from Gravesend, at least, felt that justice had been done, and 'returned home with their companion in great joy and without doing anything more'. But others apparently had larger aims. There was a particular focus on the documentary records of bondage, which the peasants decided to burn, 'so that once the memory of ancient customs had been wiped out their lords would be completely unable to vindicate their rights over them'. It may not be a coincidence that it was at this point that Wat Tyler took up the leadership of the rising, 'to maintain and advise them'.

Tyler is described by some as coming from Maidstone, but in other accounts as an Essex man, from Colchester. The story that he was provoked to rebel by a tax commissioner indecently 'examining' his daughter to decide whether she was under the age of fifteen (and therefore ineligible to be taxed) stems from a misreading of a fifteenth-century account, garbled by Thomas Paine and others in the eighteenth century. Like so much about the revolt, its best-known leader only emerges fleetingly from obscurity. All that we can deduce is that, after his appearance, the revolt seems to have proceeded with more certainty towards a series of specific targets. First was Canterbury, where the rebels put forward a demand to the monks to elect a new archbishop and executed various 'traitors' who were handed over to them by the townspeople. Then they marched to London, by way of Maidstone, where John Ball was released from prison. They camped, on 12 June, the day before the great medieval feast of Corpus Christi, on Blackheath, now part of south-east London but in the fourteenth century a place still far enough from the City for the chroniclers to describe it (exaggeratedly) as 'three leagues' (nine miles) away. On the same day, the rebels from Essex 'arrived on the other side of the water to help them and have the king's reply'. The rebels' loyalty to the King, as against their violent mistrust of his government, was maintained throughout the revolt. Their reply to the challenge 'With whom hold you?' was 'With King Richard and the true commons'.

How many rebels were there? The chroniclers mention huge figures, of 50,000 for the Kent rebels and 60,000 for those of Essex, or again of 100,000 for the total. Modern historians, bearing in mind the estimates of England's population for the period and medieval chroniclers' fondness for numerical exaggeration, estimate the rebel forces at around 10,000. Even so, that number is larger than most armies that took the field in this period, and certainly larger than anything the authorities could summon up at short notice. Whatever the real figure, the chroniclers' exaggerations only emphasize the impression that was clearly felt at the time, of a vast and terrifying force of angry men encamped threateningly outside London.

The rebels' arrival at the outskirts of London also brings us closer to another perennial point of discussion about their revolt. Were their numbers really made up exclusively of agricultural workers, the *rustici* of the chroniclers' descriptions, totally distinct from the townsmen of their counties and from the Londoners whom they would shortly attempt to co-opt? Unsurprisingly, the answer is 'no'. The 'Peasants' Revolt' is a convenient shorthand for a group of rebels that, as well as free and unfree peasants, included tradesmen, labourers, artisans, unbeneficed priests, even some gentry. The chroniclers name a few knights, like Sir John Newton, constable of Rochester Castle (which the rebels attacked to liberate Robert Belling), who were 'compelled' to join the revolt on pain of death. Some, like Sir Roger Bacon in Norfolk or Sir William Coggan in Somerset, may have taken a more positive role in representing the grievances of the commons to local authorities. John Ball's couplet, 'When Adam delved and Eve span / Who was then the gentleman?' may be the best-known rallying cry of the Peasants' Revolt, but this was never a simple class war. Minor gentry participated, although they did not take charge of the revolt.

The rising spread beyond its initial flashpoints of Essex and Kent, to East Anglia and as far as Yorkshire, as well as westwards. More than geographical extent, what made it a national rising was the direct attack on the national centres of power. It is no wonder that the contemporary chroniclers, and historians ever since, have focused on events in London. The Kent and Essex rebels who camped outside the city walls on 12 June knew that a few miles away were the vital organs of government: the person of the King himself, to whom they wished to appeal; his hated advisers, including the Treasurer, Sir Robert Hales, and the Chancellor and Archbishop of Canterbury, Simon Sudbury. John of Gaunt, the King's uncle and power behind the throne, the man blamed for corruption at home and military failure abroad, as well as the levy of the Poll Tax itself, was away in the Scottish Marches, and stayed away during the revolt. But his palace, the Savoy, opulently taunted men who had been squeezed of their every penny. In other parts of the city lay more potential targets of rebel fury: prisons, lawyers' quarters, and the houses and religious foundations of various enemies.

Most of these goals lay behind the walls of the city, or across the river from those encamped on the south side at Blackheath. But the rebels' first two targets were more easily reached. The Marshalsea Prison in Southwark, south of the Thames, was attacked first. The rebels sprang the debtors and felons incarcerated there.

Next came the Archbishop of Canterbury's manor of Lambeth, to the west of the Marshalsea on the same side of the river, where they set alight more records. Picking up support as they went, the Kent rebels had been joined by the people of Southwark. The real prizes, though, lay on the other side of the only structure across the Thames at this time: London Bridge. For their part, the Essex rebels, led by a figure whose trace on the historical record is even more evanescent than Wat Tyler's – Jack Straw – were kept out by the city gates. Both obstacles proved inadequate. The men who guarded them – either because they were 'of [the rebels'] accord' and 'favoured the rustics', or 'for fear of their lives' – agreed to open both the bridge and the city gates to the rebels from south and north. Knowing the ultimate failure of the Peasants' Revolt, we can easily underestimate how astonishing their progress was. A rising that had its origins in two apparently local disputes had seen castles, prisons, and now the capital city itself open before them.

Even the chroniclers seem to acknowledge that, once inside London, the rebels continued a targeted campaign which, however violent, did not descend into mere lawlessness. The Fleet prison in Fleet Street was opened and its inmates released. Two houses were also destroyed there, but otherwise they did 'no harm or injury' until they came either to the Temple or to the Savoy Palace (the order is not agreed upon). John of Gaunt's Savoy was burnt, but not looted, with the 'commons of London' participating enthusiastically. As well as being nationally unpopular, Gaunt was a particular hate figure to some Londoners, who four years before had been involved in a bitter dispute with him, suffering the public humiliation of having to set up a marble pillar in Cheapside to display his arms and show their respect. In 1381, they demonstrated their true feelings, as the Savoy and its luxurious contents were torched. At the Temple, a lawyers' part of the city then and now, property and legal records were again destroyed. More prisons, at Westminster and Newgate, were opened, and individuals were targeted. That day, 'eighteen persons were beheaded in various places of the town.' Others alleged the violence was more widespread, with a general slaughter of Flemish residents, an echo of xenophobic outbreaks in previous rebellions, and a reliably poisonous ingredient in many that followed.

The actions of the rebels in London were unquestionably violent, but they still gave evidence of leadership. At this moment, if anyone was unsure of what to do next, it was those around the King. Richard and his advisers had repaired to the Tower of London, the safest place in the city, from which, standing in a turret, Richard witnessed the fire and destruction taking hold all around him. But when the fourteen-year-old King 'called all the lords about him into a chamber, and asked their counsel as to what should be done in such a crisis', 'none of them could or would give him any counsel'. It was apparently the young King himself who decided to summon the rebels to a conference at Mile End, to the east, outside the city walls. Richard was fourteen years old – young enough, had he not been king, to be ineligible for the third Poll Tax that had kick-started the revolt. Yet it was he who realized that he must talk to the rebels if his government were to stand a chance of stopping them.

The next morning, Friday, 14 June, the King and a small party rode to Mile End to meet the crowd of rebels gathered there. Meanwhile, some who had stayed outside the Tower managed to force or threaten their way in. The fact that they were able to get in with such apparent ease raises suspicions about the prominent men they found there. Were these men left behind on purpose, to appease the peasants – as the chroniclers would have seen it, to satisfy their blood lust? The rebels seized and executed several hated men, among whom were the Archbishop of Canterbury (and Chancellor), Simon Sudbury, and the Treasurer, Robert Hales. To some, the killing of the Archbishop was the rebels' greatest crime. Thomas Walsingham, the monk of St Albans who saw the revolt as a morality lesson, describes the 'horrible shrieks' of the rebels as they carried out their beheadings: 'their throats sounded with the bleating of sheep, or, to be more accurate, with the devilish voices of peacocks.' Their animal savagery is contrasted with the calm dignity of Sudbury, meeting his violent fate, like Thomas Becket before him, with steady equanimity, and like Thomas becoming a miracle-worker in martyrdom. One young man who survived the onslaught on the Tower may have drawn another lesson from the experience. John of Gaunt's son, Henry of Bolingbroke, the King's cousin and only a year older than him, was also left behind. John of Gaunt, of course, was far away in the North; unsurprisingly, Henry came close to being the stand-in for his detested father. According to one report, only the intervention of an old soldier, John Ferrour, saved Henry's skin. For the fifteen-year-old future Henry IV, as for King Richard, this must have been the defining moment of his life. It helped to make him the self-reliant man he became, one whom Richard underestimated, with disastrous consequences, when Henry too turned rebel, less than twenty years later.

In 1381, while one group of rebels took their revenge, another presented their demands to the teenage King at Mile End. Accounts differ as to whether Wat Tyler was present or not, but those who were 'required that henceforward no man should be a serf nor make homage nor any type of service to any lord, but should give four pence for an acre of land. They also asked that no one should serve any man except at his own will and by means of regular covenant.' The King agreed to the requests. But the killings continued, with the rebels allegedly proclaiming that 'whoever could catch any Fleming or other aliens of any nation, might cut off their head'. Thirty-five Flemings who took refuge in a church in the City were dragged out and beheaded. Up to 160 people suffered the same fate that day.

Strange meeting

The slaughter carried on the following day, and again Richard took the lead in trying to effect a solution. On 15 June, precisely the same date that King John had been humiliated by the barons at Runnymede in 1215, King Richard took the risk of an equally public, and far more extreme, display of role reversal. He summoned the rebels to another meeting, at Smithfield, only just outside the gates of the city. There, the face-to-face confrontation between the rebel captain, Wat Tyler, and the King to whom Tyler protested his loyalty certainly took place. It is an extraordinary moment. Tyler, who had in a few days gone from being a complete nonentity to one of the most significant, if also one of the most hated, men in the country, spoke familiarly to the descendant of a line of monarchs stretching back more than 300 years. If previous encounters between rebels and rulers had an element of theatre about them, this one recalled the folk dramas in which a 'Lord of Misrule' turned the tables on his masters. It took place at a time when a public display of communal activity was expected, during the feast of Corpus Christi, but this scenario broke with all convention. Unsurprisingly, the chroniclers, to whom the thought of the two men conversing was anathema, show Tyler as uncouth, boastful, literally as well as metaphorically drunk in his hour of triumph. As he approached the King, Tyler brandished a dagger, which he 'kept throwing . . . from hand to hand like a boy playing a game'. With limitless presumption he addressed his sovereign: 'Sir king, seest thou all yonder people? . . . they be all at my commandment and have sworn me to faith and truth, to do all that I will have them.' Dismounting his little horse and only half-bending his knee, he took Richard 'by the hand, shaking his arm forcefully and roughly, saying to him "Brother, be of good comfort and joyful, for you shall have, in a fortnight that is to come, forty thousand more commons than you have at present, and we shall be good companions".'

The image of the world turned upside down is one used by later rebels, but for a brief moment on 15 June 1381 it had no better illustration than when a Kent commoner, 'with his head covered and with a threatening expression', dictated terms to an anointed king. Richard listened again to the rebels' demands. 'There should be no law but the law of Winchester' was the first, which may refer to very old customs or quite new ones. The other demands are more easily understood: no outlawry, no lord to have lordship, 'but it should be divided among all men, except for the king's own lordship'; the goods of the Church to be divided up among the laity, with only 'sufficient' provision for the clergy's own sustenance; 'only one bishop in England'; finally, 'no more villeins, and no serfdom nor villeinage'. The King had no real choice but to agree, and charters of manumission and pardon were issued. But what happened next stopped the rebellion in its tracks. The mayor of London, William Walworth, who was in the King's party, tried to arrest Tyler. Walworth resembled Tyler inasmuch as he had achieved his elevated position through his own efforts rather than high birth. But Walworth's steady progress, from apprentice, to MP, to the mayoralty had merely confirmed to him the importance of hierarchy. So his impetuous decision to take on Tyler was not a simple case of the medieval social order reimposing itself. Walworth had worked hard to get to his position. He couldn't let a jumped-up serf dictate terms to his superiors. The rebel leader stabbed the mayor, without wounding him through his armour. Walworth in turn stabbed Tyler in the neck, and another of the King's entourage ran him through. Wat Tyler fell dying from his horse, calling on his followers to avenge him.

This, of course, is another turning-point in the history of English rebellion, and of England itself. Had the rebels attacked, it is perfectly likely that they would have killed or captured the King, and prolonged their rising, with unguessable results. But they hesitated. All the chroniclers agree that, once again, King Richard's actions were the key to saving the situation, though some make it more threatening than others, who show the death of Tyler totally deflating his followers, 'who fell to the ground among the corn, like beaten men, imploring the king for mercy for their misdeeds'. According to another account, Richard and his followers were in rather more danger, as rebel archers drew back their bows.

With marvellous presence of mind and courage for so young a man, [he] spurred his horse towards the commons and rode round them saying, 'What is this, my men? What are you doing? Surely you do not wish to fire on your own king? Do not attack me and do not regret the death of that traitor and ruffian. For I will be your king, your captain and your leader.'

With the renewed promise of charters of manumission, the rebels agreed to return home. The great transgressive moment was over.

Because Tyler is such a shadowy figure, it is easy to discount his death as merely one factor in the inevitable doom of the Peasants' Revolt. It certainly seems unlikely that the rebels could have stayed together for much longer to dictate terms. But with a leader, they had a focus. The chroniclers agree that without one, once persuaded not to avenge his death immediately, they were undone. Tyler's 'arrogance' may have been his downfall, but it was also his strength. None of the other leaders was able to exert such authority, or assume that his followers' cause should find natural justice at the hand of the King. Nevertheless, the apparently genuine promise of charters of manumission seemed successful. Walsingham reproduces one in his account, and it is clear that these titles to freedom were sent across the country. But, as another chronicler wrote, this promise was duly 'quashed, annulled and judged worthless by the king and the magnates of the realm in the parliament held at Westminster' later that year. It was not only the King and the magnates who demanded the annulment. The Commons in Parliament were equally hostile to a measure that led inevitably to the 'disinheritance of themselves and the destruction of the realm'. The antagonism towards the unfree that the Commons had displayed in Parliament before the revolt was only confirmed and strengthened after it.

The immediate fate of the other leaders of the revolt in London was the same as Tyler's. Jack Straw and John Ball were 'found in an old house hidden, thinking to have stolen away', and quickly executed. Straw's 'confession' survives, in which he admitted to a plan to murder 'all the knights, esquires and other gentlemen' around the King, before forcing Richard to accompany the rebels 'around with us from place to place in full sight of all'. We can't know how much truth there is in any of this, but the idea of a puppet king at the whim of a rebel force was, after all, not far from what Simon de Montfort had briefly imposed on Henry III, between success at Lewes and disaster at Evesham in the 1260s.

The most prominent leaders of the revolt (eight are named by Walsingham) were not the only ones to die. A royal army was mustered and marched into Essex, where resistance held out for longest. To rebel envoys who thought that the balance of power at Mile End and Smithfield still prevailed, the King gave a withering answer:

You wretched men, detestable on land and sea, you who seek equality with lords are not worthy to live. . . . Give this message to your colleagues from the king. Rustics you were and rustics you are still; you will remain in bondage, not as before but incomparably harsher. For as long as we live and, by God's grace, rule over the realm, we will strive with mind, strength and goods to suppress you so that the rigour of your servitude will be an example to posterity.

Here was the rebels' royal 'captain and leader' displaying the true feelings of his class and his office. Richard's troops surrounded the woods around Chelmsford, where the rebels had barricaded themselves, and conducted a systematic slaughter. Five hundred rebels were killed. Official commissions were set up, with Tyler's killer, Mayor William Walworth, at their head, to punish rebels in London and surrounding counties. A hundred more rebels died at official hands, but revenge wasn't always carried out by due process. Far more rebels died in summary executions and in hot blood. In November, only five months after the revolt, Parliament was summoned. As well as rejecting the villeins' plea for freedom and quashing the charters that promised it, the Lords and Commons offered an amnesty to rebels who applied for a pardon before next Whitsuntide (29 May).

The aftermath

The cut-off date for the amnesty was less than a year after the revolt itself. Before that, the recriminations started. The Oxford theologian John Wyclif was accused of preaching 'to the pollution of the people', and spurring them to rise. Religion became the driving force behind many a rebellion in the next three to four centuries, but Wyclif was an unconvincing scapegoat in 1381. For a start, when writing about the revolt, Wyclif opposed it. And how are we to square Wyclif's influence with the fact that his patron was the rebels' chief hate figure, John of Gaunt? It is not even clear that the priestly elements in the revolt, like John Ball and John Wrawe (in East Anglia), were 'followers' of Wyclif. The rebels certainly objected violently to the established Church, but they were not in any coherent sense 'Wycliffites'. One unintended side effect of the failure of the revolt, however, was the suppression of Wyclif's views. The murdered Archbishop Sudbury's successor, William Courtenay, was far more diligent in stamping out Wyclif's teachings. Wyclif left Oxford not long after the Peasants' Revolt, though he continued to write and his ideas continued to spread. Without the revolt, the official backing for what was now condemned as heresy could have continued, and could perhaps have heralded a home-grown Reformation long before the ideas of Martin Luther and others crossed the Channel.

Was there any more to the revolt? There is a temptation to overplay the significance of 1381, at least for its own time. To our eyes, the violence of the revolt is distant enough for its more egalitarian, more apparently modern, aspects to dominate. We naturally sympathize with a class as oppressed as the *rustici* and *nativi* of fourteenth-century England, and instinctively identify with their appeal for freedom, their fight for a greater share in government, and their resentment of aristocratic privilege. To some, John Ball was a 'proto-Communist', whose egalitarian messages prophetically foreshadowed the battles of the nineteenth and twentieth centuries. Ball was the subject of William Morris's flight of Christian socialist imagination, *The Dream of John Ball* (1888). When the British Labour Party was looking for a rural, pre-industrial ancestry for English socialism, it was naturally to the events of 1381 that they turned. As the Labour MP (and, later, leader) George Lansbury put it in 1928, 'We are not an organisation created out of special conditions at a particular moment. No, you will find the beginnings of our story in the lives of those rebels, Wat Tyler, [and] the [sixteenth-century] Kett brothers.' Rebellion was an Englishman's birthright.

If (some of) the rebels' cause eventually triumphed, it is difficult to argue that the revolt had much to do with it. The promise of the end of bondage, first dangled before the rebels at Smithfield and permanently snatched away at Westminster five months later, was never made good. It seems extraordinary, but villeinage was never actually abolished; it just died out – and very slowly. The Kett brothers pleaded that 'all bond men be made free' in 1549, and villeins could still be found in Elizabeth I's reign. The Commons in Parliament after 1381 betrayed no sense that this was a form of tenure on its last legs, and they made it clear that it was they, not the King, who had the most interest in maintaining it.

Such a manumission [as the one offered by Richard at Smithfield] could not be made without their assent, who had the greatest interest in the matter. And they had never agreed to it, either voluntarily or not, nor would they ever do so, even if it were their dying day.

The other great target of the revolt, the Statute of Labourers, was only reinforced by the Commons in the following decades. Again, the self-interest of the Commons in Parliament prevailed over the interests of the unrepresented 'true commons'. In Parliament, the Speaker for the Commons, Sir Richard Waldegrave, did attempt to enunciate an analysis of and reforming reaction to the revolt, but, although some officials were replaced and a commission to survey the King's household was appointed, it was not long before the Lords reasserted themselves. Repression, rather than reform, was the lesson they took from the revolt. The most tangible achievement of 1381 was that no more poll taxes were levied – not a negligible outcome, but not much when set against the radical ambitions revealed that June.

Most individuals who survived the revolt seemed little affected. The career of John of Gaunt, for example, was unchanged by it, except that he perhaps gained some sympathy for the sacking of his palace by the rebels. Those who replaced the dead made few concessions: the Archbishop of Canterbury who followed the murdered Sudbury briefly combined the role of chancellor as his predecessor had done, and took a far stronger line on heresy. The individual most profoundly influenced by 1381 was the King himself, though not in the way either the peasants or his more natural allies among the peers would have wished for. Richard developed an uncompromising, sacred view of his royal authority, deluding himself of his inviolability all the way to deposition and a miserable death. It is hard not to trace the genesis of this back to the moment at Smithfield when the boy Richard was able to take command simply because he was 'your king'. But the magic only worked once. Richard could not overawe his more powerful subjects as he had the Peasants. Eventually, another man whose personality had been forged in the fires of June 1381, Henry of Bolingbroke, overthrew him.

The Peasants' Revolt may have achieved a long afterlife, but it needs to be understood primarily as an event steeped in the customs and rhythms of its time. The revolt came to a head around a newly popular medieval Christian feast, Corpus Christi, a time of processions, of coming together that could easily turn to violent protest. Because it was of its time, it failed. It was drawn from a class which in the Middle Ages had no resources to sustain self-organized and self-led mass actions. In many senses, the Peasants' Revolt is the nearest England ever came to a popular revolution, but it happened far too early to be anything more than a brief explosion.

All this is not to say that the revolt didn't matter. Less than seventy years later, Jack Cade's rebellion, drawn mainly from Kent and Essex, followed the Peasants' example to a remarkable degree, including their petitions on behalf of the 'trewe commons'. But perhaps the most abiding legacy of 1381 was as a collective, and very long, memory. To those in authority, it stood for centuries as a warning of the potential of the 'mob': Charles I invoked the spectre of Wat Tyler and the Peasants' Revolt in 1642, and Tyler's name was on Tory lips enough after the French Revolution for Thomas Paine to feel moved to spring to his defence, declaring in the second part of *Rights of Man* that Tyler and his followers' proposals 'were on a more just and public ground than those which had been made to John by the barons'. The psyche of Richard II may have been changed for ever by his experience of containing the revolt almost by personal aura alone, but the wider psychological influence of the rising has been extraordinarily long-lived. Even in our own time, the Conservative minister Nicholas Ridley argued that the miners' strike in 1984 was 'very much in the nature of a peasants' revolt'. The measure that arguably brought down Ridley's Prime Minister, Margaret Thatcher, six years later also had distinct echoes of 1381. Her 'poll tax' was only the universally adopted nickname for a local levy officially named the 'community charge'. The fact that the last universal poll tax to be raised in England (though it too didn't have that name officially) was more than 600 years before did not stop the term being instantly associated with injustice, and resistance to it with the now heroically conceived Tyler and Straw.

Much of the work in keeping the revolutionary 'tradition' of the Peasants' Revolt as a living memory had been done by Radicals and their heirs in seventeenth- and eighteenth-century England. It seems unlikely that 1990s Britain would have recalled the iniquity of a poll tax had not writers and activists as varied as the Levellers in the seventeenth century or Robert Southey, William Morris and the Chartists in the nineteenth kept its memory alive. Southey repudiated his early play on Wat Tyler when his politics changed, showing how potent a symbol of radical views association with the revolt remained. But the political opponents who uncovered the play in 1817, the year after the Spa Fields riots, which happened less than a mile from the site of the meeting of Tyler and Richard II at Smithfield, preserved an eloquent version of the fourteenth-century rebels. Southey's John Ball sounds to modern ears more like a Romantic visionary than the millenarian medieval riddler of contemporary accounts. Reinvented, he calls the oppressed to arms once again, and, ultimately, it is as a rallying cry that the Peasants' Revolt had its most lasting impact:

> The ray of truth shall emanate around,
> And the whole world be lighted!

7. Challenging the Realm

Henry Bolingbroke to Sir John Oldcastle 1388–1417

'Rebellion lay in his way, and he found it.'

William Shakespeare, *I Henry IV*, 5, i

Less than seven years after the Peasants' Revolt, in January 1388, Richard II found himself in the Tower of London again, looking out as before on a crowd demanding revenge on his government. Once again, Henry of Bolingbroke, now Earl of Derby, was in the Tower too. But this time Henry was standing beside Richard, showing him how unpopular royal government had become. The near victim of the mob in 1381 had become one of five 'Appellant' lords determined to bring Richard to heel, to drive out his favourites such as Robert de Vere, the newly created Duke of Ireland, and to force him to govern with the assent of the most powerful men in the land.

The Appellants' rebellion was a return to the aristocratic infighting of Edward II's reign, and it, rather than the Peasants' Revolt, was the harbinger of rebellions for the century to come. It had its origins in a protest in Parliament in 1385, and by November 1387 the 'appeal' against five 'traitors' who surrounded Richard (from which they took their designation as Appellants) had been heard by his councillors. Richard only stalled for time while his right-hand man, De Vere, gathered an army to confront the Appellants, rebels by yet another name. At Radcot Bridge, in Oxfordshire, in December 1387, De Vere's army, summoned by Richard to outflank his opponents, was routed by a combined force led by Henry of Bolingbroke and his fellow Appellants: the King's uncle, Thomas Woodstock, Duke of Gloucester, and the earls of Nottingham, Arundel and Warwick. De Vere fled the country, leaving Richard defenceless in London. As Henry stood beside him in the Tower, the rebel, not the King, was master.

The Appellants discussed what to do with the King. We cannot be certain how far the conversation went, as it was of necessity a dangerous and very secret one. But Richard had already been reminded in Parliament of what had happened to his great-grandfather, Edward II, when he tried to rely on unpopular favourites to govern without consent. In the end, the rebels agreed to impose their will on the King's government, but to keep him on the throne. The material relicts of Richard's reign, such as the marvellous Wilton diptych, in which the King's conception of his sacred status is given full expression, can give the impression that the idea that he developed of kingship as inviolable was widely shared. But the speed with which his potential removal from the throne was mooted in 1387–8 indicates the power of another tradition: that of the aristocratic rebel.

It may seem anachronistic to speak of a rebel 'tradition' among self-seeking nobles, but in an age acutely conscious of family example and with a much wider sense of family loyalty and affinity than our own, 'nuclear' version, it is worth pointing out that the Appellants were not only related to each other as cousins and uncles. They were also descended from rebel lords who had opposed Richard's great-grandfather, Edward II, sixty years earlier: Edward had been faced by the earls of Lancaster, Hereford, Warwick and Arundel, and Richard's opponents came from the same estates, to which they were heirs by birth or marriage (both Henry and his uncle Thomas, Duke of Gloucester, had an interest in the earldom of Hereford). Thomas of Lancaster, the Ordainer who had begun the backlash against Edward II and paid with his life for it, may not have achieved as long-lasting fame as Thomas Becket or Simon de Montfort, but he was still being talked about as a potential saint as late as 1390. The example of Edward II also meant that barons were much quicker to threaten an unpopular king with deposition, even when, as in Richard's case, there was no direct heir to propose as a replacement. It meant, too, that rebellion had become an increasingly personal affair. If the ultimate threat of rebellion was to replace the monarch with the rebels' own man, then the prospect of reform – other than reform which replaced the King's favourites with rebels – had much less mileage.

In 1387–8, deposition was certainly considered, but the Appellant rebels drew back from it. Richard was still very young; it was only in 1389 that he declared himself of an age to govern. The rebels might well have concluded that, with the proper 'guidance', i.e. theirs, the King could be moulded into the shape they required. Again, the matter of who might replace Richard if they did depose him wasn't simple. The fact that the Appellants could not agree on a replacement may have saved Richard's skin for the time being. The potential to work on that disagreement eventually enabled him to get his revenge on some of those who had humiliated him in 1387–8. Richard played a long game, declaring himself of age in 1389, and not moving against the older three of the five Appellants, Gloucester, Arundel and Warwick, until 1397. Arundel was executed, the King telling him that 'you shall have such mercy as you showed to Simon Burley', Richard's old tutor and favourite, who had been one of the Appellants' victims during their brief ascendancy. Richard's uncle Gloucester was arrested and spirited to Calais, where his former ally the Earl of Nottingham presided over his 'accidental death', an outcome later revealed to have been produced with the assistance of a feather bed and five heavies to crush the royal uncle beneath it. Warwick, the oldest of the former Appellants, was banished for life to the Isle of Man.

At this point, it seemed that the two younger members of the 1387–8 rebellion, Henry of Bolingbroke and the Earl of Nottingham, had charmed their way back into the King's circle, and been forgiven their trespasses. They were both rewarded for their assistance or acquiescence in the King's revenge with dukedoms. But the process by which both of them were alienated and, a year later, one of them removed Richard from the throne is one of the murkier stories in English history, a matter of plot and counterplot, of rumour and more or less false suggestion, that reads like a prelude to the bloody machinations of the civil war of the next century.

Towards the end of the same year, 1397, in which Richard had punished three of the Appellants and officially pardoned two – Henry of Bolingbroke (now Duke of Hereford) and Thomas Mowbray, Earl of Nottingham (now Duke of Norfolk) – Henry was riding from Brentford to London, when Norfolk caught up with him. The account of the conversation that followed only survives in versions sanctioned by Henry, so we can hardly take its veracity for granted. But what Norfolk wanted to talk about was a plot. 'We are on the point of being undone,' he told Henry. 'Why?' . . . 'For what was done at Radcot Bridge.' The conspiracy that Norfolk revealed, in which he implicated the King himself, sought to remove John of Gaunt and Henry from their lands. They had inherited them through the brother of Thomas of Lancaster, that arch-rebel of Edward II's years who had paid with his life, but not his inheritance, for his defiance of the King – but whose lands had been allowed to stay in the family. Now, Norfolk said, Richard planned to reverse that judgment. Norfolk also alleged that 'had it not been for certain people, your father the lord of Lancaster and you would have been either seized or killed when you came to Windsor after the parliament' in October that year.

How much truth there was in such allegations it is impossible to know. Perhaps the story originated with Henry, who drew it to Richard's attention as a way of moving against Norfolk. Equally well, there is evidence that one of Richard's favourites was involved in a scheme to kill John of Gaunt, so the conspiracy may have been genuine (and this would not have been the first time that Richard had wanted John dead, having ordered his execution without trial on the basis of a rumour as early as 1384). The King was brooding on the rights and wrongs of the events of his great-grandfather's reign. In the next parliament, he reversed the judgments of 1326 against Edward's favourites the Despensers, the great enemies of the Lancastrian rebels of that time. It is typical of Richard's bloody-mindedness that, while opponents sought to warn the King by drawing attention to the fate of Edward II, Richard consistently promoted his ancestor. He decorated Edward's tomb at Gloucester Cathedral with his own white hart device, and commissioned a book to record the miracles performed there. In 1397, Richard sent an embassy to the Pope to argue for Edward's canonization (the second to be dispatched), apparently part of a concerted programme in that year to rehabilitate his forebear and re-judge Edward's opponents, as represented by their descendants.

Whether the plot 'revealed' on the road from Brentford was real or imagined, Norfolk cannot have expected Henry's next move. By disclosing the contents of the conversation to Richard, Henry was, in effect, accusing Norfolk of treason. When Norfolk denied having said any such things to Henry, Richard resolved not to take sides and ordered the two dukes to decide the matter in a trial by battle – that is, by man-to-man combat between the pair. Henry had already gained a reputation as an accomplished jouster and soldier so would probably have fancied his chances in such an encounter. The occasion was set for six months later, in September 1398, and on the appointed day, with the matter still unresolved, the two dukes and the whole court assembled to witness the battle. At the last moment, Richard put a halt to proceedings and, without any proof of the guilt of either party, sentenced them both to banishment, Norfolk for life and Henry for ten years.

At this point, we encounter what might be called the Shakespeare problem for the first time in our story. We are all so aware of Richard's fate, mostly as a result of Shakespeare's play, that it is difficult to keep in mind that what happened to the King was not a preordained tragedy. Knowing how little time Richard had left on the throne, it is tempting to see this banishment as the King's fatal error. But at the time it can't have looked like it. No one objected, and the two men left the country within a month, Henry to receive a hero's welcome from anti-Richard factions in Paris, Norfolk to exile in Italy and a swift death from plague less than a year later. Could that have been the end of it? Richard had accepted Henry back into his affairs, if not his affections, before. If Henry had been allowed or compelled to serve out the ten years of his banishment, could he have returned again to a position by the King's side, taking up the role his father had played for Edward III and, intermittently, for Richard himself? One of the many instructive things about looking at England's past through its rebellions is that very little looks inevitable.

Richard's fall and Henry's return as rebel and then usurper-king might have been avoided. But the two antagonists' personalities, formed at such proximity to one another over the past eighteen years or so, certainly made it less likely that either would allow the matter to rest. And some events cannot be predicted. In February 1399, only five months into Bolingbroke's exile, his father, John of Gaunt, died. Almost immediately, what Richard really meant by the banishment was put to the test. In a sense, the quarrel between Norfolk and Henry had presented the King with the perfect opportunity to get rid of the last and most vigorous remaining rebels from the early part of his reign. The death of Gaunt seems to have struck Richard as a similar opportunity. Whether or not Richard really had designs on the Lancaster inheritance before he banished Henry, his fixation on the events of Edward II's reign made it clear that he regarded the concentration of power in the hands of the dukes of Lancaster as the source of rebellious threat to his majesty. Now he saw a chance to remove that threat. The King made Henry's exile permanent, and declared his inheritance forfeit, though a nominal possibility that Henry or his son might reclaim it was included in the announcement.

From Ravenspur to Westminster

That concession was not enough to deter Henry, who only had to wait until June that year to seize his chance. Richard was confident enough of his position to depart for Ireland, to which he had been planning an expedition for several months, leaving the kingdom to be guarded by yet another royal uncle, Edmund, Duke of York. By the end of June, Henry, with a small force, had landed at Ravenspur, at the mouth of the Humber, to reclaim his inheritance. Was that all he was after? We know that, as early as 1387, when only twenty, Henry had been confident enough of his claim to the throne to push it as an alternative to the Duke of Gloucester's when Richard's deposition was first discussed. Gloucester was now gone, and Richard still had no direct heir, though his cousin, the Earl of March, had the strongest blood claim. But Roger, Earl of March, had been killed in Ireland in 1398, and his heir was only a year old. So did Henry have his eye on the Crown from the beginning of his expedition? Possibly not. Even after Richard's return and surrender to Henry's forces at Conway Castle in Wales, Henry still issued summons to Parliament in Richard's name. Perhaps at this point, he was merely intending to use his hereditary office of Steward to become the power behind Richard's throne, following the example of previous rebels like Simon de Montfort and his own ancestor, Thomas of Lancaster. Something persuaded him to change his mind, and to go for the ultimate prize, but we cannot know what that was – perhaps no more than a combination of ambition, circumstance, and a realization that, once Richard was his prisoner, this course really was open to him. Just because his campaign proved so startlingly successful, that is no reason to assume that Henry expected it to be. He may well have anticipated that he would have his work cut out to re-establish himself in his own inheritance, let alone in anyone else's, when he landed at Ravenspur with perhaps sixty followers.

The momentum that Henry built up on his return relied on several lucky breaks. The first was Richard's initial absence. It took the King two weeks from hearing of Henry's landing to make it back from Ireland to Wales. Richard may not have been an exactly legendary military leader, and by this time Henry had added to his own reputation as a tournament fighter in mock battles with success at the real thing, not only in the Thames Valley but on crusade in Lithuania. Yet if Richard had returned more quickly (he was delayed by lack of shipping as much as by lack of will), he would have provided a rallying point for loyal subjects. His absence led to dark rumour and despondency. When the Earl of Salisbury arrived back in Wales as a royal advance party, he mustered a force of Welsh 'gentlemen' and archers, numbered at 40,000 by an eyewitness, which even at a tenth of that size would have been a serious obstacle to Henry. But 'when the Welshmen realized that the king was not there, they became downcast, and began to murmur among themselves in groups, for they thought that the king must have died of grief, and they were full of alarm and dread at the terrible cruelty of the duke of Lancaster . . .' Their loyalty could not stand the absence of the King: 'were he here, whether his cause were right or wrong, we would be eager to assail his enemies. But for now we will not go with you.'

Henry was also lucky that Richard was widely unpopular. Henry acquired important allies beyond his direct Lancastrian affinity, including the Percy family of Northumberland, who hated Richard for his interference on their patch and were anxious about their title, as they too were descended from Thomas of Lancaster, so stood to lose out if Richard did reverse the judgments made at the time of Thomas's rebellion. But their support came with conditions. The younger Percy was uncle by marriage to the only rival heir to the throne, the young Earl of March, so the Percys compelled Henry, according to some accounts, to swear only to recover his inheritance, not to claim the throne – a promise that would have consequences four years later.

Henry's next piece of luck was the performance of the man the King had left to protect his realm, his uncle Edmund, the Duke of York. York seems to have decided which way the wind was blowing ten days after the Welsh desertion. The force he summoned was draining away, and when Henry caught up with him at Berkeley church, in Gloucestershire (perhaps uncoincidentally, next door to the castle where the last king to suffer an invasion by one of his subjects had met his fate), they 'came to an agreement', and York joined the rebels. By the time Richard arrived back in the country, his delay and the betrayal of his regent had all but sealed his fate. There was no army left to defend his kingdom. For the third factor which counted in Henry's favour was the sheer popularity of his arrival. The rise of Henry and fall of Richard seem to have had a lot to do with the contrast in atmosphere around the rivals. Richard had tried to project majesty, but personal histrionics, the politics of fear and the exaction of revenge were also his stock in trade. Henry was a popular figure, a crusader who had visited the Holy Places, a trustworthy lord and an unfairly treated subject. Even bearing in mind that many contemporary accounts of his campaign were more or less propaganda, it is clear that the unpopularity of Richard's government was a reality, and that the crowds who shouted 'blessed is he who comes in the name of the Lord, our king of England' to Henry (adapting the Psalm that the people of Jerusalem had sung to the returning Jesus on Palm Sunday) were not a figment of the imagination. It was a French supporter of Richard, after all, who told the story of the King going through Wales disguised as a poor priest, for fear of being identified by his own subjects.

Henry had gathered enough support from high and low sources for the eventual confrontation with Richard to be predictably one-sided. When the two met at Flint Castle, it was Henry who dictated terms. Yet again, Richard had to listen to a rebel, but this time there was no way out. All Henry wanted was 'to reclaim, with your royal permission, my life, my lands and my inheritance'. A witness more loyal to Richard sets out Henry's purpose more broadly, and less deferentially:

My Lord, I have come sooner than you sent for me, and I shall tell you why: it is commonly said among your people that you have, for the last twenty or twenty-two years, governed them very badly and far too harshly, with the result that they are most discontented. If it please our Lord, however, I shall now help you to govern them better than they have been governed in the past.

Richard agreed, but from that moment on he was Henry's prisoner. By the time they reached London, if no sooner, Henry seems to have resolved that such an arrangement wouldn't work. Representatives of the City of London, which had had a say in the destiny of the Crown before, came to the Duke 'and recommended their city to him, under their common seal, renouncing their fealty to king Richard'.

Perhaps it was by such gestures that Henry was convinced that he could safely move to depose and replace the King. But he was also aware that a different procedure from the previous act of deposition (which had replaced Edward II with his eldest son and direct heir) needed to be found, if Henry's own claim to the throne was to be admitted. A committee of learned men was summoned, among them the chronicler Adam of Usk, not to decide 'the matter of setting aside King Richard, and of choosing Henry, duke of Lancaster in his stead', but to work out 'how it was to be done'. They concluded that the King's own conduct – his 'perjuries, sacrileges, unnatural crimes, exactions from his subjects, reduction of his people to slavery, cowardice and weakness of rule' – were all 'reasons enough for setting him aside'. When this decision was relayed to Richard, he waxed despairingly, in words that Shakespeare would adapt and immortalize, on England's rebellious habits. 'My God!, a wonderful land is this, and a fickle; which hath exiled, slain, destroyed or ruined so many kings, rulers, and great men, and is ever tainted and toileth with strife and variance and envy.' Gloomier observers might also have seen Richard as the ghost of rebellions future, predicting the doom of the house that displaced him. However popular he seemed to be in his hour of victory, Henry and his heirs would find it difficult to resist the force of his own precedent when circumstances became less favourable.

For a short time, however, Henry was able to believe he was only obtaining what was rightfully his. In 1397, he had been prevented from proving his case in hand-to-hand combat, banished and then disinherited. The form of words he chose to claim his throne was 'I, Henry of Lancaster, challenge this realm of England', as if he was daring the whole country to fight him. And it is perfectly believable of Henry that he really would have fought any rival man to man. But the claim was also a carefully worked-out compromise to turn his rebellion into a legitimate venture. Henry considered claiming the throne by right of conquest, but was persuaded that this might give potential rebels too obvious a precedent. He thought about making use of an old rumour that Edward I had not been Henry III's eldest son. The story went that Bolingbroke's own direct ancestor Edmund was Edward I's senior, but had somehow been passed over because he was hunchbacked (or because of 'mental weakness'): the committee of lawyers and wise men rejected that. In the end, his claim included elements of challenge, blood title ('I that am descended by right line of the blood coming from the good lord Henry the third') and of conquest ('that right that God of his grace hath sent me with help of my kin and of my friends to recover [the realm]'). Making a rebel into a king was a matter of subtlety and symbolism, as well as of brute force.

A dangerous precedent

Henry's first problem as king was what to do with his predecessor. Like Edward II, Richard came to a violent if mysterious end, and, as with Edward, there were rumours that he had survived long into his successor's reign. The weight of evidence, however, is firmly for a more immediate fate. Richard was taken to Pontefract Castle, the Lancaster stronghold where Thomas of Lancaster had been executed (again, the symbolic significance is hard to resist). He languished there for just over two months. An unsuccessful rebellion that proclaimed Richard king again at the time of Epiphany, after Christmas, 1399, almost certainly made up Henry IV's mind. Once this rebellion had been put down in January 1400, Richard was killed, or, at least, 'allowed' to die, probably of starvation, by 17 February, the date when a payment was made to an undertaker to remove his body to London, displaying it as he went so as to allay any argument over Richard's survival. The Epiphany rebellion had been led by die-hard Ricardians, and the fact that several were slaughtered by populist mobs during its brief course showed that Henry as king initially retained most of the popularity he had found as returning Duke of Lancaster. He reacted to the rebellion with more self-restraint than many predecessors had shown in the face of similar challenges. Although several ringleaders were executed, more rebels were shown mercy. One pardon was a favour called in from what seemed a lifetime ago, though it was less than twenty years. It went to John Ferrour, the man who had saved Henry's life in the Tower in June 1381, when the teenage Bolingbroke had found himself surrounded by rebel peasants, eyeing him up as the best substitute victim for his hated and absent father, John of Gaunt.

Henry's fourteen-year reign was not a quiet one. Despite his best attempts to finesse the problem, his usurpation had set an even more dangerous precedent for action than previous rebellions. He also found it impossible to live up to the expectations raised during his second-coming-like return in 1399, when, as well as promising more general reform, he had specifically pledged to live 'of his own', that is, from the revenues of his own (which now included the royal as well as the Lancastrian) estates, at least in times of peace. That promise couldn't last more than a year, and by the time a parliament was summoned, in January 1401, Henry was already requesting grants of taxation, which the Commons only gave on their own conditions. There were violent attacks on tax officials, one of whom was killed with his servant. Although Richard had been dead for two years, he was the focus of an aborted rebellion in 1402 by a group of Franciscans and others, who were arrested and questioned on their belief that Richard was alive. Henry had little difficulty in dealing with opposition based on such shaky foundations, but it did not make him sit any more comfortably on the throne.

From the beginning, Henry seemed to want to abide by his coronation oath to rule fairly and with consent, but he found that concessions could not guarantee loyalty. Henry had already been forced to deal with an uprising in Wales led by a disaffected minor lord, Owain Glyn Dŵr, in 1400, but this rebellion, which simmered away after a royal expedition had failed to suppress it, became much more serious when in 1403 the Welsh threatened to link up with the disaffected Percy family, led by the Earl of Northumberland's hard-bitten son Henry, known as 'Hotspur'. The Percys had only ever been lukewarm supporters of Henry, and their connection by marriage to the family of the Mortimer earls of March, the only surviving alternative candidate for the throne (whom Henry kept under supervision in Windsor), made them a potential danger. Hotspur had been instrumental in a great success against an invading Scottish force, defeated at Homildon Hill in September 1402, but was owed wages for that action and refused to hand over prisoners to the King. Henry had also previously entrusted the Percys with a mission to put down Glyn Dŵr's rebellion, but instead they had negotiated. Henry was right to be wary. In July 1403, Hotspur gathered a force and marched on Chester, where the recently created Prince of Wales, the future Henry V, was based. Cheshire was also the territory from which Richard II had drawn his most loyal bodyguard, and Hotspur hoped to find support there.

Unlike Richard, however, Henry met rebellious military challenges head on, and in person. In 1400, he had mustered a scratch army to fight the abortive Epiphany rising. Against Hotspur's rebellion a more thoroughgoing response was called for, and Henry gave it. Gathering an army as he marched on the Midlands, joining up with his own son's forces and those of the loyal Earl of Stafford, he surprised the rebel army by confronting it at Shrewsbury, and forced Hotspur to give battle. The fighting was hard and extremely intense, 'one of the wyrste bataylys that ever came to Inglonde, and unkyndyst'. During it the precedent of Henry's own usurpation found its echo in the cries of Hotspur's men for 'Henry Percy King' when it was thought that Henry IV had been killed. In fact, it was Hotspur himself who died, in a frontal assault on the King's position. For all the rebellions that had been raised in the past two centuries, this was the first time since Stephen's reign that an English king had personally defeated a rebel army on English soil. Henry had the rebel Earl of Worcester and a couple of knightly followers beheaded, and completed the operation against the rebellion by securing an oath of loyalty from the knights and squires of Northumberland. This last move would become a standard way of dealing with rebellions in the next century, and was part of the incremental way in which England's rebellious tendencies ended up strengthening the bonds of monarchy.

The Northumberland rebellion of 1403 was certainly the most

serious threat to Henry, but it was not the last. Two years later, as Henry prepared an expedition against Glyn Dŵr, the Earl of Northumberland, who had secured a pardon through Parliament for his previous indiscretion, again marched against the King. This time, Northumberland had the support of the Archbishop of York, Richard Scrope, who led an armed demonstration against Henry onto Shipton Moor, six miles outside York. Scrope was protesting against Henry's levy of clerical taxation, and he was joined by a force of around 8,000 Northern gentry, who are as likely to have been inspired by the Earl of Northumberland's moves to the north as by their archbishop's cause. Northumberland's own role in the rebellion was short-lived. When, in May 1405, he failed to eliminate his rival the Earl of Westmorland, he decided that his rebellion was doomed, and fled for Berwick, and then for Scotland. Although he lived for another three years, moving to Wales and France in search of support for yet another rebellion, he was never again a serious threat. His last attempt at rebellion ended in his death at the hands of a small local force in Yorkshire in 1408. His remains were quartered, and his head placed on London Bridge, as his son's had been placed at York after the Battle of Shrewsbury.

The more significant symbolic event of the rebellion of 1405 was in the fate of Archbishop Scrope. For three days, the Archbishop and his army waited for reinforcements from Northumberland. Instead, the man whom Northumberland had failed to capture, the Earl of Westmorland, arrived. When Scrope's armed backing melted away as he negotiated with Westmorland, representing the King, he was arrested, and brought before the King himself at Scrope's own castle of Bishopthorpe. He had already been stripped of office. Now, despite the pleas of his fellow archbishop and Henry's ally, Arundel (who had known Scrope for thirty years), the rebellious prelate of York was treated as so many secular rebels had been in the past century: he was beheaded, along with the Earl of Norfolk (son of Henry's old adversary, with whom he had been banished) and a knight who had also been instrumental in the rebellion.

Although the number of men that Scrope had been able to

summon was impressive, the swiftness with which they were uncoupled from their leader showed that, without the Earl of Northumberland, the threat from the Archbishop's rebellion was never very great. It seems surprising, then, that Henry, who had been prepared to be merciful before, became the first king since Henry II to be responsible for the death of one of his own archbishops. But for Henry IV leniency hadn't worked. The outstanding example of that was Northumberland, but since he had evaded justice for the time being, Scrope found himself as the most prominent rebel in the King's hands, and one who had appeared to have abandoned his right to clerical protection by levying war on his sovereign.

Whatever the justification for the King's sentence in the context of the times, it didn't look good. Archbishop Arundel was fully aware of that when he rode for two days to try to persuade Henry not to execute Scrope. Arundel invoked the example of Thomas Becket, and how much his murder had damaged Henry II's reputation. Sure enough, the Pope reacted to the execution by excommunicating anybody who had had anything to do with it (though Arundel refused to publish the sentence in England). Henry and Arundel might have predicted, too, the springing up of a cult around Scrope, particularly after the King had allowed him to be buried in York Minster. And, sure enough, miracles began to be reported around his tomb and the place of execution. So Richard Scrope joined a lengthening list of rebel martyrs, including Thomas Becket, Simon de Montfort and Thomas of Lancaster. In a sense, he became in death more influential than any of them, in a way that Henry could scarcely have predicted. The northern rebellions which began in Henry IV's reign were the first indication of a developing fault line in English politics, between supporters of Lancaster and York, in the great division of the Wars of the Roses. Henry V tried to neutralize the Archbishop's cult by giving it official backing in his reign, but the rise of the Yorkists found symbolic inspiration in the example of Richard Scrope, and when a duke of York became king, as Edward IV, he attempted to secure the rebel martyr's official canonization, in 1462.

In June 1405, it was on the day after Scrope's execution that Henry was taken severely ill, with a skin complaint that has never been explained. Of course, it looked like instant divine retribution, but it is perhaps more important that, despite his sacrilegious act and a state of health that would decline intermittently but steadily over the next few years, Henry was never again faced with serious rebellion in England itself. Even Glyn Dŵr's uprising had lost all its force as a result of the defeat of Northumberland. And, although Northumberland himself escaped intact for a time, his lands did not: they were confiscated by Henry and parcelled out among his family and supporters. The huge concentration of landed power in royal hands that stemmed from the combination of the royal, Lancastrian and various rebel inheritances all being under the King's control made his position practically unassailable. For eight years, Henry was able to rule, sometimes in conflict with Parliament, sometimes at odds with his own son and his followers, but without the sort of threat that he had faced at the beginning of his reign. He left a will full of regrets for his life as a 'sinful wretch', perhaps allowing himself at the last to show guilt over his usurpation (though it wasn't unusually self-incriminating for the time). But his was the most successful rebellion in English history, establishing Henry and his dynasty on the throne. How long that dynasty lasted was down to the men who succeeded him – and the rebels they faced.

Jack the rebel

Henry's son, Henry V, has been described as 'the greatest man that ever ruled England'. His nine-year reign may be better remembered for conquest abroad than rebellion at home, but the new king was forced to deal with an uprising – and a rebel – that had a surprisingly prolonged influence. Compared to Simon de Montfort or Wat Tyler, Sir John Oldcastle is a forgotten figure, but both his name and his cause resounded for more than a hundred years after his rebellion failed and he died a traitor's death in 1417.

Oldcastle might have remained an even more recognizable name to this day, had Shakespeare been allowed to stick with his first choice of names for one of his best-known characters; for Sir John Falstaff began his dramatic life in *The First Part of Henry IV* as Sir John Oldcastle. Only after an inheritor of the rebel-knight's title of Lord Cobham had complained of the knockabout treatment his famous namesake suffered at the playwright's hands was Shakespeare persuaded to change the name to Falstaff. It seems a fitting instance of the way rebellion gets pushed to the side in traditional English history that the one thing routinely obscured about Falstaff, the most indelibly English of characters, is the fact that he was modelled on a historic rebel.

As with most medieval men, the records of the real Sir John Oldcastle's life are sparse. As with any medieval rebel, they are also prejudiced; particularly as Oldcastle was not 'merely' a rebel. He was also a heretic. In the aftermath of the Peasants' Revolt a finger had been pointed – unconvincingly – at John Wyclif and his followers, the 'Lollards'. By the time of Oldcastle's moment of fame, in 1413, Wyclif had been dead for almost thirty years, and his doctrines unequivocally declared heretical, but they had also taken root in some fairly high-up places. Richard II seems to have extended a measure of toleration to the anti-clerical, Lollard practices of a small number of knights at his court. Many of the things Lollards believed in (Bible reading, an unendowed Church, symbolic rather than actual transubstantiation, the importance of preaching rather than priesthood) would become staples of the Protestant Reformation. But more-conspicuous campaigning provoked a stronger reaction in Richard's usurping successor's reign. A new law, *De Heretico Comburendo*, making heresy a crime against the state as well as the Church, and condemning heretics to be burnt to death, was passed in Henry IV's reign. Although the holocausts of the sixteenth century were some way off, two heretics were executed, and others pursued into exile, recantation, or hiding. Nevertheless, it seems that, as long as Lollardy wasn't too conspicuously espoused, it was generally tolerated under Henry IV.

The new king, Henry V, was more unequivocally orthodox

than his father, and under him Archbishop Thomas Arundel conducted a vigorous campaign of rooting out Lollard sympathizers. Sir John Oldcastle, who like Falstaff had served under Henry when he was Prince of Wales, came to greater political prominence by virtue of his marriage to Lady Cobham, which gave him a seat in the House of Lords. He was already in place in 1410 when a Lollard petition against the endowed Church was floated in Parliament, and he may well have been its chief backer. In that year, a priest in Oldcastle's household was investigated for Lollardy and was forced into hiding. A letter from Oldcastle to a patron of the Bohemian heretic leader Jan Hus survives from this time, a sign that Oldcastle saw himself as a leader in an international movement. The promotion of an international, radical religion at odds with established national loyalties has parallels for our own time, and likewise, the fears of secular authorities about the potential menace of Lollardy were to be borne out in part, and in part used to forward their own agenda.

Early in Henry V's reign in 1413, Arundel gathered more evidence of Oldcastle's heresy and he was required to answer charges in front of the King. Oldcastle tried to avoid first the trial, by barricading himself in his castle, and then the charge, by refusing to give a statement of his beliefs. When goaded into an outburst against the Pope, however, Oldcastle was condemned. His service to the King clearly counted for something, as he was sent to the Tower to be given an opportunity to recant. Instead, like the rebels Ranulf Flambard and Roger Mortimer before him, Oldcastle escaped. (Through the prism of rebellion, the famous royal prison doesn't look particularly good at keeping people in, or, for that matter, out.) For two months at the end of 1413 he hid, apparently in the home of a parchment maker, William Fisher, in Turnmill Street, not three miles from his prison.

During these two months, Oldcastle worked in secret to raise an armed force against the King. It was alleged that the rebels intended to kill Henry and his brothers, though it was unclear whether Oldcastle himself, or a more 'royal' candidate, was envisaged as a replacement. The rising took place on the night of

9 January 1414, when a small number of rebels gathered at St Giles' Fields, arriving from as far away as the Midlands. There were only around 300, to judge by the records of their pardons and punishments, though chroniclers like Thomas Walsingham conjured up a terrifying picture of a vast, countrywide conspiracy, with 'crowds of people flocking together, brought to London from almost every county of England by the extravagant promises of the Lollards'. But the plot had already been betrayed to the King three days earlier, and the rebels were quickly arrested.

Sir John himself, who can only have revealed his presence to his followers at the last moment, fled the city. He was to remain in hiding – sometimes associated with other conspiracies, sometimes with a price on his head, at others offered a full pardon by a king who seems to have retained some affection for him – for more than four years. It colours an English triumphalist view of Henry's reign to consider that, even as he was achieving his legendary victory at Agincourt in 1415, an avowed rebel and traitor who had escaped justice and led an armed uprising against the King was still at large. Granted, Henry clearly thought the scale of the threat posed by Oldcastle was small enough not to interfere with his preparation and departure for the French campaign. One might speculate that Henry had allowed the conspiracy to mature into a full-blown, if unthreatening, rebellion, in order to smoke out seditious elements in his kingdom, and he certainly took direct action against Lollard sympathizers after the rebellion, securing his own position as he did so. But it is worth considering, too, how Oldcastle might have been able to capitalize if Henry's heavily outnumbered force had suffered the resounding defeat the French had expected to inflict upon them. Before and after 1415, the course of rebellion at home could often be dictated by military fortunes abroad.

Little is known in detail of Oldcastle's activities while on the run, though he seems to have made contact at various times with potential Welsh, Scottish and aristocratic English rebels. From among the latter – Richard, Earl of Cambridge, Lord Scrope and Sir Thomas Grey – emerged the only other serious conspiracy against Henry, in 1415. This was betrayed by the man whom the conspirators hoped to put on the throne in place of Henry, the young Earl of March, Edmund Mortimer. Oldcastle himself continued to be a focus and instigator of Lollard demonstrations. He was not captured until November 1417, near Welshpool, in the Welsh Marches. He was injured in the struggle, possibly breaking a leg, and was brought by horse litter down to London, to face a parliamentary trial and his certain fate. Oldcastle proved his treason by blurting out that he owed allegiance only to his 'liege lord', Richard II, who was 'still alive in the kingdom of Scotland' (the Scottish court continued to maintain Thomas Trumpington, a Richard lookalike who claimed to be the surviving king himself, as a useful tool). At this, Oldcastle's second trial, sentence was swiftly carried out. He was executed by hanging and burning at St Giles' Field, the same place where his abortive attempt to overthrow the King had foundered. Rumours that he was to return to life in three days proved unfounded.

Oldcastle did have an afterlife of sorts. True, Shakespeare's use of him for the Falstaff character had as much to do with satires of the Cobhams of the playwright's day as with any comment on the historical knight. Comical allusions to the gallows and burning were unlikely to have been lost on his audience, however, particularly those who saw the part played under its original name. But, in any case, Shakespeare was drawing on a tradition begun around a century after Oldcastle's death by William Tyndale, that had reached its apogee in the work of John Foxe and John Bale, which made the Lollard Knight an early Protestant martyr. Although this tradition formed part of a new scheme that attempted to replace discredited Catholic saints with home-grown 'Protestant' ones, it also links back to the existing cults of rebel-saints, like Becket, Montfort, Lancaster and Scrope, all of whom found a place in more or less religious observance that their failed rebellions hadn't secured for them in their lifetimes. Bale argued that Oldcastle was a better subject for emulation in the Protestant age than Thomas Becket, the non-violent rebel of a previous one.

The Lollards rose sporadically over the next few decades, for example in 1431, when an Abingdon weaver who took the name of 'Jack Sharp' led a rebellion in the West that threatened royal dukes and magnates as well as the established Church. But the next great cycle of rebellion – in which two kings were toppled and a confident new dynasty fought its way to power – returned to older forms of defiance, stemming from a breakdown in confidence in the country's rulers. Religious rebellion would only really flower in the sixteenth and seventeenth centuries, where it became a driving force behind several uprisings and one revolution. The early case of Sir John Oldcastle was taken up in those centuries as a glorious example, only to be both immortalized and obscured in the convivial satire of Shakespeare's 'plump Jack', with his 'more flesh than another man, and therefore more frailty'.

8. Wars of the Roses

Jack Cade to Perkin Warbeck 1450–99

'A crown, or else a glorious tomb!
A sceptre, or an earthly sepulchre!'

III Henry VI, I, iv

'. . . the world, I assure you, is right queasy . . .'

Sir John Paston to his cousin, 18 April 1471

Henry V died unexpectedly, struck down with dysentery on campaign in France in 1422. The eventually disastrous consequences of one supremely capable monarch's premature death, and his replacement with the infant and, even as an adult, thoroughly incapable Henry VI, provided Shakespeare with the subject of another great cycle of history plays. They also reintroduce our 'Shakespeare problem', by which English history comes to seem like the workings of fate. It was actually a different genius of imaginative historiography, Sir Walter Scott, who christened the chaotic conflicts of the fifteenth century the 'wars of the White and Red Roses'. But Scott was inspired by Shakespeare's invented scene in Temple garden, where the two sides choose their emblems, white for York, red for Lancaster, in their 'quarrel [that] will drink blood'. The plays' epic treatment traces the fall of the House of Lancaster, headed by the ineffectual Henry VI, back to his grandfather's usurpation more than sixty years earlier. But Henry's replacement, the 'noble son of York', Edward IV, was also a usurper, so his line too was destined to fail, when the bad blood of Richard III rose to the top. Only when Henry Tudor 'liberated' the country from Richard's tyranny was England saved, by a king who managed to combine the houses and bury the feud. (He was a usurper too, of course, but as Shakespeare lived in a country ruled by his dynasty, this was best ignored.)

On this view, it looks as if rebellion was merely the agent of tragic destiny, the means by which the curse on the houses of Lancaster and York was inevitably fulfilled. Like the transformation of Oldcastle into Jack Falstaff, however, the inexorable fate evoked in the three *Henry VI* plays and in *Richard III*, not to mention the psychopathic revelling in violence attributed to the English aristocracy, is matchless poetry, but lousy history. Still, it has proved hard to shift the idea that Henry IV's seizure of the throne somehow hexed his Lancastrian successors, incubating chickens that came home to roost in his feeble grandson's reign. Historians of the past fifty years at least have struggled valiantly to recover the period from Shakespeare's dominant picture of indiscriminate slaughter, vaulting personal ambition, and dynasties destined for mutual destruction.

There are two strands to this recasting, one of which is more persuasive than the other. The first argues that we make too much of the Wars of the Roses. Henry VI's government lasted for more than twenty years without serious opposition, despite his infancy and then inadequacy. His successor, Edward IV, was able to rule for twelve years relatively unmolested. This was not a relentless war of attrition, but an on-and-off conflict punctuated by many years of relative peace. True, up to a point. The fact remains that, from 1455 to 1487, fifteen battles were fought, including the deadliest ever on English soil. Kings and heirs to the throne, as well as hundreds of nobles, knights and gentry, and many thousands of nameless followers on every side, were killed. If the aristocracy were the greatest sufferers, few classes were untouched, and this was a time of popular uprising as well as noble in-fighting.

So Shakespeare didn't invent the civil war. The second strand of recasting to replace his curse of Lancaster may be a reaction to the complex theories of various modern historians, focusing on the malign influence of 'bastard feudalism' or entrenched regional affinities. The explanation that seems to have gained most popularity is that the Wars of the Roses weren't about very much at all, just 'a power struggle between Plantagenets'. Some wars seem more futile than others, and this one comes across as an exercise in self-indulgent, blue-blooded gangsterism.

As part of England's history of rebellion, however, the Wars begin to make more sense. They were prefaced by a popular rebellion, and began in earnest with an aristocratic one, neither of which was about simple personal advancement or the tunnel vision of revenge. They were about what rebels had been contesting for the past 400 years: how the country should be ruled. As before, only when rebellion failed to provide a satisfactory answer (either by forcing the government to operate as the rebels wanted, or by the government demonstrating its strength in quashing the rebellion and ruling as it pleased) was the possibility seriously advanced of replacing one king, and one dynasty, with another. Up until the establishment of Edward IV as king, battle was actually joined around often well-intentioned attempts from all sides to make a headless body politic function. That isn't to argue that these rebels were any different from their predecessors in combining self-interest with their idea of the national interest; just that self-interest wasn't their sole motivation. Only in the two later outbreaks of violence, led by the Earl of Warwick ('the Kingmaker') in 1470 and Richard of Gloucester (Richard III) in 1483, do personal ambitions begin to trump all suits, but those episodes were the aftershocks of the fall of the house of Lancaster, not the cause.

So for about fifty years, rebels made the political running in England: powerful men like Richard Plantagenet, Duke of York, and his son Edward, the future king, as well as the Earl of Warwick and Richard of Gloucester; and men from lower down the social scale, who emerged from actual or assumed obscurity to lead risings that overlapped with, but didn't always correspond to, the magnates' causes: men like Jack Cade, Robin of Redesdale and Robin of Holderness, the 'Bastard Fauconberg', and the two impostors who challenged Henry VII, Lambert Simnel and Perkin Warbeck. True, these rebellions took on their own dynamic, and the pitiless logic of revenge worked to polarize two separate camps.

But the Wars of the Roses were only collected under that name in retrospect. People who lived through these decades would not necessarily have seen them as a self-contained sequence of events. The two parties' differences emerged slowly, and nobody could have been certain they had been settled until well into the reign of Henry VII, at least to 1497. Not until three years after the first battle of the Wars, at St Albans in 1455, did anyone even publicly acknowledge that there *were* two defined 'sides'.

Jack Cade's rising

Crucially, the prelude to this intermittently bloody, mostly aristocratic struggle was not a noble but a popular rising, one that foreshadowed the grounds on which the civil war would be fought. In modern political terms, the personalities changed, but many of the issues didn't. Jack Cade's rebellion of 1450, which began in Kent and spread briefly across the country, looks at first like a dead ringer for the Peasants' Revolt of 1381. A younger and weaker king had replaced a colossus on the throne. In France, ground so gloriously gained in the last reign had been frittered away by unworthy lieutenants, and there were fears of a French invasion: in Norfolk that year, Margaret Paston (one of that gentry family whose letters give us a unique, though frustratingly isolated, glimpse into fifteenth-century English life) wrote to her husband that 'the said enemies been so bold that they come up to the land and playn them on Caister sands and in other places, as homely as they were Englishmen'. The financial burdens that paid for these failures of government were begrudged inside and outside Parliament.

This was the background of discontent from which the Kentish rising sprang. Its leader, Jack Cade, remains if anything an even more obscure figure than Wat Tyler or Jack Straw, but like them he owed his position at the head of the revolt to personal charisma rather than the traditional affinity on which a noble could rely. Like the *rustici* of Kent and Essex before them, and at almost exactly the same time of year as in 1381, Cade's followers headed for

London, and camped on Blackheath a few miles outside the City, making their demands known in a series of ultimatums, before forcing their way across London Bridge. Despite the efforts of the leadership at restraint, there were outbreaks of indiscriminate violence. As in 1381, certain individuals, whom the rebels held responsible for the country's plight and their own, were specifically targeted. Some of them were killed.

All these aspects of Cade's rebellion call to mind its predecessor, but the differences are almost as striking. It is true that, as in Tyler and Straw's rising, so in Cade's, a class not normally associated with armed rebellion against the establishment was galvanized into action. This time, however, it was not the bondsmen and *rustici* of Tyler's bands who rose, but the smaller freeholders and artisans whose modest property and income made them vulnerable to unscrupulous, corrupt local officials, in the service of magnates whose position at court Henry VI seemed powerless to limit. These smallholders were more directly affected by the movements of court faction and politics, and their revolt was not an assault on the status quo but an appeal for its restitution. Cade's followers did not seek to abolish lordship or (despite what Shakespeare has his followers cry) 'kill all the lawyers'. They wanted a more predictable, more trustworthy world, where legal procedure and everyday life no longer depended on the whim of those who had bent the King's ear. It was a complaint that emerged in different forms again and again over the next thirty years.

Cade's rebellion began locally, but it emerged from a national crisis. While Henry VI had been a minor, his government could be run uncontroversially by magnates, preferably those with royal blood, like Henry's uncles, Humphrey, Duke of Gloucester, and John, Duke of Bedford, the former running government at home as 'Protector', the latter continuing the French campaign with initial success. By 1437, Henry's minority was coming to an end, or should have been. But it was from this time that the real vacuum at the centre began to be revealed, as the King showed himself unable to take on the true burdens of government. It is impossible at this distance to know exactly how many of the things done in

Henry's name were his own ideas or those of the men around him. It seems that the King was personally pious and that, in contrast to his father, he genuinely sought peace abroad. At home, most of the running of government remained in the hands of the council, though the one area Henry controlled directly, the distribution of patronage, was enough to get him into trouble. The open-handed King gave away most of what he had to give, even granting the same post, the stewardship of Cornwall, to two different recipients (who happened to be sworn enemies) by mistake. The death of the Duke of Bedford on campaign in 1435 deprived the government of an effective soldier and a restraining influence on his brother Gloucester. The latter's standing began to wane from 1441, when his wife was banished after being accused of necromancy for casting a doom-filled horoscope for the King. Although Gloucester himself was not implicated, Henry looked elsewhere for guidance, and throughout the 1440s the Earl, later Duke, of Suffolk, William de la Pole, emerged as the dominant force at court.

In Kent, it was allies of Suffolk, such as James Fiennes, Lord Saye and Sele, and Humphrey Stafford, Duke of Buckingham, who presided over a corrupt and extortionate local government. As long as Suffolk remained the real power behind Henry's throne, however, there was little the people of Kent, or any other locality where court influence prevailed, could do. The experiences of the Paston family in Norfolk at this time, preserved in their famous correspondence, illustrate how the law could be manipulated by allies of those in power. The Paston estate at Gresham had been taken by force, but while the criminals retained court backing, the family had no chance of legal redress. Elsewhere in the south-east, outbreaks of revolt earlier in the same year as Cade's rebellion, 1450, led by Thomas Cheyne in Kent and Nicholas Jakes in Westminster, were ruthlessly put down and their leaders executed in the now conventional traitors' sentence of hanging, drawing and quartering. But Suffolk's position had been weakened by his involvement in the increasing debacle of the French campaign. During the course of 1449, Suffolk's government had presided over the loss of Normandy, and by the end of the year Calais was the only French possession that remained securely in English hands (Gascony was lost in 1453).

When you consider that Henry VI's only visit to France had been to be crowned as French king eighteen years earlier, it is clear how far English fortunes had fallen since the apotheosis of Henry V. Suffolk was blamed by the Commons that gathered for the parliament from November 1449, and articles of impeachment were drawn up. The Commons also presented an act of 'resumption', which sought to remedy King Henry's finances and get back for him what he had so readily given away. Under the influence of those who had most to gain from his generosity, the King wriggled out of this attempt to balance the royal books. Suffolk was more difficult to rescue. Already one of the Duke's closest associates, Bishop Adam Moleyns of Chichester, had been set upon and killed at Portsmouth by disaffected soldiers who had been unpaid and unemployed, while Normandy was being lost on the other side of the Channel. Although Suffolk was able to avoid the accusations of 'great and horrible treasons', he was found guilty on charges of misprision and banished for five years.

He didn't get very far. Crossing the Channel, Suffolk's ship was taken by another, called the *Nicholas of the Tower*, whose captain was not inclined to let a man accused of conspiring with the King of France get away so easily. (If, as the name of his ship suggests, he was attached to the man in command of the Tower of London, then Suffolk had fallen indirectly into the hands of an implacable enemy, the Duke of Exeter.) Suffolk was 'tried' on board and sentenced to death. He was executed with a rusty sword, which took several blows to sever the victim's neck. Suffolk's headless body was dumped on the Dover shingle on 2 May.

The rumours of vengeance for this act of summary justice were what sparked the biggest popular uprising since 1381. It was said that Suffolk's ally Lord Saye, now Treasurer to the Crown, would turn Kent into wild forest. Across the county, Kentishmen swiftly began gathering to defend their county against this threat. No leader emerged at first, but by June the rebels had a captain: Jack Cade. What we know of Cade comes only from his actions in the

brief period during 1450 that he came to national attention. Details
about him were given on the government proclamation for his
capture that year, but these were no more securely based than
other rumours about him. It was believed, or at least put about,
that Cade's real name was John Mortimer, which connected him
to the man who would emerge as the leading alternative candidate
for the throne, the King's cousin Richard, Duke of York, descended on his mother's side from the Irish Mortimer family, and
on both sides from Edward III. The fact that this associated the
rebellion both with the rebels of 1327 (led by Roger Mortimer)
and with potential designs on the throne in the person of the Duke
of York was convenient for those in government, and strenuously
denied by the rebels themselves (as well as by the Duke, who
stayed loyally at his post in Ireland, where he was lieutenant, until
the rebellion was over). There is a record of a yeoman from Sussex
at this time called John Cade, which puts him in the same class of
freeholders as many of the rebels, but it is only guesswork whether
this is really our man.

By 11 June, Cade and his followers had arrived at Blackheath.
They posed enough of a threat to bring Henry and his court back
from Leicester, where Parliament had been moved, to London. A
group of dignitaries including the two archbishops was sent to
speak to the rebels on the heath. They were unable to negotiate
the withdrawal of Cade's force, but they returned with the rebels'
bill of petition, which set out their grievances and remedies. Surviving examples of the petitions mention the rumours of vengeance
on the county of Kent for the murder of Suffolk. They also discuss
the King's situation, alleging that 'other men . . . have the revenues
of the crown.' His councillors are not, as traditionally, men of
'royal blood', but 'persons of lower nature', who keep the King in
the dark about the state of his realm and allow justice to be served
only if they get their hands on 'bribes and gifts'. Like the commons
in Edward II's reign, Cade's followers complained about not being
paid for 'the stuff and purveyance taken to the use of the king'.
Other more specific grievances were a combination of local and
national concerns, ranging from uncertain land titles to the loss of

France. Their suggested remedies included charging named guilty men with treason, and replacing them with councillors, including the 'high and mighty' Duke of York, whose royal blood fitted them better for the job. There is little evidence here of the sort of class hatred on show in 1381.

The authorities' initial reaction to these complaints, many of which reflected petitions already heard in Parliament, was to resist them. The next day, a royalist detachment marched to Blackheath, only to find that Cade and his men had already left. This might have been the end of the uprising, with hit squads sent to hunt down the rebels in their native county. But Cade's rebellion had exposed weaknesses in both the competence and the unity of Henry's government. First, the pursuing force was set upon at Sevenoaks, and its leaders, Sir Humphrey and William Stafford, both killed. The next day, 19 June, some of the King's inner circle voiced their agreement with at least one aspect of the rebels' programme – pinning the blame on particular individuals. Most of those were away from the court, but the notorious Lord Saye, the King's Treasurer, was present, and he was duly committed to the Tower. Six days later, the King and court left London for the safety of Warwickshire, and two days after that, on 27 June, a party of Londoners sent out to check on Cade and company's movements returned with the news that they were on their way back. While violence broke out elsewhere in the country, with the Bishop of Salisbury, William Aiscough, murdered by a mob in Wiltshire, the Kent rebels camped again at Blackheath and started to make plans to cross into the City. As in 1381, the security of London's only bridge could not be relied on. On 3 July, Cade was able to gain access to the river crossing. He cut the ropes of the drawbridge so that it couldn't be raised again, and led his men into the City. Although Cade tried to control his followers by proclaiming that looters would be executed, the pent-up fury of the rebels couldn't be contained: one alderman's house in Lime Street was stripped bare.

Mostly, the rebels were more restrained, and rather than exercising mob justice, Cade simply made a judicial commission already sitting at the Guildhall turn its attentions to the rebels' 'guilty men', most of whom were convicted in their absence. One, however, was in London to receive sentence. Lord Saye was removed from the Tower and tried at the Guildhall for treason. His fate had been sealed when Henry had agreed to imprison him and then abandoned the city. He was taken on to Cheapside, beheaded, and his body dragged through the City. Saye's son-in-law, William Crowmer, sheriff of Kent, who was already in Fleet prison, was less formally tried, and beheaded outside the city walls in Mile End. For two days, Cade was undisputed master of the capital, and lethal justice continued to be meted out, though the victims were less exalted.

On the evening of 5 July, the royal and City authorities were at last able to co-ordinate a military response to the rebels. Cade had been returning at night to lodgings in Southwark, on the south side of the river, and that night an armed force attempted to retake the bridge and ensure he couldn't cross back over. Cade was alerted to the plan, and gathered his men to resist. The fighting lasted all night, with casualties estimated in the hundreds. It ended with Cade burning the drawbridge, while the Londoners closed the gates. It was not a conclusive encounter, but it was enough to persuade Cade to a truce, and to negotiations with the two arch-bishops and the Bishop of Winchester at St Margaret's, Southwark, over the next two days. The outcome was a general pardon for the rebels. They had little option but to return home. Henry's government had hardly showed leadership, and there was nothing from the feeble 29-year-old King to match the personal courage of his fourteen-year-old predecessor seventy years before, but the withdrawal from London had at least removed the possibility of direct confrontation between monarch and rebels, as in 1381. This time, the rebels had made their complaints, and got their vengeance on the most hated of enemies, but they could not force the government's hand any further.

Cade and his men had hardly been humiliated, however, and it is another contrast between this rebellion and the Peasants' Revolt that Cade continued his activities, attacking a castle in Kent and attempting to avoid capture when his pardon was, inevitably, withdrawn. On 12 July, only five days after leaving London, he was captured at Heathfield in Sussex by the new sheriff of Kent. He died of his wounds before the sheriff could return him to the capital. Cade was decapitated anyway, his head stuck up on London Bridge, where the fortunes of his rebellion had bloodily turned, and his body quartered and sent across the South to places that had shown rebellious tendencies: Blackheath, Norwich, Salisbury and Gloucester. Cade's name and his designation as 'Captain of Kent' continued to inspire risings in southern counties throughout the 1450s, but none on the scale of the original. The government at first responded generously to those who sought pardon: a commission to inquire into injustices and extortions was sent into Kent at the beginning of August. But as the year wore on, and outbreaks of popular violence continued, so the mood turned. Another reason for this was the return of the man the rebels had wanted to see installed as the King's councillor: Richard, Duke of York.

York and Lancaster

With all the royal blood in his veins, the Duke posed a threat to the childless King by his very existence. But if he had objections to the way the country was being run, let alone designs on the throne, he had only expressed them by removing himself from the court. He had been – probably spuriously – linked with the rebels from the beginning, but once it looked as if York would try to take advantage of his popularity, those around the King, led now by the Duke of Somerset, decided that a show of strength was called for. Somerset seems to have represented everything that York most objected to in Henry's government, certainly politically, and most likely personally as well. He was the military commander who had replaced York in France, presiding over the humiliating loss of French possessions, and he now seemed to have been rewarded by being promoted to fill the position vacated by the murdered Duke of Suffolk. Somerset ensured that York himself

was put on a committee to punish the Kentish rebels, surely in
order to test his loyalty, and although York does not seem to have
taken any active role, a steady number of executions built up in
the first part of the new year. The progress of this commission
came to be known as the 'harvest of heads', and it seems to have
guaranteed that, for the time being at least, any appeal York might
have wanted to make directly to popular support would not receive
much response.

Initially, he tried to do this on almost exactly the same grounds
that the Commons in Parliament, and then those who followed
Jack Cade, had done; that is, he promised to sort out the
deficiencies of the government in the king's name. There was no
indication at this stage that York had any plans to remove Henry.
A member of his household wrote a letter in October 1450 to John
Paston setting out what his master wanted, and the propaganda
campaign that was needed to promote it:

my lord has put a bill to the king desiring much which is after the
commons' own heart, with all the emphasis on justice and on arresting
those who have been indicted. . . . And, sir, many groups of commons
should be organised . . . to cry out to my lord for justice.

But when York tried to go further, getting an MP of his affinity,
Thomas Young, to request that the Duke be recognized as the
official heir to the still childless King, Young was instead sent to
prison. At this point, York must have realized that if he wanted to
oust Somerset from government and usurp his position, let alone
have any chance of the succession in the event that Henry failed
to produce an heir, he would have to resort to violence. But when
he did come out in open rebellion in February 1452, he was unable
to secure enough backing to force the royal party to battle. Instead,
after a standoff at Dartford in March (where the commons of Kent,
sufficiently cowed by the 'harvest of heads', conspicuously failed
to turn out for the Duke), Richard was forced to apologize, and
stayed out of national politics for more than a year.

It was never likely, however, that a man who took his exclusion from the centre of politics as a personal slight would retire from them permanently. Although Somerset's administration in Henry's name had some successes – making gains in Gascony for example – when it stumbled, York was on hand to take advantage. And the stumbles were difficult to miss. In August 1453, defeat in Gascony passed the region back into French hands after 300 years of almost unbroken English rule. In the same month, the King, who had merely been easily manipulated before, was suddenly afflicted with a grave, and at this remove undiagnosable, mental illness. He lapsed into a catatonic state. Unable to elicit any flicker of response from Henry, Somerset and his circle attempted to carry on governing for him over the next two months, but the fiction that the King was in charge could not be maintained. When Somerset and his colleagues attempted to exclude York from a council to discuss Henry's incapacity, the Duke looked around for allies. He found them in the powerful and well-connected Neville family, whose long-running dispute with the Percys in the North of England had recently turned violent, when a Percy group had ambushed and assaulted a Neville wedding party in August 1453. Richard Neville, Earl of Warwick, known to posterity as 'the Kingmaker', agreed to assist York in ousting Somerset. Somerset was placed in the Tower, and York was appointed Protector during the King's inca-pacity. He seemed to have achieved by political manoeuvre what had eluded him by rebellion. For a little less than a year, he held this position, using it in part to make good on his promises of good governance but also, and crucially for the process by which rebellious confrontation escalated into civil war, to pay back the Nevilles by bringing the Percys to heel. In the complex tit-for-tat arrangements between powerful families, the split in the country began to form.

York's position was not a very secure one – something like a regent's during a minority, albeit an open-ended one. Unfortu-nately for him, Henry's second childhood came to an end when, in January 1455, it was reported that 'the king is well amended and hath been since Christmas Day.' He recognized the Queen, and also, for the first time, his baby son, born during his madness:

Prince Edward. Almost immediately, the bad old days returned. York's office of Protector lapsed, and Somerset was released and welcomed back into the King's inner circle, with the Percys now firmly taking his side against York, who had assisted their mortal foes the Nevilles. It is not known whether Somerset planned any formal move against York, who refused a summons to a council at Leicester. As in 1451, York seems to have run out of options, finally settling on armed rebellion. Unlike the first time, however, he had a powerful ally in Richard, Earl of Warwick, and his father, also Richard, Earl of Salisbury. Their combined army mustered in the North and the Midlands and marched south in May 1455 to confront Somerset and the royalist forces, which hastily assembled. They met at St Albans, and this time no negotiated settlement could be reached. The first battle of the Wars of the Roses took place almost exactly five years after Jack Cade's rebellion had exposed the cracks in the half-government. At St Albans, it was the Earl of Warwick's men who turned the battle in York's favour, managing to find a way into the heavily barricaded town and to fall on the men around the King. Although Henry himself was saved, three of the most important men around him were killed: Somerset, the Percy Earl of Northumberland and his closest ally, Thomas, Lord Clifford.

For the second time in two years, York had triumphed. He appeared to have the kingdom, and more importantly the King, at his mercy. But his time in charge showed that he faced the same problem as any successful rebel who was reluctant to take the ultimate step of removing the king. Simon de Montfort's solution 200 years earlier had been to set up a formal body to rule in the king's name. By the time of Richard of York's success, high politics had become if anything even more personal, and the more recent precedents from the reigns of Edward II and Richard II far more unforgiving. But York was neither ruthless enough to kill Henry and his child in cold blood, nor visionary enough to try a new form of government. He resumed the role of Protector, his admin-istration made efforts to put the royal finances in order, and he moved to deal with the feuding between powerful families that had often been a barometer for the breakdown in central government.

York was unable to hold on to power for long, because of the emergence of a rival he had almost certainly not bargained for. Henry's queen, Margaret of Anjou, found enough support against York's attempt to push through another act of 'resumption' to block it. The result was that York felt unable to continue as Protector and resigned. In some ways, this was another polarizing step on the road to civil war. But just as important as the hardening of the two factions – the court, 'Lancastrian' party and the re-forming 'Yorkist' one – was the issue on which they clashed. A dispute over royal finances allowed York to take the moral high ground, and also connected him not to usurping rebels who merely wanted to take the monarch's place, but to reformers who wanted to help him rule more justly.

For more than two years, while Margaret strengthened her grip on the machinery of government – with her private chancellor, for example, being appointed Keeper of the Privy Seal – York did nothing actively to challenge the status quo. This was hardly the behaviour of a wanton troublemaker, or, for that matter, the swift, unstoppable descent into civil strife of the traditional view of the Wars of the Roses. The most memorable occasion of this period, indeed, was not an act of war but an ostentatious one of peace, when Lady Day, 25 March 1458, was declared a 'loveday'. This was the first time that the fault-line in the ruling classes was recognized. The heir of the Duke of Somerset walked arm in arm with the Neville Earl of Salisbury, head of the family responsible for Somerset's father's death, while York, Warwick, Northumberland, and even the Queen herself also conspicuously buried their differences, as they heard Mass for the dead of St Albans.

The Kingmaker

This late-medieval version of truth and reconciliation, however, only drew attention to the growing fissure in English politics. The next episode in the Wars was precipitated by another rebellion, though at first it was led not by York but by his ally the Earl of Warwick. The return of the 'Lancastrian' party to power meant that, although Warwick had been allowed to continue as Captain of Calais, the position to which York had appointed him, government money to pay the troops was withdrawn. This, of course, was a personal slight to a 'Yorkist' from the 'Lancastrians'. But it was also yet another occasion when a breakdown in the proper function of government – in this case paying for vital defence – was the cause of dispute. Warwick tried to get his own money by turning pirate, but the diplomatic problems caused by his attacks on foreign shipping provided the perfect pretext to summon him to court to face charges. When that summons turned into a personal violent attack on the Earl, he withdrew to gather his forces for a rebellious invasion. The royal party prepared to defend themselves, but did not include York and his closest allies (including Warwick's father Salisbury) in the preparations, prejudging their disloyalty.

Sure enough, when Warwick returned in September 1459, he marched to link forces with his father and York. Though his father won a battle against a royalist force at Blore Heath in Staffordshire, a more significant encounter with the King's army, with Henry actually at its head, at Ludford Bridge, near Ludlow, ended when Warwick and York, together with York's son, the eighteen-year-old Edward, Earl of March, were forced to flee the field after Warwick's best troops deserted him. The rebels made it back to Calais, but their rebellion had failed. It had also made accommodation impossible with Henry's government, whoever ran it. By attacking a royal army, led by the King in person, and crucially by being defeated, York and his allies had become traitors, punishable by death.

York went to Ireland, where he was able to gather his forces, while Warwick did the same in Calais. It was Warwick who invaded first, landing at Sandwich in June 1460, and gathering Kentish support as he marched north and met a royal army at Northampton. It is a corrective to the view of the Wars of the Roses as rich men's quarrels, of interest only to the upper echelons of fifteenth-century English society, that Warwick was able to recruit the 'commons' of Kent to his cause. Once again, this was advertised as an assault not on the Crown but on those bad advisers around King Henry. At Northampton, the Earl's troops were under orders to spare the King *and* the commons on the Lancastrian side. The rebels were conscious not only of the momentousness of facing their monarch in battle, but also that they would need popular backing for any regime they tried to set up. The outcome at Northampton, like that at Ludford Bridge, was decided by treachery, but on this occasion by a desertion from the royal force. Lord Grey of Ruthin's retirement allowed Warwick's men to breach the Lancastrians' well-defended position. As at St Albans, the fighting was fierce around the King himself, but, as before, Henry was spared. Some of the most influential of his lieutenants, however, including the Duke of Buckingham, the Earl of Shrewsbury, Lord Egremont (son of the Earl of Northumberland) and Lord Beaumont, were killed in the battle, defending the King's position in person. As the death toll mounted, so the potential for revenge, for simple strike and counter-strike, grew.

Only after Warwick's victory did his ally Richard of York land in Chester with his army, and begin to make his way to London. There, in October, Richard at last claimed the throne for himself. Unfortunately for him, this claim was not as well stage-managed as Henry IV's or Edward III's had been before him. Crucially, York does not seem to have received the wholehearted support of his comrade-in-arms, Warwick, whose protestations that he was invading to help King Henry, not to remove him, turned out to be more than a front. Warwick had sailed from Calais to Ireland before the invasion for a secret discussion with York, the terms of which are unknown. If the Duke's plan to usurp the throne had been discussed then, Warwick reneged on the agreement. With the Queen's forces still at large, perhaps he decided it wasn't the right time for the move. His reputation as 'Kingmaker' came from his support for Richard of York's son Edward, but in July 1460 Warwick showed he could unmake a potential king. York's claim was debated by the lords, spiritual and temporal, and a compromise was reached. It was agreed that York would succeed on Henry's death, bypassing Henry's son. This was the sort of arrangement which had placed York's distant ancestor Henry II on the throne, but in 1153 there was a formal treaty agreed to by all parties after a long period of civil war. In 1460, the compromise could only bring a very temporary lull in the fighting. Henry VI may have been under the control of York and Warwick, but Margaret of Anjou was regathering her forces in Wales.

York had got as close to the throne as he was ever going to. Shakespeare actually has him sitting on it, goading Henry to obeisance. Contemporary sources stop at the Duke's hand placed on the throne-cushion, waiting in vain for the acclamation that would encourage him to go further. In one of several unlikely reverses which add to the confusion and longevity of the Wars of the Roses, a Lancastrian army confronted York at Wakefield in Yorkshire, when he emerged from the security of Sandal Castle, and the Duke was defeated and killed on 30 December 1460, as was one of his sons, Edmund, and, after the battle, Warwick's father, the Earl of Salisbury. York's head, topped with a paper crown to mock his ambitions, was displayed over the gate to the city of York.

York's end was less predictable than that of many rebels who had gone before him, so powerful had his position seemed, even without the confirmation of the Crown. But York was a rebel who appears more than anything else to have had a very bad sense of timing. From his botched attempt to secure popular backing at Dartford in 1452, through the protectorships and the long-delayed but finally fudged claim to the Crown, down to the last miscalculation of leaving the safety of Sandal Castle for the risks of open battle at Wakefield, York's failings were not ones of ambition or imagination but of execution, and of sheer bad luck. It wasn't his fault that Henry recovered when he did during the first protectorship, and it is difficult to be too critical of him for lacking the ruthlessness to kill Henry when he got the chance. If he seems to have mishandled Warwick, the latter's actions during York's son's reign show that the Earl was an extremely difficult ally to pin down. But the ten years of opposition, rebellion and finally attempted usurpation had at least ensured one thing. By the time of the Duke of York's death, his eldest son, Edward, Earl of March, was old enough at eighteen and experienced enough, with a military command in Wales, to take up the Yorkist cause and his family's claim to the Crown. Unlike his father, Edward was born into an aristocratic rebel's life, with little option, if he wanted to claim any part of his inheritance, but to aim at all England. That was what he set about doing without delay.

Edward's killing field

Edward was in the Welsh Marches when his father died, and it was there, at Mortimer's Cross in Herefordshire, that he defeated a Lancastrian army led by the earls of Pembroke (Jasper Tudor, uncle of the future Henry VII) and of Wiltshire. Another Lancastrian force was still on the move. Margaret of Anjou hadn't been in command of the army at Wakefield, but she put herself at the head of the Lancastrians as they marched south to confront Warwick and to free King Henry. Although the Londoners refused them entry, when Warwick's army confronted Margaret's for the second battle of the wars at St Albans, it was Margaret who emerged triumphant, even resecuring her husband. But it proved only a temporary reversal for the Yorkist cause. Warwick escaped, meeting up with Edward, and they resolved to return to London, which Margaret hesitated to enter, and claim the throne. Edward IV was crowned king on 4 March 1461, only fifteen days after Warwick's defeat at St Albans, and three months after his father's death at Wakefield.

Edward's coronation had done nothing to extinguish the Lancastrian cause; it had merely raised the stakes even higher. Just over three weeks later, at Towton in Yorkshire, this unremitting civil war produced England's biggest battle, with as many as 40,000 on either side. The fighting was said to have lasted for ten hours. There was snow on the ground, and hundreds drowned in the freezing waters of the River Cock, where the crossing was fiercely contested. When the struggle came down to man-to-man combat, the six-foot-three teenage King was at the centre of the melee. Eventually, Edward's Yorkists prevailed, and the Lancastrians fled. Henry and Margaret had not been on the battlefield, but their cause was dealt a terminal blow at Towton, even if its death throes were long drawn out. The dead among the highest ranks included the Earl of Northumberland, Lord Clifford (who had killed Edward's brother at Wakefield), and the Earl of Devon, executed after the battle. But the losses among other ranks, from the gentry down, were unbearable: the lowest estimates put the number of dead at Towton at 9,000, the highest at 28,000 – more than died on the first day of the Somme, and nearly all the violence done not with shot but with arrow, sword and knife. A recent excavation at the site of Towton has cast doubt on some of those numbers, but the evidence of the victims' skulls gives a grim reminder of the way men died. The well-armoured combatants aimed high: 'in some cases', in the forensic language of the report, 'bisecting the face and cranial vault of some individuals and detaching bone in others'.

Edward's reign had begun with a bloodbath, but it did not wash the spirit of rebellion entirely away. The Lancastrian cause resurfaced one more time, and Edward, like Henry IV before him, soon discovered that a throne won by rebellion came with automatic risks. The biggest liability turned out to be Edward's closest ally, the 'Kingmaker' himself, Richard Neville, Earl of Warwick. At first, Warwick remained a loyal servant of the victorious Yorkists, as Edward spent the opening three years of his reign in a fluctuating battle to gain and keep control of the northern Marches, where various Lancastrians, in alliance with the Scottish Crown, attempted to establish a foothold. By 1464, this campaign was successfully completed, and Warwick had played an instrumental role in it. Five years later, he was in open rebellion. And, as was the case almost twenty years before, at the time of Jack Cade, it was a popular uprising that foreshadowed the aristocratic one.

Up to 1464, Warwick had little to complain of in his treatment by the King, who was in turn under no illusions about how much the Earl had done to help him to the throne. Warwick was

appointed to negotiate a potential Continental marriage alliance
for his master. But Edward had a secret: he was married already.
Elizabeth Woodville was of not very exalted background, and
she was English, so diplomatically useless. This much may have
displeased Warwick, but when Elizabeth's family started receiving
honours and preferential treatment hitherto reserved for Warwick's
Nevilles, his loyalty – which had been bought with favours –
started to waver. The deciding factor was Edward's preference for
a Burgundian alliance – promoted by his father-in-law, Earl Rivers
– over a French one, to which Warwick had committed his time
and energy. When he returned from France in 1467, the Earl did
not stay at court but withdrew to his vast northern estates.

Warwick waited, but Edward's promotion of the Woodvilles
and the business of ruling itself – together with the fact that,
although Henry VI had been captured and placed in the Tower in
1465, Queen Margaret was still at large, attempting to find support
in Scotland, then France – all meant that there was plenty of
discontent to exploit. Warwick, the consummate manipulator, was
able to work up both popular and aristocratic opposition. In the
North, Percy-inspired popular risings had demonstrated that there
was a grassroots objection in one region at least to Edward's
government. Two Robins, of Holderness and of Redesdale, had
been named at the head of these outbreaks, and in June 1469 there
was another rising which was also apparently led by Robin of
Redesdale. The man behind this rebellion may not have been the
same as the first; it seems likely that a Warwick retainer, a hardened
soldier called Sir John Conyers, had been instructed to make use
of the name and its affiliations to stir up support. While this 'Robin'
gathered a force and made trouble in the North, Warwick sailed
to his secure base at Calais, taking his daughter and the other piece
in the game, the Duke of Clarence, Edward's brother, with him.
There, the Duke and the Earl's daughter were married, a match
specifically forbidden by Edward. Clarence had thus been drawn
to Warwick's side, and he put his name to a rebel manifesto
with the Earl complaining of the bad rule of Edward's Woodville
favourites, and calling on the commons of Kent to rise. Warwick

was popular in Kent, where his acts of piracy had directly benefited many, and where the port of Sandwich provided the well-rewarded supply line to Calais. When he and Clarence landed in the county, they were welcomed, and were allowed to march westwards and enter London.

Edward seems to have underestimated the strength of Warwick's rebellion. As a result, neither of the main players was involved in the first decisive engagement. While the King was still in Nottingham gathering troops and the Earl was in London, the army of 'Robin of Redesdale' confronted a royalist force led by the Earl of Pembroke. At Edgecote in Oxfordshire, the rebels triumphed. The captured Pembroke and his brother were executed on Warwick's orders, the rebel-Earl taking it upon himself to treat royal lieutenants as traitors. Other victims of Warwick's rebellion were dispatched with even less ceremony, including the Earl of Devon, killed by a Somerset mob, and Earl Rivers, the Queen's father, and her brother John, captured and murdered in the Forest of Dean. Edward himself was unable to rally his forces, and, deserted, he gave himself up to Warwick's brother George.

Warwick's posthumous reputation as 'the Kingmaker' might lead us to expect that at this point, with Edward at his mercy, the Earl would have deposed him and replaced him with his new son-in-law, Clarence. But, instead, Warwick allowed Edward to reclaim his position, and Edward proceeded to behave as if the rebellion had never occurred, readmitting Warwick to his counsel. When the King decided to rebalance power in the North, however, restoring a Percy, Henry, to the earldom of Northumberland (and removing a Neville, Warwick's brother, in the process), this was the catalyst for Warwick to renew his machinations. Again, he took Clarence with him and, again, a popular rising, this time in Lincolnshire, was co-opted to split royal forces. On this occasion, however, the rebellious army was defeated on 12 March 1470, fleeing the battle and casting off their protective or identifying clothing with such speed that the encounter became known as 'Losecote Field'. Learning that Warwick and Clarence had backed this force, Edward went north in pursuit, and Warwick was forced to run. He and the King's brother went south and west, and sailed from Dartmouth, eventually finding sanctuary not in Calais, which was now closed to them, but at the court of Louis XI of France. There, Warwick was reconciled, after much persuasion on both sides, to Margaret of Anjou. Warwick's willingness to change affinities is less a reflection of his own personality than an indication that Lancastrians and Yorkists were never rigidly defined groups. Clarence's willingness to go along with the Earl is further proof of that, although in Clarence's case it is also evidence of an infinitely biddable, vacillating character.

Return of the King

The rebellion that Warwick led to remove Edward and replace him with Henry (still in captivity in London) was a briefly successful, audaciously played last hand. Much of Warwick's career reads like the biography of an inveterate gambler, and when he and Clarence arrived in September 1470, only six months after their previous play for the Crown, he was once again risking everything to gain everything. Amazingly, it worked – if only for a few months. Again, Warwick had orchestrated a rising in the North, allowing him to land in the South unchallenged. Again, he made for London, but this time he found much more support as the champion of the imprisoned King. When Warwick's brother John, Lord Montagu, whose loyalty Edward thought he had secured, declared instead for the rebels, Edward realized he was cornered and was forced to flee. The Kingmaker had secured the return of the old King, an episode unusual enough for a unique name, the 're-adeption', to have been attached to it. Henry VI, released from the Tower, was a broken man, even less capable of carrying out his royal duties than previously, and Warwick could have been forgiven for assuming that he would assume the dominant role in government, the crowning moment in the career of a supremely daring rebel. He was appointed to the position of lieutenant of the realm, but he had less than six months to enjoy the post. In March 1471, Edward, having secured the backing of the Duke of Burgundy, returned, landing at Ravenspur, where Henry VI's grandfather Bolingbroke had come ashore in 1399. This time it was Warwick who suffered from unreliable allies, as Clarence returned to his brother's affinity and abandoned his father-in-law.

Edward's army swelled gradually, but by the time the two forces confronted each other at Barnet on Easter Sunday, 14 April, Warwick's was still the larger, though accurate figures are impossible to come by. In thick fog, a confused battle ended with Edward's triumph. As at Towton, Edward's personal prowess was remarked upon, and may well have inspired the victory. Warwick preferred to direct operations from horseback, and it is unclear whether at Barnet he died when unusually fighting on foot in a doomed attempt to inspire his men, or was caught up with when, more characteristically for a man in whom the instinct for self-preservation was strong, he rode away from the battlefield through the woods. However he fell, Warwick's luck finally ran out at Barnet. Edward's next battle was fought only three weeks later at Tewkesbury. There, a Lancastrian army brought over by Margaret of Anjou and Edward, the (Lancastrian) Prince of Wales, lined up under the command of the Duke of Somerset, son of the man killed at St Albans. Edward IV's victory at Tewkesbury really did put paid to the Lancastrian threat, resulting in the execution of Somerset, and the death in battle of the Prince of Wales, as well as of other senior Lancastrians. Margaret, too, was captured.

A Kentish rising which marched (and sailed) on London under the pirate 'Bastard Fauconberg' (an illegitimate son of Warwick's uncle) had been terrorizing the citizens even while Edward was fighting at Tewkesbury. By the time he came to the capital, having put down a rebellion in the North, an unusually determined resistance from the City government had only just succeeded in ejecting Fauconberg's rebels, who left no Cade-like manifesto from which we can glean any higher motives. This popular explosion while the more 'traditional' aspects of the war were being decided elsewhere is another reminder that the absence of active government at times of crisis during the wars could affect all the people, not just those on the better-remembered battlefields.

Edward reigned in relative peace until his death in 1483. In the North, he placed his younger brother, Richard of Gloucester, who was a paragon of loyalty until after Edward's death, in charge of the Marches. The possibility of any further rebellion on behalf of Henry VI was removed when Henry himself was murdered in the Tower on Edward's return to London. In ordering the killing, Edward was finally following the precedent which Mortimer and Isabella had set with Edward II, and Henry IV had followed with Richard II. The only remaining Lancastrian supporter, the Earl of Oxford, was captured following a siege of St Michael's Mount in Cornwall, in 1473. Two other potential thorns in Edward's side, Warwick's brother, George Neville, Archbishop of York, and the King's own untrustworthy brother Clarence, died in 1476 and 1478, the latter after he fell foul of enough opinion close to the King to encourage Edward to have him arrested for treason.

Two usurpers

Edward IV's death, leaving a twelve-year-old heir, Edward V, and the seizure of the throne by that boy's uncle, Richard of Gloucester, less than three months later set in motion what is usually seen as the last act of the Wars of the Roses. But Richard's usurpation in 1483, and his removal by Henry Tudor two years after that, had very little to do with the conflicts that had come to a conclusion after Barnet, Tewkesbury, and the deaths of Henry VI and his heir twelve years before. Again, Shakespeare must bear most of the burden for the telescoping of these events in our minds, so that Edward IV's reign is reduced to a pause for breath in the epic bout between two warring houses. Richard's rise was the result of a palace coup rather than a rebellion, but rebellions were the almost immediate consequence, stemming directly from Richard's own actions, not from more long-term 'unfinished business'. What moved Richard to act so uncharacteristically has never been fully explained. Shakespeare's villain, murdering his way to the throne from as early as 1471, may not match up to what we know of the dutiful, trustworthy man who served his brother faithfully until the latter's death. In 1483, however, Richard did turn ruthless, dispatching Lord Hastings (a loyal servant to Richard's brother who may have opposed a mooted usurpation) and, of course, Edward's sons, the 'Princes in the Tower', the older of whom had succeeded, even if he was never crowned.

Richard obviously decided that the protectorship, the post he was meant to occupy during Edward V's minority, would not allow him to run the country as he saw fit. Whether through pure, callous ambition or through a sense of duty to the legacy of Edward IV's stable government – or some combination of the two – Richard quickly concluded that only the Crown itself would do. But it would be a mistake to see Richard's ruthlessness as efficiency. It was closer to panic. True, he embraced early the logic that his brother had taken years to accept – that direct rivals for the throne must be removed. The threat that Edward V posed was not a theoretical one: only a month after Richard's coronation, as he travelled on a progress round his new kingdom, a rebellion attempting to spring the boys from the Tower was put down. It was almost certainly in the wake of this that the princes themselves were killed. But Edward V was blameless in a way Edward II, Richard II, and even Henry VI were not: Richard was crucially unable to secure the wider loyalty that he needed to run the country he had snatched, and his cold-blooded calculation only made those outside a very small inner circle feel vulnerable, motivating them to look elsewhere for a champion. The person with the strongest blood claim was probably Edward IV's nephew, Edward of Warwick, son of the Duke of Clarence, but he was only nine years old in 1484. Richard's enemies – including the various Woodvilles whose alleged control over Edward V (son of Elizabeth Woodville) was the pretext for Richard's coup – needed an adult.

They found him in Brittany. Henry Tudor had been living in exile ever since his involvement with his uncle, the Earl of Pembroke, in the so-called 're-adeption' of Henry VI in 1471. At that time he had narrowly escaped the returning Edward IV, who had besieged the Tudors in Pembroke Castle. But how could this obscure Welsh noble possibly have a claim to the English throne? It was, in truth, a pretty tenuous one. Henry's grandfather Owen had married Henry V's widow, Catherine of France, a union so unlikely in social terms that only love, that rarest of considerations in fifteenth-century aristocratic matchmaking, can explain it. The orbit into which this drew the Tudors enabled Henry's own father to make a marriage that theoretically linked his son to the English Crown. Edmund Tudor married Margaret Beaufort, a great-granddaughter of Edward III. The fact that the Beauforts, descendants of John of Gaunt's third marriage, to his former mistress Katherine Swynford, had been specifically excluded from the succession was a technicality that didn't disturb Henry, or those casting around for a viable alternative to Richard. One effect of Edward IV's death and Richard's usurpation had been to halt negotiations for a rapprochement between Henry and the English king, who in 1482 had been almost ready to accept his return from exile and restoration to his father's title as Earl of Richmond. Richard's actions had instead legitimized a more enticing ambition for Henry.

Henry could rely on the support of foreign forces in his bid to topple the English king, but he needed English backers too. His first ally was an unlikely rebel, the Duke of Buckingham, one of the few magnates who had materially benefited from Richard III's rise. But Buckingham's rebellion was badly timed. He tried to raise a force in the Welsh Marches while the people of Kent took on their now expected role of rising against the Crown, but the numbers didn't materialize. Nor did Henry himself, unable to find a safe landing because of Richard's south-western defences and inhospitable weather. Henry returned to Brittany and Buckingham was forced to go into hiding. He was handed over by his own retainer and executed without trial.

Buckingham's rebellion had failed, and Richard tried to secure himself on the throne by removing the inheritances of an unprecedented number of rebels in the only parliament of his reign. But the real test of Henry Tudor's invasion was still to come. Henry spent the next year gathering support, including that of the French court. It was not until August 1485 that he tried again. The Battle of Bosworth, where Richard lost his crown and his life, turned on the loyalty or lack of it of two powerful families – the Percys, represented by the Earl of Northumberland, and the Stanleys. Northumberland's forces failed to commit to the battle at all, while Thomas Stanley's intervention late on in the engagement on Henry's side turned it in favour of the invader. Stanley was well rewarded, with the earldom of Derby. It is curious to think that one of the longest continuously held family titles in the country, which includes a prime minister among its ranks (the 16th earl) and is still held today (by the 19th), should have been founded on this single moment, when Thomas Stanley decided which way to lean.

Traditionally, we think of Bosworth as the end of the Wars of the Roses. Henry VII's marriage soon afterwards to Edward IV's daughter, Elizabeth of York, was supposed to represent the symbolic healing of the dynastic rift between Lancaster and York. But Henry was only very distantly a 'Lancastrian', and he fought against Richard not because Richard was a Yorkist, but because he seemed an illegitimate (and vulnerable) king. The new king relied on servants of both houses to carry out his government. Henry's experiences in the first part of his reign – when the rebellions he faced were in the names of impostors who seem to have convinced few of their assumed 'Yorkist' identity, but who nevertheless secured significant support – were tests of his own legitimacy and ability to hold on to the throne. The Tudors had less blood claim to the throne than any king since William I, but the previous thirty years' events had demonstrated a yearning for kingship, not just for a king. In some ways, Henry VII was a far less effective king than Edward IV, and the rebellions that challenged him were a sign of that. Unlike Edward, however, he had the crucial advantage of leaving an adult and (to put it mildly) vigorous successor. Even so, the two impostors Henry VIII's father had to see off, Lambert Simnel and Perkin Warbeck, were important tests of this mature student of kingship's approach to his unexpected elevation.

Faking it

Rebels had assumed aliases in the past, and one, Thomas Trumpington, had even been put forward as a true king (a resurrected Richard II). But the exotic careers of the rebel-impostors of Henry VII's reign are of a different order, and the plausibility of their rebellions gives an insight into the continuing feverishness of English politics after Bosworth. Henry's reign is often taken as a rather dull, necessary corrective to the violent excesses of the previous decades. Simnel and Warbeck are reminders that the King of England still had to live on his nerves.

Lambert Simnel was the son of a Flemish organ maker from Oxford and seems to have been taken by a priest to Ireland with the express purpose of being promoted as Edward, Earl of Warwick, Clarence's son and 'true' heir to the throne. What should have been a fatal blow to this plot was the fact that Edward himself was alive and in captivity in the Tower. Unlike Richard III with the Princes in the Tower, Henry VII was able to produce his young prisoner, but there was enough opposition to the new king in 1486–7 for this not to put an end to the rumour, or to the support it began to gather. Henry's prisoner was instead alleged to be the impostor, and the 'real' Edward, i.e. Simnel, was even crowned as Edward VI at Dublin in May 1487. He was joined by the Earl of Lincoln, a nephew of Edward IV who had not found the new court to his liking. It was important too that Henry's failure to confirm the Earl of Kildare as Deputy Lieutenant of Ireland, a role traditionally held by his family (and one of genuine power when the Lieutenant was often an absentee), had thrown Kildare and his forces into Simnel's camp. This English rebellion was in large part an Irish affair.

When Simnel and Lincoln invaded, it was with a force of around 8,000, including 1,500 German mercenaries. Although King Henry was able to gather a much larger army, the outcome of the Battle of Stoke wasn't a foregone conclusion. The rebels seem to have attacked before Henry's army had fully formed up, their best chance of neutralizing the King's numerical advantage. But the royal vanguard did their job, and the rebels fled towards the nearby River Trent, where their slaughter gave the name to a stretch known as the Red Gutter. Lincoln was killed, while Viscount Lovell, who had been one of Richard III's closest allies, fled to Scotland. Lambert Simnel, captured on the battlefield, met perhaps the most unusual fate of any medieval rebel, especially considering the dim (and usually merciless) view taken by royalty and aristocracy of the lower orders' getting above their stations. Instead of execution, Simnel experienced the ultimate act of demotion, from 'king' to scullion in the royal kitchens. He was even allowed prospects, and ended his days as a falconer.

The man Simnel impersonated, Edward of Warwick, remained in custody until 1499. He was the focus of plots only two years after Stoke, which resulted in three executions, though the prisoner himself was, once again, spared. From 1491, it was another impostor, Perkin Warbeck, who became the new figurehead of resistance to Henry. Warbeck was an even more unlikely front man for a rebellion than Lambert Simnel. He was a French silk merchant who had never actually set foot in England when, on a business trip to Cork, he was persuaded to pose as Richard of York, the younger of the two princes in fact murdered in the Tower in the previous decade. Warbeck's strings were being pulled by the King of France, Charles VIII, who hoped to distract Henry from a campaign to aid the Duke of Brittany. Six months after Charles brought Warbeck to his court, in March 1492, the French king concluded a peace with Henry VII, and Warbeck was no longer welcome. He found refuge in Burgundy, where Edward IV's sister Margaret happened to be the dowager duchess. She welcomed him as her long-lost nephew Richard, and through her influence Warbeck secured the support of Maximilien, the king of the Romans, who funded an invasion of England in July 1495. By this time, Henry had already been informed of the backing for Warbeck of several members of his own court, and had acted accordingly, with arrests and executions. The first of the pretender's two invasions didn't get off the ground, with an advance party overwhelmed by local levies as it put in at Deal in Kent. Warbeck himself didn't disembark, and now found Scottish help for his venture.

In 1497, the tax Henry was raising to deal with the threat from Scotland was the direct cause of a rebellion in Cornwall, which soon spread through the south-west as the Cornishmen marched on London to protest against taxation for a war they felt had nothing to do with them. The Cornish rebels, whose leadership included a local MP and a blacksmith, were defeated on that traditional graveyard of popular rebels' hopes, Blackheath. But when they returned to Cornwall, they were joined by none other than Warbeck, who had sailed from Scotland via Ireland, and gathered a force of about 8,000 within less than two weeks of landing on the Cornish coast. Failing to take the city of Exeter, the rebels appeared to be on course for a confrontation with Henry at Taunton, but before the two armies could meet Perkin Warbeck's had dissipated even more rapidly than it had assembled. Warbeck himself initially escaped, and even when he was captured he escaped again as Henry took him on a progress. Confined to the Tower, he was implicated in one last conspiracy, in 1499, along with the still imprisoned Edward of Warwick. Both prisoners were at last dealt with permanently. Perkin Warbeck was hanged at Tyburn on 23 November 1499; Edward of Warwick followed five days later, beheaded at Tower Hill, within sight of the fortress prison where he had spent more than half of his short life, guilty only of having more royal blood in his veins than the King.

The execution of Edward of Warwick really was the last blow of the Wars of the Roses. From this moment on, the disaffected of Tudor England were no longer able to use a 'Yorkist' or 'Lancastrian' claimant as their rallying call. As Henry's rule grew more established, rebellion ceased. But the reasons for rebellion, which lie at the heart of much of the Wars of the Roses, had not disappeared for ever with the arrival of the Tudors. Henry VIII may bestride his period as domineeringly as his Holbein portrait suggests, but he too would be faced by rebels – even if a lack of strong leadership was not their complaint.

9. The People's Wars of Religion

Robert Aske to Robert Kett 1536–49

The first Tudor king had to deal with the aftershocks of the civil war that had brought him to power, but his son's tribulations are traditionally seen as self-inflicted. Henry VIII's swollen conception of kingship, together with his indefatigable search for a male heir, defined his rule. This king's centre-stage performance seems to augur a new era, of dominant if not quite absolute monarchy, and to bring the curtain down on those messy, rebellious Middle Ages. In fact, rebellions continued not only through the Tudor age but into the modern one. Over the centuries, they took very different forms and aimed at different objectives. Yet no English monarch until Victoria – that is, until long after monarchy had become the 'dignified', rather than the 'efficient', part of the constitution – remained free from challenge, and three lost their thrones to rebellions. For his part, Henry VIII faced a rebellion that grew into the largest popular revolt in English history, and it began because of a rumour. In October 1536, the people of Louth, a market town in Lincolnshire, heard that royal officials were coming to confiscate the church silver. Their decision to do something about it culminated in the Pilgrimage of Grace, a rebellion which, at its height, held sway over the whole of England north of the River Don.

To those who cast English history as a narrative about the 'peaceful evolution' of the state, its institutions and government, rebellions can appear almost as inconvenient as they were to people in charge at the time. One way to marginalize rebels is to point out how the things that set off rebellions often seem trivially disproportionate to the massive forces they unleash. They are the political equivalent of freak weather events – intriguing but anomalous, part of history's sideshow, not the main attraction. The implication is that rebels, unlike rulers, tend to be irrational animals, unworthy of sustained attention. Rebellion, especially in hindsight, rarely looks like the rational option in England: from very early on, the institutions of government, the 'natural order' of society, the concentration of power and military expertise in traditionally more 'trustworthy' hands, as well as the example of the fates of most previous rebels, all made joining a rebellion an unreasonable thing to do. So it shouldn't be surprising that frequently, while the background to a rebellion looks explicable in 'conventional' terms, what sets it off can appear puzzlingly inconsequential or wrong-headed.

Yet in an era before political parties, broad representation, or modern media, rumours were important. Henry VIII's father had been powerless to quash reports about pretenders to the throne, and the story that Lord Saye was planning to turn Kent into 'wild forest', after the murder of the Duke of Suffolk in 1450, had provided the spark for Jack Cade's rebellion. Later, the Elizabethan obsession with 'vagabonds' stemmed in part from the concern that vagrants were precisely the sort of people who 'spriede . . . sedicious, false, and untrue rumours'. Excluded from the political mainstream, ordinary people could nonetheless be profoundly, and sometimes very personally, affected by decisions taken miles and worlds away from them. The way they found out about these goings-on was by word of mouth. In 1536, the rumours that started a rebellion focused on the issue that would drive rebellion and British politics generally for much of the next two centuries: religion.

The nationwide risings of 1536 were not the first rebellion that Henry had faced, and, contrary to his uncompromising reputation, earlier rebels had enjoyed some success in opposing him. In 1525, an attempt to raise an extraordinary tax, the provocatively named 'Amicable Grant' (government attempts to dress up new burdens on the people in friendly terms have a long pedigree), met with concerted resistance across southern England, from Wiltshire to East Anglia. Around Lavenham in Suffolk, some 4,000 rebels gathered to protest against the tax, which both clergy and laity were expected to pay. Although the Duke of Norfolk, acting for the King, arrested four ringleaders, when he brought them to

London, Henry decided to pardon them rather than punish them, and to abandon the gathering of the tax altogether. The 'grant' had been meant to pay for war in France, so the rebels' success had more than domestic repercussions. After the collapse of the Amicable Grant, Henry moved instead to make peace with the French.

There was at least a partial connection between the rebellions of 1536 and this earlier resistance. Historians have calculated that Henry's government continued to raise impressive sums of money despite the rejection of the Amicable Grant. One source of revenue was the vast wealth that accrued from the dissolution of the monasteries, which began in the year of the larger uprising. Henry moved to dissolve the monasteries for several reasons, not all of them selfish. But it escaped no one that they would be a money-spinner, and it is noticeable that when Robert Aske, the man who came to lead the Pilgrimage of Grace, set down his complaints, he discussed the dissolution of the monasteries as much for its economic effects as its spiritual ones: 'now the profits of the abbeys suppressed, . . . went out of those parts. By occasion whereof, within short space or [sic] years, there should be no money nor treasure in those parts . . .'.

But, initially at least, the dissolution was not the rebels' casus belli. If it had been, they surely would have risen months before, when the smaller monasteries were suppressed. The dissolution was part of what we now recognize as Henry's Reformation of the Church, a combination of political expediency and religious enthusiasm for new ways of worship. In Lincolnshire, the townspeople of Louth were rarely enthusiasts for the new religion, but the spark was more specific. An episcopal commission was in the county, to value benefices and possibly collect clerical taxation. There were also suggestions that the commissaries would be confiscating church goods, and examining the local clergy on their learning, to see if they were fit to hold office. Rumours that other churches had suffered confiscation had been in circulation for some time when the procession behind Louth's silver cross assembled on Sunday, 1 October 1536. There, a yeoman named Thomas

Foster remarked that this was the last time the parishioners would have the chance to follow their cross into church. After the service, a group of parishioners gathered to protect their community's possessions, and a cobbler, Nicholas Melton, emerged as the leader of the small party.

Two coincidences turned this very local rising into something bigger. The first was that a commissary from the Bishop of Lincoln happened to be on his way to the town – why we don't know, but the townsmen were convinced that it was to carry out an inventory before a confiscation. The second is that the clergy in the area were already in a mood to rebel, convinced that they were going to be examined and some excluded from their livings. As one rebel later put it:

the chief occasion of this business rose by the means of the priests . . . they with many others were there and cried with a loud voice 'go to it!', holding up their hands and [saying the commons] should lose nothing if they would go forward and win the holy cross.

Another participant said that if it hadn't been for the priests, the guarantee given by one of the Bishop's servants would have been enough to defuse the situation. Instead, the rebellion started to spread to neighbouring towns, helped by the priests' ringing the 'common bells' to gather their parishioners to the cause. What that cause was, beyond a vociferous objection to a threatened confiscation that, in fact, was never envisaged by any authority (though the fear would certainly be justified over the following decades), remains unclear. It seems that in Lincolnshire a gathering sense of disquiet over several reforming acts of the past few months coalesced around this issue and the similarly baseless threat that parishes were to be amalgamated.

At a national level, it might seem strange that it was at this moment that conservative religious elements began to make their unhappiness known. The suppression of the monasteries was already in full swing, and Henry's usurpation of the Pope's position as head of the Church, the Act of Supremacy, had been passed in

1534. Much of the origins of all this, Henry's 'Great Matter', the annulment of his marriage to the piously Catholic Catherine of Aragon and her replacement with the evangelically innovative Anne Boleyn, had been resolved in Anne's favour three years before; since when Anne had already fallen foul of Henry's jealousy, anxiety about the lack of a male heir and the workings of court gossips on the more paranoid elements of his personality. In May 1536, she had been executed on trumped-up charges of treasonous adultery. It may be that in the aftermath of Henry's unseemly haste to get rid of his wife, he wished to demonstrate that this would not remove the reforming energy from his rule. At the Canterbury convocation of clergy which met in the month after Anne's execution, further reforming measures were adopted, summed up in the Ten Articles of a faith increasingly influenced by Lutheranism. They were given royal backing, circulated in the King's name, so that they applied to the province of York as well as that of Canterbury, and they were swiftly followed by Injunctions in the name of the King's minister, Thomas Cromwell. These instructed parish priests to preach against the 'bishop of Rome', miracles, relics and pilgrimage, and for faith as against good works – unpicking various threads from the fabric of the Catholic Church, familiar from centuries of ritual and observance in parishes throughout the country.

The dissemination of these views, which the King hoped would 'establish Christian quietness and unity among us', probably accounts for the appearance of the exact opposite among the rank-and-file clergy. One specific reason is that the King and his bishops had just abolished Purgatory, or at least had become decidedly agnostic on the subject: 'the place where they [dead souls] be, the name thereof, and kind of pains there, also be to us uncertain by scripture'. This disagreement was more than a matter of doctrine. It also rendered obsolete the saying of Masses for the dead, a key source of income for unbeneficed priests (those parishless clerics who had been identified as troublemakers as long ago as the time of the Peasants' Revolt). If there was no purgatory through which to speed the dead, then no one needed to pay for priests to help them on their way. We need not be too cynical about the clergy's motives to believe that this sort of worry inspired them to take advantage of, if not actively stoke up, the rumours that moved the Lincolnshire laity to come together in the autumn of 1536. One of the best pieces of evidence we have that the priests did connect the activities of the convocation with a threat to their position is in what they did to one of its representatives in Lincolnshire, Dr Rayne, when he fell into their hands: they murdered him. Historians have spilt a lot of ink in the past fifty years over how much the Lincolnshire Rising and the subsequent Pilgrimage of Grace were genuine 'risings of the commons', and how much they were worked up by members of the gentry class, higher up the social scale. At the beginning, however, most of the running was made by a different category altogether, the lower clergy.

Having clerics as the moving force behind a rebellion meant free use of the best avenues of communication in the sixteenth century. In Lincolnshire, the rising caught on through preaching, bell-ringing and rumour-mongering, and various gentry were more or less willingly co-opted to the cause. Many tried to assume leadership in order to divert the rebels from doing too much harm, and, as the rebels were admitted to Lincoln itself, it seemed as if this tactic had worked. The rebels were persuaded to present their grievances and sue for pardon. Various sets of articles were drawn up, not all of which survive in their original form. By the time a set was sent to the King, they had been substantially watered down, and had become more pleading than threatening. A demand for no more peacetime taxes, for example, had become a complaint about the difficulty of paying a specific tax; a general requirement for the restitution of the Church had mutated into a comment on the ill effects of the dissolution of the monasteries; and the traditional rebels' beef about bad advisers, which had begun as an insistence that the likes of Thomas Cromwell, Richard Rich and Thomas Cranmer should be handed over to them for summary justice – or at least banished – had become a comment on the presence of 'counsellors of low birth' around the King, reminiscent of Cade's rebels in 1450. Perhaps sensing the equivocation in the rebels' platform, which hardly called for any specific action on the King's part, except the offer of a pardon for having dared to rise, Henry went on the rhetorical offensive. Either the rebels dispersed, or the royal army would wreak revenge. Encouraged by a silver-tongued royal herald, and nudged by their new gentry leaders, the Lincolnshire rebels gave in. Some, like Nicholas Melton, Louth's 'Captain Cobbler', thought they knew where the blame lay: 'What whoresones were we that we had not killed the gentlemen, for I thought allwayes that they would be traytors.'

From rebels to pilgrims

But one gentleman, at least, had been persuaded of the justice of the rebels' complaints. Robert Aske was a Yorkshire lawyer who happened to be travelling through Lincolnshire at the time of the Rising, and, by his own account, was caught up in it. He was required to swear an oath by a group of mounted men led by a suitably sinister figure 'having a black coat and a grey beard'. This first oath seemed an unexceptional one ('Ye shall be true to God and the king and the commonwealth'), and Aske had no trouble agreeing to swear to it. He then became a sort of outrider for this group of rebels, linking up with another Lincolnshire group. Up to this point, it is unclear what Aske thought of the rebels' griev-ances, or how much of a part he had in formulating them. The only indication he gives in later testimony is that he didn't believe the rumours of confiscation.

Crucially, the commons of Lincolnshire allowed Aske to cross the Humber into Yorkshire, where rumours of what was happening to the south had begun to spread across the East Riding. At first, Aske appears to have wanted to pacify his county, telling two separate villages not to rise unless they heard the bell of the other. What persuaded him to become a more active leader of a Yorkshire version of the Lincolnshire Rising was his reading of the articles that the Lincolnshire rebels drew up to send to the King. Only after he had seen this did Aske manage to put himself at the head of an ever-swelling number of Yorkshire rebels, who had been mustered by beacon burning and, in the case of Beverley, had been encouraged by a letter sent in Aske's name (he denied anything to do with it). On 16 October 1536, at the head of about 10,000 men, Aske entered York unopposed and made the proclamation that turned this rising of the commons into the Pilgrimage of Grace.

The oath that Aske devised emphasizes the religious conservatism of the cause ('for the love that ye do bear unto Almighty God his faith, and the Holy Church militant') and the loyalty of the 'pilgrims' to their king. Like so many rebels before them, Aske and his followers disavowed the name. He was not the first rebel leader to turn his rising into a religious movement (the Magna Carta barons, it will be recalled, formed an 'Army of God'), and the mention even in the oath of poor counsel as one of the rebellion's grievances links it to more 'secular' precedents. Elsewhere in the North, risings which would eventually be linked to the Pilgrimage were almost wholly economic and agrarian in character, taking up the name of 'Captain Poverty'. But the self-designation as pilgrims was an inspired piece of rhetoric, which doesn't mean that Aske didn't believe in it. It seems to have been on his inspiration, too, that the pilgrims took for their badge a design of the 'five wounds of Christ', examples of which still survive. The five wounds were a favourite symbol at this time, in prayers, sermons, poems, images and designs throughout the country. Christ's body was still as powerful a motivational symbol in the sixteenth century as it had been in the fourteenth, when the Peasants' Revolt had come together around the feast of Corpus Christi.

With the new oath and a committed new leader, the Pilgrimage spread its influence across the North, even as word of the collapse of the original Lincolnshire Rising arrived. Aske and his pilgrims may have been disappointed that their inspiration had faded from view, but, for the time being at least, momentum was with them. The pilgrims marched south to Pontefract Castle, which they took after a short siege. The gentry leaders already in the castle gave different shades of co-operation to Aske, and he was able to gather more reinforcements from different parts of the North, which had risen and co-opted gentry leaders such as Sir Thomas Percy (of what was by now the most inveterately rebellious family in England). A force of more than 20,000 men assembled, much larger than the royal army which was mustered on the other side of the River Don.

Aske seemed to be in a powerful position, but the reality was much shakier. The pilgrims' main problem was that Aske appears to have been the only gentry leader who genuinely bridged the gap between his own class, which contained the trained military leadership of Tudor society necessary for any successful armed insurrection, and the commons. As at Lincoln, the other leaders whom the commons had adopted were actually playing a double game, trying to pacify their followers before they went too far in their defiance and risked their own and their leaders' necks. If some of the gentry believed in the complaints of the pilgrims, and some may well have done, then they were unconvinced about how best to satisfy them. At Pontefract, Aske himself appears to have decided that the Pilgrims' best bet was to secure aristocratic backing. He got the man who conceded Pontefract Castle to him, Lord Darcy, steward of the Duchy of Lancaster, to join the Pilgrimage, although Darcy maintained that he had been forced to and was loyal all along (it's impossible to know who to believe, as Darcy had a history of disquiet with the regime, but, equally well, had little choice once his poorly defended castle was in rebel hands). Aske drew up a new set of articles to present to the commander of the royal army, the Duke of Norfolk, which was relayed to Henry. On 5 November, the King instructed the Duke, without addressing the specific points in the articles, to offer a pardon on his behalf and the promise of a parliament in York to satisfy regional discontent.

Aske had difficulty selling this settlement to his followers, and had to return from Doncaster, where he had been negotiating, to Pontefract, to persuade them to end the Pilgrimage. The pardon was read out by the King's Herald of Lancaster on 7 December, and the pilgrims disbanded, tearing off their badges and declaring, 'We will all wear no badge nor sign but the badge of our sovereign lord.' The pilgrims, no longer claiming that name, began to go home. Later that month, Aske was invited to the King's Christmas court. It appeared not only that the rebels had pressed their case, but that they were being listened to in the highest circles. Aske certainly thought so, and there survives his self-aggrandizing advice to the King on how to pacify the North, which began with a suggestion that Aske himself should be given a royal proclamation to take to the people (at least he did not call them 'my people', as he had at the height of the revolt). His detailed proscriptions on more parliamentary representation also suggest that he expected to achieve in the promised northern parliament (which was never summoned) the detail of what had been requested in the various sets of articles.

Although Aske thought he was still at the centre of events, he had in reality missed his best chance of having a real impact. At Pontefract, the Pilgrims had outnumbered the royal army by perhaps four times, and Norfolk was well aware that he should try anything to avoid battle. 'In every man's mouth it is said in our army that I never served his grace [the King] so well as now in dissolving the army of the enemy without the loss of ours,' he wrote later. Norfolk also beseeched Henry not to read too much into any concessions he might give, right up to the possibility of swearing the rebels' oath himself, if only he could persuade them to disband. Aske had begun as a reluctant rebel, who had then brought the zeal of the convert to the cause, but at Pontefract his unwillingness to shed blood prevented him from pressing home his advantage. Killing the nobility ranged against the Pilgrimage, Aske later said, would have been 'a loss to this realm and what displeasure to the king'. And so it would, but it would also have advanced the Pilgrims' cause far more than the specious promises secured from Norfolk, even if most of the rebels could rely on the pardon secured in December 1536.

One who turned out not to be able to depend on that pardon was the King's recent house guest, Robert Aske. Unrest broke out again in the East Riding in January 1537 under the leadership of Sir Francis Bigod, descendant of the family who had confronted Henry III and Edward I, though their instincts were usually for loyalty. Bigod was swiftly defeated, as was a commons rising in Carlisle the following month. But these two abortive outgrowths of the Pilgrimage (Bigod, in fact, was no conservative but a committed evangelical who thought that the King was persecuting the North) gave Henry the chance he craved to take revenge. Norfolk was sent to pacify the region, and 178 people were rounded up and sent to London for trial and, inevitably, execution. Aske did not need to be rounded up, as he was part of Norfolk's entourage. But he was summoned south, and there arrested on a charge of having raised rebellion after the date of his pardon. He was convicted and sent back north, to be executed at York, the site of his first triumph as Captain of the Pilgrimage of Grace. He was hanged by a chain on 12 July, an agonizing death that seemed briefly to become the standard for Tudor rebels (though it wasn't an original one: William fitz Osbert and his followers had suffered it in 1196).

It is impossible to know whether Aske really thought he had been taken into Henry's confidence and been forgiven his part in the rebellion. It might seem self-delusional for a country lawyer who had led an armed host against the King to expect to survive, when in the same year Henry had seen fit to execute his own wife, a crowned queen and the mother of his second child. But there is something both naïve and wishful thinking about Robert Aske, at least as he appears in his own testimony. Ultimately, he may have felt that he had little choice but to carry on acting as though he had indeed been pardoned. Aske was a new sort of English rebel, neither one of those nobles who periodically took it upon themselves to 'correct' the government by force, nor a traditional commons captain like the cobbler Nicholas Melton of Louth. Perhaps as a lawyer rather than a natural man of action, he believed too much in the power of negotiation, of written agreement, and of process. His tragedy, admittedly not one often attributed to members of his profession, was a lack of cynicism.

As for Henry's government, the King's own uncompromising nature had left his commanders on the ground in a difficult position, but it had at least meant that the rebels' hand had been forced. The result was that a rebellion which took much of its inspiration from a genuine sense of religious conservatism, involving rebels who presented themselves more than opportunistically as pilgrims, would not take the step towards full-scale military confrontation that their movement required if it was to have any real chance of success. That strengthened Henry's hand, and the cases of those who wanted to push through further reforms, men like Thomas Cranmer and Thomas Cromwell, whose positions were only enhanced by the failure of the Pilgrimage. Cromwell oversaw the completion of the dissolution of the monasteries, and was instrumental in creating a Council of the North, which took a more direct role in keeping the area of the rebellions of 1536 under much closer scrutiny than before. Henry's government was never again threatened with the kind of resistance that he had faced for a few weeks that autumn.

The Pilgrimage of Grace has been called 'England's War of Religion', and its defeat the moment that 'made the English Reformation possible'. It is certainly true that even some measure of success for the rebellion must have diverted, if not derailed, Henry's and his successors' attempts to remake the English Church in their own image. But this was not the last time that England was disturbed by religious rebellion, whether in favour of the old religion – as in an attempt to stop the tide of a Reformation that had become ever more radical, the Western or Prayer Book rebellion of 1549, against the minority government of Henry VIII's son, Edward VI – or the new, as in Thomas Wyatt's rebellion against the Catholic Queen Mary in 1554. The Reformation is often taken as one of the signs of the emergence of the modern world shrugging off the 'superstitions' of the Middle Ages. That makes the rebellions against it look like a medieval defence of a medieval religion. But the sophistication of the Pilgrims of Grace, the savagery of Henry VIII's reaction, and the fact that subsequent opposition came from both sides of the religious faultline, all do little to sustain this case. English rebels expose shallow nostrums about 'medieval' thinking giving way to 'modern'.

From West and East

1549 was a year of rebels. In this 'comocyon tyme', there were various outbreaks of protest across the country, from Yorkshire to Wiltshire. The two most significant arose in East Anglia and in the far West. The people of Cornwall and Devon marched against the imposition of a new English Prayer Book, and to oppose the removal of various observances and traditions which fundamentally (and, it should be stressed, financially) altered parish life. These western rebels were prepared to die for this cause. Fewer than 200 Pilgrims of Grace were executed after their rebellion; the Prayer Book rebels died in their thousands. In the same summer in East Anglia, another rebellion rose up that was perhaps even more threatening to the government of Edward Seymour, Duke of Somerset, the uncle and 'Protector' of the eleven-year-old King. This rebellion, like most of the other risings that year, began as a protest against the enclosure of common lands in Norfolk and was led, surprisingly enough, by a landowner whose own hedges had been cast down by the rebels, but who had been persuaded of the justice of their cause: Robert Kett. The two rebellions were very different, in character, aims and causes, but the fact that they happened almost simultaneously made them far more dangerous to the government. That July, while Kett's followers camped at Mousehold Heath outside Norwich, setting up something approaching an alternative local government (even as they professed loyalty to the Crown, in traditional English rebel style), the western rebels surrounded Exeter and reduced it to near starvation. The two popular uprisings that convulsed the country in 1549 carried echoes of the medieval rebellions of 1381, 1450 and 1497. But those echoes were not the residue of outmoded ways of thinking. They were reassertions of the understanding of a government's responsibility to its people. As so often before, the rebels' complaints focused on those gentry who abused their positions of power; they called for stronger royal government, not its abolition. As one rebel of the time put it, they 'knoweth no other lord ther then the Kings highnes'.

The trouble in Cornwall had been brewing for at least two years, and at first centred on one unpopular man, William Body. He was an ambitious layman who had got his hands on the arch-deaconry of Cornwall against local opposition, and vigorously enforced the steady stream of reforms that emerged from Somer-set's government, apparently as a means of lining his own pockets. In 1547, he gave the impression that church goods were to be confiscated, the same rumour that had sparked off the Lincolnshire Rising just over ten years before, but in view of the galloping pace of reform a much more credible one now. The new government's radical reformation had begun with a set of Injunctions in July 1547, six months after Edward came to the throne. All religious images, including stained-glass ones, were to be destroyed, and rosary beads were banned, as were church processions and church lights. That autumn in the West Country, government com-missioners went further, banning bell-ringing for the dead, cancel-ling 'church ales' (the fund-raising banquets by which most of a parish's income was gathered), and laying down strict rules about priests' vestments (for which the whole parish would contribute money). The first demonstration against William Body's part in these reforms, at Penryn in Cornwall in 1547, passed off reasonably peacefully, and was treated leniently by the government, anxious to believe that the people at large were thirsting for reform. When Body returned in 1548 to enforce the suppression of the chantries (foundations for the singing of Masses for the dead), there was a much louder outcry. At Easter that year, Body was set upon by a mob in Helston in Cornwall and murdered. The response was also more severe, with the ringleader (a chantry priest) sent to London to be executed, and ten more hangings carried out in Helston itself. But no one at the centre seems to have believed that this outbreak on the margins of the kingdom foreshadowed a deeper reaction against their reforming zeal, which powered on.

On Whitsunday, 10 June 1549, the first Sunday on which the services from the newly introduced Prayer Book were to be heard, the people of Bodmin gathered to protest. They induced a member of the local gentry, Humphrey Arundell, to lead them (they are likely to have known that Arundell's maternal grandfather, Humphrey Calwodely, had been involved in the Cornish rising that Perkin Warbeck had co-opted in 1497), and they set up a camp. In Devon, meanwhile, the residents of Sampford Courtenay took similar action when their priest used the new liturgy on Whitsunday, persuading him to hold a traditional service the following day. Nine days later, these two forces had met up at Crediton in Devon, and three days after that they were encamped a few miles outside Exeter at Clyst St Mary. The rebellion had been given added impetus by the actions of a local knight, Sir Peter Carew, who had mustered a force to resist the rebels. One of his men set fire to the barns in Crediton, and the town was abandoned in panic. The rebels drew the understandable conclusion that the gentry were 'altogether bent to overrun, spoil and destroy them'. Carew, a committed evangelical who was criticized back in London, would find roles reversed five years later, when he tried to raise the commons for his own rebellion against Queen Mary. Unsurprisingly, there were few takers.

The rebels issued various sets of articles, but the ones released as they prepared to besiege Exeter were the fullest. Of their sixteen items, all but three were directly concerned with religious matters, from lay taking of the sacrament to the language of the liturgy. Tellingly, for those who, then and in centuries to come, dismissed such conservative instincts as 'superstitious', the rebels complained that, on the contrary, it was the new service that was 'lyke a Christmas game' (reminiscent of the 'Crystemas gomen' to which the pagan Green Knight challenges King Arthur's men in that masterpiece of medieval verse, *Gawain and the Green Knight*). Moreover, for those who, like Cranmer, mocked the rebels' preference for Latin over English ('Had you rather be like [mag]pies or parrots, that be taught to speak, and yet understand not one word what they say . . . ?'), they had a ready answer: 'we the Cornyshe men (whereof certen of us understande no Englysh) utterly refuse thys newe Englysh.' Like the rebels of 1497, these Cornishmen still saw vestiges of independence from England itself in their cause. So there were certainly regional as well as social aspects to the Western Rebellion just as there had been to the Pilgrimage of Grace. Nonetheless, the overwhelming impetus was religious, as the rebels gathered to defend something that penetrated the fabric of their daily lives. Many days' ride from the centre of reform in London, and as yet un-'corrected' like the northern rebels before them, these Cornish and Devonians were more than prepared to fight for their beliefs. As so often before, they put themselves forward not as rebels but as loyal subjects who wished to correct the King's evil counsellors. In other parts of the West, there were similar, if less menacing demonstrations, and in Hampshire the banner of the Five Wounds, last seen in the Pilgrimage of Grace, was unfurled. The rebels knew that some measure of reformation had to be conceded, and they campaigned for the restitution of the articles of Henry VIII's time, rather than a wholesale reversal. But it is clear too that some saw their cause as a continuation of the one that had been raised against Edward's father.

The regional focus of the Western Rebellion is borne out by the fact that the rebels only advanced a few miles beyond Exeter, before turning round and concentrating their attentions on the regional capital. The Cornish and Devon rebels were not as numerous as the followers of the Pilgrimage of Grace, but a march on London at the same time as the eastern part of the country was in 'commotion' – particularly if the rebels had been able to bypass the force sent to deal with them under Lord Russell – would have seriously threatened the government. Instead, Russell was able first to relieve Exeter at the beginning of August, and then, when the rebellion reignited around Sampford Courtenay once more, to bring the rebels to battle, resulting in a headlong pursuit in which it is estimated that as many as 4,000 rebels were killed. With a demonstration of government force like that, there was perhaps no necessity for wholesale retribution, and, as in response to the much smaller rising the year before in Helston, the rank and file were spared. Only the ringleaders, like Humphrey Arundell, and a priest, Robert Welsh (who was hanged while decked out in 'papist' vestments from a gallows on the tower of his own church of St Thomas outside Exeter), were executed. The rebellion did nothing to halt the progress of the Edwardian Reformation, and the parishes were compelled to knuckle down under the new regime. But their true allegiances could easily resurface. When Edward was succeeded by the conservative Catholic Queen Mary, Exeter Cathedral all but emptied at the news, leaving the Protestant Bishop Myles Coverdale to preach to a handful of diehards.

The Oak of Reformation

The Western Rebellion was all the more threatening to the government because it almost exactly coincided with a rising in the East. The causes and concerns of the rebellion in Norfolk led by Robert Kett (and to a lesser degree by his brother William) were, on the face of it, very different from those in the West. There had been trouble about the steadily increasing enclosure of common land for pasture across the country, mostly in fact in western counties – like Wiltshire, Somerset, Hampshire and Surrey – at the beginning of the summer of 1549. But it was in Norfolk, in June, that these activities came to a head. At Attleborough, hedges were cast down around three villages on 20 June; then, between 6 and 8 July, at a gathering to celebrate the feast of the translation of Thomas Becket's relics at Wymondham, about five miles north-east of Attleborough, another local landlord, Robert Kett, had his hedges targeted for destruction. Instead of resisting the rioters, however, Kett took their side (possibly as a way of turning the tables on the local lawyer who had encouraged the villagers to attack the land, and with whom Kett had a long-standing feud). Kett gave the protests impetus and focus. He gathered a following and marched on Norwich. There, the rebels made a camp at Mousehold Heath outside the city, and their numbers swelled to around 12,000 while they drew up their demands. Similar camps began to spring up across Norfolk and Suffolk, and also in Kent. The events of that summer became known as the 'camping tyme'. Although the western rebels, too, had set up camp at Clyst, it is with the eastern ones that this defiantly static method of protest is associated. In the seventeenth century it was revived, and again in the second half of the twentieth, when camps sprang up to protest against anything from cruise missiles to the building of new roads and runways.

The most obvious difference between the two rebellions of 1549 was religious. While the western rebels burnt the new Prayer Book (parish priests had to buy replacements after the rebellion failed), the eastern ones used it, daily. Reform preachers, like the future Archbishop Matthew Parker, were given a cautious welcome at the various camps, and where their articles of complaint touched on religion, the Norfolk rebels showed themselves to be on the side of an evangelical clergy directed at expounding the Gospel to their flocks. Local resentment of the disgraced, imprisoned and very (Henrician) Catholic Duke of Norfolk, Thomas Howard – who had marched against the Pilgrimage of Grace but was no enthusiast for the quickening pace of reform – would partly account for the lack of conservative religious feeling among the rebels. Nonetheless, it would be wrong to assume that Kett and his followers were all uncomplicated enthusiasts of the new religion. An admittedly hostile chronicler of the rebellion, Nicholas Sotherton, thought that the rebels espoused the new forms of worship 'in order to have a fayre shew and similitude of well doing', while Protector Somerset suspected that their enthusiasm 'proceade not from the harte'. And what of the spark of the protest, the gathering for the feast of the translation of Thomas Becket's relics? Robert Kett and his brother William were both members of the guild of St Thomas, for years an uncontroversial association. But by this time, such an adherence in itself could be a mark of ambivalence about the reformed religion. Edward VI's father (see Chapter 3, p. 47) had destroyed Becket's shrine and reclassified him as a rebel. Celebrating a saint's day was in itself an act of defiance against the Edwardian reformers. Celebrating a rebel-saint's was surely doubly so. Moreover, the first victim of the

Wymondham rebels' ire was a local lawyer, John Flowerdew, who, as well as being an encloser, had angered local opinion by pulling down part of the abbey that also served as the parish church (and which was to play a grisly role in the conclusion of the rebellion).

If the Norfolk rebels cannot then be classified as diametrically opposed in religion to their western counterparts, it is still clear that the focus of their rebellion lay elsewhere. The rising began as a protest against land enclosure, and many of the articles of rebellion signed by Kett and his fellow rebel leaders are to do with land ownership and use: with 'inclosyng', rents and the rights of commons. Enclosure – which often transferred common land into private hands, and which was, at this time, frequently carried out by landholders with no legal justification – became one of the great causes of protestors and rebels from the sixteenth century onwards. In time, from the seventeenth century and through the eighteenth, landlords' enclosure would receive parliamentary backing, usually in the form of individual private members' bills for separate pieces of land. In 1549, however, the government was as likely to react as unfavourably as the dispossessed to the unauthorized enclosure of land, which challenged central authority in the provinces. In this, Somerset was continuing what the first two Tudors had initiated: there were Acts against enclosing passed by Henry VII in 1489, by Henry VIII in 1515, and again in 1534 and 1536, as well as three proclamations in the latter's reign, ordering hedges to be cast down and enclosed land to be opened up. Of course, as people would have recognized at the time (and historians have pointed out since), the fact that essentially the same legislation had to be passed again and again was evidence that it was being ignored. There was an economic imperative – broadly, the growth in the wool and cloth industry demanded more land to be enclosed for sheep pasture – that tended to override other considerations. We could compare the doomed attempts of previous governments to restrict wages in a shrunken labour market by the Statute of Labourers.

In June 1548, Somerset had issued another proclamation against enclosures, and appointed a commission to investigate the effects of the previous regimes' legislation. The work of this commission continued for a year, and was still going on when Kett's rebellion broke out. Perhaps the Protector's government was itself partly responsible for 'stirring up' the anti-enclosure feelings of the peasantry. But the apparent sympathy of Somerset's administration (though he did issue warnings against men taking the law into their own hands) might also account for the fact that the East Anglian rebels were content to make a large local demonstration. They did not march on the capital, and showed their loyalty in other ways – such as matters of religion – while confidently expecting redress on their specific, mostly economic or agrarian, grievances. In their final form, Kett's articles have even been interpreted as supporting some forms of enclosure, which could in some cases be useful to smallholders trying to keep great flocks out of their land, and not only for more substantial owners trying to extend areas of pasture.

The authorities were stretched by the simultaneous western and eastern risings, and the situation wasn't helped by the fact that the natural opponents of the rebels on the ground, the local gentry, had been summoned to a muster at Windsor. When they did return, some were able to break up the smaller gatherings. In Suffolk, the protestors' camps were dispersed on the promise of a pardon. Outside Norwich, however, a more serious response was called for. Kett's men assaulted the city and took the Mayor and two of his advisers prisoner on 23 July. The brazen behaviour of the rebels – 'brychles and bear arssyde' – drew special comment, and was even used as an excuse for the city archers' lack of resistance. Kett himself tried to maintain discipline over his followers, setting up a form of alternative local government for a time. In warrants issued by Kett, he and his men are described as Edward's 'amici ac delegati', friends and deputies, as they took on the traditional role of loyal subjects seeking reform, rather than rebels beyond the pale. But there is a streak of defiance running through the rank and file of the rebellion that bears Kett's name. So, when the Marquis of Northampton came to relieve Norwich with a force partly comprised of Italian mercenaries, the vast majority of the rebels contemptuously dismissed the offers of pardon that had succeeded elsewhere in the country, and instead took an Italian prisoner, and hanged him, naked, over the walls of Surrey Place. This was the house of the late Earl of Surrey (the Duke of Norfolk's son, executed in Henry VIII's reign) at Mousehold Heath that Kett had taken as his headquarters. The final provocation that set off the bloody denouement of the rebellion happened when a boy from the camp mooned an approaching herald, and was shot dead by the outraged government soldiers. In such defiant taboo-breaking, as contrasted with Kett's respectful, measured approach, we can perhaps see the gap between the landowning rebel leader and his followers. The rank and file were fuelled by an anger against direct experience of injustice, while Kett's was a more intellectual, or possibly more calculating, engagement with their cause. In the specific use of public nudity, we might also discern the origins of that very English phenomenon, the streaker.

Northampton's force was seen off by the rebels, who for the next three weeks consolidated their position and administered justice from Mousehold Heath. It is from this period that the utopian legend of the rebellion springs, as the benign rebel leader was seen to consider pleas from beneath the 'Oak of Reformation', like some sixteenth-century English Buddha. One of the rebels' articles, demanding that 'all bond men be made free for god made all free with his precious blood shedding' – which harks back to the demands of the peasants of 1381, as well as projecting forward to a more democratic, levelling age – contributes to this wider sense of significance for Kett's rebellion. But this was not a proto-type radical community, of the type that sprang up a century later after the Civil Wars. The demand for freedom has been con-vincingly connected to a local and specific cause, the tenants on former Howard land, many of whom *were* still in bondage. And although Kett's followers pursued those they thought responsible for maladministration, such as a royal purveyor in Norfolk (the practice of purveyance continued, and continued to be unpopular), they were still committed to demonstrating their loyalty to the King's regime, in this case by appointing an alternative to carry out the work. Such protestations counted for little, however, when Kett and his followers had actively opposed the Protector's appointed commander, Northampton, and refused the offer of a pardon. Soon, inevitably, another force was mustered.

On 23 August, a new army, under the Earl of Warwick (who was, among other things, Kett's landlord), numbering up to 12,000 men, arrived outside Norwich. It was in the negotiations with Warwick's herald, which at first seemed to hold out some prospect of pardon for all but Kett himself, that the killing of the boy took place, and the sides parted again to settle their differences in battle, after Kett had been persuaded not to meet Warwick in person. Kett moved his camp to nearby Dussindale, possibly to fulfil a prophecy. But his luck was out. On 27 August, Warwick's cavalry attacked, and in the ensuing battle around 3,000 rebels were killed. Kett himself was captured, along with his brother. Both were found guilty of treason and executed. Robert Kett was hanged at Norwich Castle, while his brother William, like the western rebel Robert Welsh, was hanged from his local church, the part-demolished former abbey of Wymondham, suspended from the high west tower for all to see.

Kett's rebellion had a long afterlife, but perhaps his decision to confine his protest to the region of Norwich has made him more of a local than a national hero. One of several oak trees identified as the Oak of Reformation is preserved on the road between Wymondham and Norwich; the rebellion is commemorated by a plaque at Norwich Castle that praises 'a notable and courageous leader in the long struggle of the common people of England to escape from a servile life into the freedom of just conditions', and a 1960s Cambridge office block is decorated with a concrete relief depicting the famous oak. Nearer to the time of the event itself, the rising became part of the radical tradition seized on by later thinkers and activists. With Wat Tyler and Jack Cade, Robert Kett became one of those 'captains of the people' who were used as inspiration or warning, most urgently in the seventeenth century. But the rebellion secured nothing in 1549. Like other rebellions, its effects in its own time were incidental and largely reactionary.

The relations between landowner and tenantry, and the position of the gentry, which Kett's articles had attempted to fix in a permanent state, continued to be fluid. The reliability of central government, and its administration of local justice, meanwhile, became ever more dependent on changes at court, not in the country. The main immediate result of the rebellion was the fall of Somerset, who had been warned that his 'levytie' and 'softnes' were the reason that the 'King's subjects [were] owt of all discipline'. He was replaced in fact if not in office by the victor of Dussindale, John Dudley, Earl of Warwick. Although Somerset was rehabilitated for a short time, within two years of the rebellion he was dead, cornered into planning his own rebellion by Dudley, who had been made Duke of Northumberland, and executed on charges of felony when acquitted of treason, in January 1552. There is an intriguing postscript to all this plotting in high places as far as Kett is concerned. Kett's own motives, as a relatively rich landowner, if not a member of the gentry, for joining the rebellion, have never been fully explained. But evidence from an ally of the future Duke of Northumberland, Sir Richard Southwell, who, though treasurer of the royal army, made payments to Kett's rebels, suggests that Kett may have been implicated in a palace plot to discredit Somerset's government. If Kett had been privately expecting the support of Warwick against the government, this may explain his confidence in his initial dealings with the Earl. Whether or not there was a conspiracy, Warwick certainly ran out of use for Kett, and by the time he confronted him at Dussindale it was clear that no deals could be struck.

10. Queens and Their Rebels

Mary Tudor to the Earl of Essex 1553–1601

'Yt was but a monthes work to overrun England.'

Bartholomew Steer, 1596

Popular rebellion was always the type that scared the authorities most, but was least likely to succeed. The rebels against the rest of Henry Tudor's line came from more traditional, aristocratic origins. In fact, the most successful rebellion of the period was led by a Tudor, Henry VIII's daughter, who became Mary I – but not without a struggle that involved the people as well as their lords. Her crooked path to the crown was traced out of the circumstances created by the defeat of Kett's rebellion. That defeat had eased the Duke of Northumberland's rise to power, directing the young King Edward VI in place of the discredited Somerset.

Northumberland used to be accused of more Machiavellian behaviour still, of engineering the royal succession towards his family, by persuading a sickening Edward to settle on his cousin, the devoutly Protestant Lady Jane Grey, as his heir. Lady Jane happened to be married to Northumberland's son Lord Guildford Dudley. This 'Device' or 'Devise', as it was known, bypassed the King's half-sisters – the Catholic Princess Mary and the Protestant Princess Elizabeth – as illegitimate, overturning the succession statute promulgated by Henry VIII in 1544. The timing of such a scheme is wrong if it is to be attributed to Northumberland's influence, however, as Edward had jotted down his own ideas about the succession if he were to die childless along these lines some months before, while the marriage of Lady Jane and Guildford Dudley took place a month *after* the 'Devise' to place Jane on the throne had been made public. But if Edward took more part in that decision than has traditionally been conceded, Dudley nonetheless took full advantage of it, and when in July 1553, two months after Guildford's marriage to the new heir to the throne, Edward died, it was the Duke of Northumberland who attempted to make the succession work. The swiftness with which Queen Jane's nine-day reign ended tends to cast an air of inevitability over Mary's replacement of her. But we should be as wary of seeing Jane's downfall as inevitable as we have been of seeing rebels' projects as 'fated' to fail. Such assumptions can obscure the fact that Mary's succession came about as a direct result of one of the most effective, bold, but least celebrated rebellions in English history.

The rebellion that put Mary on the throne was the opposite of most English rebellions, in which history written 'by the winners' consigns our rebels to a marginal or preordained losing role. The success of Mary's rebellion meant that her regime was able to present her coming to the throne as having nothing to do with a rebellion at all, merely being the swift reassertion of legitimate authority. But in July 1553 the story might have looked very different. Historians used to describe the accession of Queen Jane, masterminded by Northumberland, as a 'coup d'état', but that term, too, can only be used with hindsight. Jane succeeded in peculiar circumstances, and no one could argue that she received an unequivocal welcome, or that the men around her were sanguine about how securely the crown was placed on her head. But she became queen because her cousin the late King had wished it, and had published his wishes – even if he had died before they could be ratified by Parliament. It suited her father-in-law's purposes to take Edward's will as binding, but that does not mean that it was a fiction Northumberland cooked up. On the contrary, the fact that Northumberland was so cack-handed in controlling the new Queen's obvious rival, Princess (now styled 'Lady') Mary, is an indication that, far from being a coup, Jane's succession turned out to be a botched transfer of power. A Northumberland who conformed more closely to the scheming 'black duke' of traditional interpretations would have realized, Richard III-like (and like

Henry IV and Edward IV) that the most important way to ensure that a succession was unchallenged was to have the potential challengers in your power. This he failed to do, either through incompetence, or because he was persuaded that Mary would not resist the succession, or perhaps because he thought that the councillors, local dignitaries and foreign allies who had pledged their support for Jane were an impressive enough force to rely upon. It is easy to forget, too, that Jane's rival was hardly ideal. Mary's religion made her suspect in a great number of people's minds, including those of the most powerful men in England, and her title, though stronger than Jane's, had nonetheless been discredited ever since her father had unilaterally annulled his marriage to her mother and disinherited Mary, in 1533, despite his later attempts to reverse this judgment.

This was certainly how some observers saw the state of play. Mary acted swiftly, evading capture and issuing a letter to the Council proclaiming her right to the Crown. In it was ample evidence of that courageous defiance more usually associated with her half-sister at Tilbury thirty-five years later. She told the clique around Jane: 'You know, the realm and the whole world knoweth' that Mary was the rightful heir. But the confident words couldn't hide a desperate political situation for the would-be queen, forced into the status of a rebel. Mary hoped for support from Charles V, the Catholic Holy Roman Emperor whose son she would eventually marry. But the Imperial ambassador to England, Jehan Scheyfve, was initially convinced that her cause was hopeless: 'All the forces in the country are in the Duke's hands, and my Lady [Mary] has no hope of raising enough men to face him, nor means of assisting those who may espouse her cause.' All the power indeed seemed to be in the hands of Northumberland's party, and the secretary of state, William Cecil, drew up a comprehensive list of local magnates and gentry who could be expected to support the new queen, which he hoped to use to persuade any waverers. Though Mary had escaped Northumberland's grasp initially, moving secretly from the royal palace at Hunsdon in Hertfordshire to Sawston Hall in Cambridgeshire, Northumberland was gathering a well-armed retinue of about 600, as well as sending six ships to track her down; Mary's household numbered about sixty.

First, however, Northumberland attended the coronation of his daughter-in-law, Queen Jane, brought by barge from Richmond to the Tower for the purpose. Here, the new queen showed that she would not be entirely the pawn of the Dudleys, when she refused to countenance the crowning of her husband as king. Although the coronation was hardly the lavish spectacle of some of Jane's predecessors and successors, a couple of eyewitness details show that it was not conducted in secret, and that Jane and those around her had learnt the Tudor lesson about putting on a show. Why else would the new queen be decked out in a velvet dress embroidered with gold, or take the trouble to compensate for her tiny stature in comparison to her rangy husband by wearing stilts under her skirts?

Popular acclamation, however, was not forthcoming, and the people of London, while not actively rebellious (with the exception of one brave soul who had his ears cut off for challenging Jane's right), engaged in none of the celebrations that traditionally greeted a new monarch. Edward had died too soon after the publication of the Devise to make a smooth transition likely. A more able, or a luckier, man than Northumberland might have overcome this initial popular reluctance or indifference to his protégée. Indeed, it could be argued that had Northumberland been permitted to stay in London, as he initially planned to do, keeping the coalition around Jane together while her father, the Duke of Suffolk, went to East Anglia to capture Mary, then perhaps he could have strengthened her position. Instead, Jane objected so vehemently to her father's being sent on the potentially dangerous mission that Northumberland agreed to go himself, returning to the scene of his triumph over Robert Kett, in order to put down a more eminent, but for the time being less well-backed, rebel. Although Nicholas Ridley, the Bishop of London, had preached at St Paul's against Mary (and Elizabeth) and in favour of Jane, the absence of Northumberland left London undecided about the succession, and potentially hostile.

Everything depended on Mary's ability to evade Northumberland, and to secure enough support to challenge Jane. In this, she had more than her fair share of luck, but her decision, or that of those around her, to move from house to house in East Anglia, raising the gentry in Norfolk and Suffolk, systematically built up a groundswell against the Northumberland-backed regime. There is evidence that this was more than a spontaneous reaction to extraordinary events. During Edward's reign, Mary's Catholicism, tolerated but disapproved of by her half-brother's government, had proved a rallying point for a separate, dependable retinue, focused on East Anglia. These men, like Robert Rochester, Henry Jerningham and Edward Waldegrave, had proved their loyalty and willingness to defy authority. In the succession crisis, they helped Mary to mobilize a following with her co-religionists, and beyond. This support certainly had a popular as well as a gentry dimension, and there were risings in Mary's favour in Berkshire, Oxfordshire, Buckinghamshire, Bedfordshire and Northamptonshire, as well as the principal one in East Anglia. By the time Northumberland reached Bury, Mary had secured both noble backing, from the Earl of Oxford (with a promise of support from the Earl of Sussex, significantly an evangelical, showing that Mary's support was now reaching beyond confessional boundaries), as well as 'innumerable companies of the common folk'.

By now, Mary's army outnumbered the Duke's. The naval detachment of Northumberland's expedition was thrown off course by a storm and the captain and crew ended up, short of pay, putting in at a port sympathetic to Mary. There, one of her retinue, Sir Henry Jerningham, was able without much effort to persuade the sailors to throw in their lot with his mistress rather than with Jane. Northumberland avoided confrontation at Bury and reached Cambridge, where he pondered his next move, but events began to move too fast for him. When news of the ships' defection reached London, it seems to have amounted to a sort of tipping point among Jane's supporters. Led by the Earl of Arundel, one by one the Queen's party withdrew their loyalty and proclaimed Mary the rightful sovereign. The announcement was

greeted ecstatically in the capital, with 'everie strett full of bon-
fyres'. When this news reached Cambridge, the Duke of Northumberland decided the game was up. He too proclaimed Mary
queen, and threw himself on her mercy. When Mary entered
London, she received the welcome that had so conspicuously
eluded Jane. The deposed queen, who had spent her whole reign
in the Tower of London, remained in it as the palace reverted for
her to its traditional role as a prison. She was joined there by the
Duke of Northumberland.

Mary's rebellion was a triumph of personal leadership achieved
in part by determined household support. She manipulated her two
distinguishing features, her Catholicism and her greater legitimacy,
relying more on the latter to give her a greater chance of securing
a realm where Edward's Reformation had widely taken hold.
The personal decisions of Mary and her followers, and those of
Northumberland and the privy councillors, were crucial to the
outcome in 1553. But the commons played just as important a part
in the rising's success. Queen Jane was initially backed by almost
every powerful man in the country, as well as by those senior
churchmen who had most to lose from the accession of a conservative Catholic like Mary. For her part, Mary at first had backing
from only a few gentry and nobles. Her potential foreign allies
waited on the sidelines until the result was in before proclaiming
their support. Mary and her household may have prepared for a
disputed succession, but in such circumstances the will of the
people could prove crucial. The sailors off the Suffolk coast; the
household servants of the Earl of Oxford who forcibly 'persuaded'
him to join Mary while his relatives urged loyalty to Jane; the
Norfolk yeomen who reminded Mary later in 1553 (in a petition
rediscovered only recently) of their role in resisting the succession
of Jane when their gentry leaders had gone the other way: such
demonstrations, echoed in London on Mary's entry, showed how
in rebellion a people not formally represented could make their
voices count. Mary's succession came about as a result of a broad-
based, popular rising, not a palace coup.

Sir Thomas Wyatt and the Queen's marriage

Mary's rebellion had been founded on her conservative Catholic following, but in order to make its appeal as wide as possible her party had taken care not to make hers an exclusively Catholic cause. George Foxe, the Protestant martyrologist, and John Knox, the radical Scottish churchman, admittedly not unbiased witnesses, later agreed that Mary had promised no 'innovation' in religion when gathering her following. At the beginning of her short reign, it looked as though the new queen might persevere with this inclusive attitude. After some vacillation, she allowed her half-brother to be buried in a Protestant ceremony (which she didn't attend, hearing Mass for him with other Catholics instead). Ten days afterwards, Mary issued a proclamation that emphasized her own Catholicism and expressed the hope that her subjects would return to it. Nevertheless, although she also banned unlicensed preaching, one of the foundations of the new religion, Mary promised not to do anything to coerce her subjects without the approval of Parliament. But even before Parliament met in October 1553, the refashioning of the English Church in its old form was well under way. Mary's chancellor, Bishop Stephen Gardiner, began rooting out 'heretical' preachers, many of whom fled the country. In the first few months of Mary's reign, five bishops found themselves in prison on various charges. Not all of them would get out alive.

If the Queen assumed that Edwardian Protestantism had not yet put down real roots in English life, a London riot directed at a royal appointee who prayed for the dead at St Paul's Cross might have given her pause. But it was another aspect of the Queen's policy that provoked the only serious rebellion of her short reign, one tied to but not sparked exclusively by her Catholicism. This was her decision to marry Philip of Spain, son of the Emperor Charles V. The first moves had been made as early as 15 August 1553, and by January the following year the terms of their marriage, which were supposed to allay English fears of Philip's influence, were published (a pre-nuptial agreement that, in the time-honoured way of such agreements, at least one party did not expect to keep to). Mary, the daughter of an English father and a Spanish mother, may have seen the union as an obvious one, but she had been sensitive to the objections of most of her advisers to the match. They understandably expected that the future King of Spain would become the dominant partner, and Mary herself, though she took to her role as queen, was in no way revolutionary in her view of the roles of the sexes. In November 1553, the Queen was outraged when the Commons petitioned her against the marriage. Perhaps those closer to Mary made it a condition of their support that a hard bargain should be driven. The various restrictions placed on Philip's future role, and the emphasis on the retention of English subjects in trusted positions, might have been enough to deal with some people's objections. But for others, the new queen was moving too fast, in both matrimonial and religious affairs.

It was around an alternative candidate for Mary's hand, Edward Courtenay, that the conspiracy which has come to be known as Wyatt's rebellion turned. The idea was that four leaders, Lady Jane Grey's father, the Duke of Suffolk (who had been released from the Tower after only a few days), Sir James Croft, Sir Peter Carew and Sir Thomas Wyatt, would raise Leicestershire, Herefordshire, Devon and Kent, and converge on London. The precise plan is impossible to discern now, but part of it seems to have been to marry Courtenay, Earl of Devon, who had some royal blood in his veins, to Princess Elizabeth, and to put the couple in as the new queen and king consort, thus solving the problem of the monarch's Catholicism and her Spanish leanings at one blow. Different conspirators seem to have wanted instead to force Mary to marry Courtenay, others again to assassinate the Queen. The risings were planned for 18 March, but by 21 January, Courtenay himself had been leant on by Bishop Gardiner (who might have been worried that his own loyalty was open to question, as he had earlier put forward Courtenay as an alternative to Philip) and revealed the details of the plan. Carew tried to raise Devon (where his record in putting down the Western Rebellion in 1549 was remembered bitterly), and Grey to bring out Leicestershire, but with no result; the Duke of Suffolk's efforts in Leicester were pathetically ineffectual, and he fled for his life. Wyatt, who had been, by his own later admission, only a part of the rebellion, not its leader, found himself at its head by virtue of being the only member to manage to raise an army.

Wyatt's was not the first rebellion to make use of xenophobia – we have seen the Poitevins and the Flemish fall victim in earlier risings, and the Jewish experience had long been to fear any breakdown in law and order as much as government-backed oppression. In 1554, there was certainly also an element of Protestant resistance to Mary's Catholic juggernaut. But Wyatt assimilated what Mary herself had understood, that appeals on religious grounds were as likely to exclude potential allies as win them. 'You may not so much as name religion, for that will withdraw from us the hearts of many. You must make your only quarrel for overrunning by strangers,' he told a follower. So he concentrated on the impending foreign marriage, portraying the arrival of a Spanish embassy to negotiate it as the first wave of an invasion: 'lo, now even at hand Spaniards be now already arrived at Dover, at one passage to the number of a hundred, passing upward to London . . . with harness, harquebuses and morions, with matchlight, the foremost company where of already be at Rochester'. Publicly, he presented himself, too, in the traditional rebel role of non-rebel, wanting only to supply the monarch with 'better counsel and councillors'. But the various plans to depose and replace Mary make it even less likely than usual that this was the limit of his ambition. Wyatt's rebellion can be compared to other gentry risings based on conspiracy, such as Sir John Oldcastle's more than a century before, especially in that it was revealed to the authorities long before its planned launch. It used to be argued that the Pilgrimage of Grace was the result of a number of bungled gentry conspiracies, rather than emerging from lower down. The description fits Wyatt's rebellion far better.

The fact that the other elements of the conspiracy failed to ignite did not guarantee Wyatt's failure. His force was the nearest to London, and could become the most immediately menacing. As Mary's own experience had demonstrated (though with the added ingredient of wounded legitimacy), a rebel did not have to start with overwhelming numbers to stand a chance of success. Wyatt's followers were concentrated in north Kent, but spread throughout the county. They received a setback when a force under the rebel Sir Henry Isley was defeated at Wrotham by the loyalist sheriff, Sir Robert Southwell. Almost immediately, however, Wyatt won the next point. A force of Londoners under the aged Duke of Norfolk – recently released from prison and called on once again, as he had been eighteen years before, to resist a rebellion – defected to Wyatt's side at Rochester, running down the hill and shouting, 'We are all Englishmen.' These turncoats urged Wyatt to press on to London, which they said 'longed sore for his coming'. But Wyatt wasted time in manoeuvres against Lord Cobham, giving Mary and her government another day to plan their response. They had offered once before to hear the rebels' grievances, and did so again. When Wyatt rejected the offer, Mary denounced him and his followers as 'rank traitors', again displaying the qualities that had served her in her own rebellion, making a confident, defiant speech at the Guildhall, which also played on her unprecedented position as a queen regnant, as she offered herself in the role of loving mother to her people. By now, Wyatt had arrived at Blackheath, as Tyler, Cade and the Cornishmen of 1497 had done before him. Could he expect any different result?

Wyatt entered Southwark, where his followers attacked Bishop Gardiner's property. But when they found London Bridge closed and well guarded, their chances can only have seemed even slimmer than those of their predecessors. The rebels numbered around 3,000, which may not have been as formidable as some of the hordes that had previously gathered at London's gates, but it seems to have been a disciplined military force, and its leader was able to get it to follow orders. This was demonstrated in Wyatt's next move, a swift march westwards to Kingston, where another bridge across the Thames proved reparable and allowed the rebels to cross. They marched on London's outlying western parts, approaching the City itself from a different angle. Though they were attacked and defeated at St James's Fields, they were able to press on, and government detachments failed to confront the remnant in Charing Cross or Whitehall. In Fleet Street, one government band apparently passed them by 'without eny whit saying to them', while the body of citizens, though armed, 'stoode on both sydes, without eny withstandinge them'. But at the top of Fleet Street stood Ludgate, entrance to the City itself. There, at last, Londoners stood firm, shutting the gate to Wyatt. With his following reduced to a tenth of its strength by the march, Wyatt knew he could not hope to assault the City. As he began his retreat, the Londoners finally attacked. Forty rebels were killed, and Wyatt himself was taken prisoner.

Inevitably, there was government retribution, but it is likely that the equivocal display that the Queen and her advisers had witnessed in London reduced its severity. In all, around a hundred rebels were killed in the aftermath. Among the most prominent were the Duke of Suffolk, whose failure to take a more direct part in the rebellion was a consequence of his incompetence, not his loyalty; and Lady Jane Grey herself – who, with her husband Guildford Dudley, now paid the ultimate price for their parents' ambitions, though they were in no way directly implicated in this rebellion. They were beheaded on Tower Hill on 12 February 1554. She was sixteen years old. Wyatt himself was spared for two more months, perhaps in the hope that more information about the rebellion might be extracted from him. He was executed on 11 April.

An un-English rebellion

Although it was reported that people dipped their handkerchiefs in Wyatt's blood, he represented too many conflicting constituencies to become a rebel-martyr. Elizabeth, who had suffered directly as a result of the rebellion, when her sister had her imprisoned for a time on suspicion of involvement, would draw a lesson when she succeeded as queen about the unpopularity of Mary's foreign match that coloured her attitude to the whole question of marriage itself. Wyatt, despite his sensitivities on the subject, had stood for the Protestant religion. When it returned under Queen Elizabeth, his name might have been included in the memorials of sufferers for their beliefs. But Elizabeth and those around her preferred their martyrs to be more pliant than Wyatt, more like Thomas Cranmer, whose opposition had been personal, calling on no one's sacrifice but his own.

Here we come to one of the most significant developments in the mental world created by England's long history of rebellion and reactions to rebellion. Its origins lie in the Reformation of Henry VIII's reign, but the experiences of rulers and subjects in the three subsequent Tudor reigns all contributed to its refinement. This was the careful yoking together of English Protestantism with theories of obedience, and specifically with obedience to the Crown. This emphasis had been insisted on during Henry's reign, when William Tyndale's *Obedience of a Christian Man* was published, and Henry's propagandists explained that 'Obey ye your king' was the most important commandment (Luther had argued that obeying one's father and mother could be taken as a commandment to obey a prince, as princes were the fathers of their people). But the theory took some time to catch on. When Matthew Parker, who became Elizabeth's Archbishop of Canterbury, went to preach, as an up-and-coming evangelical churchman, to Kett's rebels at Mousehold Heath in 1549, it was his theme of submission for the common good which almost caused a riot. Though the rebels immediately demonstrated their evangelical credentials by being so distracted by the singing of a new English version of the Te Deum that they allowed Parker to get away, at this time the association of Protestantism and obedience was not yet commonly accepted. Its origins in the defiance of one establishment did not immediately suit it to propping up another. Increasingly, however, it would become a keynote of English Protestant thinking, and one widely disseminated by preaching and in treatises, pamphlets and biblical exegesis.

It was hardly a new thing for Christianity to be wedded by those in power to an appeal to the obedience of those they ruled. This principle predated the Reformation, and worked as hard in religious as in lay circles. The Rule of St Benedict, after all, which Henry's commissioners had dissolved in the acid of monastic suppression, was founded on the practice of obedience. But, elsewhere, Protestantism had come as a challenge to lay as well as Church authority, often with violent consequences, as in the Peasants' War in Germany (1524–5), or the rejection of the Savoyard prince-bishop's influence in Geneva in the 1530s. Rulers had, of course, taken up the theme of Protestant obedience elsewhere, but in England the combining of Church and state authority, and obedience to one implying obedience to the other, was to reach its fullest expression anywhere in the Protestant world. The experience of rebellion played a crucial part in this formulation. Mary's reign provided an exception to prove the rule. Protestants such as Wyatt and, more vociferously, exiled clerics like John Knox, in his *First Blast of the Trumpet Against the Monstrous Regiment of Women*, written three years after Wyatt's rebellion, argued that Mary's removal or even assassination was justified by their faith. But in Elizabeth's reign, these arguments were swept aside in the concentration on submission to the monarch. This was argued for even if the ruler was wicked, or an infidel.

Early in Elizabeth's reign, Philip was again proposed as a husband for the Queen, and other Catholic candidates were mooted, each of whom would have been expected to compel his bride to convert to his religion. Loyal Protestant subjects could not have known that their queen would never marry. The Elizabethan religious settlement did not seem to preclude her considering Catholic suitors. Even in the worst-case scenarios, however, rebellion was not justified. The distinction between Catholic and Protestant approaches to the issue of obedience and rebellion became stark. The Pope withdrew Catholics' fealty from Elizabeth, excommunicating her in 1570, while his secretary's fatwa advocated sending 'her out of the world with the pious intention of doing God service'. Catholic assassins murdered the Protestant rulers William of Orange and Henry III of France. By contrast, English Protestants were told, in the words of John Whitgift, that 'disobedience to the prince in civil matters is disobedience to God.' Here are the origins of the traditional picture of the English subject as both Protestant and loyal. It helped in these circumstances that the most eloquently radical proponent of violent resistance in the years of Mary Tudor, and one who continued to practise a more protestant brand of Protestantism, was not an Englishman but a Scot, John Knox. Knox found little favour in England, especially as his attack on the monstrous regiment, intended for the Catholic 'Jezebel' Mary, was published just as a Protestant queen, Elizabeth, was ascending the throne. Nonetheless, he was able to export his theories to his homeland, where they assisted in the overthrow of the Catholic Mary of Guise as regent, and then of her daughter, Mary Stuart.

This complicated legacy meant that Wyatt never achieved the martyr's afterlife we might expect for him in Elizabeth's reign. The failure of his rebellion, however, convinced Mary of the righteousness of her position, which she and those around her pursued with increasing zeal, although the level of violence, with around 290 heretics executed by the end of her reign, was not quite as unprecedented as Protestant propagandists would later make out. After all, Henry V had executed Lollards, and Henry VIII sent both conservatives and evangelicals to the scaffold for straying from the King's own line. Mary's half-sister later also resorted to execution as a way of putting down Catholic opposition (189 Catholics were executed in Elizabeth's admittedly far longer reign). For Mary herself, Wyatt's was the only significant rebellion in a reign whose religious violence was not universally condemned, even if the Queen's marriage was never popular.

Gloriana's rebels

Mary's successor, Elizabeth, experienced only one large-scale rising, the so-called Northern Rebellion in 1569, and although there were several conspiracies and plots, and one aristocratic rising that had more of the characteristics of a psychotic episode than a genuinely threatening rebellion, this relatively peaceful state of affairs was maintained until the outbreak of the Civil Wars in the 1640s. This was the longest period without serious rebellion since the Norman Conquest. Before we ask why this should have been so, it is worth examining the two failed rebellions of Elizabeth's reign. Both attempted to rely on a more traditional, feudal backing than those Tudor risings that counted on a wider appeal, specifically to the gentry class whose growth in status and importance was frequently recognized in the role they took either in fomenting or more often in suppressing rebellion.

The Northern Rebellion of 1569 emerged from some of the same locales as the Pilgrimage of Grace thirty-three years before, was inspired by the same Catholic cause, and even included a rebel leader, Richard Norton, now well into his eighties, who had worn the pilgrim badge of the Five Wounds that autumn, but it relied on a much more restricted constituency for its support, making it far less threatening than the Pilgrimage had been, and no more successful. Its nominal leaders were two northern earls, Charles Neville, 6th Earl of Westmorland, and Thomas Percy, 7th Earl of Northumberland. Their rebellion coincided with, but was not strongly linked to, a court dispute over the possible marriage of the exiled (Catholic) Mary, Queen of Scots, and the (Protestant) Duke of Norfolk, a match which Elizabeth refused to countenance, presumably on the basis that it would only have concentrated more power in the hands of a potential threat to her own rule by joining England's leading nobleman to the woman put forward as Elizabeth's successor, if not her replacement. When Norfolk retired to his estates on being forbidden to marry the Scots Queen, it was assumed that he would go into open rebellion. His failure to do so, or to come to any accommodation with the two northern earls – who were prepared to rebel but not, as Northumberland put it, to 'hazard myself for the marriage' of Catholic and Protestant – fatally weakened the rising that followed.

The presence of Mary, Queen of Scots, in England made her an obvious focus for Catholic disaffection, but her own involvement in the Northern Rebellion was minimal. According to North-umberland, when he was questioned after the rebellion, both Mary and her ally the Spanish ambassador advised that it was 'better not to stir'. This was a self-fulfilling prophecy. Outside the North, the reluctance to rebel on the grounds that not enough rebels were joining the rising ensured that the rebellion failed for lack of support. In the North itself, the earls did manage to secure some following, partly through the loyalty (or fear, or thrift: men were both threatened and paid to join the rising) of their tenantry, partly through a genuine commitment to the old religion. As one government agent sneeringly remarked, 'the common people are ignorant, superstitious, and altogether blinded with the old popish doctrine'. The fact that the palatine Bishop of Durham, James Pilkington, was an enthusiastic iconoclast who had presided over the destruction of the banner of the North's patron saint, Cuthbert, provided a useful reservoir of local resentment. But, from the beginning, their chances of success were minimized by the fact that the government, represented by the Council of the North with the Earl of Sussex as President, was aware that a rising was in the offing and moved, if not with undue speed, to suppress it.

In fact, the earls were summoned before the Council to explain themselves before they had actually committed to rebellion, on 9 October 1569. Their decision to press ahead in November already bore the marks of desperation. Already too there was a split in their ranks: Westmorland had actively gathered his following at his stronghold of Brancepeth, while Northumberland had to be persuaded to join by his own men. At Topcliffe, Northumberland's estate, the bells were heard to ring their chimes in reverse order, the call to arms. The rebel retinues joined, and issued a procla-mation making the usual protestations of loyalty to the Queen, and showing clearly that 'trewe and catholicke religion' was their cause. Their first act of defiance was to hold a Mass at Durham Cathedral, where they pulled down evidence of Pilkington and his supporters' 'new found religion and heresie'. Their numbers swelled to almost 6,000, while the Earl of Sussex had only suc-ceeded in raising around 400 men.

Despite their numerical advantage, the rebel earls lost their nerve. It was later observed of both leaders that their wives were bolder than the husbands. Of the Countess of Northumberland, Lord Hunsdon commented at the time, 'Hys wyfe beyng the stowter of the too, dothe hasten hym, and yncourage hym to persever.' Geed up, the rebels reached Bramham Moor near Tadcaster in Yorkshire on 22 November, but, after staying there for two days, they turned back. They had not yet decided to disband, but any sense that the rebels would threaten the seat of Tudor power, and try to liberate Mary, who had been moved southwards to Coventry, out of harm's way, had been lost. The rebellion became a regional show of strength, a major difficulty but still a local one that Elizabeth's government was more than capable of dealing with. The rising continued through a freezing winter, with a siege of Barnard Castle on the River Tees for just over a week before the castle fell to the rebels, while the town of Hartlepool was also taken. But two days after Barnard Castle came into their hands, the earls fled north again on the rumour of the arrival of a large royal army. Their infantry scattered, and only a small party met a loyal force under Sir John Forster at Hexham on 19 December. The only other fighting of the rebellion came after its principal leaders had fled across the border, when 500 rebels were killed in February 1570 in a battle at Naworth, about fifteen miles from the Scottish border, between a rebel landowner, Leonard Dacre, who had returned from a legal battle in London after the main action, and Lord Hunsdon who, with the Earl of Sussex, had been entrusted with resisting the rising.

The two earls had never presented an entirely united front in a rebellion that didn't convince as a genuine menace to Elizabeth's authority, or that of her Church. So it seems fitting that their fates were very different. While Westmorland continued his flight as far as the Netherlands, where he lived out his days as a pensioner of the Spanish king, the unlucky Northumberland fell into his sovereign's hands when he was betrayed in Scotland and passed south. His responses to questioning give one of the best insights into why the earls rebelled, and why they failed. Unlike Mary

Tudor, or indeed Thomas Wyatt, Northumberland was not prepared to compromise his message to broaden his appeal. 'Our first object . . . was the reformation of religion and preservation of the person of the Queen of Scots, as next heir,' he declared. It was a cause that no one south of Leeds was willing to join, and so the Northern Rebellion spread even less far down the country than the Pilgrimage of Grace, which had at least made inroads as far as Doncaster (and Lincolnshire, if the initial stir is taken into account). The Council of the North, constituted as a permanent body in the wake of the Pilgrimage of Grace, had done much, if hardly with great dispatch, to eliminate its successor. There was no sense in 1569, as there had been in 1536, that with a little bit more nerve, or more luck, the rebels might really have threatened the Crown. As for Northumberland, like Robert Aske after the Pilgrimage, he was executed at York, though his noble status at least ensured he was beheaded rather than hanged. Elizabeth pressed for a similarly bloody fate for 700 more rebels (the Tudor reputation for mercilessness shouldn't only be attached to her father and her half-sister), although it seems that a much smaller number eventually died.

There was one more, far more pathetic, aristocratic rising at the end of Elizabeth's reign, led by the Earl of Essex, but the Northern Rebellion was the last major rising of the Tudor age, and the last revolt of any substantial number of subjects before the Civil Wars. The Queen of Scots continued to attract conspiracy, a threat of which the English queen's super-vigilant secretary of state, Francis Walsingham, was well aware. It was Walsingham who made sure that the last attempt to spring Mary from captivity and to topple her cousin, in the so-called Babington plot, was known to the authorities in all its details, as all the secret messages passing between the Scots queen and the plotters had been intercepted and deciphered. With a little bit of embellishment, the incriminating messages persuaded a reluctant Elizabeth to order Mary's execution in 1587. (Mary drew attention to the tampered evidence, embarrassing Walsingham but having no effect on the verdict.) But the failure of the northern earls' appeal to Catholic sentiment and a Catholic succession demonstrated that no rebellion was likely to succeed on

'*Et fuga verterunt Angli*', 'And the English have turned to flight': the last panel of the Bayeux Tapestry (as we have it) gives a misleading impression that William's conquest was the work of a few hours.

Effigy of Geoffrey de Mandeville, d. 1144, in Temple Church, London. Geoffrey died excommunicate, while in open rebellion, so he was not granted a Christian burial until twenty years after his death, when his son, who had been granted Geoffrey's earldom of Essex by Henry II, appealed successfully to the Pope for absolution.

Leaden tokens and an ampulla worn by pilgrims to the shrine of Thomas Becket. The ampulla (*top left*) was designed to carry holy water. The inscription, '*optimus agrorum medicus fit toma bonorum*', 'may Thomas be the best doctor of the worthy sick', is testament to the rebel-saint's reputed healing powers.

GREAT NORFOLK WINDOW

KING JOHN signing MAGNA CHARTA

The drama of Magna Carta, as seen through nineteenth-century eyes. This drawing of the design for a window in Arundel Castle shows King John in the act of signing the Great Charter. In fact, he attached his seal to the document. The Duke of Norfolk (and Earl of Arundel), who commissioned the window, chose to have himself portrayed in the person of one of the rebels, Robert Fitzwalter. The holder of the earldom of Arundel in John's time, William D'Aubigny, was actually a favourite of the king's, who never withdrew his support.

The execution of Thomas of Lancaster, from the Luttrell Psalter (*c.*1325–35): 'forasmuch as he was the queen's uncle and the son of the king's uncle ... he was neither drawn nor hanged, only beheaded in like manner as this same Earl Thomas caused Piers de Gaveston to be beheaded' (*Chronicle of Lanercost* 1272–1346).

Simon de Montfort's death and dismemberment after Evesham, 1265, in the *Chronica Roffense* (fourteenth century).

A fifteenth-century illustration from Froissart's *Chronicle* shows the meeting of Wat Tyler with Richard II, and Tyler's death at the hands of William Walworth, in a graphic narrative, with the young king witnessing the rebel's death on the left and speaking to his troops on the right.

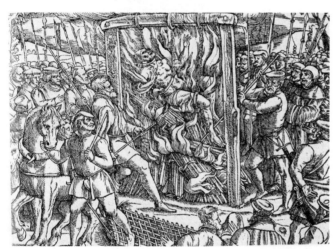

A Protestant rebel-martyr: Sir John Oldcastle is hung in chains and burned. An illustration from John Foxe's *Book of Martyrs* (1563): 'As gold in the fornace doth God try his elect, and as a most pleasant brent offering receiueth he them to reast.'

'Lord Saye and Sele brought before Jack Cade', an engraving by W. Ridgway; the original by Charles Lucy (1814–73) was deposited in Broughton Castle – still the seat of Lord Saye and Sele – which may account for the depiction of Cade as conducting mob justice in the open, rather than in more formal circumstances at the Guildhall.

'Robert Kett, under the Oak of Reformation at his Great Camp on Mousehold Heath', 1549; an engraving based on Samuel Wale's painting of this subject (*c.*1746).

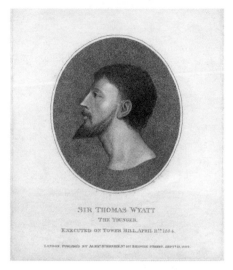

Sir Thomas Wyatt the younger, an engraving of 1800 of a mid-sixteenth-century portrait by an unknown artist.

Severed head of Guy Fawkes, an illustration from *Mischeefes mysterie: or, Treasons master-peece, the powder plot* by Francis Herring (1617), part of the outpouring of loyal literature after the plot.

A drawing of the 'Powder Plot Cellar' beneath the Houses of Parliament, demolished in 1833.

John Lilburne, the Leveller who fell foul of the Commonwealth; a drawing from an account of his trial in October 1649. Although he was acquitted, Lilburne soon provoked the authorities again and was sent into exile in 1652 and imprisoned on his return in June 1653.

The execution of James Scott, Duke of Monmouth, illegitimate son of Charles II, after his uncle James II's rejection of his pleas for mercy.

John Wilkes Esqr.
Drawn from the Life and Etch'd in Aquafortis by Wilm. Hogarth.

William Hogarth's drawing of John Wilkes, 1763. Wilkes was certainly cross-eyed, and used to say that it took him half an hour to talk his face away. But Hogarth had been attacked by Wilkes's paper, the *North Briton*, and this caricature looks more like revenge.

NO POPERY or NEWGATE REFORMER.

Tho' He Says he's a Protestant. look at the Print.
The Face and the Bludgeon, will give you a hint,
Religion he cries, in hopes to deceive,
While his practice is only to burn and to thieve.

James Gillray's print of a Gordon Rioter (1780), with Newgate prison in flames behind him.

The arrest of the Cato Street Conspirators, 1820.

An engraving of the Chartist meeting at Kennington Common on 10 April 1848, from the *Illustrated London News*, based on a daguerreotype (which is thought to be the first photograph of a crowd). The paper was full of praise for the police and barely concealed *Schadenfreude* that the Chartists' 'demonstration was in every respect a failure'. Considering that the last but one number of the periodical had been devoted to reporting the 'revolutionary movement' across the Continent, from France to Lombardy, the writers' relief was understandable.

The General Strike, May 1926, from the *Illustrated London News*. This was one of the few violent incidents recorded in a special edition, which concentrated mostly on 'How England Carried On', and reported the 'surrender of the Trades Union Congress'.

The Home Secretary, Reginald McKenna, force-feeding a suffragette in prison, May 1913.

The Angry Brigade 'Stoke Newington 8' in the dock, as seen in *Oz* magazine 42 (May/June 1972), drawn by Roy Knipe.

A demonstration against the 'Poll Tax', 31 March 1990, descends into violence.

such grounds. The English Reformation had been a play in several acts, and the rebellions of 1536, 1549, and 1569 were its bloodiest scenes. But they represent a disaffection concentrated in specific areas, not spread evenly across the country, and 1569 was the last year in which Catholicism was mooted as a cause with popular appeal. The Northern Rebellion was old-fashioned in another way, too, representing an attempt to turn the clock back almost to the fourteenth century, when powerful nobles with an armed following might expect to influence royal government. By Elizabeth's time, far more of the population had a stake in that government, which was run by professionals like William Cecil and Walsingham on less personal lines. An aristocratic rising, particularly one which concentrated its support so narrowly, had little chance of success.

A carpenter's revolt

The lack of aristocratic (or gentry) rebellion before that of the Earl of Essex at the end of Elizabeth's reign (rebellion was usually more likely when a regime was new or not yet established) also contributed to a relatively unthreatened rule. But the absence of rebellion was not necessarily a sign of a contented society. The monetary inflation of the sixteenth century, especially when combined with a dearth of food, fell hardest on the poorest in the country. In the 1590s, successive harvest failures led to food riots which culminated in an abortive rising in Oxfordshire in 1596, in which a carpenter from the village of Hampton Gay, Bartholomew Steer, planned to lead a mob from manor to manor decapitating those he blamed for their enclosure of land and hence for the people's growing hunger.

Although the rising failed utterly (despite its would-be leaders' early attempts to recruit, only four men met at the appointed time on Enslow Hill), it was taken extremely seriously by the authorities, who questioned and certainly tortured Steer and four other alleged conspirators. Two of them, including Steer, seem to have died before they could be convicted. The other four were sentenced to be hanged, drawn and quartered for levying war against the Crown. The savage overreaction to a threatened rising that never got anywhere near off the ground, together with the faintly paranoid interrogations about Gypsies and off-duty soldiers, are an indication that Elizabeth's government did not feel entirely secure internally, despite the relative lack of rebellion in her reign. The combination of enclosure and famine was always a potent one, and mention in a prophecy of the same year of the example of Robert Kett and his 'camp' would have sent shivers down government spines.

Bartholomew Steer was a spectacularly unsuccessful rebel, but that was not for lack of trying. The nervous, non-committal responses he received to his entreaties are evidence of a cowed people, not a contented one: time and again, those who were asked to join said that they would if everybody else did, clearly too nervous to take the first step. Steer did not even approach those in the slightly more prosperous classes, such as the yeomen, richer farmers who had figured prominently in previous popular risings, like that of Jack Cade or those of 1549. Some were included in the roll call of intended victims. The most convincing explanation of this is that the 'middling sort' now had too much to lose. They were players in Tudor society, increasingly literate, and increasingly litigious, more likely to be enclosers than their victims. The expansion in Commons membership, for which 40-shilling freeholders had a vote, might also have given yeomen the impression that they were increasingly represented. All these developments meant that the yeoman's sympathies were more likely to lie with the gentry than with the labouring class. Their gains had left the labouring poor behind, with the added effect of divorcing the two classes politically. Disconnected, misunderstood, feared and increasingly demonized as 'monstrous' – the 'Hydra' and its 'horn and noise o'th'monster's' of Shakespeare's *Coriolanus* (1608) – a rebellious peasant class could be disciplined and destroyed rather than accommodated. The repression that met an attempt – even one as malformed as Bartholomew Steer's – to voice the poor's own complaints is the other side of the familiar picture of

'Gloriana's' reign. Some very dirty work had to be done to keep the glory of an ageing queen untarnished.

The spurned Earl

The effectiveness of the security machine that had grown up under Elizabeth's eye was, in truth, barely tested right at the end of her reign when another rebellion, this time from the opposite end of the social scale, posed a similarly unconvincing threat to the realm, with similarly dire results for the perpetrators. Robert Devereux, Earl of Essex, led an old-fashioned rising stemming from his own exclusion from court (with echoes of Richard, Duke of York, in the fifteenth century), but one which attracted nothing like the support of earlier aristocratic rebels. Essex had risen to the position of the Queen's favourite, taking over almost seamlessly from his stepfather, the Earl of Leicester, after Leicester's death. But Essex's own preoccupations, which centred on his military career and dovetailed nicely with his passionate belief that Spain, and Continental Catholicism, should be attacked on all fronts, clashed with the more subtle realpolitik of Elizabeth and the Cecils (Robert had succeeded in his father's role in 1596). Essex's fall from grace, which led eventually to his underpowered half-demo, half-coup, had begun in July 1598 when the Earl, perceiving an insult from his Queen, had turned his back on her. Elizabeth slapped Essex about the head, and he reached for his sword, though his hand was stayed by the Lord Admiral. Essex didn't return the attack, but he still stormed from the room, throwing insults at Elizabeth before he left. Amazingly, Elizabeth forgave the Earl. He missed out on the redistribution of patronage and power that followed the death of William Cecil, Lord Burghley, while he was absent from court. But Elizabeth allowed Essex to return to court later the same year, where, after much wrangling, he was appointed to a command against the rebellious Irish Earl of Tyrone, who was making large gains in the Queen's second kingdom.

Essex's previous military action had displayed in both success and failure a somewhat free interpretation of his orders. When this led him to excessive action, as at the sack of Cadiz, Essex could still emerge with credit. In Ireland, the reality of his position led Essex in the opposite direction, to a compromise with the man he was supposed to be confronting. The Earl knew that he had made enough enemies at court for such negotiations to prove damaging to his reputation. If interpreted as consorting with the enemy, this could have had potentially more dangerous consequences. He can be forgiven the speed with which he returned from Ireland to make his case directly, though he was characteristically unsubtle in contriving to burst in on the Queen half-dressed as soon as he arrived. Essex often attributed his difficulties with his sovereign to the fact that she was a woman, and this last faux pas made it all too clear that he found it hard to make the necessary concessions to her sex. Although the Queen was willing to talk to him later, it was nonetheless in her Council that the decision to place the Earl under house arrest was taken, beginning in June 1600. Essex still benefited from Elizabeth's personal favour, and although he wasn't allowed back to court (thus putting an end to his political career), the arrest was lifted before three months were up.

At the age of only thirty-four, Essex was not exactly ready for retirement. Although the traditional image of him as vain and superficial is belied by what was a pretty serious interest both in the more reforming, 'godly' end of Protestantism that was beginning to be known as 'puritanism', and an active passion for scholarship, he was still a man of action. He was also broke. For years he had relied on the monopoly on the customs for sweet wines, but when this wasn't renewed in October 1600, it tipped Essex and his cronies into more active seeking of alternative ways to find favour, leading to a direct appeal for help to Elizabeth's likely (and eventual) successor, James VI of Scotland. James was far too cautious an operator to have anything to do with any scheme that might jeopardize the succession, but the manoeuvrings of Essex and his friends were enough for the Earl to receive a summons to explain himself in front of the Council. When he refused, and locked up representatives who came to ask him why, Essex was set on the course of rebellion. With a following of about 300 men, he marched from Essex House just outside the City to the house of the sheriff of London, brandishing weapons, but not bothering with armour. When the gates of the City were barred to him, the rebels retreated back to Essex House. Although their number included three earls and various lords, there was no popular support and none from those close to Elizabeth. Essex surrendered the same day, 8 February 1601. He was tried and executed less than two weeks later.

Although Essex did represent something other than himself – a dissatisfaction with the waning powers of the Queen, with her ever tighter circle of advisers, as well as a genuine fear for England's Protestant future if James's succession wasn't confirmed – his was far too personal a rebellion to present much more of a threat to Elizabeth's government than Bartholomew Steer's 'popular rising' five years earlier. Though Steer had a more urgent basis on which to appeal for support – an empty belly and a conviction of the causes – the two very different rebellions foundered on an almost total lack of following. The night before his rising, Essex's circle backed a revival at the Globe of Shakespeare's *Richard II*, with its king who 'must . . . lose the name of King'. But as a spur to popular action this was a little too attenuated. Rather than being the tool of aristocratic rebels, Shakespeare allowed himself to comment allusively on the divisions that led men like Steer to attempt to rise. It has been argued that *As You Like It* – probably written around the time of the Oxfordshire revolt – in which Orlando is displaced from his land by his cruel brother, is in part a dramatization of the sort of agrarian conflict that men like Steer experienced in more basic circumstances. Steer's reported exhortations to make a 'merrier' world are reflected in the play's disquisition on merriment in a divided countryside. On this reading, 'Under the greenwood tree', with its refrain 'Here shall he see / No enemy', is not a ditty about a rural idyll but an expression of longing for a return to an 'unenclosed' existence.

As the early years of James I's reign showed, Catholic plotting could still present a genuine threat to the Crown, although one which the intelligence gathering of Elizabeth's regime was well equipped to contend with. There are a lot of differences between plots and rebellions, but the most obvious is numbers. As Catesby, Fawkes and co. were to show in 1605, Catholic threats to the Protestant succession might resurface, but (despite efforts to generate a rising) they were small, targeted plots because Catholics could no longer expect the sort of popular support demonstrated in 1569, let alone in 1549 or 1536.

The marriage of Protestantism itself with obedience to the Crown had been a masterstroke, but one that could not cope with the rise of nonconformity, those manifestations of the Protestant faith that were responsible for a whole new set of disagreements. Elizabeth and her ministers had not 'solved' the problem of rebellion: in any case, lack of rebellion was itself no indicator of a successful polity. But they had made it a less attractive option to more people. It would take the repeated mistakes of a determinedly provocative king to rekindle rebellion in the seventeenth century. It wasn't until James's son was on the throne that, to adapt Max Beerbohm, the nonsense knocked out of the English monarchy during the Reformation was gently put back. The result was a cause with enough appeal to make several rebellions, civil war and a revolution.

11. Republicans and Revolutionaries

Robert Catesby to Oliver Cromwell 1605–60

Our brutish fury struggling to be free

Andrew Marvell, 'The First Anniversary
of the Government under His Highness
the Lord Protector, 1655'

The 'incessant peals of muskets, great guns and mortar pieces' came to be the mood music of seventeenth-century England. But towards the beginning of this rebellious century, people noticed the silence. When Elizabeth I died in 1603 without leaving a direct heir, the accession of the new king passed off unexpectedly smoothly. It was noted in London that 'there was no tumult, no contradiction, no disorder in the city; everyman went about his business as readily, as peaceably, as securely as if there had been no change.' Despite the disadvantage of his 'foreign' birth, James VI of Scotland was able in 1603 to succeed with relative ease to the English throne that Elizabeth had occupied for so long, and with so little willingness to name a successor. The King made an unhurried progress south on hearing the news, and spent the day of the old queen's funeral near Huntingdon, being richly entertained at the house of Sir Oliver Cromwell – whose nephew would, less than fifty years later, hasten James's son to the executioner's block with all the trappings of legal process. That prospect would have seemed not just monstrous but inconceivable to James as he feasted on his new subject's hospitality. No one had seriously threatened the monarch, let alone the monarchy, for almost forty years. But it took effort, attention to detail and luck to avoid rebellions, and the Stuarts were eventually found wanting on all three fronts.

James started well enough. He understood that the key to an

untroubled succession, once Elizabeth had indicated her own preference for a successor (which she did only on her deathbed, by touching her hand to her head when James's name was mentioned) was the support of those who controlled Elizabeth's government, men like Robert Cecil, the younger son of William, Lord Burghley, who had taken over his father's role as Secretary of State. Characteristically for this micro-manager of a ruler, James also paid attention to less powerful, but still potentially troublesome elements. One of the ways in which he tried to please all the people all the time, at least until the crown was securely placed, was to indicate, without ever actually articulating, a more tolerant attitude to England's Catholic minority. Nonetheless, it was members of that minority who, two years later, led one of the most daring and most memorialized, if not exactly best-remembered, rebellions in English history: the Gunpowder Plot.

English Catholics had much to resent. Under Elizabeth, they had to pay fines for non-attendance at Protestant church services, were prohibited from public office or even taking university degrees, and had their movements restricted. Catholic priests, after the papal bull in 1570 that excommunicated the Queen and called for her overthrow, were deemed traitors. To celebrate a Mass was to risk your life. Even sheltering 'perpetrators' could be fatal, as Margaret Clitherow of York discovered in 1586, when she was pressed to death – literally, squashed beneath heavy weights – for that offence. Even before his succession was confirmed, Catholics were hopeful that James, the Protestant son of a Catholic 'martyr', Mary, Queen of Scots, might take a more enlightened attitude.

To begin with, he did. Records of fines for 'recusants', those Catholics who did not attend Protestant services, were markedly reduced at the beginning of James's reign. From a high of £9,126 in 1601, the fines fell to £1,414 in 1604. But this did not buy everyone's co-operation. In James's first year on the throne, there were two foiled plots against him, known as the 'Main' and the 'Bye' plots. Only the latter was a Catholic conspiracy, designed to hold the new king prisoner while the maximum concessions to English Catholics were extracted from him. The 'Main' plot, by contrast, was an old-fashioned dynastic intrigue, to put another candidate, Lady Arabella Stuart, on the throne instead of James. Both were revealed quickly, and James took notice that it was the two leading Jesuits who reported their suspicions of the 'Bye' plot to the Privy Council, shopping fellow Catholics rather than risking the inevitable crackdown if and when the plot failed. One element of the other plot of that year, which was more Puritan in character, was its anti-Scottishness. Arabella was English (she would have had the unique distinction for a British sovereign of being born in Hackney), and this fact appealed to Englishmen of all religious persuasions who were suspicious of the new king and especially of the Scottish friends he put in high places. James had encountered this hostility in his first parliament, when his proposed Act of Union was rejected. Anti-Scottishness would be a feature of the Gunpowder Plot, and ran deep with the conspirators. Before joining the plot itself, when Guy Fawkes appealed to the Spanish for help in his struggle for Catholic freedom, he referred to the 'natural hostility between English and Scots' as one of the reasons why a rebellion would find support.

The Gunpowder Plot

In fact, Spain, like England, was getting used to a new ruler with less appetite for the religious fight. In 1604, Philip III and James I agreed a peace treaty, which withdrew English support for rebels against Spanish rule in the Netherlands, and promised on the Spanish side not to lead or support action against the English king. This put paid to any English Catholic hopes that Spain would help them overthrow their Protestant king. English Catholics liked to imply that there were legions of conformists who would return to the old religion if given a lead. But visible Catholics were in a tiny minority, perhaps 1 per cent of the population, and it would have been bizarre if the new king, an inquisitive and devout Protestant himself, had leant very far to accommodate a feared, hated and politically marginalized minority. James's apparently more relaxed attitude, as well as the withdrawal of Spanish support for any English Catholic insurrection, led the more thoughtful elements in English Catholicism to conclude that co-operation with the authorities was their safest option. Once we turn to the men who led the Gunpowder Plot, however, it becomes clear that rational thinking was not their strong suit. The plotters were fanatics, and like many fanatics their legitimate grievances found expression in disproportionate violence and misguidedly optimistic expectations of support for their actions. The temptation to draw present-day parallels is so strong that it should almost certainly be avoided, but it was definitely the case with the 'terrorists' of 1605 that their cause was immeasurably damaged by their actions. One can only speculate how much worse it might have been had they actually succeeded.

The plotters' leader was not the figure the English still burn every year, Guy Fawkes (who changed his name to 'Guido' to advertise his Spanish sympathies), but Robert Catesby, known to his friends as Robin. A Catholic gentleman with connections to various eminent recusant families, Catesby had form as a rebel, having taken part in Essex's failed coup at the end of Elizabeth's reign. One reason why the Essex rebellion never convinced at the time or later as a rising for Puritanism was the involvement of several disaffected Catholics. Only four years later, Catesby and three other young Catholics who had followed Essex conspired in a plot for their own religion, to blow up the King, his family, the Lords and Commons at the opening of Parliament on 5 November 1605. The avalanche of literature that has followed the plot for four centuries includes one element that casts doubt on its genuine existence at all. Some writers have argued that the Gunpowder Plot was a government set-up, designed by Cecil and the Puritans to push the lenient King into more extreme anti-Catholicism, and to ensure that Catholics could not aspire to positions of power for the foreseeable future (though even Cecil and his friends might have been surprised that this would mean more than 200 years thence). It is more generally agreed that, although Cecil might have known more, and earlier, than he let on, there is far too much evidence of a real plot (including the actions of a party outside the city who continued with their plans to 'raise' the country even after the plot's discovery) for it to have been a fiction. That still leaves us with the problem of explaining why men who only four years before had been willing to follow a Protestant, and who were now living under an ostensibly more tolerant regime, which had come to terms with the Catholics' most likely outside supporter, would conceive of such a massively violent rebellion.

One explanation must centre on the fact that the plotters were a tiny minority within a tiny minority. Although the government implicated the Jesuit superior in the plot, Father Henry Garnett, to whom details of it had in fact been confessed, it is clear that 'mainstream' Catholics followed Garnett in thinking the plot 'most horrible'. Garnett was under instructions from Rome to discourage any action against James, who seemed a far better prospect than his predecessor. So the plotters were 'unrepresentative', even if their disappointment that more tolerance was not being extended to Catholics was shared. This makes it more important to concentrate on the individual motivation to rebel, and that, of course, at such a distance, is difficult to do, especially as much of what the plotters said came out in their trial, and as a result of torture.

The repressive conditions under which Catholics lived might have resigned most of their number to quietism. In the minds of frustrated, active young men, it is perhaps not surprising that they produced instead fantasies of violent revenge to set alongside the violence visited on their co-religionists. Guy Fawkes was an experienced soldier who had fought on the Spanish side in the war in the Netherlands. He seems to have brought to the conspiracy a single-minded dedication and reliability. As the man charged with storing the gunpowder and setting the fuses he had, of course, to be unrecognizable, so his absence abroad favoured him for the role. Masquerading as 'John Johnson', he got very close to realizing the plans. But it was Catesby – flamboyant, charismatic, and not a little histrionic – who was the guiding force, and who drew supporters to him, most of whom were related by blood or marriage (with the notable exception of Fawkes). At the treason trial after the plot, two conspirators, Ambrose Rookwood and Everard Digby (it is unfortunate that such desperate men are burdened with names that sound quite so effete to modern ears), spoke of Catesby as the motivating force. Rookwood said that he 'loved [him] above any worldly man', and actually seemed to believe that pleading this as his motivation for joining the plot (at a relatively late stage) would get him off. Rookwood had been brought into the conspiracy for his horsemanship (and possession of fine horses), and his way of preparing for it was by buying a 'very fair Hungarian horseman's coat, lined all with velvet, and other apparel exceeding costly, not fit for his degree'. Digby, too, was something of a dandy, and he also pleaded affection for Catesby in mitigation at his trial. Catesby's svengali-like influence on his friends may have been the most important factor in bringing the conspiracy so close to fruition.

Like Digby and Rookwood, Catesby seems in some ways to have treated the plot as a piece of theatre. Certainly, the choice of Parliament at its opening was a deliberately dramatic one. We know from present-day experience what an impact a successful attack on a symbolic landmark can make. Catesby's plan was a perfect example of 'asymmetric' warfare. If it had worked, the amount of gunpowder stored under the Palace of Westminster has been calculated as having the potential to destroy all buildings within 40 yards of the blast, and to cause damage within 500. The crowds assembled for the opening would all have been killed. The fact that the other elements of the conspiracy – which included plans to raise Catholics and other sympathizers in the Midlands, and to seize James's nine-year-old daughter, Elizabeth, and proclaim her queen – were so vaguely worked out also seems to point to a conviction that it was the great explosion itself that would magically achieve Catholic freedom. The plot was revealed by another device out of melodrama, a secret letter sent to warn the recipient to stay away from the opening. When the addressee, Lord Monteagle, took the letter to Cecil, the latter too seems to have decided to be complicit in continuing the 'performance', not even showing the letter to James until five days after it had been passed to him. It was another four days before the final, charged scene, of the 'booted and spurred' figure of Guy Fawkes discovered in a storeroom beneath the palace of Westminster, could be played out.

Nevertheless, just like modern terrorist spreaders of what Mikhail Bakunin called the 'propaganda of the deed', Catesby and his followers realized that their performance invited their own death as clearly as it aimed at the death of others. Guido suffered dreadful torture, nowhere better attested than in the hauntingly feeble signature on his eventual confession, dragged out of him on the rack. Catesby was able to suffer the action man's death he had half expected, shot while waving his sword outside a fortified house in Staffordshire. Those who were captured were not so lucky, and met the traditional traitors' agonizing end of hanging, drawing and quartering. Francis Tresham, the conspirator who is most likely to have revealed the plot to the authorities, whether or not he actually wrote the 'Monteagle letter', fell ill and died in captivity, but his body was decapitated and the head displayed as the familiar warning.

The posterity of the plot, of course, went far beyond the traditional grim object lesson of the rebels' body parts being displayed throughout the country. From the night of its discovery, the foiling of the plot became a cause of national rejoicing, one which is still celebrated, however divorced from its origins, in annual Bonfire Nights. The first of these was in 1605 itself, and seems to have been a more or less spontaneous response to the 'delivery' of the King and Parliament. But the marking of the day was also swiftly co-opted officially, and nowhere more directly than in the institution of a 'Public Thanksgiving to Almighty God every year on the fifth Day of November' from 1606. The sermons that accompanied these services tended to remind listeners of the Catholic threat and the divine providence that had delivered England from popery. The service remained in the Anglican calendar until 1859, thirty years after Catholic Emancipation and nine years after the reintroduction of the Catholic hierarchy into Britain. In some ways, the Gunpowder Plot had the most long-lasting legacies of

Always by the Great Bishop Andrewes in James 1st presence.

any rebellion in English history, but from the rebels' point of view they were all negative. Even the leading rebel's name has been popularly forgotten, his place silently taken by the impressively mute Guy, a blanker screen onto which all sorts of fantasies have been projected. As the officially endorsed 'representative' rebellion in English history, the plot has effaced far better supported, frequent or more justified rebels from popular memory. The plotters were English rebels, but they were unusual ones.

History Wars

King James, who liked to point out that his life had been threatened since even before he was born (it was true: plotters had pointed a dagger at Mary, Queen of Scots' pregnant belly), died in 1625 of disease, not the attentions of assassins. His son was less fortunate. Whereas the Catholic Gunpowder Plotters had wanted to kill James *in* Parliament, as the appropriate site of 'all the mischief' done to them, Charles I was condemned to death *by* Parliament, a body he had attempted to rule without, and had eventually so provoked in the course of two civil wars that some of its members felt compelled to impose the ultimate sanction.

Very little about this period is agreed on for long. Even naming the events of roughly 1640 to 1660 has proved contentious. For more than 300 years, the changing fashions of nomenclature have reflected a constantly shifting set of arguments and understandings, about what these events meant then, and mean now. Our difficulty with names is important because it shows how much about the fundamentals of the period remains up for discussion. In a history of English rebellion, it is tempting to go back to one of the earliest designations, the Royalist Edward Hyde, Earl of Clarendon's no-nonsense 'the Rebellion'. But the 'rebels' of the middle of the seventeenth century, perhaps more absolutely even than their pre-decessors, rejected the name. Though those who went on to sit in judgment on the King and preside over a republic could hardly cling to the old defence that they were loyal to the monarch, most were convinced that their actions were loyal to the Constitution and, perhaps more importantly for these godly men, to the true religion of England. Much later, it became the fashion to refer to these events as 'the English Revolution'. The scale of change, the death of the King and the (temporary) abolition of monarchy, bishoprics and House of Lords – not to mention the tumultuous swirl of political and religious ideas that sprang up in the 1640s and '50s – all make this a perfectly justifiable option. But what happened was both more and less than an (let alone 'the') English revolution: more, because these events fundamentally affected all three kingdoms over which the Stuarts ruled – England, Ireland and Scotland – as well as Wales, where several serious engagements took place; and less, because of the connotations which subsequent revolutions, in France, Russia and China especially, have projected back onto this term when applied to seventeenth-century Britain. Despite years of trying, it has proved almost impossible to impose a Marxist, class-based (or even, very persuasively, economic) interpretation on Britain's experiences. Of course, not all revolutions have to conform to Karl Marx's strictures, but the word's associations may be too bound up with them for it to be a comfortable fit.

The 'War of the Three Kingdoms' became the acceptable term more recently, taking into account that the violence began in Scotland, carried on in part in Ireland, and ended with an army from Scotland (though not of Scots) coming into England to effect a Restoration. But since it has been the intention of this book to focus on English rebels very specifically, in part to emphasize the fact that there were just as many, and they were just as important, in England as in the other of the 'two kingdoms' (and the principality), the 'Three Kingdoms' option isn't completely helpful here either. But, as Hugh Trevor-Roper said, 'one has to call it something', and for our purposes the 'English Civil Wars' seems a good enough way of referring to the part of these events that we will focus on: England's troubles (though without ignoring those that originated in Scotland and Ireland), and what they led to. And while the focus on England alone may not be the fashion for historians nowadays, it perhaps gives an insight into Anglo-Saxon attitudes of the time, at least if Clarendon is to be believed when he writes that 'the truth is, there was so little curiosity in the Court, or in the country to know any thing of Scotland'.

The Civil Wars became so complex and generated such a lot of words that full-scale treatments of them sensibly confine themselves to the century in which they happened. But even events as cataclysmic and apparently *sui generis* as those of the mid-seventeenth century were not totally unprecedented. The men and women who lived through them drew comparisons with earlier times, and even if such comparisons, as so often, proved no reliable guide to the way things would unfold, it helps us at this distance to understand what contemporaries made of their own circumstances, by bearing in mind how they contextualized them. One reason to do this is to show how *un*helpful to a proper understanding of what was going on such comparisons could be. If Charles I and his contemporaries thought they were witnessing (or participating in) the sort of opposition their forefathers had carried on, it would have affected the way they behaved. In Charles's case, it might help to explain his total inability to come to terms with it, even to the extent of 'martyring' himself. When faced with a powerful and intransigent Parliament, he clung to the example of 'Our blessed Predecessor Queen Elizabeth' (though without any of her genius for compromise), and warned that the way Parliament was going would mean that 'this splendid and excellently distinguished form of Government, [would] end in a dark equall *Chaos* of Confusion, and the long Line of Our many noble Ancestors in a *Jack Cade,* or a *Wat Tyler.*'

On Parliament's side, men like the lawyer Henry Parker also invoked historical example, declaring that:

vast power itselfe is justly odious, for divers reasons. First, because it may fall into the hands of ill disposed Princes, such as were King *John, Henry* the third, *Edward* the second, *Richard* the second. These all in their times made England miserable, and certainly had their power beene more unconfineable, they had made it more miserable.

The implication was that Parliament was now best placed to play the role once taken by the barons or by alternative claimants to the throne. The Civil Wars were not fought in a historical vacuum. Later participants would look even further back in English history for their interpretation, seeing the removal of unjust monarchy as the throwing off of the 'Norman yoke' imposed by William the Conqueror. However unexpected the consequences of the different parties' actions were, they all looked to historical precedent as a guide.

Divine Rights

The other precedent that had equal force in people's minds in the seventeenth century (almost certainly more) was religious and biblical precedent. James I had been able to make political capital out of the failure of a 'popish' plot to destroy him and his government in 1605. Charles, who was married to a Catholic but had no thoughts of extending toleration, let alone his own conversion, became the victim of anti-Catholic insinuation, as the 'godly' party in Parliament jumped to conclusions about where Charles and his Archbishop William Laud's 'innovations' in their Church would lead. The Civil Wars were in part a dispute over political sovereignty, and they certainly became one once the momentous step of executing the King had been taken. But their character, and the dynamic which seemed to drive the dispute further than anyone had realistically contemplated, stemmed from something that made seventeenth-century people's blood pulse much more quickly than politics: religion. It is perhaps no surprise to find the famously godly Puritan Oliver Cromwell repeatedly 'seeking God' before taking significant decisions. A fear of 'popery' provided much of the fuel for the initial rebellion. As it went on, Parliamentarians became increasingly convinced in their belief that they were agents of divine Providence. The designation of their New Model Army as an 'Army of God' was far more justifiable than in any previous 'rebel' force. The New Model had their own Soldiers' Bible, and were accompanied by army preachers (though many soldiers were also part-time preachers). But such convictions were not restricted to the Parliamentary side. Before the Battle of Naseby, Charles, his forces outnumbered, justified his decision to engage the enemy: 'I must say that there is no probability but of my ruin; yet as a Christian, I must tell you that God will not suffer rebels or traitors to prosper.' When both fighters believe God is in their corner, it is less surprising that the fight is to the death.

Charles's religious beliefs have traditionally been more associated with the political theory of the 'divine right of kings', the concept elucidated by his father but embraced with less compromise by the son. But to assume that Charles's 'divine right' was a kind of backward-looking, superstitiously unrealistic view of kingly power is to prejudge the issue. In other European monarchies at this time, it was precisely this kind of thinking that was reducing the part played by the 'Estates' in government and exalting the monarch's. Charles's problem was that he attempted to expound this theory in a political atmosphere that was widely unreceptive to it, and that he seemed to possess the diplomatic skills of a spoilt child. The King inherited a war with Spain and an unpopular favourite, George Villiers, the Duke of Buckingham. Charles addressed Buckingham affectionately as 'Steenie', the name James had given him because he thought the Duke, like St Stephen, had the face of an angel. Buckingham held Charles in thrall almost as thoroughly, though perhaps without the sexual element to the relationship, as he had James, and his influence over court patronage was widely resented. Buckingham was blamed, too, for the failures of the war with Spain, and in the fighting with France that soon followed.

The early experiences of his reign made Charles see the summoning of Parliament not as a necessary element in government, but as an intolerable imposition, and he came to conclude that it was not the only way to cure a chronic lack of funds. His struggles in the first three parliaments of his reign, up to 1628, to impose himself and to obtain money, also saw the rise of a more fully rounded alternative theory of sovereignty to that of the King. But the issues around which this grew up were hardly new. The

Commons attempted to impeach Buckingham (the King ignored them) and, in the third parliament of the reign, they presented the 'Petition of Right', which referred the King to his predecessors' promises to restrain arbitrary government. But if parliamentary opposition began as an essentially retrospective movement, trying to secure the rights already granted by past rulers, it was radicalized somewhat during the twelve years of the King's 'Personal Rule', in which he didn't call a parliament. What emerged was little less than an equivalent, and equally divinely sanctioned, theory of parliamentary sovereignty to challenge Charles's 'divine right'. The champions of this alternative were men like Parker, like Sir Edward Coke – who saw the 'rule of law' as the counterbalance to the king's exercise of arbitrary power – and John Pym, the Parliamentary leader who first put forward Parliament's position as 'the soul of the commonwealth, that only is able to apprehend and understand the symptoms of all such diseases which threaten the body politic'.

This was the backdrop against which time-honoured disputes about tax, about religion, and about the king's councillors ended up in the public trial and execution of a king, and the abolition of monarchy itself. The Parliamentarians who brought the Grand Remonstrance in 1641, let alone those who presented the Petition of Right in 1628, cannot have conceived of such an outcome. But Charles and Parliament's increasingly uncompromising interpretations of their sovereignty, fuelled by equally extreme adherence to their religious positions, made war possible. War in turn made almost anything possible.

Of course, the English Civil Wars were not just a clash of semi-detached ideologies. They were a clash of personalities, of people. And of all the conflicts discussed in this book, they had the most devastating human consequences, accounting in all three kingdoms for an estimated half a million deaths. This was the first English rebellion to be fought in a kind of media spotlight, coinciding as it did with the invention of the printed weekly newsbook, the forerunner of the modern newspaper. Something of the rhetorical and dramatic flavour of the war has survived in the phrases that still pepper our history books: 'Pride's Purge',

'Barebone's Parliament', 'the Sealed Knot', 'the Good Old Cause'. But this evocative shorthand mustn't be permitted to prettify the essential fact about the wars: that hundreds of thousands of men and women died in them. Looking back after the Restoration in 1660, who would have been able to say it was worth it?

Pym and the King

Of the dozens of people who played their part in originating, directing and driving the English Civil Wars, the two most obvious were Charles I and Oliver Cromwell, matched in conviction perhaps, but one completely outfaced by the other in terms of ability. Cromwell did not emerge as a leading player until the Civil Wars were under way, and while the King's favourites, Buckingham and then the Earl of Strafford, were the most important figures on the 'Royalist' side before war broke out, on Parliament's it was at first John Hampden and then John Pym who defied the King most eloquently.

Charles was able to rule without Parliament for almost twelve years, and it is perhaps only in retrospect that public attempts to resist his more arbitrary measures, such as the raising of 'Ship Money' – which was rightly seen as a tax that had not been voted by Parliament – seem ominous. The MP and Buckinghamshire gentleman John Hampden first came to prominence by refusing to pay Ship Money in 1637, for which he was tried and found guilty, though by a slim majority. We might see this as a moral victory for Hampden, whose stance was definitely of the 'won't pay' as against the 'can't pay' party (the charge was £1). His counsel made public the case for parliamentary taxation, but as long as Charles could avoid summoning Parliament, such protests were never likely to become more threatening. Yet the King needed more money, especially when, after 1637, he had to muster an army to fight his own subjects, the Scottish Covenanters.

The Covenant was a document drawn up and sworn to by large numbers of Scots after the introduction of the Scottish Prayer

Book in July 1637. The attempt to introduce what the Scots saw as English-style, 'popish' forms of worship was met almost immediately with violence. The first blows of the whole British conflict were struck not with musket or pike, but with prayer stools, hurled at the Scottish Archbishop, Archibald Johnston. And the violence was perpetrated not by trained soldiers but by a group of women, whom the ministers of the Scottish Kirk had encouraged to protest, perhaps because they thought they would avoid retribution. Over the following year, this religious protest had coalesced into a nationalist uprising, and Charles raised an army to deal with it. But a humiliating retreat in the Scottish borders had Charles negotiating peace with the Scottish rebels. This was an ignominious end for the King to the first 'Bishops' Wars', and it was unlikely to be a permanent one. The positions of the two sides were too far from each other, and neither side had established a military advantage. It was only a matter of time before battle was rejoined.

A matter of time, and of money. There was no way that Charles's piecemeal taxation could fund a war, and in April 1640 he summoned his first parliament for twelve years, to secure financial backing. It was in this 'Short Parliament' that the MP for Tavistock, John Pym, emerged as the leader of the anti-Royalist group in the House of Commons. Pym's two-hour speech was the most memorable episode in a session that lasted only three weeks, passed no bills, and was dissolved by Charles before any agreement on taxation had been reached. In it, Pym described some of the faultlines along which the King and his Parliament would split. He complained of arbitrary taxation, of monopolies, and the abuses of the Court of the Star Chamber. At the heart of his case, however, and the inspiration for a defiance of which his earlier career had given only hints, was the urge to protect the Church, for the 'greatest liberty of the kingdom is religion; thereby we are freed from spiritual evils, and no impositions are so grievous as those that are laid upon the soul'. Pym was a fanatic anti-Catholic who made egregious calls for 'papists' to be hunted out, even to wear distinctive clothing. In his speech to the Short Parliament, he warned of the 'great encouragement given to popery', but he also made it clear that it was Protestants in high places who were leading the King astray:

It was now . . . grown common for ambitious and corrupt men of the clergy to abuse the truth of God and the bond of conscience; preaching down the laws and liberties of the kingdom, and pretending Divine authority for an absolute power in the king, to do what he would without persons and goods.

Pym's ancestor Alexander had supported Perkin Warbeck's attempted invasion in 1497, but this was the only whiff of rebelliousness in his family history. Pym was an unlikely rebel, a man with a government job as Exchequer receiver for three counties, and one who, by the time Parliament was recalled in 1640, was severely in debt after a failed investment in a colonial venture, a situation that might have made a less principled man keep his head down. He did not represent a 'county interest', as many other Members of the House of Commons did. Pym's family were from Somerset, where his estates were, but he sat in Parliament first for a constituency in Wiltshire, then one in Devon (which he seems never to have visited, his election apparently secured by his patron, the Earl of Bedford). Perhaps 'Pym's junto', as the group around him was known, and which included peers as well as Members of the Commons, can best be compared to those traditional groups of aristocratic rebels who had tried to control their monarchs for hundreds of years. Nonetheless his speech, which was copied and widely circulated (and, in the following year, appeared in a printed version), singled out the 'commoner' Pym, ahead of his aristocratic allies, as the leader of opposition to the King. He was not a rebel yet, but by the beginning of 1642, when he had to slip out of the House with four colleagues to avoid the King's personal attempts to arrest them, he had certainly become one, in Charles's eyes at least.

What became known as the 'Long Parliament' was summoned in November 1640, by which time the King's attempts to fight the Scots without Parliament-voted money had failed even more starkly than his previous efforts. The Scots had defeated an English army at Newburn, outside Newcastle, and had then occupied the city. At York, the Covenanters, who had gone into war defending their own conception of the Scottish Kirk and the Scottish nation, were able to demand rather more. Charles conceded that the Covenanters' army would remain in occupation of the six English counties it had overrun, while his government would pay it £850 a day for the privilege of being partially occupied. The Parliament that assembled in November 1640 held more cards than its defeated, intransigent king, and played them mercilessly, if not yet with complete certainty of how the game would turn out.

The first play was for the King's favourite, Thomas Wentworth, Earl of Strafford. The shift in the balance of power between Parliament and King is well illustrated by comparing the attempt to impeach Buckingham at the beginning of the reign with the proceedings against Strafford. Charles had simply dissolved Parliament before the impeachment process against Buckingham could be finalized, and relied on a forced loan for the money he needed. Strafford, like Buckingham, had been put in command of the King's forces, and, like him, had failed to deliver a victory while appearing to support a 'tyrannical' conception of the monarch's powers. Pym launched impeachment proceedings against him in November 1640, partly because Strafford himself had advised the King to charge MPs like Pym with treason for conspiring with the Scottish enemy (with whom they had certainly communicated).

Although the Lords agreed that the trial should go ahead, it took a long time to build a case against the Earl, who had been a loyal servant to the King, especially in Ireland. But, determined to get their man, the MPs merely altered their line of attack. Instead of impeachment, they drew up a Bill of Attainder, which carried the death penalty, and could be passed as an Act of Parliament, without requiring the proof of guilt needed for a successful trial. Its final passage was accompanied by frustrated plots on the King's side to spring Strafford, and, on the other, noisy demands by Londoners outside the House for Strafford's execution. The peers weren't impressed by either side, but a majority of those who attended voted for the Attainder. Even after the Bill was passed, the King still hoped to save Strafford, writing to him on St George's Day, 1641, 'upon the word of a king you shall not suffer in life, honour, or fortune' at 'the strange mistaking and conjuncture of these times'. But suffer the Earl did. Exposed in his machinations, presented with a united House and a riotous capital, Charles assented to the Bill. Strafford was executed, less than three weeks after the King had assured him he would be safe, at Tower Hill on 12 May 1641. Even Charles's appeal to 'reprieve him until Saturday' was ignored.

If Charles imagined that his assent would at least make Parliament more co-operative, he was mistaken. While the King prepared to go north to finalize peace terms with the triumphant Scots, the Commons kept up the legislative pressure. Their concerns fell into two broad categories, the political and the religious. Under the former, measures were enacted against the Star Chamber (the special court that Charles had used to pursue his own agenda), while Ship Money and Tonnage and Poundage (customs duties) were abolished; there was also a bill that meant only Parliament could dissolve itself. On religion, there were measures against episcopacy, vocal denunciations of Catholic influences, and more 'Puritan' moves against church images, dancing on the Sabbath, or bowing at the name of Jesus. Over the latter issues there was far more of a range of opinion in the House, not just between Commons and Lords. However, guided by the zealous Pym, and taking advantage of the return of less 'committed' members to their homes as the capital was threatened with smallpox and plague through the summer, Parliament continued its reforming work. It was not yet 'revolutionary' work. Pym and his supporters' alternative to the King's 'personal' government was still government in his name, by various commissions, broadly on the model of those arrangements when the King was a minor or, like Henry VI, mentally incapacitated. Their outlook has been compared convincingly with that of Simon de Montfort. None of it was very original, but the precedents didn't give many grounds for optimism. They had all been accompanied by rebellion, and in some cases civil war.

Role reversal

Events in Charles's 'third' kingdom, Ireland, changed the atmosphere back in London and brought war much closer. Parliament was discussing the details of the document that became the Grand Remonstrance when news arrived of a great rebellion in Ireland, accompanied by lurid (and not entirely invented) tales of atrocities against Protestants. Pym and others may have genuinely suspected the King of some complicity with the rebels, and they were emboldened to summon an army on parliamentary rather than royal authority to deal with the uprising. Despite an atmosphere in Parliament that suspected popish plots around every corner, the Remonstrance was only just passed. In 204 clauses, it set out a view of 'those evils under which we have now many years suffered', and went into detail as to how the King was to rectify them. It began with the threat of 'Popery', and the way that recent Church reforms had provided encouragement to those elements. The Remonstrance went on into a breakdown of all the abuses of taxations, monopolies and legal process that had taken place in the reign, before blaming them, in a style familiar for at least 400 years, on 'evil counsellors'. Not all of it was what we might call 'grand', as it stooped to deal with everything from herring fishing to the Commission for Sewers, but even in this, it was in good constitutional company: Magna Carta had dealt with fish-weirs and standard weights and measures. The Remonstrance was presented to the King in December 1641, and he took his time in replying to it; but when he did, more than three weeks later, it was an unusually placatory message, concentrating on the 'purity and glory' of the Church, and the King's role in maintaining it against all attacks, whether 'popish' or the work of other 'schismatics and separatists'. In a sense, he was appealing over the heads of Parliament to the country at large, just as the Remonstrance had appealed over the head of Charles.

It might have worked, but rumour would once again play a large part in tipping peaceful resistance into rebellion. On this occasion, it was Charles whose hand was forced by a story that Parliament was about to impeach his (Catholic) queen, Henrietta-Maria. It wasn't true, but it seemed to galvanize the King. He charged five Members of the House of Commons and one Lord with treason. They were Pym, Hampden, Denzel Holles, William Strode and Sir Arthur Haselrig, as well as Lord Mandeville. The terms of the impeachment, which echo some against Strafford, suggest that Charles was still hurting at his inability to save his favourite. When the Lords procrastinated about going ahead with a procedure that had never before been initiated by the Crown, Charles took matters into his own hands. The next day, 4 January, accompanied by several hundred armed men, he descended on Westminster. The five MPs had taken their seats but, forewarned, made their escape by river. When the King, accompanied by eighty or so soldiers, burst into the Chamber and took over the Speaker's chair, a wholly unprecedented breach of parliamentary privilege, there was no one to arrest. From this moment, with the King's humiliation so public, and at the hands of the institution that sought to control him, civil war became possible, if not yet inevitable. It is absolutely right when looking at the origins of the Civil Wars to emphasize the religious and political background, complicated by the different needs and desires of three nations under one king. But it is also the case that violently opposed personalities, and spectacularly ill-judged gesture politics, and consequent loss of face, did as much to set the country at war with itself.

When Charles's repeated attempts to make the arrests failed, the Parliamentarians moved to control the administration of the City of London, including the armed forces the City leaders could raise. This was the sign for Charles to leave the capital. When he returned, seven years later, it was as a prisoner, on trial for his life. Two separate wars would be fought before then, but it is worth pointing out how early the traditional roles of king and rebels were reversed, well before Charles faced the ultimate punishment. At first, he went to Windsor, where he was joined by only a handful of loyal servants. When he tried to secure the important strategic port of Hull, a Parliamentarian was swiftly installed to prevent him.

Sensing the weakness of his position, he held out the possibility of a compromise, dropping the impeachment of the five Members and assenting to two of the House's bills. But both sides were stalling for time, and another break came when Charles refused assent to the Militia Ordinance, which gave Parliament control over summoning an army – an understandably delicate subject when it was unclear against whom that army would be directed. Both sides sought popular backing, but Parliament was able to do so with more apparent legitimacy, putting into effect a village-by-village programme to swear to the Protestation (a more digestible summary of the grievances that were later expanded on in the Grand Remonstrance). This was not the kind of oath that rebels had sworn to in the past, when a relatively small group promised to act for the greater good, as had happened in the Provisions of Oxford back in 1258. It was in fact much closer to the sort of countrywide, 'official' declaration of loyalty that King John had insisted on even longer ago, in 1205. But in 1642 it was Parliament, not the King, that received the homage.

Moves like this forced Charles into the role of rebel in his own kingdom. He tried to call his opponents' bluff, marching on Hull to 'inspect' the arsenal there, but was refused entry. Although the war of words continued between the King and his Parliament, preparations went on for real action, with the Navy throwing in their lot with Parliament. In July, Parliament appointed Robert Devereux, Earl of Essex (whose father's rebellion had temporarily disinherited him at the age of twelve), as commander-in-chief of their army. The following month, Charles raised his standard at Nottingham. The English Civil Wars had begun. Charles's ceremony was more reminiscent of the rebel calls to arms of Thomas Wyatt or the Earl of Northumberland in the previous century than of the actions of an anointed king. It was a disappointing gesture too, as he 'found the place much emptier than he thought the Fame of his Standard would have suffered it to be', according to Clarendon. On a blustery day, the standard itself fell down, and 'could not be fixed again in a day or two till the tempest was allayed'.

From Edgehill to Marston Moor

In fact, though a skirmish at Southam, near Warwick, took place the following day between Royalists led by the Earl of Northampton and a Parliamentarian force which included John Hampden among its commanders, neither side that summer was in a position to fight. This, the first Civil War, lasted four years, in part because it took that long for Parliament to press home the advantage that it seemed to have had from the beginning. In October 1642, the two sides fought the first pitched battle of the war, at Edgehill, by which time Charles had gathered a more substantial force based on the personal levies of loyal nobles and gentry (including a substantial number of Catholics, despite an explicit ban). It was hard fought, and afterwards Charles wrote about the 'defeat of the rebels', but actually, the battle was inconclusive. If the Royalists had gained an advantage, they failed to capitalize – by not moving in on the capital. That was because the citizens of London made a great enough show of force to deter them. The Civil Wars were rarely a simple case of the 'people' versus the 'ruling class'. Regional loyalties counted for more than class ones. But in London, at least, the anti-Royal mood that had grown up around the parliamentary disputes of the past two years was sustained.

What became clear in the first two years of conflict was that neither side had quite enough resources for total victory, and although both sought outside help – the 'rebels' from the Scottish covenanters and the King in Ireland – the situation initially favoured Charles. Throughout the wars, there were large parts of the country that remained resolutely neutral, though 'pacification treaties' signed early on did not last. Nor was organized violence restricted to the official armies. Several counties had more or less spontaneous uprisings of 'Clubmen', so-armed to defend their territory against the incursions of either side, though their conservatism tended to favour the Royalists. On one occasion, at Hambledon Hill in Dorset, Oliver Cromwell was faced by a force of around 2,000 making demands, and a few were killed, the rest imprisoned overnight, after Cromwell realized they would not disperse quietly. Many thousands fought, and many thousands died in the Civil Wars, but most men and women tried to stay out of the main conflict.

In 1643, there were even some abortive peace negotiations, which, despite being overwhelmingly favourable to Charles, only failed to pass through Parliament by seven votes. For all the King's military vulnerability, and despite the development of a new, parliamentary theory of government, the position that Parliament found itself in, while its supporters clung to a belief in monarchy, was not very different from that of so many rebels before. Unless they could provide an alternative candidate for the throne (and none was available), sooner or later they would have to treat with Charles. Later, the Civil Wars took an unprecedented, and unforeseen, turn, but for six years, at least, the essential problem facing Parliament was the same that faced the barons of John or Henry III's time. The leadership of the Parliamentarian army, which included Essex, Edward Montagu, Earl of Manchester, Lord Fairfax and his son, Sir Thomas, is another indication that this was not, or not yet, so very different a rebellion from those predecessors, which had been commanded by men of the same rank. The King's advantage was succinctly described by Manchester, to the rising star of the Army, the MP for Huntingdon, Lieutenant-General Oliver Cromwell:

The king cares not how oft he fights, but it concerns us to be wary, for in fighting we venture all to nothing. If we beat the king ninety-nine times he would be king still, and his posterity, and we subjects still; but if he beat us but once we should be hanged, and our posterity be undone.

This remark was made after Parliament's greatest victory so far, in one of the largest battles ever fought on English soil, Marston Moor in Yorkshire, 2 July 1644. There – especially if you read the Anglocentric reports of the London press which ignored the Scottish contribution – Cromwell's cavalry had excelled, charging the Royalist lines just as a storm broke in the evening, after a tense face-off lasting the whole of that day. Cromwell himself had ignored a flesh wound in the neck, and it was from this time that the press christened him (and later by extension his troops) 'Ironside'. The victory at Marston Moor of Manchester, the Fairfaxes and Cromwell, with their Scots allies, gave Parliament control over the North, and should have spelt the end for the King. But the advantage was again allowed to slip away. Manchester, Essex and Cromwell all made mistakes in the autumn of campaigning that followed. At Newbury, Cromwell didn't use his cavalry quickly enough to assist Manchester, with whom he was falling out. In the West, the Earl of Essex was forced to surrender and escape alone after defeat at Lostwithiel in Cornwall.

Army of God

The effect of these setbacks was the birth of an institution which, perhaps more than any other, put England on the road from rebellion and civil war to revolution: the New Model Army. In the beginning, the New Model was a purely military solution, and not a particularly radical one, to the problem of how to direct the military effort more effectively. The Self-Denying Ordinance (the fact that it was still called an 'ordinance' gives a clue to the conservative mindset which prevailed in Parliament; it could not become an Act without royal assent) excluded Members of both Houses from positions of command in the Army. This had the happy effect of dismissing the ineffectual Essex and Manchester. Their overall replacement, Sir Thomas Fairfax, was a young but experienced, no-nonsense professional soldier, who respected and admired Cromwell. Cromwell was at first the only MP who secured an exemption from the Ordinance, though this arrangement had to be renewed periodically. The creation of the Army was followed by an almost unbroken string of victories over the following year, with Cromwell at the forefront. Successes at Naseby, Langport and Basing House among others culminated in the surrender of the Royalist capital at Oxford, and the flight of the King to surrender to the Scots at Newark, in June 1646.

The spectacular course the war had taken increasingly convinced Cromwell that Providence was at work. He hoped that what seemed to him the clearest of indications that 'the face of God' was smiling on Parliament would help to heal the rifts that had emerged in their camp, particularly along religious lines, over the past four years of civil war. The man whom the Royalists called 'King Pym' had died in 1643, and no convincing leadership in the Commons had emerged to replace him. There was nothing so contained as a political party at this time, but religious affiliation counted for much, particularly where the Scottish alliance was concerned. The Scots had taken up arms for the Presbyterian Kirk, and the only grounds on which they had agreed to fight for the English Parliament was if a victory would introduce Presbyterianism to England. Thus a split developed in Parliament between English supporters of this position, the Presbyterians, and 'Independents', whose religion embraced various shades of 'Puritan' practice, but who at least, like Cromwell, hoped for some degree of 'tolerance' (though that did not extend to the Laudianism of Charles's Church, let alone to Catholics). It was no coincidence that Charles surrendered to the Scots, although he was handed over to the English Parliament on the payment of £200,000 (inflation had apparently not much affected the price of a king's ransom since Richard the Lionheart's day) and placed under house arrest at Holdenby in Northamptonshire. The King still hoped to play one party off against the other.

More immediately, he might hope to benefit from the rebellion within a rebellion that surfaced between Parliament and the Army, and within the Army itself. The first of these ruptures occurred when the grateful Parliament, and in particular its Presbyterian supporters, did what civilian leaders so often do once an army has done their dirty work. The politicians turned on the soldiers. Although it was conceded that the Catholic rebellion in Ireland would need military resources, the New Model was to be drastically reduced. It was also not to be paid properly. When the Army petitioned Parliament to guarantee its pay and working conditions, Parliament responded with the 'Declaration of Dislike', which branded the Army that had so brilliantly (and so recently) secured Parliament's cause, and at such cost, as 'enemies of the state'.

This was a split between the mainstream of the Army, including its leadership, and Parliament, but there was another movement among the soldiers, and another petition at this time, that perhaps accounts for the MPs' overreaction. A number of pamphlets had begun to circulate in the past year, most of them written by one of, or a combination of, three men: John Lilburne, Richard Overton and William Walwyn. These writings associated religious nonconformity with political freedom. The 'Levellers', as their enemies christened them, were moved at first by what they saw as the monolithic threat of Presbyterianism, which would leave no place for the sectarian congregations that had sprung up in London in particular, but which were also mirrored by religious arrangements in the Army itself. Many took a long view of the origins of their oppression, blaming not Charles in particular but the 'Norman yoke', which even the repeated resistance of rebels had not thrown off. 'It is wonderful', Overton and Walwyn wrote in *A Remonstrance of Many Thousand Citizens* (1646):

that the failings of former kings to bring our forefathers into bondage (together with the trouble and danger that some of them drew upon themselves and their posterity by those their unjust endeavours) had not wrought in our latter kings a resolution to rely on and trust only to justice and square dealing with the people.

When would they ever learn?

The Levellers' 'Large Petition', which came to the attention of Parliament in March 1647, was more forward-looking, ascribing more power to the Commons alone than they seemed willing to accept. It called too for the abolition of tithes, the reform of the law, and the removal of the royal veto and of the Lords' jurisdiction. If Parliament had made more of a distinction between this radical programme, which was duly burnt by the common hangman later in the year, and the unexceptionable demands of the Army's leadership for fair treatment, it could surely have avoided the confrontation that was to unfold over the coming months, from which Parliament's authority would not recover until well after the Restoration. Instead, Parliament followed up the intemperate Declaration of Dislike with further provocations over the next three months, culminating in a peremptory order for the Army to disband. The Presbyterians controlling Parliament reckoned that their control of the trained bands of London, which amounted to around 20,000 men, would enable them to resist any 'mutiny'. Soon enough they were proved wrong, as the Army came out into open revolt, taken up after some hesitation by Fairfax and Cromwell. The Army's first move was yet another example, on an individual scale, of the law of unintended consequences that was the most consistent factor throughout the Civil Wars. A junior officer in Fairfax's life guard was sent to prevent the removal of the King by the Presbyterian party. Instead, Cornet Joyce himself abducted Charles from his house arrest. It is hard to believe, but apparently true, that it was the King who suggested going to Newmarket, for the air. It just so happened that that was where the Army was gathering to consider its next move.

The Army met at Kentford Heath, outside Newmarket, on 5 June 1647, and issued its *Solemn Engagement* under Fairfax's name (though it is thought to have been written by Cromwell's son-in-law, Commissary-General Henry Ireton), addressed to the Speaker of the House of Commons. This was no Levelling document but a reiteration of appeals for fair treatment. It did, however, give notice of a reorganization within the ranks, the formation of a General Council of the Army to canvass and represent the soldiers' views. As well as senior officers, this body was to include two officers and two common soldiers from each regiment. This made it an institution based on a far more representative model than Parliament itself, and the fact that the Army had been formed as a national body meant that it could claim to speak for a fairly wide swathe of the country's opinion. More important than what was said, or how, however, was the fact that the Army was on the move. Day by day, it made a slow advance on London. As the Army advanced, its demands became tougher: its enemies in Parliament were to be impeached, Members who had abused their powers should be purged, parliamentary sittings and representation were to be reformed. The Army was hardly hell-bent on forcing the issue, however, and for two months the soldiers debated and considered how to proceed. Only when Parliament, and then the King himself, now at Hampton Court, rejected any chance of compromise, did Fairfax enter the city, at the beginning of August. The trained bands offered no resistance.

The Putney debates

Looking from a twenty-first-century perspective, with all our experience of military coups, of the rules of generals and colonels, even in countries with democratic traditions, it seems remarkable that in 1647 in England, a country with no such tradition, the entry of the Army did not precipitate an immediate, complete takeover of government. True, some Members of Parliament were dismissed, and proceedings continued under the Army's shadow, but Fairfax removed his troops to Putney. What followed instead was talk, and of a kind never before witnessed in England: an open debate under the auspices of the new General Council on how the Army, and by extension the country, should go on. The Putney Debates were extraordinary not just for what was said, though some of that has resonated to this day, but for the fact that they happened at all.

The Levellers, several of whom had been made members of the General Council, set the agenda for the debates with the issue of two pamphlets: *The Case of the Army Truly Stated*, which has been justly described as 'long and rambling', and the more succinct, more revolutionary statement of first principles, *An Agreement of the People*. The *Agreement*, in which the authors discussed 'at how high a rate we value our just freedom', and made a declaration of their 'native rights', was read out in full at Putney and then discussed at length, and in detail. In the transcripts of these discussions we hear the voice of those outnumbered men who were struggling to articulate something that we would now instantly recognize, but which they could not yet name: representative democracy. Colonel Thomas Rainsborough stated the case most memorably:

For really I think that the poorest he that is in England has a life to live as the greatest he; and therefore truly, sir, I think it's clear that every man that is to live under a government ought by his own consent to put himself under that government . . .

Ireton, who spoke for the ruling body of the Army, was incredulous: '*That's* the meaning of this "according to the number of the inhabitants"?' (the passage from the *Agreement* that was under discussion). Ireton's statement of the more conservative case, 'that no person has a right to an interest or share in the disposing or determining of the affairs of the kingdom . . . that has not a permanent fixed interest in this kingdom' – by which he meant property – was far more in keeping with the temper of the age. It was also, and this point tends to get lost when past politics are refracted too much through the prism of the present, closer to what the Levellers themselves stood for. Rainsborough, who had not previously been associated with the Levellers, took at Putney a more radical position than they had. The *Agreement* itself, for example, did not discuss voting rights. A later version, published as a manifesto for a full-scale mutiny, did, and specifically excluded servants and recipients of alms.

There was an attempt at a mutiny, following the closing of the Putney Debates by Cromwell in November 1647, but it was headed off almost without bloodshed once Fairfax had managed to address the concerns of the men. John Lilburne continued to be a thorn to the Army's conscience, and was in prison for most of his remaining years, but his Levelling energy was transformed into the less overtly political emerging faith of Quakerism in 1655. Other Leveller leaders, such as Richard Overton and William Walwyn, survived the wars and they too gave up their cause. The mutiny that Fairfax and Cromwell put down at Burford in 1649, summarily executing three ringleaders, had to wait until the 1970s to find the sort of recognition accorded to other pre-Socialist martyrs. Every year, on the anniversary of the executions, at Burford church in the Cotswolds, the Levellers are remembered, their complex legacy channelled to the uncontroversially good causes of justice and democracy.

Cruel necessity

The rebellion that the leaders of the Army faced was not their main concern in these years. Charles, whom even most Levellers believed could still be accommodated at the top of a reformed constitution, was about to take a step closer to the block. He had attempted to escape from Hampton Court, been recaptured, and was now confined on the Isle of Wight, but he was still allowed to receive visitors, and he still kept up negotiations with Parliament, while secretly sounding out the Scots, who did not want the King to come to an agreement with a Parliament now dominated by Independents. The day after Christmas, 1647 (celebrations had by now been officially prohibited), Charles made the alliance known as 'The Engagement', and the Scots leaders agreed to raise an army to fight the King's enemies. They might have reflected that they had come full circle, that the Covenanters who had precipitated the Civil Wars in England were now to fight on the King's side. But the King himself was still a prisoner, and when Fairfax and Cromwell defeated the Scottish and Royalist attempts to co-ordinate an armed invasion, the second Civil War, which lasted less than four months, was over. As hostilities resumed, Charles was excoriated by the Parliamentarians as a 'man of blood', who levied war on his own people – much like an incorrigible rebel, in fact.

Was Charles doomed from the moment he signed the Engagement – unless his allies had pulled off a very unlikely win, that is? Historians used to say so, and the mood of the Army, of Parliament, and possibly of the majority of the country, which cannot have relished the return of war, was certainly unsympathetic. But even at this late stage the King's fate might have been different. True, Ireton called for 'exemplary justice' for Charles in *The Remonstrance to the Army*, but the document was rejected by Parliament. Perhaps the only man who could have saved the King, and dissuaded Parliament from the 'purge' (presided over by Colonel Pride, but orchestrated by Ireton) in December 1648 that removed those Members who rejected the Remonstrance, was Cromwell. He had by now emerged as the driving force of the Army in whom were united military ability, political will and religious certitude. But for the time being he stayed away, conducting the siege of Pontefract at which Ireton's debating adversary Thomas Rainsborough was killed, leading to a great outpouring of grief in the capital, which can only have increased the mood for revenge on the man who had brought the country to war again.

Cromwell delayed his return longer than necessary, staying away until just after the Purge, and after the King had been brought to the mainland. Perhaps he was wrestling with his conscience, trying, without a hint of cynicism, to decide whether God, who had once again smiled on the Army, was insisting that the 'man of blood' must pay for all that he had spilt. If Cromwell had decided that Charles's death was not a spiritual, but merely a political obligation (when the deed was done, Cromwell himself described it as a 'cruel necessity'), it is possible that he could have steered his comrades away from it. There were hopes that the King could be persuaded to abdicate, but when he refused, Cromwell took his place among the specially invented court that sat in judgment over 'the said Charles Stuart', and signed the death warrant along with fifty-eight others. The King defended himself courageously, sticking to his conception of anointed kingship and refusing to plead for his life. The reaction of the watching public at the execution, crying out in horror and then dipping handkerchiefs in the royal blood (just as they had dipped them in Thomas Wyatt's), hardly spoke of a people crying out for a revolution. In death, Charles had proved a far better advertisement for the sanctity of monarchy than he ever had in life.

The rejection of the idea of 'replacing' Charles with his younger son, the sort of solution that would almost certainly have been taken in earlier rebellions, shows that, for all its similarities to previous episodes in English history, the logic of the Civil Wars created something new: a gathering sense that monarchy, not just the monarch, was the root of the country's ills. Why else would divine providence have presided over so public and legally justified a condemnation of Charles? John Milton, who at this time had almost given up poetry to bear official witness in prose to the great events of his day, even as his sight deserted him, praised his fellow countrymen, to whom God had given 'such strength of heart that you did not shrink from being the first men to pass judgement in a notable trial upon a king, conquered and made captive by your arms, and to execute him when he had been found guilty'. Milton was still against tyranny rather than monarchy per se when he wrote those lines. But the idea that monarchy must be abolished had taken hold in much of the Army, and in the 'Rump' of Parliament that remained. No one, however, was under much illusion that it was shared in the country at large. The popularity of *Eikon Basilike* ('the royal image'), the forged meditations of Charles I 'in his solicitudes and sufferings', demonstrated that the mystique of kingship had not been extinguished, and Parliament was moved to commission Milton to write a reply, *Eikonoklastes* ('image breaker'), which never made it into a second edition. The Commonwealth and then the Protectorate that followed never risked any real exposure to the electorate, even on the limited franchise that still obtained. Cromwell's record as leader of his country stands favourable comparison with any monarch's, but if it achieved a measure of popularity, his refusal to transform his appeal into the anointed magic of kingship made it almost impossible for his office to outlive his death. Richard Cromwell, the son who succeeded him, was not the hopeless incompetent of Royalist propaganda, but he had not achieved the special position of his father either. How could he? Oliver Cromwell was a one-off, a man who had risen to power purely by his own ability, and who, for all his 'warts' – including the streak of Protestant zealotry that makes him so hard for a modern observer to warm to – had done so for the purest motives.

Heaven in earth

In the year of the King's execution, 1649, the sense that alternative ways of arranging society, of living and being governed, might flourish in these unique conditions took shape in various groups. The best-remembered, though their impact at the time was hardly epoch-making, were the Diggers of Gerrard Winstanley. Winstanley, a failed clothes merchant whose life had been transformed by a vision that 'the earth should be made a common treasury of livelihood to whole mankind, without respect of persons', tried to put his revelation into practice. On 1 April 1649, a small group occupied common land on St George's Hill in Surrey and planted parsnips, beans and carrots, as the modest first step in a programme of economic and agricultural revolution. Although a few other such camps briefly sprang up, exactly a century after the 'camping tyme' of Kett and his followers, Winstanley met with no more success in the long term. On the complaints of local landowners, the Diggers were monitored by the Army, and when the camp transferred onto Cobham Heath, they were forcibly removed. The sites of these two proto-Communist experiments are now respectively occupied by a private golf course and the dream homes of Chelsea footballers (this was not the first place of rebellion to suffer such a fate: Blackheath, where Tyler, Cade, the Cornish and other rebels had gathered, became the first golf course in England when the game was imported by James I). The English Civil Wars may have prompted a political earthquake, but – despite the fears of contemporaries and the wishful thinking of later observers – the social world was never truly 'turned upside down'.

Winstanley called his movement '*True* Levellers', not to mark his philosophy out as more politically radical than others of that name but as more genuinely Christian. For, like other millennial movements of the period – such as the Fifth Monarchists, whose looking towards an imminent Second Coming to be preceded by a 'rule of saints' appealed for a time to Cromwell's strongest religious instincts, or the libertarian Ranters, whose public cursing, fornication and displays of nudity emphatically didn't – the Diggers were inspired by scripture, not by secular distractions. Their suppression, along with the more violent reaction visited on the Levellers themselves that year, shows how conservative the 'English Revolution' was. In this, Cromwell and his fellow Parliamentarians were like the majority of English rebels who went before them. They took up arms reluctantly, protesting their loyalty to much of the status quo; and if they met with success, their instincts were not to continue to push for change, but to restrict those who did. As the events outside Burford church demonstrated, they were perfectly prepared to use force on 'their own people' to do so.

Despite attempts by philosophers like James Harrington to give it a theoretical underpinning, English republicanism proved to have very shallow foundations, particularly after it was concentrated in one man. That happened in 1653, when Cromwell disbanded the Rump Parliament that remained after Pride's Purge, as it refused to agree to new elections, and took the role of Lord Protector. The choice of title was perhaps another indication of Cromwell's essential conservatism, as he searched for a role with a precedent – although the examples of previous Protectors, from Richard of York, to Richard of Gloucester, to the Duke of Somerset, were hardly auspicious ones. The 'Good Old Cause' for which the Civil Wars had been fought, and which was invoked on Cromwell's death in pamphlet after pamphlet, meant different things to different people. But in the right hands it might have proved a rallying point for resisting resurgent Royalism. When Cromwell died in 1658, the Restoration of Charles II was not a foregone conclusion. Charles had failed to make a dent in the Commonwealth seven years before, when he headed a Scottish invasion that was defeated at the Battle of Worcester. This was the episode remembered for Charles's escape in disguise, and the most famous night of rough sleeping in English history (in Richard Penderel's 'Royal Oak', which has proved a more popular pub name than Kett's Oak of

Reformation). Colourful it may have been, but it was also a Royalist disaster. Later Royalist uprisings met with equally little success, particularly when they were organized by the timid and unenterprising 'Sealed Knot' of Royalist exiles (it seems odd that the vigorous present-day re-enactors of Civil War battles take their name from a group whose record of inaction and failure was unbroken).

This was true even after Richard Cromwell had been removed by the machinations of his brother-in-law, Charles Fleetwood, and the Commonwealth returned, with the Rump Parliament. A series of Royalist risings in the summer of 1659 came to nothing, even though there was growing fear of the influence of religious radicals, such as Fifth Monarchists and Quakers (who were not yet committed to the pacifism with which we associate them), which fuelled a reaction to republican politics. The Royalist cause seemed to have been crushed for good when Sir George Booth, leader of the only sustained rebellion that summer, was defeated by a Commonwealth army on 19 August at Winnington Bridge in Cheshire, often cited as the last battle of the Civil Wars (so that, curiously, they ended with a Parliamentarian victory).

But the tensions in the Commonwealth proved far more effective in breaking it apart than the threat of the King over the water. The division that had never been effectively bridged was between Army and Parliament. When the brief truce between the Army and the restored Rump Parliament broke down, Army leaders attempted to enforce their solution as they had in 1648. Instead, the clamour grew for free elections. General George Monck, a trusted Cromwellian veteran who had held aloof from the death throes of the Protectorate, marched south at the beginning of 1660 from his posting in Scotland. Waiting until the threat of opposition had melted away, Monck entered the capital on 3 February. He restored the Long Parliament, which duly dissolved itself on 16 March. In the subsequent elections, although Royalists were supposed to be excluded, sixty-one managed to be returned. Within the week, they had issued a declaration of loyalty to King Charles II, in exile in the Netherlands. A week after that, the King returned, to general if not universal rejoicing. Whether Monck had meant to do so from the beginning of the year, when he began his march south, or whether he had been convinced that there was no other workable alternative as the atomization of the Commonwealth became clear to him on his entry into London, he had somehow effected a bloodless coup. In this sense, like Mary I's 'replacement' of Queen Jane, the Restoration of Charles II was an unusually successful English rebellion.

The Restoration was certainly a defeat for much of the 'Good Old Cause', and the retribution visited on the 'regicides', in some cases posthumously, their bodies exhumed and put on display, showed that the new regime was not going to ignore what had happened. The new King was at first able to manoeuvre fairly freely over the matters of army command and religion that had fuelled the animosities of the Civil Wars, although Parliament's role in approving taxation was established. It would be difficult to argue then or now that this small achievement had been worth the bloodshed. When later observers claim to see a revolution in the 1640s and '50s, they allude to the great changes in politics and society that seemed to have taken place. But for seventeenth-century observers, the idea of 'revolution' was much closer to the medieval concept of the wheel of fortune. By 1660, the great wheel of English politics seemed to have turned full circle.

12. Good and Glorious

Thomas Venner to the Immortal Seven 1660–88

The bonfires and loyal toasts that greeted the return of the King gave a false impression of a united country. The traditional view of the first part of the reign of Charles II is summed up by Gilbert Burnet (1643–1715), historian and Bishop of Salisbury who wrote a *History of My Own Time*: 'the reign of King Charles was pretty serene and calm at home. A nation weary of a long civil war was not easily brought into fears and jealousies which . . . might end in confusions and troubles.' In fact, fear and jealousy were at times the staple diet of the Restoration, and from the beginning. The return of the Stuarts frustrated the hopes of those who thought monarchy itself was anathema, and led some convinced republicans into sporadic, but isolated, rebellion. In the longer term, it was another of the issues that had underpinned the Civil Wars, religious controversy, and which was fudged at the Restoration, that returned as the deciding factor in precipitating two major rebellions. The second of those would be remodelled as a revolution; in reality, it bore many of the hallmarks of another conquest.

The Republic had shallow roots when compared to the monarchy, but there were still men and women prepared to fight for it. This form of rebellion was enmeshed with a spectrum of religious practice that had thrived in the Interregnum: dissent. The years of the Civil Wars had seen a proliferation, if not an explosion, of Protestant sects and 'gathered' churches, such as George Fox's 'Friends of the Truth', nicknamed the Quakers, as well as growing numbers of Baptists and the above-mentioned Fifth Monarchists (the previous four monarchies, by the way, were the Assyrian, the Persian, the Greek and the Roman). All of these posed genuine or imagined threats to the restored monarchy and Church. True, Charles seemed prepared to take a measured attitude to these dissenters. The manifesto on which Charles was welcomed back into the country, the Declaration of Breda, made specific reference to these 'differences of opinion in matter of religion' and promised 'liberty to tender consciences, and that no man shall be disquieted or called in question' for them, as long they did not 'disturb the peace of the kingdom'. But the actions of one diehard rebel, Thomas Venner, went a long way to making sure that Charles went back on his promise.

Venner was a London cooper who had sampled a colonist's life in New England, where he was converted to Fifth Monarchism, but returned in 1651. His first efforts to hasten the arrival of the kingdom of Heaven came in 1655, when he talked about making use of his position as Master Cooper at the Tower of London to blow the place up. Although he was arrested and lost his job, he was free later that year and began discussing plans for a coup against the Protectorate with committed republicans. Although these too came to the attention of the authorities, Venner was still at large the following year, when he took part in an actual rising, backed by manifestoes, an emblem (of a lion 'couching with this motto round it, Who shall rowze him up?'), and a clandestine organization of cells. But in April 1657 government soldiers swooped on about twenty-five rebels at Mile End Green before their plans for a theocracy and government according to biblical lore had been put to much of a test. Venner was sent to prison again, without a trial, and by the time of the Restoration he was free once more. His zeal was undimmed, possibly because no one seemed to take him seriously enough to prosecute him for what were undoubtedly treasonous acts. In January 1661, Venner led the last of his attempts to overthrow the government. He and about thirty-five followers made an attempt on the City, were chased off by a detachment of the Lord Mayor's troops, but returned, after a night in Highgate Woods, for a last stand at Cheapside, where they fought off a regiment for half an hour. Twenty of their number were killed, and Venner and others were taken prisoner. Samuel Pepys expressed the general amazement that such a small number of 'Fanatiques . . . should dare and do so much mischief . . . We did believe them . . . to be at least 500.' Less than two weeks later, while going about his daily business, Pepys passed Venner and another condemned rebel 'upon a sledge', on their way to be hanged, drawn and quartered.

The presence of known republicans as well as millenarians like Venner in the conspiracy gave the impression that the rising was more broadly based than it really was. As Fifth Monarchists were few in number, the reaction fell hardest on fellow dissenters who seemed to espouse alternative forms of government, and most especially on the Quakers, who were arrested by the thousand, and only began to be released when it became impractical to keep them in such large numbers. The intolerant tone set by this early response was echoed in the first Parliament of Charles's reign, called after his Coronation in April 1661 (the Parliament that had welcomed him back was not officially entitled to the name, not having been summoned by the king, so is known as the 'Convention'). The 'Cavalier Parliament', which sat from 1661 until 1679, passed in its first four years the body of laws that came to be known as the 'Clarendon Code', after the Lord Chancellor (and future historian) of the time, though Clarendon himself was no great supporter of them.

The King also had to be coerced into support, being far more convinced of the need for the sort of toleration he had espoused in the Declaration of Breda. Parliament, on the other hand, used the continued discovery by a network of spies of a number of conspiracies – some more genuine than others – as a means of whipping up support for their repressive policies. Those policies had as much to do with pursuing their own agenda of a Laudian Church and a 'loyal' urban population as the actual suppression of rebellion. The revelation of the republican 'Tong plot' in November 1662 was followed not only by a further round of executions, but also by the more rigorous enforcement of the Quaker Act, which was aimed at anyone who refused the Oath of Allegiance. Quakers would not take oaths as part of their faith, so the measure fell particularly hard on them. Quakers suffered even more after some of their number were convicted of involvement in a rebellion which began around Derwentdale, County Durham, in 1663, spreading even as its conspirators were discovered into Yorkshire.

There were widespread arrests and twenty-four executions. The Conventicle Act followed in 1664, this time with the full support of the King, who referred to the 'late treason in the North' in his speech at the opening of the new session of Parliament. The Act had a series of escalating penalties for any adult who attended an unorthodox religious gathering of more than five, including imprisonment and transportation to the colonies. Two hundred and thirty men and women were forcibly removed to the colonies, and hundreds more were imprisoned. Occasionally, their courage and forbearance impressed even those who were meant to guard them: in Bristol, for example, one crew refused to transport three Quakers. Quakers were the main victims of the Act simply because they saw it as their duty not to avoid its penalties. Other sects – whether Presbyterian, Baptist, or congregationalists – were happier to dodge the authorities. As the terms of the Act meant that a meeting had to be interrupted as it was happening, an early-warning system, if you were willing to stoop to one, could be effective. So the Act merely strengthened the Quakers in their convictions, and committed them to pacifism, while doing nothing to halt potential insurrections. Once again, rebellion shapes our history in unexpected ways. Without the experience of the failed Venner and Northern uprisings, followed by this period of oppression, the Quakers might not have latched on to the doctrine of pacifism that still defines them, and which has proved an inspiration across centuries and continents. Mahatma Gandhi was not 'much struck' by the Quaker practice of sitting in silence: 'in India, it will fall flat,' he wrote. But he also commented that 'the history of the Quakers has been made glorious by non-violent non-cooperation'.

The last republican plot of Charles's reign came in its fifth year, and it had nothing to do with the Quakers. The year 1665 was remembered as one when the bubonic plague returned to London, and those who could do so left the city to escape the deadly epidemic. One loyal servant who stayed behind was General Monck, now Duke of Albemarle and Commander-in-Chief of the Army. Ordered to root out widely rumoured rebellions, Albemarle and his men uncovered plans for a rising on the significant date of

3 September, the anniversary of Cromwell's death and his two great victories over the Scots at Worcester (when Charles had had to run for his life) and Dunbar. It was alleged that there was a plan to set the city alight, an allegation that was to bear significant fruit in the following year, when London did go up in flames and conspirators (though Catholic ones) were blamed. The leader of the plot was Henry Danvers, who had conspired (like Thomas Venner) against the Protectorate and had been implicated in previous schemes against Charles such as the 'Tong plot'. Danvers, a Baptist turned Fifth Monarchist and a committed republican, seems to have led something of a charmed life. To the government, he was a rebel Scarlet Pimpernel. Albemarle had him arrested on suspicion of a plan to assassinate Charles and re-establish a republic, but, on the way to the Tower, Danvers was rescued by a crowd of supporters. He was able to slip away and avoid recapture, despite the efforts of the normally efficient Restoration spy network. This was by no means the last that would be heard of Danvers. He turned up again in the two later causes célèbres of Charles's reign, the Rye House plot and the Popish plot (though he became an informer in the put-up job of the latter). Still avoiding arrest, he tried to assist with the Duke of Monmouth's uprising against Charles's successor, James II, in 1685, and, when that failed, made his escape to the Netherlands. In an age when rebels died by the hundred, many on very little evidence, Henry Danvers was able to take a leading role in at least four rebellions, and died in his late sixties in his own bed.

Eight other conspirators were not so lucky: they were hanged, joining the lengthening list of victims of the Merry Monarch's sense of humour failure when it came to potential attempts on his life. More broadly, the victims of Danvers's conspiracy were dissenters in general, who were once again subjected to a round of arrests, with the added risk that prison overcrowding in a plague year could be even more lethal than usual. Parliament, sitting in Oxford, also passed the 'Five Mile Act', the final repressive measure to which fear of rebellion had given impetus. The targets this time were those Anglican ministers who had already been ejected as a consequence of the earlier Act of Uniformity, which had made the Prayer Book and Laudian ceremonial compulsory and resulted in the expulsion of 961 clergymen from their positions. These almost universally unrebellious souls were now, in the wake of the Danvers affair, forbidden to live within five miles of the parish from which they had been ejected, or to find work as schoolteachers (a natural outlet now closed off), unless they declared their loyalty and rejection of rebellion. Some moved, some willingly made the declaration, and very few were prosecuted. But this was hardly the 'liberty to tender consciences' the King had promised from Breda.

Catholic panics

Nonetheless, this final stone in the edifice of repression constructed by the Cavalier Parliament could have been argued to have done its job. For ten years, Charles was able to govern in relative peace (though he chose to wage a costly war, against the Dutch). The trigger of the final crisis of his reign, of one real and one imaginary plot, of a full-scale rebellion in his successor's reign, and finally of another revolution, lay closer to home than the stirs of Venner, Danvers and co., or the perceived threats of those self-possessed Quakers who still refused to remove their hats in the presence of their betters. The Popish plot, Exclusion Crisis, the Rye House plot, Monmouth's rebellion and the Glorious Revolution, all packed into the ten years from 1678 to 1688, revolved around Charles's brother James, Duke of York, and future King of England (Charles, despite his rugby team of illegitimate children, never produced an heir). In 1672, in secret, James converted to Catholicism. By 1676, he had ceased attending Anglican services, and his 'secret' was widely known. What was not known, and might have occasioned an even more hysterical reaction than the campaign against James that followed, was that Charles himself had also flirted with Catholicism, and had taken the incredible risk of letting Louis XIV of France in on his soul-searching. The generally cynical character attributed to Charles has made some historians doubt the sincerity of his leanings at this time, but he did convert on his deathbed, so the King's religious conscience, such as it was, ultimately inclined towards Rome. In the immediate term, Charles dropped the idea when his alliance with Louis broke down, but James was already committed, and there was no doubting his sincerity.

The realization that the next king would be a Catholic promoted an atmosphere in which plots, or rumours of plots, might flourish. The more influential of the two conspiracies which arose in the latter part of Charles's reign was the one that actually never existed, the 'Popish plot' 'revealed' by a fantasist with an apparently mesmeric power over his audience, Titus Oates. Oates's lurid, detailed and ultimately contradictory stories of Catholic schemes to kill the King, overthrow the government and raise the nation in rebellion were brought before the Privy Council, and then before Parliament. Oates even implicated the Duke of York himself in the conspiracies, though James was eventually able to get his accuser convicted of libel. This was after Oates's stories had led to the deaths of thirty-five men and played a direct part in bringing about the so-called Exclusion Crisis that caused a break between King and Parliament as serious as any before the Civil Wars. What Parliament wanted to exclude was the succession of a Catholic, something the brother of the Catholic in question would never agree to. The split over this issue led to the great divide in English party and national politics between 'Tories' and 'Whigs': the former, defenders of the rights of royal succession despite any difficulties of religion; the latter seeing a Catholic on the throne as the first step towards an absolutist monarchy, which would force popery onto the country at large. (Both names began as insults: whig for a Scottish raider, tory for an Irish outlaw.) Charles perhaps read the mood of the nation better than his father had done, because in dissolving the second and third of three parliaments which attempted to bring in Exclusion, he did not precipitate a civil war, and his brother did, if only for a short time, succeed him.

Nevertheless, the last plot of Charles's reign, the Rye House plot, showed that Whig disaffection had a more extreme wing. The man around whom this plot centred, although he disavowed personal knowledge of it, was one whom many Whigs would like to have seen succeed Charles instead of his brother: James Scott, Duke of Monmouth. Monmouth was Charles's illegitimate son by Lucy Walter, a Welsh courtesan with whom Charles had had an affair when in exile. As a child, James had been snatched from his mother's side by his father's agents, only to be placed in the dubious care of one of the King's gentlemen of the bedchamber. Until the age of nine, he seems barely to have been educated and was not able to read or count. As a young man, he was feckless and spendthrift, but these were not necessarily qualities to disbar him from his father's affections, and he was eventually much indulged, set up with a marriage to a Scottish heiress, a dukedom and various sources of income. It was only after Monmouth began to listen to those who wished to see him instead of his uncle succeed Charles that relations between father and son became strained. In 1682, as Monmouth's popularity with certain sections of opinion was being loudly proclaimed, Whig leaders such as Anthony Ashley Cooper, the Earl of Shaftesbury, and William, Lord Russell, began to formulate plans for Monmouth to secure the succession, or, ultimately, to force it. Although Shaftesbury died soon afterwards, the schemes continued, eventually emerging, in so far as they can be reconstructed, as a plot to assassinate the King and his brother as they returned home from Newmarket races, combined with a general insurrection throughout the country and a simultaneous rising in Scotland.

The plot was revealed in June 1683 by one of the conspirators, and, as before, Charles and his government took the opportunity to cast their net wide to catch anyone who might be, or might be made to seem, involved. Though several plotters fled or traded evidence for their freedom, Lord Russell and the Earl of Essex were both arrested. Essex committed suicide, apparently cutting his own throat. Russell was sentenced to death. Monmouth himself had fled, but surrendered on the promise of a pardon, though his backsliding on that infuriated his ever-forgiving father so much that he spent nearly all the rest of the reign in exile. One man who was less fortunate was Algernon Sidney, who was certainly a committed republican (and therefore could be inculpated in the plot to remove the King, though not to replace him), but against whom only one witness could be found. The presiding judge, George Jeffreys, remembered for his vengeful part in the final act of Monmouth's life, decided that the words of Sidney's unpublished *Discourses Concerning Government*, which argued that 'seditions, tumults and wars, are justified by the laws of God and man', provided the vital second witness for a treason trial, and Sidney was duly sentenced to death, taking his place as a Whig martyr in the following century.

Monmouth's rebellion

Though it appears that Monmouth wanted to embrace a quiet life in exile in the Netherlands, the Rye House plot proved a dry run for the larger tragedy that was enacted two years later, when the Duke led a rebellion that saw the last pitched battle on English soil. This, in turn, prefigured the more successful, less bloody, end to James II's brief reign in the Glorious Revolution. Plans for an uprising against James were brought forward almost as soon as it was reported that Charles had died, of a stroke on 6 February 1685. It was perhaps this haste, more than anything else, that ensured that, when he landed in England, Monmouth did not discover the depth of support he had hoped for; he had not given James any time to lose the confidence of his people, merely assuming that the new King's religion – which was always associated with absolutism – would be enough to engender a spontaneous rising of all but diehard Tories and fellow Catholics against him. As James was careful at first to protest his innocence of any designs on the Protestant Church or the faith of his people in general, most of his subjects seemed to have been prepared to trust him, if watchfully.

Monmouth had consulted with Scottish allies, and, as with the Rye House plot, his rebellion was meant to be a co-ordinated affair. The Earl of Argyll duly raised the Highlands, and on 11 June, after battling difficult winds in the Channel, Monmouth landed at Lyme Regis in Dorset, with a tiny following of eighty-two men. Argyll's rising had already failed, and the following day he was in

Edinburgh prison, but Monmouth knew nothing of that yet, and in any case would have little choice but to press on. In his 'Declaration' issued on landing, the Duke alleged that James II had, Claudius-like, poisoned the King, Monmouth's father, but he was careful not to claim the throne himself, leaving that decision to Parliament. The refusal to put himself forward as king may have been more than a tactical move. Monmouth's declaration had been drafted by his chaplain, Robert Ferguson, a Scottish propagandist who had connections to exiled republicans. Ferguson was also a veteran conspirator who had been involved in the Rye House intrigue and was said to have exclaimed then that he would 'never be out of a plot so long as I live' – a promise that, like Henry Danvers, he was able to keep while saving his own skin. For its part, Parliament, filled with Tories, made its position clear when it had the Declaration burnt by the common hangman and issued a Bill of Attainder against Monmouth for high treason.

Initially, it looked as if Monmouth's plan to recruit his army when he arrived was working, as James II's government was slow to send a force to confront him. He was heartily welcomed in and around Lyme, an area he had toured five years before, establishing his 'royal' credentials then by 'touching for the king's evil', that quasi-religious ritual laying-on of hands for sufferers of scrofula in which the Stuarts revelled. In 1685, the Duke managed to raise about 3,000 men, which was more than the force that would eventually face him; but Monmouth's troops were poorly armed amateurs. His efforts were hampered by a lack of gentry support: without the leaders of local power, Monmouth could not hope to match a professional army. In an effort to gather more support on his return, Monmouth eventually proclaimed his right to the throne and reprised his royal 'cure'. Whatever its medical effects, as a recruiting tactic it was a failure. Monmouth's rebellion remained largely populist, and hardly any gentry joined it. Although the rebels were able to tour the West Country for almost a month, the commander-in-chief of the King's army, Lord Feversham, claimed he was only waiting until he was confident of defeating Monmouth with the fewest casualties. Feversham later became the butt of

Restoration wags, and he certainly had several natural disadvantages as a representative of England's establishment: he was a naturalized Frenchman (named Louis Duras), had more experience than expertise as a military commander – and he had a hole in his head, having been trepanned after he was nearly brained by falling timber. It came as no surprise to Feversham's critics back in London that Monmouth caught him napping. It was reported that the Earl, who had not bothered with proper reconnaissance, was still in bed when the Duke launched his night attack at Sedgemoor in Somerset. But by that time, with news having reached Monmouth of the failure of Argyll's rising in Scotland, and of a tightly controlled London's refusal to rise at all, the rebels were desperate men.

A short account of the battle was given by one of Monmouth's followers who had journeyed from London: Daniel Defoe, a church dissenter in the wholesale hosiery business from Stoke Newington, whose literary career had barely begun. Defoe was never very expansive about his part in Monmouth's rebellion, for which he secured a pardon two years later. But in his *Tour of the Whole Island of Great Britain* he wistfully describes how, if it had not been for bad luck or betrayal, which revealed the Duke's advance a moment too early, 'he had certainly cut the Lord Feversham's army all to pieces . . ., but by these circumstances, he was brought to battle on unequal terms and defeated: The rest I need not mention.' The rest, for a great number of rebels and followers, was death, either on the battlefield or at the gallows. Monmouth's rebellion, perhaps more than any since William the Conqueror had harried the North, is recalled principally for the reaction it met.

The Duke himself escaped the battlefield, but was captured two days later. It is usually seen as a sign of the pathetic circumstances of his rebellion that he was taken while disguised as a shepherd, hiding 'in a ditch'. Monmouth's own father, of course, had also once been a disguised fugitive, who had to take what cover was offered him after a defeat, but you won't find any 'Royal Ditch' pubs to commemorate the experiences of Charles II's bastard son. The Duke was brought to London and sentenced to death without a trial, none being needed as an Act of Attainder had already been passed. He did not bear his sentence stoically, requesting a personal audience with his uncle the King and begging for mercy. But James, as he had every right to be in the circumstances, was unmoved. Monmouth was braver at the executioner's block, where he joked grimly with the headsman, Jack Ketch, who had made a mess of Lord Russell's beheading after the Rye House plot. It did him no good. Whereas Ketch had taken three blows to finish off Russell, with Monmouth he needed five, one witness describing how, after the first stroke, the Duke 'lookt up, & after the third he putt his Leggs a Cross, & the Hangman flung away his Axe, but being chidd tooke it againe & gave him tother two strokes; and severed not his Head from his body till he cut it off with his Knife.' Ketch's incompetence or deliberate cruelty so incensed the watching crowd that he barely managed to escape with his life.

Monmouth's followers had at first been hunted down and summarily dispatched by soldiers under Colonel Percy Kirke known wholly inappropriately as 'Kirke's Lambs'. But a more thorough-going response was called for, and preparations for a special session of court sittings had already been made before the rebels were defeated. The 'Bloody Assizes' that decided the less eminent rebels' fates, remembered as the sole work of Lord Jeffreys (in fact, he was accompanied by four fellow judges), are just as much a contribution to the mythology of rebellion as the Harrying of the North. That is not to deny that many rebels, perhaps as many as 200, were executed. Among them was the widow Lady Alice Lisle, sentenced by Jeffreys to be burnt for harbouring rebels, though the sentence was commuted to hanging. It has been pointed out, however, that Lisle and many others were given short reprieves by Jeffreys so appeals to the King for mercy could be made. They were denied. Jeffreys was certainly a zealot who bullied witnesses and did his utmost to secure convictions. But judges of this era had an examiner's role, not the supervisory one we associate with British judges today, and Jeffreys was not unusual in the partiality with which he carried it out. Far more Monmouth rebels were sentenced to transportation than execution, about 2,400. This, of course, could also be a death sentence, as the voyage was perilous, and the destination, in this case the West Indies to labour alongside slaves, was a harsh one. Rebels had long known what fate they risked, and few can have been surprised (with the pardonable exception of those, like Alice Lisle, who hardly took an active part in the rising) that the law showed them no quarter. But if anyone deserves special opprobrium for his role in the punishments, it is the King himself, who was happy to suspend laws on different occasions but made sure the letter was enforced in 1685.

After the Glorious Revolution, when Jeffreys had died in the Tower as one of James's most loyal supporters, a pamphlet was published entitled *The Western Martyrology, or, The Bloody Assizes* by a radical journalist whom Jeffreys had sentenced to be whipped. It was this that crystallized the episode and the judge's reputation. Macaulay's endorsement of this view of 'that circuit of which the memory will last as long as our race and language' has perpetuated it. But the 'Bloody Assizes' were no bloodier a retribution on rebels than those visited on, say, the Pilgrims of Grace. More recently, three dozen innocents had been executed on the false evidence of Titus Oates. In an age that saw rebellion as an unforgivable crime, it would be surprising for James II, let alone his loyal servants, to break with convention.

Monmouth was one of the last Englishmen to live the peculiar afterlife of the popular favourite whose death was so unconscionable to his supporters that it was simply denied. It was rumoured, or perhaps more accurately fantasized, for many years that the Duke would 'in his glories / Unto his English friends appear'. At his execution, as at his grandfather's (and the rebel Thomas Wyatt's), onlookers crowded round to dip their handkerchiefs in his blood. In the West Country, his followers had been mostly drawn from the peasants and smallholders, and it is as the 'last popular rebellion' that 1685 is rightly remembered. (The popularity lasted; it was reported that at the 300th anniversary re-enactment of Sedgemoor, all the volunteers were for the rebels, not Feversham's loyalists.) Three years after Monmouth's failed rising, it was demonstrated once and for all that if you wanted to remove the King, you needed more than the people on your side.

Revolution or invasion?

It has become fashionable in recent years for historians to point out that the Glorious Revolution was 'neither glorious, nor a revolution'. The removal of the reigning monarch with, in England, relatively little loss of life and no military engagement might be said to fit the description, but the name certainly conceals a lot more than it explains. And despite historians' confident revisionism, self-delusion persists on a wide scale. An official parliamentary website alleges that 'The Glorious Revolution is a term used to describe the peaceful way in which Parliament asserted its rights over the monarchy in 1688', which gives an embarrassment of hostages to fortune. The traditional way of narrating the events of 1688–9, by which the Catholic James II was replaced as King of England, Scotland and Ireland by his own son-in-law, the Protestant Stadholder of the United Provinces of the Netherlands, William III, fits neatly into a history of English rebellion. The rebels in this case are headed by the 'Immortal Seven', disaffected Tory grandees (actually, three were Whigs) who in the three years of James's rule saw all their faith in hereditary principle 'betrayed' by a king apparently intent on imposing 'popery' on his subjects. The final spur to action on this reading is the birth to James and his queen, Mary of Modena, of a son, James Edward Stuart. Unquashable (if specious) rumours that this birth wasn't genuine, that a baby had been 'procured' for the royal couple (and smuggled into the Queen's room in a bedpan), couldn't alter the overwhelming likelihood that it meant a Catholic successor, and a perpetuation of what had seemed a bearably temporary anomaly when Tories had backed James's rights to succeed despite his religion in the Exclusion Crisis ten years before.

The Tories in Parliament, who had backed James again by providing the money for the force that routed Monmouth, had been repaid by a number of provocations seemingly calculated to extinguish their loyalty. The army that had been raised on that occasion had remained in arms, and its Catholic officers, tolerated in an emergency, had been retained. A standing army was one sure sign of a Catholic absolutist, of whom there was the pre-eminent example across the Channel in Louis XIV (with whom James seemed altogether too friendly, even when Louis began a form of anti-Protestant ethnic cleansing after revoking the Edict of Nantes in 1685). James's attempts to rule without Parliament, and to suspend laws passed by Parliament on his own prerogative, were further signs of nascent absolutism. When James issued his Declaration of Indulgence, which suspended laws against both Catholics and Dissenters, in 1687, even the usually passive Anglican bishops were moved to protest. Seven of their number presented James with a petition requesting that they not be forced to read out the Declaration in church, which James took to be a 'standard of rebellion'. When the bishops were acquitted by a court that had seemed to be rigged to give James the verdict he wanted, rebellious Englishmen had found a cause. The King had also been busily removing opponents from positions of authority throughout the country, in anticipation of 'packing' Parliament with supporters when he recalled it, and had confronted the Fellows of Magdalen College, Oxford, by insisting on his own candidate being elected as President against their will.

That, in brief, is the story of the strain under which the Catholic King is seen to have placed his Protestant nation, and the arrival of William at the invitation of the Immortal Seven is seen as the result. Thus parliamentary government was saved. At the time of the Civil Wars in the 1640s and '50s, no alternative candidate for the throne could be found, but in 1688 William, champion of Protestant Europe against the encroachments of absolutist France, was part of a dream ticket. Married to James's (Protestant) daughter by his first wife, Mary, and grandson of Charles I (William's mother was James's sister), the Stadholder seemed a readily available substitute, whose wife, up until the birth of the Prince of Wales, had stood next in the line of succession. When the English invited their Dutch cousin in, they were able to dictate their terms to him, and establish at last a constitutional monarchy and a Protestant succession.

The problem with this narrative of the ultimate triumph of the English (establishment) rebel is that it robs the principal player in the drama of his motivation. What was in it for Willem Hendrik, Prince of Orange, Stadholder, known to us as King William III? It is true, for example, that William received a coded message from England assuring him that 'the people are so generally dissatisfied with the present conduct of the Government in relation to their religion, liberties and properties . . . that your Highness may be assured there are nineteen parts of twenty of the people throughout the kingdom who are desirous of a change'. But the reason that William understood the cipher was because he had set it up, with the help of an English Whig exile with a vested interest in revenging himself on the Tories: Henry Sidney, brother of the 'martyred' Algernon. This was an invitation that the Prince had been hoping for, and which his agents in England had sought out, but it was not the 'reason' he decided to invade. Although William was sympathetic to Protestant fears, he wasn't a natural friend of their established Church. His form of Calvinism was far closer to that practised by some of the dissenting congregations in England than to Prayer Book Anglicanism. And although he had the most reason to be disappointed when the arrival of the new Prince of Wales cut him out of the succession, he had already begun making secret plans for his invasion before the birth.

William's intentions had far more to do with Continental politics, and with the man who had tried to dazzle seventeenth-century Europe into submission, Louis XIV. Louis's brand of militant anti-Protestantism and unquenchable expansionism constantly threatened the Netherlands. Although the States General, on whom William depended for money to defend his country, were always inclined first to seek a business-preserving peace over an expensive war, even their representatives realized, as Louis continued to take measures against Dutch commercial interests, that the French King could not be trusted. And as James's weakness and natural inclination as a Catholic monarch to look to the leader of royal Catholicism drew him ever more strongly into the Sun King's orbit, William resolved that he had no choice but to alter the orientation of England away from France and towards the Netherlands. It is partly the consequence of William's invasion that England looks to us like a great prize, which any ambitious leader might be tempted to tilt at, but that was not a view shared in Continental Europe. The 'caprices of the English, whose moods are as inconstant as the waves' were notorious. Here was a country that had executed its king, been racked by civil war, and was clearly still divided both about how to worship and how to be governed. By comparison with the Netherlands, England was also poor, with no central bank or stock exchange to set beside the Dutch examples, and with a king who, like his predecessor, lived hand to mouth and had to rely on French subsidies. Then there was the fact that with England came Scotland and Ireland, both of which could prove a lot more trouble than they were worth. The states of English constitutional and confessional politics were both good reasons to stay away. Only the imperatives of Continental realpolitik compelled William to come.

From his point of view, it was a good thing that William didn't take the message from the 'Seven' at face value. When he did land at Torbay on the auspicious anti-Catholic date of 5 November 1688, he met with no resistance, but no support either. Twenty out of twenty Englishmen preferred to stay at home. Luckily (though luck had nothing to do with it), he didn't need any military assistance. William had gone to the trouble of assembling easily the largest invasion force ever to come to England. His fleet was four times the size of the Spanish Armada that Elizabeth I's rather more galvanized forces had only 'defeated' with a lot of help from the weather. In William's case, even the weather was on his side, as the 'Protestant wind' hastened his crossing while keeping the English Navy in port. He was able to land a force of around 21,000 troops unopposed.

James, too, had a very large army, and at first he marched it to confront William in the west. But William had put in place an extremely effective propaganda effort (he had brought a printing press with him) which did much to sow doubt in an already disaffected English army, and magnify the early scale of defections to his side. Even so, the King should have been able to challenge William's advance, but he lost his nerve, and retreated back to London. After that, the defections increased, including major figures such as the Earl of Clarendon's son, Lord Cornbury, as well as the Duke of Grafton (who days earlier had assured the King that 'I for my own part will fight and die for your Majesty's service') and John Churchill, co-victor of Sedgemoor and one of James's most trusted generals. When his own daughter, Anne, fled to join an uprising led by the Earl of Devonshire in Nottingham, James decided that the game was up. It was William's Whig supporters who later made much of the workings of 'Providence' that had delivered the kingdom bloodlessly to their champion. In that conviction, they were only following a tradition of both rebels and rebelled against that had coloured the century, from the benign deliverance from the Gunpowder Plotters, to the victories of the New Model Army, to the Restoration. And James too seems to have believed that something beyond his control was at work. He was afflicted with nosebleeds as he tried to command his army, and his decision not to stand and fight has an air of fatalism about it that is difficult to divorce from his whole-hearted, and somewhat self-lacerating, embrace of Catholicism. Once his fate seemed to have been made clear to James, he ensured that his wife and precious son were safely dispatched before attempting to flee himself. Although James was captured, William had no desire to be faced with the prospect of dealing with a rightful king who had mismanaged himself out of a job, and allowed him to escape again. William's entry into London was a carefully stage-managed procession, in which all native troops had been replaced by Dutch. The city was occupied by foreign troops until the spring of 1690. Only after William was offered the crown, jointly with his wife, were native troops allowed to return.

The events of 1688–9 were the consequences of a Dutch invasion, not an English rebellion. There were some home-grown risings in Yorkshire, Cheshire and Nottinghamshire, and anti-Catholic riots in London, but these would hardly have threatened James (nor, undoubtedly, would they have taken place at all) without William's presence in the country. The only way in which the invasion does fit into the history of English rebellion, and it is an important one, is the manner in which it was presented. William put his case in classic English rebel's terms. His *Declaration of Reasons for Appearing in Arms in England*, which was issued in thousands of copies, did not claim the throne and blamed all James's failings on our old friends, 'evil councillors'.

It is conceivable that William at first had little intention of seizing the throne himself – that is, that he took on the rebel's role of wielder of targeted violence, as against out-and-out usurper. If he had been able to impose a guarantee of a more 'Protestant' foreign policy on James, William might have been satisfied. Although James's flight opened the way to the throne for the Dutch prince, the role of his more 'rebellious' English advisers is also important here. Men like Robert Ferguson (back on English soil having escaped after Monmouth's rising) and John Wildman, inveterate Whig and republican plotters who came over with William's force, may have been disappointed that William, despite being at the head of a unique republican arrangement himself, seemed little inclined to promote the Good Old Cause. But William also had more 'mainstream' Britons in his following, including another Scot, Gilbert Burnet, whose *History of My Own Time* did much to set the standard 'Whiggish' narrative of the 'Glorious Revolution'. Burnet resisted James's efforts at a compromise with William, dismissing the possibility of calling a parliament (before James had gone) and reacting to talk of a treaty with pronouncements about 'a suppositious child' – the Prince of Wales who was the obstacle to any Protestant security. Burnet was at first in favour of a regency after James's departure, but soon came round to the idea that William should be offered the crown, jointly with his wife, Princess Mary, the nominal next in line after James had 'abdicated' (or 'forfaulted' according to the Scots).

The offer of the crown did come with some conditions, and it is here that we might be able to locate the rice-paper-thin foundations of the apparently still 'official' line that 'parliament asserted its rights over the monarchy'. But the Bill of Rights that William and Mary passed was not a document designed to restrict the authority of monarchs in any novel way, and it is important that it was issued at the same time as they took the throne, but not as a direct condition. It required an oath of allegiance to the Crown, had a resolution against a Catholic monarch, and applied that to the succession. There were also various curbs on 'arbitrary power', examples of which had been perpetrated by James II, but in essence the Bill of Rights went no further than the Petition of Right of more than sixty years before. One way in which Parliament did 'assert their rights' was in quashing a bill supported by the King that would have extended membership of the Church of England to many dissenting congregations. Instead, the Toleration Act was passed, which removed the enforcement of yearly Anglican communion, thus allowing dissenters to worship in peace, but retained the insistence that only Church of England members could hold public office. This was the Act that turned dissent into Nonconformity. The unintended side effect of this not very generous measure was that some people gave up going to church at all.

The ship that brought over the new Queen Mary from the Netherlands also carried a returning English exile, whose own views of government were shortly to be published and dedicated to 'our Great Restorer, Our present King William'. John Locke's *Two Treatises on Government* had been long in gestation, and had certainly been influenced by the author's time in exile. They form the most cogent statement of the right to resist arbitrary government yet formulated. But in their espousal of the right to rebel they were hardly representative of the settlement that prevailed in 1689. Whig supporters and their successors among historians used to argue that the reason Britain had never experienced another revolution after 1689 was that the settlement achieved bordered on perfection. The truth is that the 'Revolution' of 1688–9 was much closer to a coup, and that English rebels, acting in an increasingly British context, continued to rise up against different aspects of that 'perfect' settlement for a very long time to come.

13. Returners and Rioters

From the Old Pretender to the Seamen's Strike 1715–75

If ever you will leave your Posterity free from faction and rebellion,
this is the time.

Daniel Defoe, *The Shortest Way with Dissenters* (1702)

For more than 600 years English rebels had taken up arms or taken
up pens, marched together in the open or plotted in private,
promoted a conviction held unto death, or jumped on a band-
wagon for personal gain. The first rebels that emerged to contest
the post-'Revolutionary' settlement after 1688, the followers and
heirs of James II who came to be known as 'Jacobites' (after
'Jacobus', James in Latin), did all these things, and something else.
In Scotland and Ireland, they merged with a nationalism that was
given new life in the former by the 1707 Act of Union, under
which some Scots felt they had been 'bought and sold for English
gold'; and in the latter by the further dispossession that their early
failure inflicted on the vast majority. If Jacobitism was a political
movement, then it was a British one. But it did have an English
element, and the behaviour of English Jacobites extended the
lexicon of English rebellion, to include such subversive acts as
drinking 'loyal' toasts while your glass is held over a bowl of water
(to adumbrate that really your loyalty is to the 'king over the
water', i.e. the exiled Stuarts), or wearing a tartan waistcoat. The
flip side of the Walter Scott, Robert Louis Stevenson Highland
romance of the loyal follower of the Old and Young Pretenders
was, in England at least, the sense that Jacobitism could be reduced
to a set of poseur's gestures. Here are the origins of rebellion as a
fashion statement.

There is more to the Jacobites in England than that. The fact

that, over the sixty years after James II fled, there were two risings
which penetrated to English soil, and half a dozen plots that
recruited English support, all aimed at overthrowing the Williamite
and then the Hanoverian monarchy, means that the Jacobites are
part of the story of English rebellion. Many English Tories seem
almost instantly to have regretted their revolutionary rush of blood
in 1688. Some persuaded themselves that the Stuarts, somehow
transformed by their experience of exile, might combine greater
legitimacy with acceptable behaviour. At first, however, English
grumblings were caused more by the cost of dealing with Jacobite
threats in the two other kingdoms. First to rise was Scotland, where
Viscount Dundee's small army inflicted an unexpected defeat on
the Williamites in 1689, but failed to make anything of it because
Dundee himself was killed in the process.

In Ireland, less than a year after he had been forced to quit his
kingdom in shame, James II led an army that reclaimed most of
another of his former possessions. The small force that William
sent was unable to stem the Jacobite tide, and William himself,
gathering a multinational army, crossed to face James again. So the
confrontation that might have happened at Salisbury in November
1688 took place instead on the banks of the River Boyne, north
of Dublin, in July 1690. Whereas William's invasion force had
been outnumbered in England, in Ireland he had perhaps 11,000
more troops. At the Boyne he used them to full advantage to rout
James's Irish followers. William was injured by a musket ball that
could easily have killed him. Yet once again James's resolve went
limp at real opposition. He fled the field (earning the Irish nickname 'Seamus an chaca' – 'James the Shit') and put himself on the
next boat for France. For the time being, the Glorious Revolution,
stained now with more blood than its Whig propagandists liked to
remember, had achieved its purpose. There were Jacobite plots
and conspiracies in William, Mary and then Anne's reigns, but the
combined strengths of a government spy network and a decent
defence on the lookout for any Continental invaders kept the
threat to a minimum.

The years William spent fighting his real opponent, Louis XIV, the only man whose opposition could seriously threaten William's place on the throne, saw the Jacobite cause in England retreat underground. But the fact that England was involved in such a protracted and, on several occasions, unsuccessful war, against an opponent who seemed a more immediate threat to William's country of origin than his adopted kingdom, created the circumstances in which the alternative of Jacobitism could survive. There were a few abortive invasion schemes (which were stymied by weather, bad communications, betrayal – and measles). But the strongest evidence that Jacobitism was still a going concern was in the never-ending stream of anti-Williamite pamphlets, lampoons and ballads. This was a cause with a grassroots following: Jacobite publications were self-funded, not sponsored from James's court in exile at Saint-Germain near Paris. The more elevated of these productions dealt squarely with the history of English rebellion – not to embrace it, of course, but to cast aspersions on William by comparing James II's experience with the iniquitous fates of Edward II, Richard II and Charles I. William, for his part, was compared to Henry IV, Henry VII and Cromwell. In this theoretical battle, the Jacobites certainly had the force of history on their side. The Restoration had been effected on the widely accepted basis of the Stuarts' legal, hereditary right. It was only Whig revolutionaries like John Locke who had to return to first principles and the 'law of nature' rather than historical precedent to show the English how they should be governed, and what rights they had to resist bad government. The traditional Tory – and Jacobite – view was still that of the Protestant martyr Hugh Latimer, burnt by Mary I in 1555: 'If the king should require of thee an unjust request yet art thou bound to pay it and not to resist and rebel.'

Remarkably, despite James's defeat at the Boyne, the failure of the conspiracies, the uncontested succession of Queen Anne, the death of James II himself in 1701, and the growing Whig grip on Parliament and patronage, Jacobitism did not die out in these 'quiet' years, even in England. It was given new blood by the rump of Protestant clergy who refused to swear the oath of allegiance to William. These so-called Non-jurors were dismissed from the

Church of England, and formed a breakaway organization, which was always a refuge for disaffected Tories, who could blame their exclusion from government on the great mistake of having got rid of James in the first place. When Anne, the last Protestant Stuart, died without leaving a direct heir in 1714, the Crown passed to the Lutheran Hanover dynasty represented by George I, a successor and a court far more remote from England than the exiled Stuarts in Paris. Jacobites took the opportunity to profit from revived Tory disaffection. In the year after his accession, when a Whig majority was returned to Parliament, and George showed himself happy to exclude Tories from positions of power, there were enough elements of discontent for another attempt on the throne to have a real chance of success. James II's heir, the 'Old Pretender' James Francis Edward Stuart, relied on French backing, which was not always forthcoming, but he had also managed to recruit eminent English politicians to his cause. The greatest coup in this respect was the defection of Viscount Bolingbroke and the Duke of Ormond, two of the Tory ministers who had helped to negotiate the Treaty of Utrecht with France in 1713, and who were harassed by the Whigs when they returned to office. In fear of arrest, they both fled to France, where Bolingbroke was made an earl and Secretary of State by the Old Pretender, and Ormond was made Captain-General. They were instrumental in planning for what in some respects was the most serious attempt to reinstate the Stuarts, the Jacobite rising of 1715.

The ground seemed well prepared for an invasion. There were popular riots in support of the Jacobites, openly proclaiming 'King James III', in the winter of 1714–15. But when the potential leaders of a rising were supposed to act, in England at least, their contribution was stifled at birth. One of the consequences of Jacobite intrigue was the development of a sophisticated government spy network, working to uncover threats to the Crown just as Walsingham's spies had unearthed Catholic plotting more than a century before. In 1715, while Scotland raised the standard of rebellion under the Earl of Mar, English Jacobites like Lord Lansdowne and Sir William Wyndham were arrested before they could gather any support (though how hard they were trying is open to dispute). In the North, English Jacobites made more of a fist of their rebellion, as the Earl of Derwentwater and Baron Widdrington, together with two MPs, Thomas Forster, Member for Northumberland, and Sir William Blackett, Member for Newcastle and local mine owner, raised a force that was meant to co-ordinate with French landings and Scots marching south. A group of Jacobite Lowland Scots did march south of the border, and together the army got as far as Lancashire. At Preston, however, it met government opposition, and after brief resistance the English Jacobites infuriated their Scottish allies by surrendering. By the time the Old Pretender landed in Scotland in December, the English part of the Jacobite rising had already been over for a month. It lasted a little longer in Scotland, but by February 1716 it was over there too. James departed for France, never to return. In England, Derwentwater was beheaded the same month, but Forster managed to escape from Newgate Prison and made his way to the Continent, where he ended his days as steward to James's household, now established much more distantly in Urbino.

The failure of expected French support to materialize was as important for the collapse of 'the '15' as the lack of widespread English action. On the other hand, the relative success of the Scottish part of the rising, and the support of senior Tories, demonstrated that, given the right military backing, even in England Jacobites could be a serious threat to a new and unpopular regime. Continuing Jacobite intriguing was uncovered in another serious manifestation seven years later, when, in 1722, Francis Atterbury, high Tory Bishop of Rochester, made contact with the exiled court to plan a rising at the time of the next election. Unfortunately for Atterbury, the political situation on the Continent had swung definitively against French backing for the Jacobites, after an Anglo-French alliance had been secretly negotiated in 1716. When the Jacobite court approached the French for support, Cardinal Dubois let the Hanoverian regime know about it. The British 'turned' the Earl of Mar, who now hoped for a pardon and a return home, and so agreed to act as a double agent. The plot was allowed to mature long enough for evidence to be gathered against the principals before they were arrested. The government even took the precaution of mustering troops in Hyde Park, as the rising was supposed to centre on a London coup, but they were never called into action. Atterbury was lucky enough only to be sent into exile. His co-conspirator, Christopher Layer, by contrast, a London lawyer who had secured the Old Pretender and his wife as god-parents to his child, as bona fides of the conspiracy, was hanged, drawn and quartered in November 1723. His head was said to have been taken from the scaffold, and retained as a more gruesome Jacobite relic than the white roses and oak leaves often affected by Stuart supporters.

Ten years later, a cooling in Anglo-French relations combined with troubles at home for Robert Walpole's government when his Excise Scheme was greeted with riots across the country. The scheme was put forward after the bursting of the 'South Sea bubble' left the government in need of funds. Walpole argued that an extension of duties on staples like salt (and wine and tobacco) could compensate for a reduction in Land Tax. The proposal struck the non-voting (but eating, drinking and smoking) classes as manifestly unfair, and they took to the streets with slogans that proclaimed their fear that their 'English' liberties were threatened with Continental-style despotism. 'Wooden Shoes and No Jury' was the fate of the oppressed across the Channel, and it was one English subjects were prepared to resist. This was a long way from the rhetoric of parliamentary reform, and eventually of democracy, that emerged in the nineteenth century. But it showed how effec-tively the Glorious Revolution and Protestant settlement had infil-trated the popular consciousness as a uniquely English arrangement, with the catch-all notion of 'liberty' its touchstone.

Because the Excise Scheme was a Whig measure, Jacobite Tories could hope to benefit by the agitation, despite the fact that, if the Stuarts were ever to return, they would be backed by the sort of Continental government that the marchers and rioters abhorred. (Not to mention the fact that James II had been thrown out in the first place precisely because of the same fears of 'Continental' absolutism.) The plot that attempted to revive the Jacobite cause on the back of the agitation centred on the young Lord Cornbury, a protégé of Bolingbroke who had met the Old Pretender while he was on the Grand Tour and had offered to work for his 'restoration'. Once again, however, the French balked at providing support, though they didn't betray the details of the plan. With no prospect of success, Cornbury was able merely to drift away from Jacobite politics, one more dilettante whose rebellious instincts never flowered into convictions. For his part, Walpole was frightened enough by the more general display of opposition to the Excise to back down.

The last throw of the Jacobite dice was more energetic, though it centred on a no less whimsical figure. The Young Pretender, Charles Edward Stuart, led the Jacobite rebellion in 1745 that almost – and in spite of its internal contradictions – managed to deliver the triumph that had been yearned for over nearly sixty years. 'The '45' is seen primarily as an episode in Scottish history, where, despite his own personal failings, 'Bonnie Prince Charlie' is more fondly remembered than his grandfather was in Ireland. As always, the scheme turned, and ultimately fell, on the dashed hope of French support, and it was in Scotland that most of the drama, and the tragedy, of the rebellion was played out. The clans rose in support of the Prince, sharing in an unlikely series of successes, before facing the ultimate extinction of their cause, and many of their followers, at the Battle of Culloden in April 1746. As with the '15, there was an English dimension to the '45, during which the Jacobites made their greatest inroads into England itself, reaching as far as Derby. There, on 5 December 1745, the Jacobite army held a council to decide whether to advance on London. The two Hanoverian armies in pursuit of the Jacobites were not in a position to defend the capital, which was forced to rely on the militia. Although the Jacobites had marched south without any English support (English followers were waiting for the French to show their hand), two Jacobites south of the border finally decided to declare for the invaders if they reached London. They were Lord Barrymore, an Irish landowner who sat as Tory MP for

Stockbridge in Hampshire, and Sir Watkin Williams Wynn, the greatest landowner in Wales and another staunch Tory MP. The message, taken by Barrymore's son, reached Derby two days after the Jacobites had left. The whole council except for Charles had agreed that they couldn't proceed without French support, which Charles had promised, but which turned out to be a fantasy.

The '45 was the end of serious Jacobitism, particularly as its leader proved a bottomless and ungrateful recipient of supporters' funds. But the Jacobite cause continued to be a touchstone for opposition to a ministry that was dominated by Whigs. The Whig 'philosophy', if ever one existed, was repeatedly compromised by years of government during which Walpole's manipulation of patronage and electoral politics were rightly seen as the corruption of an oligarchy. A decade and a half of 'Robinocracy' made clear that the only remaining Whig principle was staying in power, and even after the fall of the 'grand Corrupter', the Whig supremacy continued in one form or another for almost another twenty years. Any opposition found it fairly easy to occupy the moral high ground. Nonetheless, it is surprising to see one legacy of Jacobite rebellion in those areas of their support that shaded into the more general and supremely un-Tory opposition that would later be known as 'radicalism'. It can be traced faintly in the followers of John Wilkes in the 1760s – some of whom had been Jacobites, though Wilkes himself was quite the opposite – and the symbols of blue cockades and ribbons they adopted, the same as those of Jacobitism. Samuel Bamford, the weaver and radical activist who was present at the Peterloo massacre in 1819, wrote about the connection explicitly when discussing his grandfather's part in the Old Pretender's rising in Lancashire. Passing over his own parents' influence, he confides, 'Such were the men and women from whom I derived my being. The rebel blood, it would seem, after all, was the more impulsive; it got the ascendancy – and I was born a radical.' Often, rebellion is less to do with a set of political positions than with a tendency of temperament. And, in part, the history of English rebellion is the history of the new forms this temperamental alignment could take.

'The madding crowd's ignoble strife'

With the falling away of Jacobitism, a distinct chapter in the history of English rebellion closes – one which, at least since the fourteenth century, had been dominated by the question of who should rule. Of course, even over this period, when no alternatives for the throne presented themselves, that did not guarantee freedom from rebellion. The Civil Wars had been fought not over who should rule, but how. Yet after the Jacobites, although there were some English rebels who thought there should be no monarch at all, there were very few who were prepared to rebel to put a different one on the throne.

In part, this naturally reflected the rise of Parliament, and the gradual transfer of power away from the monarchy and towards parliamentary government. This process still had a long way to travel in the eighteenth century, and even during the nineteenth the monarchy was hardly a negligible factor in English politics. Nor was it a predictable progress, under which each successive monarch gave up more power to ministers. George III, in the early part of his reign at least, certainly took a more active part in government than Queen Mary or Queen Anne (and arguably more than his Hanoverian predecessors). Nonetheless, as power began to be concentrated more and more in the ruling ministry, so rebellion would be directed against the government's representatives. And while we have seen already that those who formed part of the active political classes, able to vote or enter Parliament, could become involved with extra-parliamentary rebellion, it was during the eighteenth century that a new political force emerged: the 'mob'. Unpredictable, sometimes politically radical, at other times jealously conservative, the mob could also be violent and xenophobic, but occasionally surprisingly principled, all in the traditions of English rebellion.

Popular politics and popular rebellion were not a creation of the eighteenth century, and although it was some time before those who came onto the streets consciously espoused the example of their more 'ancient' forebears, opponents from the seventeenth century onwards were quick to cast 'ordinary' rebels as the inheritors of Wat Tyler. At the time of the Protectorate, the Royalist John Cleveland, for example, told his readers that:

The beginnings of the second Richard's reign are turmoyled with a Rebellion, which shoke his Throne and Empire . . . a Rebellion never to be believed but in the age it was acted in, and our own, in which we find how terrible the overflowes of the common people . . . must prove.

But the term 'mob', first heard in 1688 (a contraction of the Latin 'mobile vulgus'), conveniently describes something that does seem new. (It is also the term used here, though it is not intended to carry any of its contemporary or subsequent pejorative associations.) These often organized, sometimes openly led, sometimes covertly manipulated gatherings usually focused their anger on specific issues, and conducted their business in a number of ritualized ways. The mob is most associated with London, where high-political and legal disputes were likely to be played out, but mobs rose across the country, and became an almost expected element, for example, in electoral politics. How they were raised is not always clear, though the distribution of rapidly printed handbills often played a part, and word of mouth must have been almost as important. The regular rituals once they were under way were more easily recorded by participants or eyewitnesses, and included the targeted destruction of property, chanting of slogans, forcing neutrals or opponents to demonstrate their support (for example, by 'illumination' at windows, or by joining in with slogans), and often burning in effigy. Although mob agitation could descend into more serious violence, and such rituals had often been seen before, it was in the eighteenth century that they began to combine into an almost self-contained performance, to be enacted in any number of scenarios. And, like audiences attending the premieres of avant-garde plays, it took some time for those at whom this new 'theatre of protest' was directed to understand it. On several occasions, the monarch and ministers mistook mob action for more widespread rebellion, refusing to believe that the principles on which people rose could be genuine, and genuinely focused, fearing instead that, unless they took the hardest of lines, the foundations of the constitution would be threatened. The printer William Strahan reckoned in 1768 that the ministry was 'more afraid of the mob of London than of the potent houses of Bourbon'.

Dr Sacheverell's mob

The mob's most lasting legacy may have been in the growth of repressive legislation, beginning with the Riot Act of 1715. The establishment's reaction to public disorder could, as after the Gordon riots of 1780, condemn other popular causes by association. But mob action could also be remarkably, and directly, effective. Rioting was often extremely conservative in motivation, and in those cases, even if it represented the more violent extremes of Tory thinking in response to a usually Whig-dominated government, it could change the political climate inside Parliament as well as 'outdoors'. That is what happened in 1710, when London and then the country at large witnessed the greatest popular agitation for more than a hundred years, larger than anything seen during the Civil Wars. The commotion began because on 5 November 1709 the High Tory chaplain of St Saviours decided to dust off one of his old sermons.

Dr Henry Sacheverell was an Oxford-educated clergyman, moderate in means but in little else, who, by the age of thirty-five, had established a reputation as a violent and incendiary preacher. He claimed to be committed to the Tory principle of non-resistance, but his words gave a different impression. A sermon directed against dissenters (his most frequent target) in Oxford in 1702 sounded like a call to rebellion, with its encouragement to 'hang out the bloody flag and banner of defiance'. The Nonconformist former rebel Daniel Defoe certainly thought so and published his heavily satirical *Shortest Way with Dissenters* shortly after this sermon was printed. Defoe advocated a logical extreme of Sacheverell's position, that 'the poison of [dissenters'] nature makes it a charity to our neighbours to destroy these creatures.' It was a while before some of the more rabid High Churchers detected the irony.

In 1705, Sacheverell first delivered in Oxford the sermon on 'False Brethren' that would later lead to his impeachment. Four years later, he responded to an invitation to preach at St Paul's church to the Lord Mayor and aldermen of London by haranguing the congregation from the same text for an hour and a half, on the subject of those men in high places who protected dissenters. For their part, Sacheverell argued, dissenters were the direct inheritors of the tradition not of the papists whose foiling in 1605 was officially being celebrated, nor of the Whigs of 1688 who had welcomed Stadholder William as he arrived on the same auspicious November date, but of the regicides of 1649. The sermon was interpreted, as it was surely meant to be, as an attack on the Revolutionary settlement of 1689, under which toleration had been granted. Sacheverell ignored a ban on printing the text, and when a massive print run of 100,000 copies was sold out, the Whig-dominated Parliament decided that such a flagrant attack on its rule could not be ignored. Sacheverell was impeached before the House of Commons for high crimes and misdemeanours. The trial was delayed until the end of February 1710. It was as the prosecution opened the case that there was an unprecedented show of 'mob' strength on the streets of London.

On 1–2 March, groups of up to 3,000 London citizens gathered to launch attacks on dissenters' meeting-houses around Lincoln's Inn and points west, smashing the windows and removing the furniture to be burnt in the street. The very specific targeting of the dissenters' places of worship, as well as the cries of 'High Church and Sacheverell', made it clear what the rioters' motivation was, though their leadership has never been positively identified. They were well equipped for their task of destruction, bringing the right tools to be able to strip out a meeting house in as little as three quarters of an hour. The response of the military, without a riot act to read (that was still five years off), was less co-ordinated, though mercifully restrained. In fact, though it might have been terrifying to be caught up in the events of that night, there was an air of restraint about all of it. The rioters made sure not to set light to anything apart from the dissenters' furnishings, and even dragged them some distance to avoid potential harm to 'innocent' lodgings and businesses. The disturbances lasted for about three hours before troops were belatedly deployed to deal with them. Only two people were killed on the night, which is perhaps a demonstration of the general discipline of both sides. The leaders of this well-planned action were never caught, and even the two followers who were arrested and convicted of treason escaped with their lives.

The reason for the show of mercy was that, by the time of the conviction, the ministry had changed from a Whig- to a Tory-dominated one. Sacheverell himself had been found guilty, but the peers who sentenced him had bowed to popular pressure by making his sentence a light one. The election was more or less a direct consequence of the case and the riots. The Whigs' handling of both had been so poor that the Tories were able to put huge pressure on the Queen to dismiss her ministers and dissolve Parliament. At the subsequent election, Whigs who had played a part in the impeachment of Sacheverell almost all lost their seats. The election was accompanied by as much violence as any in the century, and most of it was 'in support' of the Doctor, and therefore of the Tories, of whom 332 were returned, as against 181 Whigs (in England and Wales). Never before had a show of 'mob' agitation exercised such a direct (intended) effect on the political orientation of the country. The Sacheverell riots seemed to demonstrate an unpalatable truth to the 'natural rulers' of society: that the general public might be excluded from the direct political process, but they had methods of making their views known, and, more worryingly, of getting their way. It was only possible to dismiss the mob as 'manufactured' by the Tories if one ignored the genuine sense of grievance that the rioters evinced. Since the Reformation, motivating crowds of Englishmen on religious grounds had never proved very difficult, and this was far from the last time this proved to be the case. 'Anti-Popery', which usually provided the spark, could, it seemed, be easily converted into anti-dissenter feeling. It is perhaps less of a surprise that in the long term, the lesson that the government learnt was a more negative one, that mob violence should not be allowed to go unchecked, particularly when motivated by such a widely popular 'cause'. Though the eighteenth century continued to earn its reputation for riot, London – and the country at large – didn't see such an impressive demonstration of mob power for another seventy years.

That is not to say that mob action did not continue to play a direct part in political affairs. We have seen its effect with the Excise Bill, and popular clamour also did for the Quarantine Bill (1721), when the government was forced to soft-soap measures introduced to stop an outbreak of plague from spreading. Mob power was in evidence again after the introduction of the so-called 'Jew Bill' (1753), a statistically negligible measure to allow some resident Jews to be naturalized, which brought out the ever-reliable xenophobia of the English. As with the Sacheverell riots, the mob was often liable to confound later ideas of what constitutes a good cause. They were not always predictable at the time either. A case which demonstrated the gulf between what was politically acceptable at a parliamentary (i.e. landowning) level and what would be tolerated in the country came with the passing of the Militia Act in 1757.

On the face of it, a measure brought in by William Pitt the Elder's new ministry, firmly to re-establish locally raised militias, and to reduce the need for a professional, standing army, or for hired foreign troops, might have seemed potentially popular. After all, the Stuarts' resistance to militias and reliance on foreigners (including Catholic Irish) had been instrumental in the divisions of the Civil Wars and the Glorious Revolution. But the popularity of a militia with MPs tended to rely on the fact that they didn't have to serve in it. Even at the time of the New Model Army, when there was a civil war to fight and an inspiring cause to draw in recruits, keeping troop numbers up had been notoriously difficult, as men slipped away as soon as they got the chance, particularly after a victory. By the time of the Militia Act, the Jacobite threat was receding, and what became known as the Seven Years War was being fought on the Continent, and from India to Canada (though the fact that the enemy was France meant that potential invasion was hardly inconceivable). Despite specific assurances to the contrary, it was widely believed that conscripts to the militia would have to serve abroad, not resist attacks at home.

The mechanism by which the militias were to be raised and paid for was also manifestly unfair (though not, it seemed, manifestly enough). Enlistment of able-bodied men between the ages of eighteen and fifty was to be decided by ballot, but a payment of £10 or the provision of a substitute would ensure you avoided your three years' service. And although this meant that landowners and the rich could get out of serving, the funds for the force were not to be raised from the Land Tax (as the militia had been before) but from general taxation. This meant that the 'middling sort' would find themselves paying twice for it (£10 to avoid service plus the additional tax), while the poor would pay the tax and serve. Finally, it hadn't yet been made clear whether enlisted men would be paid for their time.

The reaction to the Act was more general than the political protesting which had met the Excise or Jewish Naturalization Bills. While the mob, urged on by pamphleteers and their own self-interest, had tried to influence Parliament over those measures, in the case of the militias, it was only when the Act had passed and the lists of recruits had been drawn up that the counties began to rise in response. The timing was unfortunate for the government, as a bad harvest for two years running had resulted in food shortages and their inevitable eighteenth-century accompaniment, food riots. In the summer of 1757, several mobs numbered in the thousands descended on Justices of the Peace at their county meetings, as they began the selection process from the militia lists. The rioters forced the magistrates or parish constables to hand over the lists for destruction in Bedfordshire, Cambridgeshire, Yorkshire, Lincolnshire, Nottinghamshire, Kent and Hertfordshire. The Duke of Bedford was in no doubt of what the defiance signified:

'the bad example of suffering a giddy and riotous populace to stand in opposition to an Act of Parliament'.

Although, this time, Parliament did not completely cave in to popular pressure, an Act 'explaining' the Militia Act had to be passed, in which it was made clear, for example, that militia men would be compensated for their service. The disturbances did not end immediately. Taken with the food rioting of the time, the anti–Militia riots look like an extension of general agrarian unrest. The risings were much more virulent in agricultural areas than urban ones, and the argument was heard (in Yorkshire) that the Act was 'a great hardship upon the country, by compelling the poorer sort of people to contribute equally with the rich'. It was the historian E. P. Thompson who, partly in response to evidence of eighteenth-century mob violence, outlined the idea of the 'moral economy' – under which ordinary people expected protection for their customary rights in return for their support for traditional holders of power. This notion applies most neatly to ordinary economic transactions, and it was in relation to the origins of food riots, where farmers were attacked for attempting to alter the 'customary' price of wheat or other essentials, that Thompson first expounded it. But it can be (and has been) applied more widely, and it looks like the same set of values was being put to the test in the Militia riots. Although the militia became accepted, particularly after an invasion scare in 1759, the ordinary Englishmen who were supposed to serve in it first needed to be persuaded that it was a just measure, not a case of the ruling classes trying to con them. Many of the disturbances of the eighteenth century revolved around the idea of attacks on 'traditional' or 'ancient' liberties. Horace Walpole referred to the Militia rioters as 'peasants', and although that hardly describes all the participants, there are reminders, too, of that grandfather of all popular agrarian risings, the revolt of 1381; not only in the perceived injustices, but in the particular method of attacking them, by destroying the documents on which those injustices were based. In 1381, it was manorial records. In 1757, it was militia lists. In both cases many of those involved in the risings would have been illiterate, but they still knew that without their pieces of paper their 'betters' were power-less – if only for a short time.

While the Militia riots represented an eighteenth-century devel-opment of a tradition of rural protest, the century also saw the growth of an industrial version. This didn't coalesce into what we would recognize as the modern Labour movement for many decades, but it could prove remarkably effective, despite the fact that trade unions, or 'combination' for collective bargaining, were outlawed until 1871. In fact, the ban on lawful combination meant that workers who wanted to improve their conditions had little choice but to take more direct action. In many industries, this could consist of machine-breaking or destroying produce, on the understanding that a simple strike would often be ineffective because there was nothing to stop employers using alternative labour. Perhaps the most extraordinary example of industrial action eighteenth-century style was in the Liverpool seamen's strike of 1775. When an employer on one ship in the port attempted to cut wages, the crew tore down the rigging and went on strike. This was a criminal offence, and the culprits were duly hauled off to gaol. More than 2,000 sailors marched on the prison to free them. Perhaps emboldened by this success, the sailors tried to improve their conditions, marching to the Exchange to ask the Mayor to speak for them. When they returned the next day, however, Mayor Rigby had summoned troops to disperse them. The seamen, unarmed, were fired on, several were killed, and perhaps as many as forty were injured.

Other insurrections before and since might have been cowed by this savage response. The sailors merely decided they must protect themselves. This they did by breaking into warehouses containing small arms and, more alarmingly, taking cannon (esti-mates vary between two and six) from a whaling ship, with which they bombarded the Exchange. For a day, the sailors had the city at their mercy, forcing merchants to give them money and taking large quantities of liquor. Perhaps their over-consumption accounts for the fact that a detachment of troops summoned from Man-chester was able to disperse them with little difficulty the following day. The official reaction to what had the potential to be one of the most serious outbreaks of popular violence in the century was remarkably muted. No one was hanged, very few were brought to justice, and even those who were convicted (twelve of them) were allowed to join the Navy instead. Whether or not this was a rare case of the authorities recognizing that little was to be gained by judicial revenge, industrial violence had not exactly been discouraged by the episode. The story of industrial relations in England is too vast to be told in any detail in the context of a history of rebellion. But, like other forms of legitimate dispute that were only latterly accepted in the law, the English trade union movement can trace its origins to the actions of English rebels. It is noticeable, too, that in the case of the Liverpool seamen's strike the 'language' of protest was closer to that of military rebellion – complete with arms, drums, flags and a siege of the 'enemy' at the Exchange – than to modern ideas of an industrial dispute.

14. Agitators

John Wilkes to the Nore Mutiny 1760–97

'This is not the clamour of a rabble, my Lord, but the voice of liberty, which must and shall be heard.'

John Wilkes, 3 May 1763

The history of rebellion is in part a history of once unconscionable causes or ways of protest becoming respectable. Men and women who had once risked imprisonment or worse could find themselves as lawmakers, while lawmakers who dismissed rebels' ideas as absurd or unworkable were either persuaded or replaced by those who defended such ideas as inalienable rights. A prime instance of the rebellious origins of a latterly respectable cause is parliamentary reform. The first person to speak in the House of Commons for universal (male) suffrage and reform of the increasingly corrupt basis on which the British were 'represented' in Parliament was a veteran of 'mob' rule, though only once did he ever march at the head of a mob: John Wilkes. Coincidentally, it was another, less sympathetic raiser of mobs whose actions probably put back the cause of reform by more than twenty years, though his own grievance had nothing to do with that cause: Lord George Gordon.

Wilkes, though he usually had personal reasons for raising agitation, championed a series of causes under the broad heading of 'liberty' that challenged the arbitrary and oligarchical tendencies of parliamentary government. It would have been difficult to predict such a career from its conventional origins. Wilkes was the son of a prosperous London 'trade' family who married into the country gentry. Although the marriage did not survive Wilkes's libertine tendencies, the association with the parliamentary seat of Aylesbury did. Wilkes was returned for the borough on the second attempt in 1757. But his future commitment to the cause of parliamentary reform would hardly be discernible from his behaviour at the next election, in 1761, when he bribed a majority of the (only 500 in total) voters. In Parliament, too, he did not shine, making little impression with his first speech, in support of Pitt, who had resigned from office.

It is difficult to say in the case of John Wilkes whether his provocative temperament led him to his principles, or whether his principles were sustained by his talent to offend. Whatever the truth of the matter, Wilkes was a 'demagogue' who found the written word more effective than the spoken, and it was his writings that first got him into trouble. He founded the satirical magazine *The North Briton* in response to the rise of George III's favourite, Lord Bute, who became Prime Minister in 1762. Although Wilkes's constant criticism was instrumental in persuading Bute to resign, it was under his successor, George Grenville, that the Member for Aylesbury emerged as a champion of liberty. In the edition of his magazine printed on St George's Day, 1763, No. 45, Wilkes lamented that the King in his speech closing Parliament had been forced to endorse the Treaty of Paris, which had ended the Seven Years War. The article could legitimately be interpreted as an attack on George III himself, and Wilkes was duly accused of seditious libel. But Grenville's government played into Wilkes's hands by issuing a general rather than an individual warrant for his arrest. This allowed government officers to arrest the 'authors, printers and publishers' of the edition without specifying anyone by name. It was obviously a recipe for arbitrary punishment, and one that affected the population at large when it was used by excise and customs officers to search warehouses and shops. It was against the general arrest warrant that Wilkes found his first popular cause, and the one that first associated his name with the cry of 'liberty'. Although the government substituted a personal for a general warrant, and tried Wilkes under that, he had found the way to stir up a 'respectable' mob. It was not until 1766 that the House of Commons condemned general warrants, but by that time they had already twice been criticized by two Lord Chief Justices who in all other respects found Wilkes's behaviour a dangerous effrontery. Wilkes himself fled to Paris to avoid the judgment of the court.

If Wilkes had only achieved the abolition of general warrants, he would still deserve to be remembered as the 'father of civil liberty'. But general warrants did not exhaust his talent for harnessing public opinion to righteous causes (in which he himself generally had a material interest). He took up three more, and it was only on the last, parliamentary reform (about which, it must be admitted, he seems to have been more lukewarm than on the other issues), that he met with failure, or more accurately, indifference. The first was the question of the rights of voters. After four years in Paris, Wilkes was so heavily in debt that only a return to Parliament, where his debts would be suspended, seemed to offer itself as a solution.

Characteristically, Wilkes was able to turn the entirely self-centred origins of his behaviour into an indisputably principled campaign. His status as an outlaw was still unclear on his return, and Wilkes challenged it in characteristic fashion by twice standing for election to Parliament. When he was returned on the second occasion as Member for Middlesex, the Commons were forced to decide whether to accept him back as an MP or not. Wilkes's outlawry had been overturned, but a new prosecution had been instantly launched on almost exactly the same grounds as the first. This one succeeded, and Wilkes was confined to the King's Bench prison for twenty-two months. Throughout the dispute, Wilkite mobs kept up the pressure on both the courts and the government. One demonstration in May 1767, in St George's Fields, Southwark, by the prison where Wilkes was being held, resulted in troops being called out and as many as eleven 'rioters' were shot dead. This did nothing to quell popular support for 'Wilkes and liberty', which continued for much of the rest of the year. Although Wilkes was kept out of Parliament for the time being, the dispute brought down the Duke of Grafton's ministry. When, after rising in the new sphere of City of London politics, Wilkes did reclaim his parliamentary seat in 1774, he continued his campaign to have his earlier expulsion overturned, once again showing that his principles could outlast their practical application. And the principle was a good one, even in as corrupt an electoral framework as that of eighteenth-century Britain: if a candidate is allowed to stand for office, and wins a popular vote, it is not in Parliament's power to decide to deprive him of his seat. 'If ministers can once usurp the power of declaring who shall not be your representative, the next step . . . is that of telling you who you shall send to Parliament, and then the boasted constitution of England will be entirely torn up by the roots.'

Wilkes became an alderman, sheriff and eventually Lord Mayor of the City of London, but it was in his first capacity that he struck his next blow for civil liberties. In a move as choreographed as the case of general warrants, Wilkes challenged Parliament's ban on reporting of parliamentary debates (which was deemed a breach of privilege). Here was another clear case of the oligarchical tendencies of the political classes, who wished to be able to conduct their business without outside 'interference'. Wilkes was not alone in connecting this issue to the others he had fought on. An ally, John Almon, wrote that 'When the spirit of the nation was raised high by the massacre in St. George's Fields, the unjust decision upon the Middlesex election, etc., Mr. Almon resolved to make the nation acquainted with the proceedings of Parliament.' Wilkes, who had been joined in the City government by a number of supporters, used the City's powers of exclusive jurisdiction to have Almon's printer, who had been accused by Parliament of breach of privilege, 'wrongfully' arrested within the City boundaries. When Wilkes threw out the case and had the citizen who had made the arrest charged with assault, Parliament's hand was forced again. Proceedings were instituted against the Lord Mayor, Wilkes and one other Alderman. But Wilkes refused to attend and was quietly ignored, while Mayor Crosby and Alderman Oliver were sent to the Tower, to the accompaniment of 'amazingly great' crowds. As the printers continued to defy Parliament and report debates, it was clear which side had won. Although reporters were still excluded from the House on occasion, and it was some years before they were permitted openly to take notes, Wilkes and his supporters had once again used the power of general ridicule to force Parliament into turning a blind eye.

Wilkes spent most of his life chronically short of funds, and the origins of the high-sounding Society of Gentlemen Supporters of the Bill of Rights were almost exclusively to do with supporting him rather than his principles. The group split after two years because some of its members, led by the radical John Horne Tooke, wanted it to be directed towards more general reform, and Wilkes himself supported a reorientation of the Society in that direction in 1771. The Society dissolved in 1775, but Wilkes became the first MP to advocate manhood suffrage as part of a programme of parliamentary reform a year later, when he returned to Parliament. In words that recalled Thomas Rainsborough's in the Putney debates, he argued that 'the meanest mechanic, the poorest peasant and day labourer has important rights respecting his personal liberty.' This cause, of the 'full and equal representation of the people', would at times come to dominate British political life over the next century. The new manufacturing districts and 'industrious' middle classes, and increasingly the workers themselves, saw how little they or their interests were represented in an unreformed Parliament, based on a system that came to be known as 'Old Corruption'.

Wilkes had spent a huge amount of time, energy and money (most of it not his own) securing his place in Parliament, and it would be satisfying to report that, once he was there, this speech crowned a career of crusades for civil liberties. In fact, Wilkes's re-entry to Parliament marked the decline of his influence. If there are any doubts about the importance of the Wilkite mobs, we need only look at what Wilkes was able to achieve without one. In 1776, the House did not even bother to vote on his speech, and there was no agitation 'outdoors'. Outside London, the Yorkshire Association founded by a clergyman, Christopher Wyvill, gained fairly wide support among the 'middling sort' for a programme of mainly economic reform, with some associated parliamentary reform that fell well short of universal suffrage. This was the first in a series of more or less radical reforming organizations that sprang up over the next five decades. From our own vantage point, it can seem puzzling how long it was before a popular campaign for the vote really got under way. Our own knowledge of the Levellers' arguments more than 100 years before Wilkes and Wyvill can make the 'denial' of universal suffrage look even more protracted. But that is to project democratic notions back onto a society that remained to be convinced of the benefits of 'democracy' (for a long time to come, still a dirty word). That applies not just to the 'landed interest', which might be expected to protect its own stake in government, but also to the disfranchised. To this fissiparous class, which struggled variously under a savage criminal code, economic injustice, a ban on unionization and discriminatory religious policies, it was not immediately clear that expanding the vote and redrawing constituencies for a Parliament that at most times must have seemed ineffably remote was a panacea. It took a different sort of publicizing genius from Wilkes's to make that popular connection. At this formative stage, and without the example of a specific injustice that he had previously been able to latch on to to inspire support, Wilkes was unable to provoke any popular enthusiasm for his more radical proposals. It would be unfair to accuse Wilkes of abandoning his principles, though he did embrace a less fractious existence, and told an old woman who shouted 'Wilkes and liberty' to him in the street, 'Be quiet, you old fool. That's all over long ago.' But his career is a demonstration of how much more could be achieved by adopting the language of 'rebellion', backed by mobs, marches, slogans and handbills, than by trying to effect change from within.

The Gordon Riots

Wilkes was as aware as anyone of the power of the mob, and his fellow MPs would have done well to listen to him when in 1779 he warned about their reaction to mob violence that had arisen in Scotland. Riots in Glasgow and Edinburgh were the Scottish response to a measure for the relief of Catholics, which had been introduced the previous year by Lord North's ministry in England and Ireland, where it had passed without noticeable opposition. Although it was presented as the mildest of relaxations of punitive measures against Catholics, it was (rightly) suspected of being motivated by the desire to raise Catholic soldiers from the Highlands to fight the American colonists, whose cause was in the ascendant. The disturbances in Scotland persuaded the government to withdraw the Bill there, and Wilkes warned that it could now expect a similar response in England. Unfortunately, there was in the Member for Ludgershall, Wiltshire, just the man to fulfil the prophecy.

The second son of the Duke of Gordon, Lord George Gordon had been prominent in the agitation in Scotland, and in November 1779 the English Protestant Association invited him to be their President. Gordon was a 29-year-old MP of extreme, mostly 'radical' convictions. His first speech to the House was against the American war, but his anti-Catholicism was of the classic strain which associated the taint of Popery with that of tyranny and absolutism. The numbers of Catholics in England may have been negligible, but Gordon was in no doubt that the Act had been formulated, as he explained in a personal audience with George III, 'for the diabolical purpose of arming the Papists against the Protestant colonies in America'. If Wilkes's unspontaneous public speaking and repeated pleas for the mob's restraint make it difficult to pin the title of 'demagogue' onto him, no such scruples attach to Gordon. He determined to make use of the very large support at his command to present a petition for repeal of the Act in the House, and force a debate on it. At St George's Fields, where Wilkes's supporters had been gunned down thirteen years before, a huge crowd of around 60,000 gathered on 2 June 1780. They were given blue cockades, the colour of the Tories, but also of Wilkes. Unlike Wilkes, Gordon was prepared to make direct appeals and thinly veiled threats to 'his' mob, who marched in three divisions over Westminster, Blackfriars and London Bridges to gather outside Parliament.

The government, which cannot have been unaware of the

gathering commotion, seems nonetheless to have done nothing to
stop it. Gordon was not only allowed to speak on the petition, but
to dart in and out of the House to give updates to the crowd on
how the debate was going. He was reported to have told them
that in Scotland the people had achieved nothing 'until they pulled
down the mass houses'. A clearer case of incitement to riot would
be difficult to conceive of, and yet, apart from the threats of a few
individual MPs (including his own uncle promising to run him
through if the mob entered the House), Gordon was allowed to
act unopposed. The business of the House could hardly continue
in such an atmosphere, with many Members of both chambers
attacked by the crowd as they arrived. In the midst of all this, the
Duke of Richmond introduced his motion for manhood suffrage,
which was debated (and rejected) the next day. This seemed hardly
the time, when Members' very lives were threatened by 'the
people', to give the same entity, no matter how narrowly defined,
more power. Of course, the Secretary of State who replied to
Richmond on behalf of the government did not put it like that,
preferring to argue that the British constitution was 'the wisest that
had ever been created'.

Gordon's mob may have done little by association for the cause
of parliamentary reform, and inside the House at least, his motion
to have his petition considered was heavily defeated. But as nothing
had been done to quell or discourage the mob, this was hardly
likely to be the end of the matter. On the night the petition was
rejected, two ambassadors' Catholic chapels, in Lincoln's Inn and
Soho, were attacked, and one was burnt down. Although the
following day was relatively quiet, there were more attacks on
Catholic chapels and schools for the next two days. When Parliament met again, Gordon wore a blue ribbon, making plain his
support for the movement against relief, although he did not
oppose a motion against the rioters. The Guards had been called
out, but they did not receive positive orders as to how to proceed,
so the mob was able to continue, and increase, its destruction as
the week went on. The agitators destroyed the house of a magistrate who read the Riot Act, and then marched to Newgate Prison,

which they burnt and threw open. By the middle of the week, every prison but one in London had been stormed, and fires raged throughout the city, including one at a Catholic distiller's where the flames were inadvertently fuelled by gin being pumped on, instead of water.

The government and city magistrates seemed unable to put a concerted plan together to oppose the rioters. In Paris less than ten years later, the throwing open of a single prison and the release of just seven inmates would herald a revolution. In 1780, London was at the mercy of a mob with over 1,500 convicts freed (though admittedly most were debtors rather than criminals). Unlike Louis XVI, however, George III did not think that 'nothing' was happening in his capital. He summoned the Privy Council and got them to declare martial law. Although it took a day before the soldiers were able to restore order, and the rioters continued their attacks, expanding their targets to include the Bank of England and the Blackfriars Bridge toll houses, the Gordon riots were eventually put down by an unprecedented show of force. As many as 210 people were shot, and seventy-five were wounded. Among those resisting the rioters was Alderman John Wilkes, who wrote in his diary that he had shot two insurgents who attacked the Bank. 'Liberty' did not mean anarchy.

The unpalatable cause of intolerance that the rioters were fighting for makes it difficult for modern observers, as with the Sacheverell riots, to view the Gordon mob in the same light as mobs that rose with Wilkes, or against the militia, or over food prices, or for any number of 'better' eighteenth-century causes, from the excise to turnpikes. The Gordon rioters are further proof, if it were needed, that 1688 had not 'cured' England (or Britain) of religious bigotry. The causes of English rebels, like the preoccupations of their rulers, were not suddenly secularized by the Glorious Revolution. Whatever the initial connection to fellow feeling for the 'oppressed' American colonists, a week into the riots, the motivation seems to have been purely sectarian. But it is worth pointing out that, although the Gordon riots were far more destructive of property than anything which preceded them, they too were targeted and, to some extent, restrained. The attacks on Catholic institutions were confined to the more prosperous, indicating that, as with the Sacheverell riots, it was the success of the hated group as opposed to their existence that was resented. And Catholics themselves had less to fear from the Gordon rioters than did MPs, who were roughed up on their way into and out of Parliament. The Gordon riots are hardly the most glorious chapter in the history of English rebellion. But they are not anomalous either. The rioters, with their blue ribbons, clearly thought they were as justified in marching behind Lord George Gordon as they had been in following Wilkes. In one sense, they were right. The same Parliament that ignored them over the issues Wilkes brought up was ignoring them over Catholic relief. Perhaps the most pathetic moment of the whole episode came when the Duke of Richmond, trying to speak on a motion that would actually offer men a greater say in their own affairs, was forced to deplore the 'riotous proceedings' outside the House of the people who stood to benefit from his proposal. The Gordon riots gave the people a bad name.

As for Gordon himself, he was hardly the first English rebel to relish the drama of his actions (reminiscent in that respect, though it is a comparison he would have abhorred, of the Gunpowder Plotter Robert Catesby). But it is difficult to discount the verdict of his contemporaries that Gordon's behaviour went beyond brinkmanship. Gordon, who in some ways was commendably brave, both in his personal conduct and in his taking up of less-popular political positions than the one which made his name, was also a little mad. As a fellow MP put it, he 'had got a twist in his head'. There seems little doubt that it was the issue of Catholic relief which had unbalanced him, or more exactly, the popular response to his embrace of it. While he had taken up 'radical' positions before, speaking against the war in America, and, when in the Navy, complaining about slavery, Catholic relief was the issue over which he found a following. Although he did not take a direct part in the riots, he did little to discourage them. Nonetheless, when he was indicted for treason, the fact that he had not actively participated was enough to secure his acquittal.

Gordon continued the campaign against Catholic relief, but was eventually gaoled in 1787 for publishing a pamphlet attacking the new sentence of transportation to Australia and for libelling Marie Antoinette. The most unexpected sequel for a man who had so strongly paraded his Protestantism was Gordon's prison conversion to Judaism. But, characteristically, he took this to extremes as well, not only having himself circumcised, but then refusing to converse with Jews who shaved their beards (Gordon grew his own to match his long and unkempt hair). It has been suggested that Gordon's conversion stemmed from a proto-Zionism, and a belief that the Second Coming would be hastened by the return of the Jews to Israel. He adopted the appropriately inspirational name of Israel Abraham. But his bizarre impact on eighteenth-century England ended in comparatively mundane fashion. Languishing in Newgate, the only partially rebuilt prison that his own followers had once torched, he caught a fever and died in 1793 with the French Revolution's call to arms, the 'Ça Ira', on his lips.

Gordon's choice of defiant farewell is a reminder that what had happened in France in 1789 had become the dominant political obsession on the other side of the Channel. The question of why Britain – with a constitution riddled with corruption, a 'foreign' monarchy, a lost colonial war and an apparently far more rebellious populace than France's – did not follow her neighbour into revolution is perhaps one of the most frequently asked in British history. One reason it keeps being posed is that it is even more difficult to explain why something didn't happen than why it did (and the alternatives begin to multiply). Perhaps the question becomes easier to answer if we accept that Britain's politics for at least the rest of the century, and indeed until after the Napoleonic wars, unfolded in reaction to what happened in France. In the first years after the French Revolution, there was certainly a significant movement to celebrate it, and perhaps to use any popular enthusiasm for it to push for reform at home. Provincial English Revolution clubs may have first been formed in the 1780s to celebrate 1688, not 1789, but after the fall of the Bastille many began to mark 14 July with the same vigour as 5 November. The domination of these clubs by dissenters and Whigs naturally hastened the formation of rival loyalist, Church and King clubs. As the Revolution slid towards ever greater violence, however, the balance between its supporters and opponents in England shifted towards the latter. And once France declared war on Britain, in 1793, although support for revolutionary principles did not vanish in an instant, the only way a British revolution would follow the French was if the French managed to impose it.

Viewed in this light, the quasi-heroic story of the founding fathers of English radicalism in the late eighteenth century, culminating in the mass movements for parliamentary reform of the nineteenth, and eventual manhood suffrage in the twentieth, looks a more fractured one, broken by the brute fact of war with France. In the wake of that war came a top-down reaction which treated reformers as potential rebels, and which sanctioned suspensions of habeas corpus and prosecutions of reformers for sedition and treason. These moves were accompanied in the 1790s by frequent acts of popular loyalist violence, of 'Church and King' mobs who were far more energetic and numerous in making clear their dislike of reform, seen as French 'Jacobinism' in disguise, than ever the radicals were in promoting it. In the suspicious atmosphere of post-French Revolutionary England, the leading voices for radical reform were unable to gain the parliamentary support they needed to be effective. Major John Cartwright, whose *Take Your Choice!*, published in 1776, had advocated parliamentary reform and universal (male) suffrage and annual parliaments; Thomas Hardy, the shoemaker who founded the London Corresponding Society in 1792 to promote the same cause; and even Thomas Paine, veteran of the American Revolution, whose *Rights of Man* – a response to Burke's conservative *Reflections on the French Revolution* – sold more than 200,000 copies: all found that, in what one MP called the 'hurricane season', no one in power was prepared to commit himself to repairing the national house.

These men and their followers all raised their voices against the establishment, and some fell foul of the law for doing so. Yet there was little chance at this moment of their becoming the sort of

English rebels who could actually change their country. Paine eluded arrest for sedition and fled to France. Hardy was tried for treason along with his fellow radicals John Horne Tooke (Wilkes's old associate) and John Thelwall in 1794. Although they were acquitted, they were marked men from this time. When mass meetings of the LCS were (unjustly) linked with subsequent attacks on the King as his carriage was drawn to Parliament in 1795, it gave William Pitt the Younger's ministry a pretext to pass Acts against Treasonable and Seditious Practices and against Seditious Meetings. These measures made the activities of such organizations as the Corresponding Society almost impossible to carry on. In any case, the war continued to inspire more manifestations of loyalist feeling than of radical ones. The Society's defendants may have been cheered in the streets after their acquittal, but Hardy's wife had been attacked in their home by loyalists while he was awaiting trial (she was pregnant, and subsequently both she and her baby died in childbirth). Hardy's house was attacked again three years later when he refused to illuminate it in 1797 after a victory over the French (he remarked that illuminating hadn't stopped the mob from attacking his wife). The LCS stopped holding mass meetings in 1797 and it was wound up in 1799. Other radical organizations, such as the London Revolution Society and the Society for Constitutional Information, also folded in the 1790s. Cartwright, from a more 'respectable' background, was able to continue campaigning, and the goal of reform wasn't forgotten. But any concerted action was almost impossible to orchestrate. None of this is to dismiss the significance of late eighteenth-century radicalism. But for this period, the radicals' actions have only a minor place in the story of English rebellion.

Where reformers were implicated in more-vigorous agitation, it tended to be as a direct consequence of the war, to which most radicals were opposed. In July 1795, radicals – 'well-dressed men haranguing the populace in true Parisian style' – were accused of fomenting the so-called 'crimp house riots'. Crimp houses were hated unofficial institutions, into which men were tricked or forced before being handed over as army 'recruits'. When a man was found dead outside one house in Charing Cross, with his arms and legs tied, it triggered several days of riotous attacks. As there were also food shortages at the time, it is unsurprising that cries for bread as well as 'no war' and 'no Pitt' were heard. If radicals were involved, however, they could not sustain the popular anger for long, and the riots died down after a week. Outside London, there were renewed Militia riots in 1796 on a similar pattern to those of 1757, after Pitt's government passed a new Militia Act to raise more troops. Again, the belief that recruits would be forced to serve abroad was the source of rioters' fears. These disturbances were fairly easily diffused, especially after a public information campaign was put in place to tell the people that militia men would not be expected to serve overseas.

Mutiny

If England ever did come anywhere near a revolution during these years, it was not in the meetings of Reform Associations, on city streets or in the fields. The rising that had the most serious potential to threaten the security of the country, and thus to raise the prospect of invasion, took place at sea. Success in the war depended on the Navy, and during the war its numbers had expanded from 16,000 to 114,000 by 1797. One way that had been achieved was by the introduction of quotas for naval recruits, which led to an increase in men from various non-maritime backgrounds, who were often more politically conscious than the average naval rating. In any case, one didn't have to be a revolutionary to find naval life objectionable. Seamen were paid at the same rate in 1797 as they had been in 1653, and two years after the Army had received pay increases, sailors were still awaiting a similar improvement. They were rarely allowed shore leave, as so many deserted, and the food on which they subsisted was semi-officially docked by the ship's purser. Such conditions, combined with the sometimes savage discipline meted out by some captains, had resulted in mutinies on individual ships, including the most famous, on the *Bounty*, in the year of the French Revolution (in fact two and a half months before the fall of the Bastille). A fleet mutiny among a group so rarely permitted the chance of unofficial contact was more difficult to arrange. When ships lay together at their anchorages off Portsmouth at Spithead, or at the Nore off the Kent coast, however, some communication could take place. In February 1797, the Admiral in charge of the Channel Fleet at Spithead, Lord Howe, received several identical petitions requesting improved pay. Although he did pass on the requests, and petitions were also sent to Parliament, nothing was done. For two months, the sailors went about their duties, but when they were ordered to weigh anchor, they refused. By then, a sort of alternative hierarchy had emerged, centred on one ship, the *Queen Charlotte*, and carried on by 'delegates' from each ship with almost a replica of ordinary naval discipline.

The delegates' refusal to set sail brought the dispute to a head, and faced with such unyielding demands, combined with the spread of the mutiny to ships off Plymouth, the government began to cave in. The mutineers were careful to secure a royal pardon for their actions, and improvements in their pay and conditions were voted through Parliament. Eventually, with their demands met, the Spithead mutineers returned their ships to the officers' command. Although their actions had raised the spectre of rebellion or defection, the delegates had been at pains to show that they retained their loyalty and would resist any enemy that appeared. The same could not be said of the mutiny at the Nore anchorage, where the crews of ships gathered to blockade France's Dutch republican allies came out with what at first seemed similar demands to those of the Channel fleet. But when the Admiralty offered the Nore mutineers, now joined by ships from the North Sea fleet, the same terms that had been agreed at Spithead, their leader, a disrated midshipman with radical leanings called Richard Parker, persuaded his fellow sailors that they could press for more. They then took the far graver step of sailing to blockade the Thames, threatening to cut off London from access to the sea.

If Parker had been able to maintain his blockade, the Nore

mutiny might have been the means by which the French Revolution was imported to England. He was happy to contemplate
defection to the Dutch if the mutiny failed, but instead, after the
Admiralty and the government held firm, the mutineers' resolve
began to crumble. As ship after ship sailed away, Parker threw
himself on the King's mercy, hoping to be granted the same pardon
that had been offered at Spithead. The Admiralty correctly saw his
insurrection as a far more serious matter and unsurprisingly gave
Parker, as well as twenty-eight others, no quarter. All were hanged
from their ships' yardarms on 30 June 1797. The same number
of mutineers were imprisoned and nine were flogged. Some
mutineers did manage to escape, probably to France, where they
avoided sentence. The Nore mutiny split apart because the
example of Spithead had shown that the Admiralty would respond
to a disciplined, 'loyal' strike. Whatever the sailors' grievances
against bad officers and poor conditions, they had clearly been
pushed beyond their intentions by Parker (though he maintained
he was not the ringleader). Both these naval rebellions had the
capacity to bring the country far closer to the brink of revolution,
if only by opening the possibility of invasion, than any number of
meetings and speeches on parliamentary reform in London or
Manchester.

15. Revolutionaries and Reformers

Colonel Despard to the Chartists 1802–67

Peaceably if we may, forcibly if we must

Motto adopted by the first General
Convention of Chartists, February 1839

The paranoid atmosphere of war made agitation for reform look like rebellion, and rebellion look like revolution. That mindset took a long time to change. It was not until the French Revolutionary Wars ended in 1802 that the possibility of a more active challenge to 'Old Corruption' from outside Parliament re-emerged. But for years to come, opponents inside both Houses tended to view all 'outdoor' political activity with suspicion, and memories of the Gordon riots were long. Even Lord Erskine, a moderate Whig supporter of reform, recalled his readiness in 1780 to 'blow the mob to the devil' when considering the government's latest crackdown on protestors in 1819. Any attempt to divide radicals or reformers into two distinct violent and non-violent camps is likely to impose the wisdom of hindsight. The two approaches alternated (and overlapped) in groups and even in individuals, right up to the Chartists' debate in the 1840s over whether 'moral force' or 'physical force' was most likely to succeed.

Shortly after the war ended, it was physical force that worried the government. Its concerns focused on an Irish military engineer who had once worked closely with Lord Nelson but had become disaffected after his dismissal as superintendent of Honduras: Colonel Edward Despard. In a plot that harked back almost to the days of the Earl of Essex or at least to Rye House, Despard seems to have attempted to combine the forces of two revolutionary movements, the United Irishmen (who had been involved in an unsuccessful French-backed rising in Ireland in 1798) and the less well-known United Britons, in a plan to attack the opening of Parliament. 'Seems' because he was arrested, on 16 November 1802, in a pub in Lambeth, well before any such plots had come to fruition. At his trial in February, the government employed what might be seen as the opposite tactic to the one it is charged with using against accused terrorists today. Modern juries are presented with the most extreme interpretation of terrorist plots, complete with mocked-up explosions and estimates of potential casualties. In 1803, Despard and his fellow suspects were portrayed as crackpots with little connection to any wider network.

There were a few scraps of evidence that pointed to a more impressive conspiracy. Cards identical to those found on Despard, calling for 'an equalization of Civil, Political, and Religious Rights', also turned up in Yorkshire and Lancashire. Intelligence sources not used at the trial implicated some known Jacobin sympathizers in the plot, which was meant either to strike at the opening of Parliament in November or to come together more widely the following year. Whatever the real magnitude of the conspiracy, the evidence presented at Despard's trial was enough to send him, along with six others (and despite Nelson himself appearing as a character witness), to the gallows. As many as 20,000 people were reported to have watched his execution, and more 'mainstream' radicals later claimed him as an inspiration.

A man who mostly represented the more law-abiding side of radical reform, but one who in his time was treated barely more generously than Despard himself, was Sir Francis Burdett. This fifth baronet was hardly an example of a self-made man, but his politics were always popular and reformist. In a number of ways, his challenge to the government ran along similar lines to that of John Wilkes. Like Wilkes, this enemy of Old Corruption owed his initial entry into Parliament to family influence, in Burdett's case to his grandfather's purchase of a pocket borough. But, coming to see the contradiction of sitting for an unrepresentative seat while espousing parliamentary reform, Burdett stood, in the same year as Despard's conspiracy, for Wilkes's old county seat of Middlesex.

Like Wilkes, Burdett was prevented from entering Parliament despite winning the popular vote. He spent the next five years attempting to get re-elected to Parliament, finally being returned for the now habitually radical seat of Westminster.

Although Burdett spoke consistently for reform, there was little support in the Commons. He wanted to provoke the government, led by the Tory Spencer Perceval, into demonstrating its repressive character, and thus to set off a popular reaction. Three years after returning as an MP, he found the cause that, according to some supporters as well as opponents, came close to unleashing a full-scale rebellion. In 1810, Burdett published criticism of the government's exclusion of reporters from a parliamentary debate (again taking up Wilkes's torch). The Commons voted to imprison him in the Tower for the duration of the parliamentary session. Burdett refused to submit, declaring the warrant illegal. Retiring to his house in Piccadilly, Burdett challenged the authorities to take him by force. There was yet another echo of Wilkes in Burdett's appeal to the City authorities to protect him from those under Parliament's command, and one City sheriff responded to the call. The final Wilkite resonance was in the 'mob' that supported Burdett, once again donning the blue cockade which happened also to be Burdett's 'colour', and shouting for 'Burdett and liberty' as they had for their earlier hero. For four days, crowds kept an arresting party at bay, and the Riot Act had to be read to disperse them. It was at this time that what is said to be one of the few barricades ever erected in the course of an English popular uprising was put up by Burdett's supporters, quickly gathering material from a building site to obstruct a detachment of troops coming to arrest them. Actually, barricades had been a feature of rebellions in London since 1215.

When Burdett himself was arrested on the fourth morning of the 'siege', before the crowd had reassembled, he happened to be engaged in the thoroughly appropriate act of listening to his son, down from Eton, translating Magna Carta. Burdett had been persuaded from taking a more robust stand against the ministry's troops by the lack of arms, though the normally 'moral' rather than 'physical' force radical Francis Place had no objection in principle to Burdett using violence. 'Many and perhaps nearly all the troops in London would have revolted,' Place thought, if Burdett had managed to 'promise effectual resistance'. As it was, the drama was not over, and at his release at the end of the session large crowds gathered again expecting to cheer Burdett home, prompting more fears on the government side of riot and possible insurrection. But Burdett refused his last performance, later explaining that he did not want to be the 'cause of a single accident, or the death of any person', and slipped away by boat from the Tower to avoid the crowds.

The Burdett affair seemed to reawaken some of the popular reforming zeal that had been so carefully snuffed out in the 1790s. But it also showed the limits of spontaneous, threatening 'mob' agitation, and began again the impetus for organized pressure. The year after the affair saw the founding of the Society (later Union) of Friends of Parliamentary Reform, and the year after that the formation of the first Hampden Club, named after the Member who resisted Charles I over Ship Money. The choice of name, like Burdett's son's choice of homework, and the later adoption of the People's Charter (to reflect Magna Carta) are all aspects of a crucial element of eighteenth- and nineteenth-century radicalism: the conscious adoption of an alternative radical, rebellious history of the country, which had achieved the 'ancient liberties' of the people. Paine had pointed out in *Common Sense* (1776) that 'in the distracted kingdom' of England since the Norman Conquest, there had been '(including the Revolution) no less than eight civil wars and nineteen rebellions'. Less famous radicals, such as the chairman of the London Corresponding Society in 1793, a silversmith called John Baxter, expanded on the same theme.

It is vain and ridiculous to tell us, that Resistance to a Government on all occasions is Rebellion; for in this Country in particular, it is a Maxim essential to the Constitution, and has been acted upon at various Times: it was amidst the din of arms that Magna Charta was wrested from that weak and profligate Prince King John; and again renewed in the reign of his son Henry, when the gallant Earl of Leicester supported by the other Barons and the People, compelled him to new model the Parliament . . .

It was an essential plank of the reformers' arguments that their cause was not newfangled, or some foreign import. It was home-grown, and this 'Tree of Liberty' had deep roots.

At Hampden Clubs, as Samuel Bamford reported, working men were introduced to the writings of William Cobbett, whose *Political Register* made clear in the plainest of language that the 'weight of taxes', the source of the country's misery, 'has all proceeded from the want of a Parliamentary Reform'. From 1811 and then sporadically over the next four years, it was economic hardship that inspired the most active demonstrations of resistance. 'Luddism', named after the fictional 'Ned Ludd' who was said to be the leader of the agitation, was a semi-organized movement of machine-breaking whose entry into popular parlance has given it an unfairly boneheaded popular reputation. The Luddites were not simple-minded opponents of 'progress' and technology. They were men who used the only weapons at their disposal (in an era when trade unionism was banned) to demonstrate for better wages and working conditions. By breaking or threatening to break the machines used in framework knitting and in the cotton and woollen industries, the Luddites tried to put pressure on the owners. Their activities overlapped with bread riots, and occasionally became more overtly political, though it is hard to substantiate the argument that the Luddites were organized revolutionaries. Less of a 'rabble' than their enemies made them out to be, they nonetheless showed little sign of wanting to transform their protest into a concerted attack on the constitution. No doubt some Luddites were also radicals. But they tried to keep their identities a secret, so we only know about those who were caught (like George Mellor, who was convicted of the murder of a mill owner in 1812, and who got up a petition for parliamentary reform while in prison). Just as often, they behaved in ways that recalled past rebels, setting up 'courts' or championing liberties in extremely traditional fashion. And like old-fashioned rebels, they were killed in large numbers: frame-breaking was made a capital offence and seventeen Luddites were hanged at York in 1813.

Spa Fields and Peterloo

A figure almost as difficult to pin down as Ned Ludd is Thomas Spence, who, particularly posthumously (he died in 1814), inspired some of the more extreme attempts to hasten the revolution. Spence was a bookseller and writer whose 'land plan' was closer to Gerrard Winstanley's communism than Karl Marx's. He wanted land to be redistributed among the population, but he didn't call for it to be nationalized. It was as a proponent of direct action, however, in favour of an armed coup led by a few thousand 'inspired' men, that he was taken up by disciples such as Arthur Thistlewood. Thistlewood was involved in organizing a meeting that he hoped would become an insurrection in Spa Fields in Clerkenwell, in December 1816. Again, the overlap between violent and non-violent radicalism was in evidence. The popular (law-abiding) radical Henry 'Orator' Hunt had been persuaded to address two meetings of 'Distressed Manufacturers, Mariners, Artisans and others of the Cities of London and Westminster' and their vicinity by the Spenceans, and agreed to do so on condition that their programme was not invoked. Hunt took a petition to the Prince Regent, and addressed a second meeting to relay the response it had yielded (none at all, in fact).

It was at this second meeting that, as *The Times* reported, 'a person mounted a coal-waggon with three flags, on which were inscribed certain mottoes'. This was James Watson, whose father (also James) was a prominent Spencean. The younger James had been treated for madness, and there was certainly something reckless about his performance that day. He invoked rebels of the past, and said that, since the petition had failed, 'We must do more than words. We have been oppressed for 800 years since the Norman Conquest. . . . Wat Tyler would have succeeded if he had not been basely murdered by a Lord Mayor. . . . The Ministers have not granted us our rights. Shall we take them? (*Yes Yes from the Mob*).' With that, he jumped from the cart and urged the crowd to follow him. In fact, only a small section did; most stayed to hear Hunt, who had deliberately delayed his arrival so as to miss any potential incitement. About 200 men marched through the City towards the Tower, arming themselves from gunshops on the way. But an even smaller number actually made it to the walls of the Tower, and when they failed to induce the guards to open the gates, a detachment of cavalry dispersed them and made arrests. Watson himself got away. The whole episode was reminiscent of the doomed march of Thomas Venner in 1661, though the relative lack of bloodshed made it more of a farce than a tragedy. After the first Spa Fields meeting, *The Times* merrily printed a mock obituary of Hunt, who was said to have fallen down drunk (after 'large and repeated potations of the pure *patriotic* British gin') on his way back to see the Prince Regent. Despite the best attempts of Hunt and his supporters to dissociate themselves from violence, as far as opponents were concerned all radicals were either dangerous, deranged, or dipsomaniacs.

The lack of evidence of the Spa Fields rioters' real intentions helped to secure the acquittal of their leaders. But there were indications from government spies that a more widespread rising had been planned (the signal in the country would come when the mail coaches stopped running). Only three months after the Spa Fields trial, there was an aborted attempt at another rising at the Bartholomew Fair in Smithfield. That failure seems to have persuaded the Spenceans to try a different approach. Two years later, Thistlewood and four others were caught in the middle of plans for a Rye House-style attack on the Cabinet at a private dinner. Thistlewood resisted arrest, stabbing and killing a Bow Street officer. Athough the conspirators briefly escaped, they were quickly captured. This time, with the evidence of a government spy who had acted as an agent provocateur, the Spenceans' conviction was assured. All five of the so-called Cato Street conspirators (the echoes of Republican Rome, and Cato's part in crushing the Catiline conspiracy, were not lost on the classically educated establishment) were found guilty of high treason and hanged on May Day, 1820. Like the Gunpowder Plotters, Thistlewood and his associates hoped that their act of mass assassination would be followed by a more general rising, although it is impossible to say how much of that was a fantasy either of the conspirators or of the government's spies. This was perhaps the last time that English rebels planned to topple the government by violence. And, by the time of Cato Street, the more peaceful side of radical reformism had received a blow that they did their best to translate into a propaganda coup: 'Peterloo'.

Henry Hunt had not been put off from an alliance with the Spenceans by the debacle of Spa Fields, and in September 1818 he put a new proposal to a meeting called by James Watson senior. Instead of a petition, the supporters of reform should issue a Remonstrance (the parallel with Parliament at the time of Charles I was clear) to demand their rights. At the meeting, one speaker again summoned up the rebel tradition: 'Why not go forth as the Barons of old with a Sword in one hand and the Bill of Rights in the other and demand your birthrights', and there were references to 'Magna Charta' and the fates of Charles I and James II. This seemed to be a platform upon which the more extreme and more moderate sides of radicalism could stand together. Hunt used the Remonstrance to recruit supporters to a national Political Union, and meetings were held throughout 1819 in which more provocative measures were adopted, such as electing 'legislatorial attorneys' for places like Birmingham and Leeds that were unrepresented in Parliament. Throughout the year, it seemed as if the radical reformers were increasing the pressure on the Tory government. Revolutionary slogans ('bread or blood') and speeches were heard at meetings in Stockport and Oldham. Watson was duly instrumental in the plans for a mass meeting to be addressed by Hunt at St Peter's Fields, Manchester, on 16 August 1819. The Manchester authorities, who had banned this meeting a week earlier, were clearly sceptical about the public assurances that nothing illegal would be attempted. When they saw groups of reformers practising drill on the eve of the meeting (the reformers said this was so their progress would be even more orderly), they became all the more twitchy.

On that morning, more than 60,000 men, women and children gathered, armed, as Hunt had requested 'with *no other weapon* but that of a self-approving conscience', and a number of banners with slogans such as 'Annual Parliaments and Universal Suffrage'. The *Times* report commented condescendingly on the group of 156 women reformers from Oldham whose white silk banner was 'by far the most elegant displayed during the day', but pitied 'the delusion which had led them to a scene so ill-suited to their usual habits'. When Hunt himself arrived, the Manchester yeomanry made their way through the throng to arrest him, presumably on the assumption that, despite his assurances to the contrary, he was about to be adopted as the 'legislatorial attorney' for Manchester, a gesture the government had declared illegal. Although the soldiers managed to get to Hunt, they couldn't make their way out, and the arrival of a force of Hussars to effect their exit caused the panic that led to most of the deaths that day. As the crowd fled from horses and sabres, some were trampled to death. Eleven people died, and over 400 were wounded. Among them were 140 who had been cut with sabres, a sign of the excessive force the cavalry had used in breaking up a peaceful meeting. It was not long before the press had christened the events 'Peterloo', a shaming defeat to set against Wellington's great victory four years earlier. *The Times*, no friend to Hunt, nevertheless condemned:

the dreadful fact that nearly a hundred of the King's unarmed subjects have been sabred by a body of cavalry in the streets of a town of which most of them were inhabitants, and in the presence of those Magistrates whose sworn duty it is to protect and preserve the life of the meanest Englishman.

For the reformers, Peterloo was a victory, 'the triumph of calumni-ated reform' as the radical paper *Black Dwarf* put it.

The Manchester meeting had been an entirely peaceful protest, and the response of the authorities combined incompetence, panic and indiscriminate force. Only in one respect was their (over) reaction understandable. Many of the same people who had been involved in the Spa Fields meetings – some, like Watson, in the insurrection that followed – were involved in Manchester. The idea of a peaceful mass meeting is familiar to us today, because the inheritors of the tradition of Peterloo have enshrined it in British life. But in 1819 large crowds usually meant trouble. This was, in fact, not the first time that a meeting at St Peter's Fields had been broken up. In March 1817, a group of around 5,000 Lancashire weavers known as 'Blanketeers', after the rolled-up blankets they carried with them, was dispersed by cavalry after the Riot Act was read. The Blanketeers were proposing to present a petition in London, but there had been rumours that their intentions were more revolutionary. In the same year, a general rising in the Midlands had failed to materialize, but a night march on Nottingham of a few hundred men from the nearby town of Pentrich, led by Jeremiah Brandreth, had alarmed the government enough for it to try forty-five men for high treason. Brandreth and two others were executed, while another thirty were sentenced to transportation. The government's response to Peterloo, passing laws against mass assembly and prosecuting Hunt, demonstrated that the idea of peaceful protest was not yet accepted. Peterloo became a rallying call and an inspiration to later generations of campaigners, but in 1819 the natural assumption of the establishment was that all such activists were potential rebels. Some certainly were. There were risings in Glasgow and several in Yorkshire the following year. The Spenceans' attempts to take advantage of popular feeling after Peterloo met with failure, and persuaded Thistlewood and others down the path of conspiracy that led to the gallows. By that time, Hunt had broken off all contact with his former allies.

In March 1820, Hunt was convicted for holding an unlawful assembly and 'arousing hatred and contempt of the government and the constitution'. He was imprisoned for two and a half years, giving him ample time to reconsider his approach to radical reform. His conclusion was that the 'mass platform' hadn't worked, and on his release, as well as trying to rebuild his fortune with such products as shoe blacking and 'breakfast powder', he formed the less confrontational Radical Reform Association with William Cobbett, and, when that failed, the Metropolitan Political Union in direct emulation of the Birmingham Political Union, in 1830. The Political Unions played an important part in the agitation for reform that eventually bore (tainted) fruit in the Reform Act of 1832. Hunt quickly saw through that measure, which fell so far short of what he had been campaigning for over so many years. But for a decade after Peterloo Hunt allowed others to take the lead in generating the sort of mass appeal that he had seen so spectacularly crushed in August 1819.

The 1820s were bookended by two displays of rebellious behaviour that recalled earlier times. The first was the rioting in 1820 and 1821 that accompanied the 'trial' and then the funeral of the estranged consort, Queen Caroline, of the new king, George IV. Radicals such as the MP Henry Brougham and Thomas Denman (a lawyer who had acted for the Pentrich rebels) made use of Caroline's dispute with her husband to try to embarrass the King and his ministry. In November, when the Bill of pains and penalties against the Queen was dropped, there was rejoicing and rioting not just in London but across the country. The affair seemed to have exhausted the Queen, and she died the following year. At her funeral the mob secured another victory, when they forced the funeral procession (by strategic use of barricades – again) to take a route through the City. If the big triumph of a reformed Parliament still seemed a long way off, small successes like these nevertheless demonstrated that 'outdoor' pressure could not always be ignored.

The agitations that began the new decade seemed to reflect an even older tradition, of agrarian protest, though the targets, such as threshing machines, were entirely modern. These rural uprisings, mainly in the South and East, lasted from 1830 to 1832 and were 'led', like those of the Luddites, by a mythical figure: Captain Swing. They typically involved threatening letters, an appeal to local leaders, and the destruction of machinery, sometimes accompanied by arson. Despite the fact of growing popular political participation in the decades leading up to 1830, it has proved almost impossible to sustain a link between wider agitation and Captain Swing. Many employers were sympathetic to the rebels, but their sympathy counted for little when both Tories and Whigs (the ministries changed during the course of the disturbances) reacted without a trace of compassion. Despite the fact that no one was killed in the Swing riots, and the orderliness of the rioters impressed onlookers, 252 death sentences were passed, and nineteen carried out, while 600 were imprisoned and nearly 500 transported. But unlike the Luddites in the factories, the Swing rioters do seem to have achieved one of their primary aims: the removal of threshing machines. Their actions brought home particularly to small and medium-size farmers the unpopularity of the machines, and also their dubious economic justification when labour was cheaply available. As the historians of the movement have put it, 'The real name of King Ludd was Swing.'

The People's Charter

The Whig administration led by Lord Grey that suppressed the Swing riots also at last brought in a measure of parliamentary reform in 1832. The Reform Act created new seats in some towns and abolished some of the unrepresentative boroughs. But it extended the electorate only fractionally, enfranchising fewer than 200,000 more men to give a total of around 652,000 voters, out of a population of around 10 million. The fact that Parliament reformed itself, and that it extended the franchise on such limited terms, would seem to argue that rebels and rebellion, even in the broadest of interpretations of the term, had little to do with the change. Certainly, much of the horse-trading between Whigs, Tories and the new king, William IV, which preceded the Act was far removed from the grassroots of agitation outside Parliament. But it is impossible to believe that the demonstrations, threatening language and wholesale rioting that broke out over the two-year period running up to the passing of the Bill could be completely ignored by the people at whom it was directed. When, for example, the House of Lords rejected the Bill, there were huge riots in Bristol, and smaller disturbances throughout the country. Meeting Lord Grey, a group of radicals determined that the best tactic was to 'frighten' the Whigs.

This 'language of menace', the threat of an uncontrollable surge of public opinion waiting to break over the establishment, resulted in the expected increase in repressive measures. But it also made reform very hard for any government to dismiss, once the principle, however diluted, had been accepted by a mainstream political party. When the Whigs resigned over the rejection of their first Bill, the King would not allow the Tories to form a ministry unless they brought in reform. The Tories' inability to govern on that basis left the way open for a return of the Whigs, and the passing at the second time of asking of the Reform Act. The fact that the necessity for reform had penetrated even as far as St James's Palace was an indication that popular pressure, which had often in the past meant more to the monarch than to Parliament, had played its part. Francis Place reckoned that when the Tory Duke of Wellington had appeared to be about to form a ministry, 'we were within a moment of general rebellion'.

It didn't take long for the realization to sink in of how far from the goal of universal suffrage the passing of the Reform Act left the country. In Birmingham, a huge meeting of 180,000 heard of the 'treachery' of the Act. At Cold Bath Fields in Clerkenwell in May 1833, a police constable was killed in a violent demonstration of would-be revolutionary fervour. The Metropolitan Police had only been introduced four years earlier, replacing a system that had operated since Tudor times. Although preventing crime was the reason the Home Secretary, Robert Peel, gave for setting up the force, it was used almost from the beginning in the politically sensitive role of supervising demonstrations. The origins of the police at the same time as the agitation for reform ensured that they would nearly always be cast in the role of deciding the difference between protest and rebellion.

Henry Hunt, who had been elected to Parliament for Preston, had seen through the false promises of the Reform Bill from the beginning, and had opposed it, which did not endear him to his former radical allies. Some, such as those in the Birmingham Political Union, even allowed their organization to lapse in the vain hope that the Reform Act was just the beginning of more far-reaching changes which a broader-based Parliament would bring in. When it became abundantly clear that this would not be the case, that the Act was seen as an end, not a beginning, the movement for reform began to reassemble. The organization that took up the cause was even more widespread than Hunt's mass platform of the previous decade, linking up with Scottish and Welsh radicals, as well as Irish Home Rulers, to form the first truly British national political pressure group. This movement attracted the support of the likes of the re-formed Birmingham Political Union, of the Glasgow combined trades, and of the London Working Men's Association. They came together around a document that was deliberately given a title with a pedigree over 600 years old, 'The People's Charter'.

In an age that was becoming increasingly sophisticated about the role of gesture and theatre in popular politics, the launch of the Charter wasn't a triumph of slick choreography. The pamphlet had been promised for almost a year by the time Arthur Wade, the representative of the London Working Men, waved a proof of it on 21 May 1838 and announced that he held 'in his hand a charter – a people's charter'. Although the meeting he was addressing, held on Glasgow Green, was attended by about 100,000 people, many had drifted away by the time Wade came to speak. Nor had he brought any copies of the People's Charter to distribute. Nonetheless, by the end of the year, the People's Charter, and the idea of a national petition to present it to Parliament, had taken hold. The combination of those two elements was an arranged marriage between London and Birmingham. But it was a third party who ensured that this union of Unions would hold the popular political stage for the next decade. The man who emerged as the driving force behind what became known as Chartism was

by birth not an English rebel but an Irish one, the former MP for
County Cork, and failed candidate for William Cobbett's old seat
of Oldham, Feargus O'Connor.

   O'Connor had not been present at the mishandled launch of
the Charter, and he was not universally popular with the London
radicals who first drew it up. He had fallen out, too, with his
original parliamentary leader, the Irish 'Liberator', Daniel O'Connell. The split with O'Connell committed O'Connor more completely to English radical concerns, although universal suffrage was
an idea that appealed across national borders. On the death of
Henry Hunt in 1835, O'Connor explicitly put himself forward as
the Orator's radical heir. He promised to 'fill up the vacancy caused
by the death of Henry Hunt', after failing in the Oldham election.
This he did by forming the Marylebone Reform Association and,
two years later, founding a new radical paper, the *Northern Star*.
The *Star* promoted Chartism and O'Connor in equal measure,
but, crucially, it secured northern radical affiliation to a Midlands
and London movement.

Moral and physical force

The Charter itself was nothing very new. All of its six points could
be found in the writings of reformers from Major Cartwright
onwards, 'embracing the principles of Universal Suffrage, No
Property Qualifications, Annual Parliaments, Equal Representation, Payment of Members, and Vote by Ballot'. What was new
about Chartism was the name, the campaign, and at its head
a rebel in a vainglorious, gentlemanly tradition reaching back
through Hunt, Burdett (O'Connor's godfather) and Wilkes. There
was something more. Chartism had an Irish landowner as its
figurehead, and its leadership included solid middle-class activists
such as the economist Thomas Atwood, founder of the Birmingham Political Union, and later the lawyer Ernest Jones. But it was
still a genuine working-class movement, its founding document
almost entirely the work of the cabinet-maker William Lovett, and

its message adopted by labouring men – and women – of all kinds. The hostile press was shocked to realize that it even included non-whites: one of the most committed of Chartist leaders was William Cuffay, a London tailor and the son of a St Kitts slave. Cuffay, who was born either on board ship bound for England, or in the port of Chatham, explored the limits of the freedom his parents gained on arrival in England. He was transported to Tasmania for levying war on the Queen in 1848.

Yet it might be argued that Chartism shouldn't really feature in a history of English rebellion. It was not exclusively English; for many of its leadership, it hardly represented a deviation from a well-trodden path of organized reform agitation that was closer to modern protest movements than traditional rebellion; and the ultimate failure, after the deliveries of mass petitions to Parliament in 1839, 1842 and 1848, to find another way of keeping up the pressure on MPs made most Chartist 'rebels' less ready in the final analysis to confront their masters than their predecessors had been. But in at least two respects Chartism fits very well with the story of the English rebel. The first is that Chartists saw themselves as part of that tradition. We have already mentioned the most obvious way in which this manifested itself, the name of the Charter itself. But we only need to listen to the speeches at a single Chartist meeting to hear the inspiration taken from English rebellion of the past. At Hartshead Moor, Yorkshire, in October 1838, one speaker, Abram Hanson, a shoemaker, referred to the condition of his fellow working men as that of 'serfs', the state that Wat Tyler and John Ball had encouraged the peasants to throw off. Another speaker, the Methodist preacher Joseph Stephens, was even plainer: 'The Lord Jesus Christ', he said, 'was the prince of Jack Cades!', a comparison the *Northern Star* reported as being received with 'Tremendous cheering'. There may have been as many as 250,000 people at that meeting. If the *Star* is to be believed, such references (however they were relayed in an age before loudspeakers) did not pass over their audience's heads: they inspired them.

Chartists made clear their connection to rebels past, but the other way in which they are central to the story of the English rebel is in their link to the future of the tradition. The people Chartism attracted, the issues (in addition to universal suffrage) its members championed, and the tensions created about how to conduct that campaign, all connect it to this next chapter. It took until the next century for the vote finally to be secured for all adult Britons, and Chartism was long dead by that time. Yet the Chartists established once and for all the political identity and participation of ordinary English men and women, and what they had in common with their fellow disfranchised in the other countries of the Union. As the son of a Chartist handloom weaver, Ramsden Balmforth, wrote in 1904, 'It would be a great mistake to suppose that the Chartist movement was really fruitless. No movement of its magnitude and intensity can be fruitless. . . . It was an excellent means of political education for the working classes.' More than that, Chartism lasted long enough to create something like an alternative culture, based around self-expression and independent action, and sustained by its own publications, art and literature, that would last long after its political campaign had waned.

'Political education' did not begin with the adoption of the People's Charter in 1838. The 1830s had witnessed two important radical political campaigns that would feed directly into Chartism. One was the agitation against the Poor Law Amendment introduced in 1834, which condemned those who sought poor relief to the ordeal of the workhouse (where, among other indignities, families were separated). It was against this measure that the fiery Methodist Stephens trained all his energy; although he was happy to address the great meetings that Chartism could raise, he was not actually interested in universal suffrage, seeing it as a distraction from the greater inequities imposed on ordinary Britons. The other campaign was on behalf of the Tolpuddle 'martyrs', six Dorset farm labourers who had been sentenced to transportation in 1834. The leaders of the successful campaign to reprieve those men included William Lovett, main author of the Charter pamphlet, and Arthur Wade, the LWMA representative who would announce the Charter in 1838. When it came to nominating delegates for a General Convention of Chartists, George Loveless, leader of the

Tolpuddle six, was chosen for Dorset. (He was in Australia at the time and, even though he returned after his reprieve, he couldn't find a substitute to work the land he had been given by the campaign, so he never actually attended.)

The General Convention, the first meeting of which in London coincided with the opening of Parliament in February 1839, papered over the cracks that necessarily existed in a movement bringing together so many different localities, not to mention nationalities. But the essential problem – the historic dilemma of the 'loyal' rebel – could not be avoided. This was what to do if (and most of the Convention and its supporters thought it would be 'when') the National Petition was rejected by Parliament. There were proposals for a 'National Holiday' – what we would call a General Strike – to last a week, or perhaps a 'sacred month'. There were also threats of more direct action, powerfully expressed, but never producing universal agreement. A meeting of the London Democratic Association, whose leader, George Julian Harney, was a delegate at the Convention, passed a resolution at the time 'to meet all acts of oppression, with immediate resistance', adding, 'we hold it to be the duty of the Convention, to impress upon the people the necessity of an immediate preparation for ulterior measures'. Such talk frightened off some Chartists, including James Cobbett, son of William, who had always been a lukewarm radical in comparison to his father and who now proposed presenting the petition and no more, which was no different from what the Home Secretary announced the Chartists should do.

The reaction to Parliament's rejection, on 12 July 1839, of the Petition for the Charter (signed by 1.2 million people) was perhaps predictably disjointed. Five days after the parliamentary vote, the Convention called for the 'sacred month', but less than three weeks after that it was called off. Although 'moral force' Chartists continued to meet, organize and decide on their next move, the initiative had passed, for the time being, to the supporters of 'physical force'. There had already been riots in Wales and Birmingham earlier in the year. On the night of 4 November 1839 (eve of another rebellious anniversary), John Frost, a Newport tailor and a veteran radical who had been a magistrate and a mayor of his home town, led a group of 3,000 armed men in an attack on the Westgate Hotel, where a detachment of troops was guarding Chartist prisoners. In the battle that followed, twenty-two Chartists were killed and more than fifty wounded. It emerged later that this had not been meant as an isolated attack, but a combined three-pronged rising on Abergavenny, Newport and Brecon, aimed at blackmailing the government by controlling these important economic centres. Disturbances in Wales earlier in the year, at Llanidloes and against new tolls in the 'Rebecca riots', might persuade us that the Newport rising was a specifically Welsh venture. But English Chartists knew about it: Frost had appeared at several English Chartist meetings in the months leading up to the rising, and consulted with a mysterious 'tall working man' from the North of England at the end of October. Feargus O'Connor, who maintained that he knew nothing of the rising, was shocked to discover that the editor of the *Northern Star*, William Hill, *had* known of it and done nothing to stop it. The line between 'physical force' and 'moral force' Chartism was never as sharp as those two categories make it sound, but the appearance of real violence clearly shook even the more aggressive leaders of the movement.

Frost and two others were tried and convicted of high treason, and a huge appeal for a reprieve was initially denied by a meeting of the Whig Cabinet. Frost's execution was scheduled for 6 February 1840, only four days before the royal wedding of Queen Victoria and Prince Albert. It is sobering to think that this celebration of the fount of 'Victorian values' might have taken place so soon after a quasi-medieval ritual of hanging and posthumous decapitation (the fate Thistlewood and his fellow conspirators had suffered after Cato Street). Whether it was that uncomfortable juxtaposition, or simply the opinion of the Chief Justice in favour of clemency, that eventually persuaded the government, Frost and his fellow conspirators William Jones and Zephaniah Williams all had their sentences commuted to transportation for life.

By the time of Frost's reprieve, there had been two more

attempted Chartist risings, in Sheffield and Bradford, at the beginning of the year. Neither was as serious as Newport, but all three incidents irrevocably deprived Chartism of its hard-earnt reputation for orderliness and respectability. The formation of a National Charter Association under Lovett in 1841 gave 'moral' Chartism renewed impetus, although the founding of the Complete Suffrage Union in Birmingham the same year showed that unity had been lost. The National Association agreed on another petition for the Charter, this time even bigger. It was presented to Parliament in May 1842, with more than 3.3 million signatures, but was again rejected. More MPs bothered to debate it, but although this meant three more votes for the Petition, it also resulted in fifty-two more against. Once again, the question of how to react tormented the Chartists.

In a way, their decision was made for them, as a dire economic situation led to widespread industrial unrest and the outbreak of strikes in the North, beginning only three months after the rejection of the Petition: the start of the so-called Hungry Forties. The government and establishment opinion in general were in no doubt that Chartists were responsible for the agitation, along with the anti-protectionist Anti-Corn Law League (a 'middle-class' movement with which the Chartists eschewed any alliance, but whose single-issue campaign met with far more ultimate success). These strikes of factory workers who, an inspector reported, had to choose between 'employment on any terms, or starvation', were nevertheless christened the 'Holiday insurrections' or 'Plug plots' (from the tactic of removing the plugs from the boilers of pit engines) by opponents who saw rebellion in all working-class organization. Chartists were certainly involved in the strikes, which spread through coalfields and mills in north Staffordshire, Lanarkshire, Lancashire, Cheshire, Yorkshire and across the east Midlands and north-east, as well as south Wales. Such widespread action could not fail to include supporters of the Charter. In some areas, such as Manchester, there were attempts to link the two more specifically. It seems that the connection was made to an already existing strike movement; no Chartist 'conspiracy' was needed to start it. Although the 'Plug plots' were accompanied by several outbreaks of violence, the lack of trade union organization meant that no strike could be supported for long, and by the end of August men were going back to work.

For almost six years, the energies of Chartists were directed into alternative schemes, such as the 'Land Question', which resulted in the setting up of several model communities, including 'O'Connorville' at Heronsgate, Hertfordshire, divided into small holdings by ballot. The adoption of this 'promised land' attracted new recruits to the cause, such as Ernest Jones, a young barrister who would become one of the leading voices of Chartism's latest phase. But the reinvigorated movement still put its trust in its tried and failed method. In the European revolutionary year of 1848, on 10 April, a mass meeting at Kennington Common across the Thames from Parliament was called to present the latest petition to MPs. The original plan was for the crowd to march to the House en masse, but institutional memories of the Gordon riots hadn't dimmed, and the whole city seemed to anticipate an insurrection. At the British Museum, stones to throw at insurgents were stockpiled on the roof. About 85,000 special constables were drafted in to resist the revolutionary crowd. Faced with such measures, some Chartists stayed away, although the gathering of around 150,000 was still impressive. Feargus O'Connor consulted with the Metropolitan Police Commissioner and agreed to abandon the march. He made a speech dispersing the crowd, and the petition was delivered in a fleet of hansom cabs. When it was discovered that many of the signatures were reproduced or for invented names, the petition was mocked in the House. O'Connor, who was by this time an MP himself, reacted to the barbs by challenging a fellow Member to a duel. Although he withdrew the challenge, his blustering reaction, and the general suspicion that the petition was a put-up job, did great damage to the cause. Once again, what to do once the petition was dismissed divided Chartists. There were riots in Bradford and London, and Jones was arrested for making an inflammatory speech. But a planned uprising in August, to take place simultaneously across Lancashire and London, was efficiently dealt with by a well-informed police. A wave of repression followed: forty-six arrests in Lancashire, twenty-one in London, a combined total of nearly 300 Chartist leaders eventually convicted, with sentences of transportation or long imprisonment, though death sentences were again commuted.

Chartism continued in different forms for another ten years, but even the fiery Harney realized that its 'outward and visible form . . . perished in 1848'. Many attributed that to the rising prosperity of those years, although those benefits did not always trickle down to rank-and-file Chartists. The more likely explanation of Chartism's 'failure' was a defeat. The movement was eventually beaten by the combination of indifference, ridicule and repression with which it was met by the people it hoped to persuade: the Members of the 'reformed' Parliament. The fate of Chartism's most charismatic leader seems appropriately undeserved. In 1852, Feargus O'Connor was declared insane. He spent the rest of his life in an asylum in Chiswick, only being taken out by his sister to die at her home in Notting Hill, in 1855. Fifty thousand people attended the funeral in Kensal Green of an Irishman who should certainly be counted as an English rebel.

After the demise of Chartism, Britain inched towards democracy. Expansions of the electorate in 1867 and 1884–5 were directed, like the first such exercise in 1832, mostly from the top down. The equivocal development of English rebellious traditions that Chartism represented seemed to have no place in this process. But Reform agitation outside Parliament did not vanish. In July 1866, for example, the short-lived Reform League protested against the banning of meetings in Hyde Park by marching there, and a section of the crowd turned violent, breaking down the railings and fighting with police. A second meeting the following year defied a government ban, gathering up to 200,000 people peacefully to hear speeches on reform. An Act did follow, but it had been in discussion for five months before the demonstration. Although, at the time, conservative publications like the *Quarterly Review* ascribed the passing of the Act to the actions of the 'mob' in Hyde Park, it is easier to show that the meeting established

Hyde Park as a venue for such protests (no mean feat in itself) than that it secured the second Reform Act. Disraeli, the reluctant architect of the 1867 Act, said he was motivated by two things, a desire to 'destroy the present agitation and extinguish Gladstone and Co'; the agitation was mentioned first, but Disraeli's more consistent obsession was with his great political adversary.

In any case, even after the further expansion in 1884–5, more than a tenth of the adult male population remained ineligible to vote. The difficulties of registering to vote made the actual numbers enfranchised smaller still. Three years before the First World War, only 63 per cent of adult males were registered. And these statistics ignore half the population. No woman had the vote before the First World War ended. The rebels outside Parliament who campaigned for universal suffrage through to the mid-nineteenth century meant by that, with a few honourable exceptions, votes for men. As their energies were diverted into other causes, such as the Chartist land experiments or the rise of trade unionism, British women (with some male allies) took on their own fight for the vote themselves. Some of them did so in the best traditions of English rebellion.

16. Women and Workers

The Suffragettes to the General Strike 1905–26

'The argument of the broken window pane is the most valuable
argument in modern politics'

Emmeline Pankhurst

Throughout English history, the achievements – or even the
example in defeat – of one set of rebels has marked out the path
for another. This pattern is visible at least since the popular rebels
of the Middle Ages began marching for the liberties that other
groups, from freemen to the represented commons, had already
achieved. It continued even as the nineteenth century came to an
end and English women began to campaign actively for the right
to vote. Calling the Chartists 'English rebels' involved some special
pleading. When it comes to the campaign for female suffrage, one
qualifier – that the organizations were British rather than English
– applies again. But the more militant campaigners positively embraced their role as rebels. It was Emmeline Pankhurst – matriarch
of a family inspired and then more or less consumed by the cause
of women's suffrage – who declared at the Albert Hall on
25 October 1912, 'I incite this meeting to rebellion.' Less than a
year later, she elaborated on her theme in another public speech:
'I know that women, once convinced that they are doing what is
right, that their rebellion is just, will go on, no matter what the
difficulties, no matter what the dangers, so long as there is a woman
alive to hold up the flag of rebellion. I would rather be a rebel
than a slave.'

Pankhurst also made reference to the Chartists, and it is striking
that it was not until after the demise of Chartism that the campaign
for women's suffrage began to emerge as a separate cause. It took

another four decades for this movement to take up militancy. The reappearance in the early twentieth century of direct, rebellious tactics aimed at the ruling classes was treated in some quarters as an anomalous, 'un-English' phenomenon. In 1908, an anonymous female correspondent to *The Times* deplored the 'shouters' who 'by their violent and unbalanced behaviour, show how unworthy they are to legislate'. This writer was convinced that she spoke for the vast majority of her sex in rejecting 'rowdyism' and trusting in 'our Englishmen, whose whole nature and training produces [*sic*] more evenly-balanced minds and judgment'. If this did represent a widely held view, one reason is that women, particularly after their popular sentimentalization in publications like Coventry Patmore's *Angel in the House* (1862), were now widely thought of as far too delicate to engage in rebellion. But that reflected a Victorian cast of mind, not an unchanging axiom. The roots of British feminism can be traced to the 1790s and the writings of Mary Wollstonecraft; more directly political feminism suffered a similar fate to most English radical causes after the French Revolution, although women took part in much of the wider agitation of the early nineteenth century. Before that, women had long been the chief instigators of bread riots (they bought the bread and were first to know when the 'customary' price changed). In the movement for parliamentary reform, women created separate organizations under the umbrella of campaigns such as Hunt's mass platform or Chartism itself. They also participated in the less militant (but more successful) campaigns to abolish the slave trade and the corn laws.

For both sexes, the reign of Queen Victoria after 1848 proved one of the least rebellious in English history, and this fact alone may account for the impression that direct action of the kind championed by the suffragettes, and at other times by the more militant trade unions or the unemployed, was exceptional in England. On the contrary, the relative decorum of Victorian politics was the anomaly. Attempts to recapture some of that period's combination of deference and self-confidence have occupied sections of political opinion ever since. You don't have to be an authoritarian bigot to want to bring back some Victorian habits (though it probably helps). But, across the longer span of history, rebels from the Pankhursts to the General Strikers were picking up the scent that had been buried by Victorian prosperity, not importing an alien tradition.

Suffragists into Suffragettes

The campaign for women's votes started genteelly enough. At the outset it relied on men to bring it to public attention. In 1832, Henry Hunt had introduced a petition to grant the vote to unmarried women who met the property qualifications (but were therefore 'unrepresented' by their husbands, the argument that did for married women's political rights for so long). The only result was the specific exclusion of women in the first Reform Act. After the Chartist defeats, the first women's group to discuss female suffrage was the Langham Place circle in the 1850s, from which the Kensington Society emerged in 1865. When John Stuart Mill was elected to Parliament that year on a platform that included women's suffrage, he was approached by Barbara Leigh Smith Bodichon, a founder of the Langham Place circle, to submit a petition to Parliament on the issue. This provided the impetus for the first local Women's Suffrage societies, with Manchester and London predominant. Mill's amendment to the 1867 Reform Act (to substitute the word 'person' for 'man' in the Bill) was rejected, prompting a National Society for Women's Suffrage to bring together the groups in London and Manchester, and to take in similar societies in Edinburgh, Bristol and Birmingham. Women's suffrage had begun to emerge onto the national stage.

Until the turn of the century, the most rebellious thing about the women's suffrage movement was its very existence. There were differences of opinion on the ways to approach the campaign. Should it be limited to suffrage or address other issues such as the iniquitous Contagious Diseases Acts (which forced 'common prostitutes' to be registered and examined for venereal disease in garrison towns)? Exactly which women should be given the vote (married as well as unmarried, propertied or not)? Such issues split fragile national alliances more than once, but throughout the 1870s suffrage bills were presented to Parliament (and rejected). A growth in party political support for women's suffrage (initially greater among Conservatives, who expected well-to-do women – the likely beneficiaries of most early proposals for an extended franchise – to vote for them) kept hopes alive, but also meant that party politics could play a part in defeating proposals. In 1897, a new organization, the National Union of Women's Suffrage Societies, reunited around a Special Appeal that had begun earlier in the decade to gather signatures nationally, and across a far broader social spectrum of women than had previously been the case. That year, a bill proposed by a Conservative MP actually passed a second reading, but the government refused to grant it any more parliamentary time.

There is no doubt that the gradual, painstaking approach adopted from 1867 until the turn of the century made women's suffrage a serious political issue that could not be ignored. Other develop-ments, such as securing participation in local democracy and women's growing role in the increasingly efficient Liberal and Conservative party organizations, made it harder to argue that women should not also have a part to play in formal national politics. Much had been achieved, and with hindsight it could be argued that the national campaign had come far closer to securing its goal than Chartism ever had. But to some in the campaign, the near miss of 1897 (and subsequent parliamentary votes in favour of women's suffrage, after which successive governments nevertheless failed to make room in their legislative programmes) merely dem-onstrated that what the Chartists had called 'moral force' hadn't worked.

Yet the resort to militancy, and the rise of the Pankhursts – mother Emmeline, and her daughters Christabel, Sylvia and Adela – did not come about quickly. Emmeline Pankhurst, born Emme-line Goulden in 1858, came from a radical Lancashire family which supported the women's suffrage movement and took their fourteen-year-old daughter to hear the Secretary of the National Society for Women's Suffrage, Lydia Becker, speak. But Emmeline's own political activism began very much in the shadow of her husband Richard Pankhurst, who campaigned for women's emancipation as a Liberal and later as a supporter of the Independent Labour Party. It was for the ILP that Emmeline was elected as a representative on the Chorlton-upon-Medlock Poor Law Board of Guardians in Manchester in 1894. This involvement in local politics, and her association with a husband who never made much of a success of either his legal or his political career, gave no indication of the historic role she and her daughters would assume ten years later.

Richard's death in 1898 put a temporary stop to Emmeline's political activity, as she concentrated on the problem of providing for herself, her three daughters and one son (Harry, a sickly boy whose frailty his mother never really accepted: he died aged twenty after contracting polio). When she returned to active politics, little had changed. The Independent Labour Party and the Labour Representation Committee (forerunner of the Labour Party) still had more pressing priorities than female suffrage, and the other two parties, though all containing broad support for the issue, were not unanimous and certainly would not make it part of their declared policy. It was a display of completely conventional sexism by the Pankhursts' own party in 1903, banning women from entering a social club (in Pankhurst Hall in Salford, built as a memorial to Richard Pankhurst, and decorated by Sylvia), that persuaded Emmeline of the necessity of setting up another women's suffrage group separate from Independent Labour: the Women's Social and Political Union. The choice of name may have owed something to the Political Unions of the nineteenth century. At first, the methods the new organization adopted were not very different from such predecessors in the male or female suffrage campaigns. Even the more provocative moves, such as nominating Emmeline as a parliamentary candidate, were in the tradition of John Wilkes, of standing when 'outlawed'.

It was the eldest Pankhurst daughter, Christabel, who initiated the decisive change of policy in 1905. Though she was still a law student, aged twenty-five, she began behind the scenes to assume the dominant role in the Union. Concluding that the campaign was 'making no headway', she resolved to get herself arrested. At a Liberal Party meeting at the Manchester Free Trade Hall, she and Annie Kenney disrupted Sir Edward Grey's speech and unfurled a banner on which was emblazoned the bold new slogan 'Votes for Women'. The police were content to eject them quietly, but Christabel made sure of arrest by spitting in a Superintendent's face and hitting an Inspector in the mouth. When the two women refused to pay the magistrates' fine, Christabel and Annie were sent to prison for seven and three days respectively. The point of the exercise was to generate publicity, and it worked. National newspapers reported the women's release, which was greeted by 1,000 supporters, and one suffragist later wrote that 'twenty years of peaceful propaganda had not produced such an effect.'

For the next five years, the WSPU grew in stature – and funds – as it attracted women of all classes, from the 'factory girl' Annie Kenney to Lady Constance Lytton, whose brother was a Tory earl. It conducted concerted campaigns to disrupt by-elections and major politicians' speeches (Winston Churchill, although a mild supporter of women's suffrage, was a particular favourite) and to 'rush' the House of Commons. After being arrested for the last offence, Christabel achieved the coup of summoning the Chancellor of the Exchequer, David Lloyd George, to the witness box, and later exposed the Home Secretary, W. E. Gladstone's son Herbert, as having advocated exactly the sort of 'direct' methods for which the suffragists were now being condemned. Christabel concluded, 'We are here, not because we are law-breakers; we are here in our efforts to become law-makers.'

By this time, the name given by hostile sections of the press to the militants, 'suffragettes', had been adopted by the campaigners themselves (in the fine tradition of English party-naming, just as Tory and Whig began as insults). For centuries, acts of rebellion had exposed the prejudices of the rebels, from the followers of Simon de Montfort to the Gordon rioters. The suffragettes, too, had their hobby horses, but what their campaign revealed more acutely was the depth of prejudice against women. Rowdiness at elections spilt over into physical attacks on individual women. One campaigner wrote of the 'mob [which] played a sort of Rugby football with us', while even policemen were alleged to be 'rough and indecent'. After one demonstration, a protestor described how 'for hours one was beaten about the body, thrown backwards and forwards from one [policeman] to another, until [one] felt dazed by the horror of it.' The argument about whether militancy delivered or delayed the vote to women still continues. It probably did both. What must be conceded is that suffragette militancy, for all its initial focus, involved far more than the vote: it showed what women were capable of, and it held up a mirror to British society.

The two most notorious suffragette tactics were not initiatives of the Pankhursts, though they soon adopted them. The first concerted act of window-breaking occurred after a march to deliver a petition in June 1909 had ended in the usual round of arrests. The same evening, a group of suffragettes began throwing stones at the windows of the Home Office, the Privy Council and the Treasury. At first, Emmeline apologized for their actions, but window-breaking, together with chaining oneself to railings, soon became a staple of militancy. The original suffragette hunger-striker was Marion Wallace Dunlop, who refused food in Holloway Prison and secured early release. Subsequent hunger-strikers were subjected to the horrors of forcible feeding. A tube 'two yards long' was inserted through the nose or mouth down to the stomach, and milk or raw eggs were poured down a funnel attached to it. As one prisoner reported, 'the sensation is most painful – the drums of the ear seem to be bursting, a horrible pain in the throat and the breast'. Another described how 'as the nozzle turned at the top of my nose to enter my gullet, it seemed as if my left eye was being wrenched out of its socket.'

By 1910, it looked as if these sacrifices had not been in vain. A bill for female suffrage with cross-party backing, and sponsored by a well-known journalist, Henry Brailsford, appeared to be about to succeed where so many others had failed. The suffragettes, who had temporarily exhausted their own and the public's appetite for militancy, were content to suspend their actions in the anticipation of victory. Once again, however, the government (led by the Liberal Herbert Asquith) feared that the measure, known as the 'Conciliation Bill', which did not enfranchise married women, might harm their party's interests. Equally, the Conservatives were not strongly enough in favour of the Bill to call the government's bluff. Like previous measures, the Conciliation Bill made it to a second vote before running out of parliamentary time. As Christabel had warned, if this Bill, which had seemed to generate so much consensus, was denied by government inertia, despite the suffragettes' re-adoption of constitutional methods, 'Mr Asquith will have shown how necessary militancy is.'

It was after this setback that the march resulting in the 'rough and indecent' police misconduct took place. November the 18th, 1910, became known, after a *Daily Mirror* headline, as 'Black Friday', and it was followed less than a week later by the 'Battle of Downing Street', when Asquith's car was set upon and windows were broken in government offices. The twentieth century would be sprinkled with days coloured black and red, the work of a popular press and efficient propaganda machines, but the suffragettes were the first to make use of the custom. The behaviour of the police in these two encounters led to a change in tactics as well. The Pankhursts decided after Black Friday that attacks on property were a safer form of militancy than contending bodily with policemen who did not always play by the rules. Emmeline's rationalization of this could stand for any number of acts of 'targeted violence' in the story of English rebellion:

Property to them [governments] is far dearer and tenderer than is human life, and so it is through property that we shall strike the enemy. . . . We want [property-owners] to go to the Government and say, 'Examine the causes that lead to the destruction of property. Remove the discontent.'

The return to militancy heralded by Black Friday and the Battle of Downing Street was delayed until another attempt to pass the

Conciliation Bill had failed. But this was to be the final phase of the campaign. It was permanently interrupted by the First World War.

Up to 1912, the suffragettes' campaign, as opposed to the on-going, though less headline-grabbing, suffragists' one, had succeeded in keeping the issue of women's votes at the top of the political agenda. After 1912, however, as both Sylvia and Adela discovered when their mother and elder sister excluded them from the Women's Social and Political Union for not toeing the line, the struggle itself seemed to displace the practical end of securing a suffrage bill. This was true of Emmeline, who continued an extended campaign of hunger-striking after the passing of the so-called 'Cat and Mouse Act', which provided for the release of fasting prisoners and their re-arrest on recovery. It was even truer of Christabel, who spent from March 1912 until after the outbreak of war evading arrest in France. In her preface to a book by Sylvia, *The Suffragette*, published in 1911, Emmeline was already revealing how militancy had seduced her:

Perhaps the women born in happier days that are to come, while rejoicing in the inheritance that we of to-day are preparing for them, may sometimes wish that they could have lived in the heroic days of stress and struggle and have shared with us the joy of battle, the exaltation that comes of sacrifice of the self for great objects . . .

Whereas previous militant innovations had been improvised, Christabel and the leadership of the WSPU directed the escalation between 1912 and 1914. Not all acts were sanctioned by them: the most famous suffragette demonstration of all, Emily Wilding Davison's fatal encounter with Anmer, the King's horse, at the Epsom Derby in 1913, was a 'freelance' action by a suffragette who was never employed by the Union. It is not known whether Davison intended her act as one of martyrdom (she died four days later, without having regained consciousness). But the Union made some capital out of her funeral, and the newsreel footage of her, ducking under the rails and apparently attempting to halt the race as all but one of the horses thunder by her, brings Davison's sacrifice unnervingly into the modern era (though it is still a shock to find it on YouTube, complete with the usual 'debate'). At the time, Davison's act – described by one of the royal household in a telegram to the injured jockey as 'the abominable conduct of a brutal and lunatic woman' – made less impression than the fact that the favourite and first past the post of the best-attended Derby in years was disqualified in favour of a 100–1 outsider.

Davison may have worked alone, but other acts – of arson, window-smashing with hammers and stones, the bombing of empty premises, and various attacks on property – were all more or less centrally orchestrated. The radicalization of the campaign caused internal dissension as well as disagreement in the country at large. Sylvia Pankhurst, who refused to stop working with men after Christabel had introduced a total ban on male participation, was expelled from the Women's Social and Political Union. Although she continued a militant campaign, she was invited to meet Lloyd George. Her mother and elder sister, meanwhile, had apparently lost all connections to the centres of power. It was Sylvia's breakaway organization, the East London Federation, that secured an undertaking in June 1914 from Asquith, the Prime Minister, to put through a more 'democratic' (i.e. full male and female) suffrage measure. The Federation's support for this (while Emmeline and Christabel insisted on a purely female bill) demonstrated a sharper understanding of where radical pressure on the government was likely to come from. The East London Federation, with its working-class membership and strong links to the Labour Party, was far better placed to ally itself to the growing pre-war labour and unemployed agitation than was the increasingly marginalized, anti-Liberal and Labour, and apparently anti-male WSPU. The diversion of Emmeline and Christabel's campaign into the 'sex war' that opponents had always accused it of fighting may have struck a blow for feminism, but it did little to gain votes for women. The Pankhursts' unwillingness truly to transcend the stereotypes of the 'weaker sex' also made difficulties. One disaffected member summed up the problem of combining militancy with feminine 'injured innocence' as a 'crooked course' or 'double shuffle, this game of quick change from the garments of the rebel to those of the innocent martyr'. Sylvia Pankhurst, on the other hand, may still have been a middle-class woman at the head of yet another suffrage group, but the journey of the campaign from its origins in fashionable Kensington to impoverished Bethnal Green was an illustration that, with sympathetic leadership, women's suffrage could be a genuinely popular cause.

On 28 June 1914, in the same month as the apparently significant contacts between Sylvia's organization and the Liberal government, Archduke Franz Ferdinand was assassinated in Sarajevo, setting in train the series of ultimatums and missed deadlines that would result in H. G. Wells's 'war that will end war'. Britain entered the conflict in August, and the women's suffrage campaign, which had always competed for political attention with everything from Irish Home Rule to the reform of the House of Lords, was for the time being forgotten, at least at Westminster. Perhaps unexpectedly, Emmeline and Christabel were complicit in the collective amnesia. They suspended 'suffragette' activities, showing a sense of realism about the impact of violence that had seemed increasingly absent in the months leading up to the war.

Unlike Sylvia, who continued a combined campaign for women's and workers' rights (her organization's paper changed its name in 1917 from the *Woman's Dreadnought* to the *Workers' Dreadnought*), Emmeline and Christabel had also run out of energy. The constant round of arrests, hunger-strikes and re-arrests was no longer generating the same sort of publicity, and, without political backing, had ceased to have any effect on the government. The war gave Christabel and Emmeline a new, far more popular cause to support, and it sealed their move to the right, away from Emmeline's radical Lancashire roots (and from her daughter Sylvia's 100 degrees proof socialism). As war patriots, Emmeline and Christabel brought the same zeal to conforming as they had to rebelling (their paper changed its name, too, from *The Suffragette* to *Britannia*). The diversion of WSPU funds to support the war effort, while many suffragettes were pacifists, broke up the Union for good; but even before the war the organization was tottering and isolated.

Until 1916, the women's suffrage issue was drowned out by the sound of guns. The prospect of a general election in the middle of the war, however, which on the existing system would have excluded most servicemen from voting as not meeting the residence qualifications, allowed the movement to re-emerge. At the Speaker's Conference that was called to try to reach a general agreement among all parties, the moderate National Union of Women's Suffrage Societies, led by Millicent Fawcett, made the case for women's votes. Emmeline Pankhurst, now as immersed in the war effort as she had once been in the struggle for women's votes, had actually withdrawn her support for women's suffrage in case it stopped the enfranchisement of servicemen. The compromise that was reached, and actually passed as the first Representation of the People Act in 1918, still restricted the female vote to those women over thirty who were qualified municipal electors or the wives of male municipal electors, which enfranchised about 8 million women. It was not until ten years later that the voting age was reduced to twenty-one, all other restrictions were lifted, and women actually achieved parity in voting with men.

The partial success of the women's suffrage movement in 1918 was less than convincingly claimed as a triumph for their methods by Emmeline and Christabel Pankhurst. In Christabel's posthumously published account of the struggle, it was 'our Votes for Women victory', in which 'the sacrifice of the militants had been rewarded.' Attempts were made to get Christabel into Parliament, backed by a newly formed Women's Party. Though the result was a close one, the Pankhursts had made little attempt to forge links with the constituency (Smethwick in the west Midlands), apparently believing that their 'war work' (which had principally consisted of encouraging speeches and editorializing directed at industrial workers) would cancel out a reputation for anarchy. It didn't. Christabel lost, and her interest waned after an attempt to be adopted for the Westminster Abbey Division failed. She later became a born-again Christian, lecturing audiences in California on the Second Coming, while her mother temporarily retired to Canada to lecture on social hygiene until the winters became too much for her.

This bathetic ending to such spectacular careers in women's politics should not be allowed to colour all the Pankhursts' efforts. They were certainly not the first agitators to lead a campaign of violence, or to foster a cult of personality. Still less were they 'un-English' in their actions. These English rebels were overtaken by the forces of moderation represented by Millicent Fawcett's group, from which they had once identified the necessity of escaping. Yet the militant suffragettes didn't merely harm a cause that was always going to prevail. The extremes they went to became an end in themselves, but their campaign still succeeded in some of its primary objectives: keeping the issue of female suffrage in the forefront of the public consciousness and demonstrating that women would not tolerate the 'slavery' of their condition. The First World War was a far more epoch-shifting event than anything the suffragettes – or the suffragists – could have effected, and ultimately it was the repercussions of the war that expanded the franchise to women. Fawcett and her allies certainly thought that the Pankhursts had become a liability (they were 'above all extraordinarily silly', Fawcett believed). But to argue that militancy only damaged the women's cause ignores both the gains made at the beginning of the WSPU's campaign and the fact that the still very militant Sylvia did manage to meet the Chancellor of the Exchequer on the eve of the Great War. All the Pankhursts were drawn to heroics and the grand gesture, but, as rebels have consistently shown, some gestures are impossible to ignore.

The match-girls' strike

The rise of the Labour Party, which partly coincided with the women's suffrage campaign, was an example of the way traditionally 'rebellious' causes, from universal suffrage to trade unionism, would increasingly be drawn into 'official' politics. Men and women who in previous ages had to break the law to be heard were being granted or had acquired more legitimate ways of operating. The growth of trade unionism after its legalization in

1824 lies mostly outside the scope of this book, as those who engineered it were consciously distancing themselves from the confrontational politics of the pre-legal days of workers' 'combinations'. But there are some exceptions to this pattern, when the fight for workers' rights moved beyond what had become conventional collective bargaining and into an attack on the status quo. We have already seen one example, in the so-called Plug plots which overlapped with Chartism in 1842. Another, less violent, but in a way equally challenging episode was the Bryant and May matchgirls' strike of 1888, the first occasion when women formed an exclusive trade union. This episode also makes an intriguing contrast with the preoccupations of the women's suffrage campaign, to which the matchgirls seemed to have enjoyed no specific connection.

The strike stemmed from an article entitled 'White Slavery in London' written by the Fabian free-thinker Annie Besant in a paper called *The Link*. Besant had heard of the bad conditions in which girls as young as twelve were employed making matches in the firm's factory at Bow in the East End of London. Her own investigations revealed a workplace where poor pay and long hours (from 6.30am till 6pm in summer) were allied to a system of fines for all sorts of 'offences', such as having an untidy workbench, and to casual brutality from foremen ('one, who appears to be a gentleman of variable temper, "clouts" them "when he is mad"', Besant wrote). The girls, who 'had to stand the whole time', had also been forced to contribute to a fund for a statue of Gladstone (they alleged that they had cut their arms over it, to show that it had been paid for 'by their blood'). When the article was printed, three girls were sacked for having talked to Besant (though the employer denied that was the reason), and a party of up to 200 match-girls congregated outside the office of Besant's paper to ask for her support in reinstating the dismissed workers.

The campaign that followed was in some ways an old-fashioned one, reflecting the relative lack of political education (or any other form of education) of girls and women at the bottom of the social scale, as compared with their male counterparts, who had been organizing for decades. Although a deputation of the match-girls was adopted as an organizing committee, Besant and her Toynbee Hall allies made all the running in the dispute. Besant dared Theodore Bryant, one of the firm's directors, to carry out his threat to sue her for libel. He declined. She also initiated a subscription to support the girls who came out on strike, while making sure their cause was publicized not only in the sympathetic press but also in less well-disposed places, such as *The Times*. A correspondence there lasted the course of the strike, during which the Union of Women Match Workers was formed. It ended with an almost complete capitulation by the employers, who agreed to abolish fines, improve working conditions (providing somewhere for the workers to eat away from the phosphorous that was contaminating their food, for example), and accepting the Union as speaking on the match-girls' behalf.

Glimpses of the match-girls' own militancy show a rebellious streak in a group whose room for independent action had been almost entirely closed off. The demonstration at the statue of Gladstone and the cry of 'We don't want no holidays', after they were given 'time off' to save the company money showed that their action was not the put-up job hostile journalists and Bryant and May's management alleged. But it is noticeable too that, in the report of the meeting to announce the negotiated end to the three-week strike, *The Times* dutifully named the male members of the London Trades Council who brought the good news, but the representatives of the match-girls themselves were only designated as 'eight young women'. The relative success of the match-girls did not turn the match factories into ideal workplaces; the perils of 'phossy jaw', the agonizing and disfiguring disease brought on by prolonged proximity to phosphorous, were still present. But the strike showed how even the most marginalized of groups could improve their lot if they were given a voice. At this time, that voice, even if it could be a female one, was still more likely to come from a middle-class outsider like Annie Besant, whose assaults on convention included living apart from her estranged husband and loudly championing atheism and contraception, rather than from the workers themselves.

General Strike

In the history of the labour movement, the Bryant and May strike, and the London dockers' strike of the following year, together heralded a spreading of unionism into unskilled labour, from its previous concentration among craftsmen. But in the history of rebellion, the 1880s are the beginning of the end of the long, sporadic struggle for what we now recognize as fundamental employee rights. The conventions of collective bargaining, of limited strikes and other 'industrial action' were the norm in the new century – even, it should be remembered, during two world wars, when, despite no-strike agreements and government and public pressure, strikes were called across industry. Digging for victory sometimes became a work to rule. By the end of the First World War, for example, strikes, particularly among munitions workers worried about the 'dilution' of their working practices by unskilled hands, cost 5.8 million working days, compared with 2.9 million in 1915.

Three times in the twentieth century, however, large-scale strike action went beyond straightforward trade disputes and took on some of the characteristics of a rebellion. The latter two came in the 1970s and then in 1984–5, when showdowns between the ruling government and the unions, especially the National Union of Mineworkers, produced two different answers to Edward Heath's famous question: 'Who governs Britain?' The first came eight years after the end of the First World War, and in a pattern that would become familiar it was the miners who were at the forefront of a campaign that the Conservative government treated more as an assault on the constitution than as a workers' dispute: the General Strike. For nine days in 1926, the 'national holiday' that the Chartists had talked of as a technique of political persuasion became a reality.

Since miners formed the backbone of the most serious industrial disputes of the century, it is worth recalling what their work entailed. By the 1970s, coal was just one of several important sources of Britain's power (though the oil crisis of that decade increased its significance). But at the beginning of the twentieth century it was the only one. Transport, electricity, industry, domestic heating all depended on coal. This put the people who got it out of the ground in a potentially powerful position. But the miners' strength was not merely economic; it was also moral. It stemmed from the conditions that miners had to endure. Miners' work was dirtier, harder, more dangerous than almost anyone else's. Accidents were frequent and often fatal; even if a miner avoided them, his life expectancy was short. Not the least of the ways in which Arthur James Cook, the General Secretary of the Miners' Federation of Great Britain, reflected his membership was in dying before he reached the age of fifty. Cook's passion for his members' rights had its origins in his own experiences in the mines of south Wales (he was originally from the West Country, but had moved at the age of eighteen in search of work). On his very first day down the pit in the Trefor colliery in the Rhondda Valley, Cook helped to carry a miner who had been killed in a roof-fall home to his family. A Baptist lay preacher, Cook became a Communist, though he left the Party in 1921. That combination of moral certainty and radical activism was reproduced in mining communities across the country, and made them an admired, if sometimes exasperating, force in the union movement. Herbert Smith, the President of the Miners' Federation, was from an even tougher school. Born in the West Riding in 1862, he was placed in the workhouse as a baby: his father had died in a mining accident days before he was born, and his mother shortly afterwards. Adopted by the couple who gave him his surname, Smith started down the mines at the age of ten. As he rose in the ranks of the miners' union, he became well known as an uncompromising negotiator. His catchphrase was 'nowt doin'.

Opponents feared the influence of Continental philosophy on British workers: first syndicalism – the revolutionary trade unionism conceived in France though never successfully practised there – and later Bolshevism. Both creeds influenced miners' leaders, and money from Soviet miners was gratefully accepted during their strikes. In 1920, dockers had refused to load a ship, the *Jolly George*, with weapons for the Poles to defend themselves against the advancing Bolsheviks. The atmosphere of paranoia about Soviet communism was demonstrated in 1924, when the *Daily Mail* printed the forged Zinoviev Letter, promising Soviet help to British workers to bring about a revolution. The Letter was thought to have played a large part in Labour's electoral defeat and their replacement by the Conservatives. But a far more important part of the British miners' make-up than any 'red' affiliations was the mixture of religious Nonconformity and the separate mentality created by their village communities and their unique experiences. Miners have never fitted the stereotype of the urban working class; they were in many ways a class apart, industrialized agricultural labourers whose crop happened to be hundreds of feet below the ground.

Before the war, a 'triple alliance' between the unions that represented mineworkers, railwaymen and transport workers attempted to strengthen their claims over pay and conditions by always agreeing on mutual support in industrial disputes. There were attempts to revive this alliance after 1918. In 1921, the mines returned to private ownership after temporary wartime national control, and the owners immediately tried to impose pay cuts. When the miners came out on strike, they found themselves acting alone after the second 'Black Friday' of the century, 15 April, when their 'allies' abandoned them. In a pattern that would repeat itself over the years, the miners held out in isolation, only returning to work, defeated, in July that year. But four years later, the miners appeared to win an equally important victory. In April 1925, under the Conservative government of Stanley Baldwin, Britain had returned to the Gold Standard, which overvalued the pound and squeezed exports. The move had been resisted by the Chancellor of the Exchequer, Winston Churchill, but, once it was taken, he was prepared to fight hard over the consequences. One of those consequences was a sharp decline in export profits from coal, which the mine owners proposed to make up not only by cutting pay, but also by extending working hours. The miners' response was summed up in the slogan Cook later made famous: 'Not a penny off the pay, not a second on the day.'

As the deadline of 1 August approached, after which the owners threatened to lock out the miners if they failed to agree, the government intervened. Fearing that, in the event of a solid national strike, as Lloyd George had explained to the miners five years before, 'we are at your mercy', Baldwin attempted to reach a compromise, despite both sides' intransigence. The history of the miners' industrial relations at this time is a four-part disharmony, with the colliers and owners at opposite ends, and the government and the general council of the Trades Union Congress attempting a more moderate approach in the middle. When a government-commissioned court of inquiry pronounced broadly in favour of the miners, it gave Baldwin some room for manoeuvre, despite the refusal of the owners to contemplate its recommendations. In order to allow more time for a solution to be found, the Prime Minister took the expedient, but politically and financially expensive, step of subsidizing the mining industry for nine months. Black had turned to 'Red Friday', in the newspapers at least.

When this result was announced, the right wing of the Tory party saw it as the ultimate capitulation. Lord Salisbury, the Lord Privy Seal, concluded that 'the moral basis of the Government seems to have dropped out'. Baldwin was a pragmatist who did not think the country was ready to face a national strike in 1925. He hoped that the Commission initiated at the same time as the subsidy might find a solution, and dispense with the need to impose one in nine months' time. But in the meanwhile, the government made discreet preparations to do just that, in case no agreement could be reached. On the unions' side, momentous steps to empower the TUC to negotiate on behalf of the miners, and more importantly to call a sympathetic, 'national' strike if negotiations failed, came only days before the deadline for the end of the subsidy. Of the two sides, it was the government that was far better prepared for what it insisted on calling a 'General Strike'.

There was a more constructive attempt to solve the mining industry's problems in the months before the strike: a report commissioned by the government, chaired by Sir Herbert Samuel, a former Cabinet minister, the High Commissioner for Palestine, and a future leader of the Liberal Party. Unfortunately, the recommendations he came up with were unacceptable to all parties for different reasons. The government, which was opposed to all forms of nationalization, didn't like the proposal to nationalize royalties (which has been described as 'public ownership of coal but not the coalmines'). The owners didn't like Samuel's rejection of extended hours for the miners. And the miners didn't like the suggestion of wage cuts. Instead of making his own objections clear, Baldwin allowed the owners and the unions to be the ones to reject the report as a basis for agreement.

In the hopeless negotiations before the deadline for the subsidy expired, it is difficult to believe that either side expected a breakthrough. The TUC believed it had some room for manoeuvre, but the mine owners hardly shifted their ground at all. Although the TUC was committed to a national strike if negotiations failed and the miners were locked out, its leaders had little enthusiasm for such a move. Negotiations were in fact broken off a day early, after the government chose to interpret two union actions – the sending of telegrams around the country authorizing a strike, and the refusal of the compositors at the *Daily Mail* to set a loyal editorial entitled 'For King and Country' – as the final provocations. Neither was meant to be. The telegrams were merely preparatory, while the *Daily Mail* compositors had acted independently. Churchill had visited the *Mail*'s offices earlier in the day, and the paper was the only one that chose to print an editorial alongside the government's advertisement appealing for volunteers in the event of a strike. So it is quite possible that the provocation was from the other side. For the second time in two years, the *Daily Mail* was instrumental – and less than entirely scrupulous – in helping the Conservatives. Churchill's friend Lord Birkenhead thought the spat at the paper was a 'bloody good job'. Baldwin had been preparing the country for the eventuality of a strike throughout the year, signing up volunteers to help run essential services, and it almost seems as if he wished to get the worst over with. The night before the deadline expired, when the TUC negotiators were still making last-ditch attempts to find a settlement, Baldwin went to bed. The TUC men were unable to deliver their reply to the government's ultimatum. Their bluff had been called, and twenty-four hours later, on 4 May 1926, the General Strike began.

The strike was initially confined to 'first line' industries. Transport workers, miners, dockers, printers, and workers in the iron, steel, chemical and power sectors downed tools in unprecedented numbers. Such an impressive turnout across so many vital sections of British life seemed to justify the idea broadcast by Baldwin, and his Chancellor Churchill, as editor of the special government newspaper the *British Gazette*, that the strike was not just an industrial dispute – it was an attack on the constitution. The reality of the strike made it difficult to sustain this picture. To begin with, thousands of volunteers – some of them the middle-class would-be train drivers of popular myth, but others non-union workers, or the unemployed – stepped in to provide skeleton services. Very few trains ran, but many buses did, while an efficient commandeering of food supplies reduced the potential for panic. One post-war fact of life that a national strike had failed to confront was the rise of road transport. Although the majority of freight was carried by rail, it wasn't too difficult to shift things like food supplies onto the roads, where un-unionized hauliers, or volunteers, could bypass the strike. Added to the fairly efficient strike-breaking, there was also very little sign of any political edge to the strike. The miners' fellow trade unionists showed their willingness to support their comrades, but neither the TUC nor any individual union used the General Strike as a cloak for revolution. There were outbreaks of violence between pickets and police, but in Plymouth the two sides played a football match against each other. Finally the government had ensured that large quantities of coal had been stockpiled in the months leading up to the Strike, so the miners' stoppage wouldn't be critical for several weeks, by which time, if the miners hadn't gone back to work, arrangements to import coal could be put into action.

The Strike lasted nine days. The strikers continued to demonstrate an impressive solidarity – A. J. P. Taylor compared this
loyalty to the cause to the 'spontaneous generosity' the same class
had shown in volunteering for the trenches in 1914: 'the first was
whipped on by almost every organ of public opinion; the second
was undertaken despite their disapproval.' On the eighth day, the
TUC even called out 'second-line' workers, but it had become
clear by then that the Strike hadn't brought the country to a
standstill, and still less had it brought the government or the owners
back to the negotiating table. The brief intensification of the Strike
was of a piece with the 'war by timetable' element of the whole
dispute. Just as the deadline and the TUC's agreement with its
members had committed it to a national strike on 4 May, so the
'second-line' call-out was part of a pre-planned strategy that was
manifestly not working. A day later, the TUC negotiators went
to Downing Street and gave in, not even, to the astonishment of
Ernest Bevin, one of their number, securing the slightest guarantee
of protection for their members from employers' reprisals, or any
concession at all for the miners, whose dispute was still unresolved.
Bevin confided to his colleagues on 12 May, 'we have committed
suicide'.

Some workers, particularly on the railways, did suffer as a result
of the strike, but it was the miners, who continued their defiance
for another five months, who lost most heavily. Not only were
they forced to accept terms that were even worse than those offered
in 1925: the strain of the strike had broken up their union and
hobbled them as a force in industrial politics for the next twenty
years. It was, indeed, twenty years later, when the Labour government repealed anti-national-strike legislation introduced in 1927,
that Ernest Bevin, now Foreign Secretary, tried to set the record
straight about the General Strike: 'This was not a strike against the
state. It was a strike in support of people whose wages were at the
lowest possible level.'

In the sense that it was not the intention of the strikers to 'bring
down the state', Bevin was right. But a national strike is to some
extent always an act of rebellion, if not of revolution, as the

Chartists had recognized in their abortive attempts to organize a 'national holiday'. May 1926 looked like a very modern industrial dispute, influenced by a global economic reality on one side and by the example of revolutionary socialism on the other. It makes more sense, however, as yet another contribution to the long history of English rebellion as theatre. We have seen it in operation across the centuries, at Runnymede in 1215, in the dramatic gestures of aristocratic rebels like Bolingbroke or Essex, in the would-be 'spectacular' of the Gunpowder Plotters, or the histrionics of Lord George Gordon, in the public provocations of John Wilkes or Henry Hunt, and the calculated headline-grabbing of the suffragettes. The miners had a genuine grievance, and the TUC wanted to help them, but the only way it could think of doing so was by putting on the most impressive show of industrial defiance seen anywhere in Western Europe. This wasn't a show that could run for very long, and Baldwin's government knew it. By the time the curtain came down after nine days, the audience had merely become even less sympathetic to the miners' distress.

The General Strike was not the end of industrial strife between the wars, but it was certainly the end of industrial rebellion. The depressed economy of the 1930s put employers in a far more powerful position than workers whose jobs were threatened. The most effective left-organized protests in those years were hunger-marches which took place throughout the 1930s. The ranks of the unemployed, like the Blanketeers of more than a century before, gathered from 'depressed areas' to march on London, simply to show how low their fortunes had sunk. They were organized under the banner of the Communist-led National Unemployed Workers' Movement, and in October 1932 over 100,000 came to Hyde Park to greet them. Two years later, more than double that number turned out, after the Conservative government only fractionally increased the scales of unemployment benefit. Although this public support was reflected by Labour voices, such as Clement Attlee's, in Parliament, the official response was dismissive enough to persuade some unemployed to take more militant action in 1938. Anticipating today's 'anti-capitalist' protestors, and once again applying the lessons of rebellion as theatre, they targeted sites of conspicuous consumption as well as purely political ones. Some walked into the Ritz Hotel, sat down at tables, and offered 2d for a cup of tea, while others lay down in Oxford Street. A mock funeral of an unemployed man was carried to Downing Street, while a banner was hung from the Monument warning 'For a Happy New Year the Unemployed Must Not Starve.' As with the suffragettes, their predecessors in the art of militancy, however, the hunger-marchers' tactics were overwhelmed by global events. In 1939, a new war at least brought full employment.

17. Outsiders

Cable Street to the Poll Tax Riots 1931–90

It might seem that the different strands of English rebellion over nine centuries had nearly all been sewn into the fabric of legitimate political life, leaving only the loose thread that represented the views of marginalized labour, the unemployed, or revolutionary socialists. Rebellion in modern times is usually associated exclusively with the political left, a link that can also colour the way rebels of earlier ages are categorized. As we have seen, 'left-wing' is often the last adjective that could be accurately applied to rebellions from the Middle Ages to the early twentieth century. Nor is it always the best way to describe those of a more modern period. If rebels are men and women who challenge the status quo in 'unacceptable' ways, at times putting themselves beyond the law, then there was a classic example of English rebellion between the wars that emerged from the opposite end of the political spectrum. In the words of its leader, it was 'an explosion against intolerable conditions, against remedial wrongs which the old world failed to remedy'. Like the suffragettes', this movement started in legitimate politics, but failure led its leader to adopt more extreme tactics.

In March 1931, Sir Oswald Mosley, who had been the rising star of the Labour Party (he was MP for Smethwick, the seat Christabel Pankhurst had once tried to win), formed his own 'New Party' to implement the version of Keynesian economics that he thought was the only answer to the slump and rising unemployment. At the next election, the New Party fielded twenty-four candidates, though none was returned. Mosley had already been tempted by some of the authoritarian doctrines of fascism, inspired by a visit to Mussolini's Italy. The electoral wipe-out merely pushed him further down that path, to the conclusion that a real crisis brought on by revolutionary communism would require a movement of 'discipline, effort and sacrifice' to defeat it. The New Party had enjoyed the support of left-wingers like A. J. Cook, who saw in it a genuine alternative to the failures of the Labour Party. Mosley's next move was not, in fact, an abandonment of socialism, but it lost him the support of most mainstream socialists. In October 1932, he announced the formation of the British Union of Fascists. The Blackshirts, a political party with the trappings of an army, were born.

Many of the rebels and rebellions from at least the nineteenth century onwards would have abhorred what Mosley stood for. His British Fascists might seem an unexpected addition to a story that has become increasingly 'radical'. It is certainly true that there is a lot about the BUF and its leader that was peculiar to Mosley and his time. Fascism was a doctrine with shallow roots, despite the attempts (espoused by Mosley as well as Continental fascists) to link it back to Roman precedents. Mosley himself looks like a one-off, a would-be Hitlerian *Übermensch* who enjoyed the gossipy frivolity of high society. His own English political hero was the Earl of Chatham, William Pitt the Elder, hardly a rebel. But it is not difficult to place Mosley in a rebel tradition. Oddly enough, it was Hitler himself who saw that kind of precedent for Mosley. The Führer told Unity Mitford, who was a Nazi groupie and later became Mosley's sister-in-law, that he should have called his party the 'Ironsides' after Cromwell's regiment. The idea might have appealed to Mosley, a confirmed follower of the historian Thomas Carlyle, whose 'great men' in history included the Lord Protector. If Mosley was no Cromwell, we have nonetheless encountered something like his brand of rabble-rousing, xenophobia and personal magnetism at least once before, in the person of Lord George Gordon. English crowds had often been incited by upper-class demagogues appealing to their worst instincts.

Two episodes ensured that Mosley had less impact on London than Gordon, let alone Hitler. The first was the British Fascists' Olympia meeting of 8 June 1934. The second, which has perhaps understandably grown into an anti-fascist myth out of all proportion to what can be reconstructed of the actual events, was the

'Battle of Cable Street' in October 1936. In the year and a half before Olympia, Mosley's Fascists had attracted the support of Lord Rothermere's *Daily Mail* (how different might the century have looked without this great institution?), where he was described as a 'new leader of genius'. The *Mail* provided free tickets for the Olympia meeting in Kensington in west London, which ensured that anti-Mosleyites had no difficulty in getting in. But Mosley's supporters were also out in force, including representatives of Mosley's own class: Lord Erroll, philandering Kenyan émigré of the 'Happy Valley' set; Sir George Duckworth-King, Nelson's great-great-grandson; and Diana Guinness, née Mitford, Mosley's lover but not yet his wife. After the entry of the great leader to cries of 'Hail Mosley', he began to be heckled by opponents, some of whom were probably, as Mosley alleged, Communists there specifically to disrupt the meeting. The Fascists' own stewards 'ejected' each one with shocking force. The police were on hand, but they kept outside the building and reported no incident that night, despite the fact that fifty people ended up needing hospital treatment, and five were seriously injured. A Conservative MP who attended the meeting wrote to the *Daily Telegraph* to complain of the 'gross brutality' and 'disgusting behaviour' of the Fascists. Although Rothermere did not withdraw his support immediately, the British Union of Fascists was finished as a 'respectable' force.

Over the next two years, while his party was kept under close watch by the security service, Mosley concentrated his efforts in the East End of London. There was a substantial Jewish population in this area, and the anti-Semitic rhetoric which now became a staple of his public speeches attracted relatively warm support from those who blamed Jewish businesses and workers for their own economic plight. Again, there was nothing very new about a rebel whipping up xenophobia, and London's Jewish population had good cause to fear outbreaks of rebellion since at least the days of Simon de Montfort.

It was in this context that a march was arranged, in October 1936, from the Royal Mint along Cable Street to Bethnal Green, to celebrate five years of the BUF. There was a concerted attempt on the part of local opponents, both Jewish and non-Jewish, to have the march banned, but when it was allowed to go ahead the anti-Fascists decided to stop it themselves. 'The Battle of Cable Street' that followed was not to any degree a fight between Fascists and their opponents, but between anti-Fascists and the police. This set a pattern both for Mosley's own party and for extreme right-wing demonstrations ever since, where the police protection afforded the extremists becomes the focus of anger when the real object cannot be reached. In Cable Street after the protestors managed to barricade the road (yet another example of a barricade in England's supposedly non-street-fighting history), the police requested that Mosley reroute the march, which he did, going westwards before his followers dispersed. The victory did nothing to keep Fascists out of the East End permanently; a meeting was held in Victoria Park in East London for 12,000 only a week later. But as a symbol of opposition to Mosley, it combined with the Olympia brutality to drain away wider support. The 'defeat' was noted in Italy, for example, where Mussolini threatened to withdraw his financial backing. The violence at Cable Street also persuaded the government to bring in the Public Order Act, which banned the wearing of uniforms and gave the police the power to stop marches. When Mosley tried to repeat his East End march in 1937, the police prevented him.

Mosley's final bid for serious power came during the abdication crisis. When it looked as if Baldwin's Conservatives would insist on the new King Edward VIII's giving up the throne if he married the divorced Mrs Simpson, Mosley was outraged. He also saw an opportunity to gather a 'King's party' around a monarch who had been willing to meet Hitler and seemed well-disposed to Mosley (Churchill, it must be said, seems to have had a similar idea). Whether Edward himself led Mosley on (Mosley later claimed that he had continued a secret correspondence with the King), it is impossible to say. Certainly those around Mosley reported that the leader was in a high state of excitement, as he saw the chance of bypassing the electorate if Edward simply asked him to form a government (a doubtful constitutional assumption, never mind a political one). In the end, if he had ever really taken the possibility seriously, Edward came to his senses and let Mosley down with 'polite thanks for his offers of support'. The King abdicated on 10 December 1936.

The growing threat from Nazi Germany and the increasing likelihood of war made Mosley's position even more precarious. He denied formal links to the Nazis and maintained to old age that he would not have been a quisling in the event of an invasion. Yet that was really the only way in which Mosley was ever likely to have achieved his dictatorial ambitions. Mosley and other British Fascists were imprisoned at the outbreak of war in 1939. He was released only in 1943, and then on medical grounds, by which time the threat of invasion was long past. Mosley re-emerged after the war, though he eventually officially repudiated Fascism. He continues to hold an odd fascination for the British public. Although he wanted to lead an extra-parliamentary British revolution as a 'new Caesar', his fate was rather closer to those English rebels of the past whose appeal to such reliable constants as xenophobia and economic inequalities sustained a following, but not one with enough appeal to overcome the inherent obnoxiousness of their programmes, or their personalities.

Ban the bomb

The Second World War, like the First, witnessed a wholly predictable decline in English rebelliousness. The economic hardship that had fuelled so much dissatisfaction was suspended by the requirements of a war economy. As well as employing restrictive legislation against potential traitors that even Churchill admitted was 'in the highest degree odious', the wartime coalition worked hard to present a united home front. There may have been more exceptions than is generally realized to this picture – strikes, for example, which declined in the first two years of the war, began to rise again. In 1943, 3.7 million working days were lost to industrial action, a figure that wouldn't be exceeded until 1955.

An independent party, Common Wealth, whose socialism owed more to the Diggers and Spenceans than to Soviet Communism, won four seats in Parliament at by-elections, while Labour stuck to the wartime agreement between the established parties not to contest them. But rebelliousness, confined in one historian's memorable phrase to 'Celts, Reds and Conchies', was not the most pressing of the nation's problems.

After the war, with the defeat of Churchill's Conservatives, and the landslide election of the first-ever majority Labour government, the mood of optimism prevailed for a time, despite continuing austerity. As we move closer to our own day, it can seem strange to talk of 'rebellion' in the same way that it has been used throughout this book. But there are connections between the protest movements, labour disputes and social complaints of more recent times and the history of English rebellion, even if some links were more explicitly embraced than others. The post-war period is also the first in which being a 'rebel' became not just acceptable but attractive. When Emmeline Pankhurst declared that she would rather be a rebel than a slave, it was still a shocking statement, which tapped into the residue of the idea that rebellion was a form of treason. The rise of youth culture, of pop music and teenage fashions, made rebellion part of growing up. Democracy, the relaxation of social boundaries and the sense of new beginnings after the Second World War all contributed to an acceptance of a certain degree of rebellion as part of a healthy society. Rebels had long understood the power of gesture, of protest as theatre when more conventional challenges invited certain defeat. But the rise of cultural rebelliousness took the gesture ever further away from the cause. Pretty soon, rebelliousness became just another way of marketing product. One of the effects of consumer culture's assimilation of counter-culture was to drain much of the subversion from opposing the establishment. This is perhaps why outbreaks of violence or obstruction – of genuine protest, as opposed to its affectation – could be greeted with such incredulity by the press and politicians. Rebellion seemed to have been 'tamed', so it was, and still is, a shock when it becomes ungovernable.

After the war, there was one subject for protest that was entirely new: nuclear weapons. Agitators against nuclear weapons tried two tactics with a long pedigree in English rebellion: the march and the camp. The Campaign for Nuclear Disarmament – founded in 1958 and led by Bertrand Russell as President and Canon John Collins as Chairman, with support from such well-known figures as J. B. Priestley, A. J. P. Taylor and Michael Foot – was in some ways a deliberately unrebellious pressure group, though one that hoped for mass participation, in the tradition of the campaign to abolish the slave trade, or the Anti-Corn Law League. The Campaign's most famous actions, the Aldermaston marches that took place over the next five years, were, unsurprisingly for a movement of pacifists, almost entirely peaceful affairs. But, like the suffragettes and the Chartists before them, the campaigners against atomic weapons disagreed over the question of more 'direct' action. Even the Aldermaston marches were initially the subject of dispute between the campaigners, though the marches' popularity persuaded the mainstream that this much 'direct action' was desirable. Russell made further moves to promote support for a campaign of mass civil disobedience from a 'Committee of 100' eminent figures.

Russell, aged eighty-six at the inception of CND, was a veteran anti-war campaigner who had gone to prison during the First World War for 'prejudicing Britain's relations with its ally': he had written an article suggesting (wrongly) that American troops would be used to break up British wartime strikes. His standing as a philosopher had not been greatly affected (he received the Order of Merit in 1949), and by the time of the Campaign for Nuclear Disarmament he was old enough to command respect even from political opponents. In embracing direct action, and courting arrest for holding unauthorized protests and sit-ins, Russell and the American student who encouraged him to form the Committee, Ralph Schoenman, had come to the same conclusion as previous campaigners about the effects of militancy. The authorities duly obliged by arresting Russell in 1961 for a breach of the peace and sentencing him, aged eighty-nine, to two months in Brixton (later shortened to a week on account of his age).

Despite the success of Russell's 'martyrdom' as a propaganda coup, CND failed because it attacked something so central to the government of the country – the decision to have nuclear weapons – without representing a majority view. Other minority single-issue pressure groups achieved success only when conceding their case became less important to the ruling classes than getting on with other business, let alone losing power. But inside Parliament in the 1960s, the number of MPs in favour of unilateral disarmament remained negligible. In 1965, CND went into abeyance. It was revived in the 1980s, but it was the women's Greenham Common protest beginning in 1981 that brought the nuclear issue back to public attention. At Greenham, a very modern protest – feminist, anti-nuclear, non-violent – drew on some very old rebel traditions. Not only did the women set up a camp, a practice that can be traced back through the Diggers and Kett's rebels, all the way to the 'greenwood' outlaws of the English resistance to the Norman Conquest: their use of common land to do so was also a tactic with historical resonance, connecting their protest to the long campaign for land as a 'common treasury', not to be enclosed. Greenham Common in Berkshire was the American air base chosen as the site for cruise missile deployment at the beginning of the decade. The women's protest, a camp that lasted for nineteen years (actually outstaying both the missiles and the air base itself), began as a march of Welsh activists from Cardiff. Using to their advantage the fact that the base as well as the camp were sited on common land (it meant they could not be arrested for trespass if they broke in), the protestors tried to disrupt the arrival of the missiles and the construction of buildings to house them. Like the suffragettes, Greenham women implausibly claimed victory for their campaign on the removal of the missiles, which began in 1989. It seems unlikely that President Reagan or General Secretary Gorbachev, who had signed the agreement leading to weapons reduction, were influenced by a peace camp in Berkshire. Nonetheless, the protest, which at its height, the 'Embrace the Base' event in 1982, involved 30,000 women, was a constant reminder of the threat of the Cold War, and of nuclear weapons. With

CND, it contributed to the culture of protest and rebellion that survived into the 1980s despite the apparent total defeat of that culture's causes in mainstream politics. Greenham was also an impressive demonstration of the power of non-violence. As one protestor put it, when persuading a comrade not to react violently to intimidation, 'we're beaten if we ever do it that way. We can stay here for ever, provided we're not violent.'

Grosvenor Square and the Angry Brigade

This was not a sentiment that all protestors after the war would have recognized. In the late 1960s, most teenagers (a new concept in itself) might have hoped to be described as 'rebels', confining their rebellion to choices in clothes and music, and occasional run-ins with rival tribes – as Teddy Boys gave way to Mods, Beatniks to Hippies. A significant proportion of British youth nonetheless took a more active role in political protest. A very small number took their grievances with mainstream society further still, into a form of rebellion more familiar in Continental Europe than in England. Many of the supporters of the Campaign for Nuclear Disarmament could be found at more 'direct' actions, such as the demonstrations against the Vietnam War in 1967 and 1968. In March and again in October 1968, up to 8,000 student protestors fought running battles with the police who were protecting the US Embassy. The leaders of the students, such as the Pakistani-born Tariq Ali, were adherents of various strains of international socialism, which allowed the press to make much of their 'un-English' approach, although Ali's Vietnam Solidarity Campaign stayed away from Grosvenor Square on the third occasion. But the name of the group's radical newspaper, *Black Dwarf*, tells another story. According to Ali, it was chosen by Christopher Logue, who had discovered the radical paper of that name published between 1817 and 1824. (It was *Black Dwarf* that had seen Peterloo as a moral triumph for radicalism in 1819.) Its slogan affirmed to the activists of the 1960s that what they were doing connected to an English tradition: 'The right of the People to resist oppression always exists and the requisite power to do this always resides in the People.' As Ali wrote in his memoirs, 'this pre-dated all of the socialist classics'.

Some of the student socialists in Grosvenor Square had more extreme ideas about how to promote their message. Interviewed years later, Ali recalled being approached by someone claiming to represent a group called the Angry Brigade, proposing to plant a bomb at the American Embassy. 'I told them it was a terrible idea. They were a distraction. It was difficult enough building an anti-war movement without the press linking this kind of action to the wider Left.' But the 'Angries' were not put off. For a year from August 1970, they conducted a carefully targeted (and deliberately small-scale) bombing campaign, against the property of government ministers, banks, embassies, events like the Miss World contest and even Biba, the fashion store. They published 'communiqués' under the name of the Angry Brigade, in which they talked up their revolutionary intent. 'The question is not whether the revolution will be violent. Organised militant struggle and organised terrorism go side by side.'

After a year, and twenty-five bombs (injuring only one person, perhaps more by chance than anything else), the police arrested eight suspected members of the Angry Brigade, four men and four women, in Stoke Newington, north London. They were middle-class student drop-outs, from Cambridge and Essex Universities. A ninth member, who was picked up in Notting Hill, Jake Prescott, could genuinely claim to be from what the Brigade's communiqués called 'the autonomous working class'. Guns, ammunition and explosives were found at their flat, and five of the accused were convicted of conspiracy to cause explosions, and sentenced to ten years each. The Angry Brigade's communiqués showed their debt to the French 'situationists' of Guy Debord (the attacks on 'spectacles' were picked up by an alert Special Branch policeman as a telltale sign of this influence). More than any other rebels in our story, theirs was an imported culture, but it had some uniquely English elements. The deliberate targeting of property, not people, was in the tradition of the suffragettes and the hunger-marcher militants, while the Angries gave a home-grown spin to the language of international anarchism: 'The Labour Party, the Unions and their minions, the CP [Communist Party] with its productivity craze, the same bastards who always sell us out, will try and fob you off with gestures like one day strikes and one day occupations, petitions etc. which will achieve bugger all.' And like other English rebels, from John Wilkes to Emmeline Pankhurst, these anarchists could become respectable citizens. One of the accused, Angela Weir, was later awarded the OBE (as Angela Mason), for her campaigning for gay rights on behalf of the group Stonewall.

'The enemy within'

The early 1970s are better remembered for a more traditional, and more successful, confrontation between the establishment and the 'autonomous working class', the strikes of 1972–4 that led eventually to the fall of Edward Heath's Conservative government. They were also the proving ground for a Yorkshire miners' leader who, according to one of his comrades, 'thought he was the reincarnation of [the miners' leader of the 1920s] A. J. Cook': Arthur Scargill. The miners' battle with the government in the 1970s was the middle round of a contest that began with the General Strike and ended with the strike of 1984–5. Seen as a whole, this fight was representative not just of the story of British industrial relations, but of the course of English rebellion. And like so many English rebels before him, Scargill was persuaded by his initial victory – one of self-advertisement as much as of practical politics – that the same result could be achieved again in very different circumstances.

The miners voted in January 1972 for the first national strike since 1926, over the issue of wages. Their moderate leader, Joe Gormley, brought his members out with some trepidation, but Scargill was convinced that the strikers could learn the lessons of the 1920s. Scargill introduced Britain to the concept of 'secondary picketing'. Since there was no need to picket the mines themselves, where the strike was solid, the strikers could concentrate on the next stage of coal's journey from the ground to the power stations. At Saltley Gate cokeworks in the west Midlands, Scargill and 12,000 supporters outnumbered the police by twelve to one and forced them to shut the plant down. Scargill called it 'the greatest day of my life'; 'we were in a class war,' he said later, 'not playing cricket on the village green like they did in 1926.'

The action at Saltley Gate was part of a nationwide campaign to stop all but 'essential' coal moving around the country. Saltley may have made Scargill's name, but the picketing across Britain did the real damage. This strike took place in the middle of winter rather than in a mild May, so that it did not take long to force the government to negotiate. Lord Wilberforce, who was appointed to a commission of inquiry, had to work quickly, as a three-day week had already been instituted and 1.6 million workers had been laid off. After two days, Wilberforce delivered his recommendations, including doubling the pay rise originally offered (from 7.9 to 18.5 per cent). The miners were able to secure even more concessions from Heath before they returned to work at the end of February.

As with 'Red Friday' (and again after the first strike under Margaret Thatcher's government), the 1972 result was unlikely to be a permanent one. During 1973, a foreign exchange crisis, rises in oil prices and the government's attempts to keep down inflation with statutory pay deals led to a series of strikes across different industries. In 1974, the miners came out again, and Heath called an election. The result was close, but after Heath failed to form a coalition with the Liberals, Harold Wilson formed a minority Labour government and the miners' strike was called off. The strikes that brought down Heath's government seemed to demonstrate the power of militancy compared to traditional TUC compromise. In his memoirs, the Conservative Cabinet minister Nicholas Ridley wrote that 'Arthur Scargill drew the lesson that brute militant force would always secure him victory. Keith Joseph [later an originator of Thatcherism] learnt the lesson that such tactics must never be allowed to prevail.' It would be ten years before Margaret Thatcher, as Conservative Prime Minister, put those theories to the test. In 1984, it turned out that it was Thatcher, not Scargill, now leader of the National Union of Mineworkers, who had learnt the right lesson.

The fundamental economic fact about British coal was that it was unprofitable. The Thatcher government was not willing to extend subsidy indefinitely, and the corollary of that would be pit closures. The Prime Minister's preparation for what she saw as an inevitable confrontation with Scargill included legislating against 'secondary action', the tactic that had worked so well for the strikers in 1972. Her ministers also followed the example of Baldwin's government in 1926 by stockpiling coal, and making plans to move it around the country. They even had their own version of Red Friday when, in 1981, before plans to resist a national miners' strike were completed, the government was forced to reprieve the closures of thirty pits announced by the chairman of the National Coal Board. This was Joe Gormley's last success, when the balance of power in a national industrial dispute still lay with the miners. When he retired, Scargill won the leadership contest to replace him. With a combative, union-hating new Chairman of the NCB installed, the Scottish-American Ian MacGregor, both sides were prepared for a battle.

The way in which the strike began, however, was of neither side's choosing. On 1 March 1984, a surprise announcement was made that a hitherto 'safe' pit, Cortonwood in south Yorkshire, was to be closed in just over a month. It employed 839 miners, whom the NCB promised to transfer to other pits. But as far as the local union was concerned, to accept this closure out of the blue was to give in on the whole principle of pits closing and jobs being lost. They voted to strike, as did miners in Scotland, where Polmaise colliery in Alloa was also threatened with closure. The reaction of the national executive of the NUM, directed by Scargill, was to extend the strike nationwide, but without holding a national ballot. The official justification for this was that a national ballot would 'compromise' those who were already out on strike, but the lack of a ballot fundamentally weakened Scargill's case.

For a man so steeped in mining history, a man who, as a fellow unionist put it, 'was always on about what happened in nineteen-ought-blob', Scargill was strangely neglectful of precedent. When the miners had succeeded before, it was not just because of tactics, still less because the economic arguments were on their side. In 1972, a national strike ballot had given them the moral high ground. In 1984, Scargill's refusal to hold a national ballot surrendered it. When he tried to re-fight another old battle, attempting to relive Saltley Gate at the Orgreave coking plant near Sheffield, Scargill found that police tactics had changed too. Five thousand pickets were met by police from ten counties, and battles between pickets and police armed with riot shields and batons, many on horseback, left twenty-eight strikers and forty-one officers injured. Orgreave stayed open, and MacGregor claimed to have stockpiled enough coal for a year. The final lesson that Scargill had failed to learn, though admittedly given the government's preparations it may not have made very much difference, was not to call a miners' strike at the end of winter, when power demand is reduced.

The miners' strike of 1984 was of a different character from the other union confrontations of the Thatcher years. The Prime Minister affected to see it as a revolutionary menace, talking of the 'enemy within'. While this was hardly fair on the average miner, threatened with redundancy, it was a legitimate enough characterization of Scargill, who saw himself as engaged in 'class war'. Lives were lost in this war, three to violence (two pickets and one taxi-driver) , as well as 100,000 jobs and £6 billion. After Orgreave, Scargill attempted to negotiate with the Coal Board, but he was in no position to do so. As in the miners' long lock-out of 1926, the government added to the strikers' problems by imposing the strictest of interpretations on welfare provisions. Despite its efforts to keep money away from the courts, and to secure it from overseas (another echo of 1926), the NUM did not have enough funds to continue strike pay to its members. The war would end not in a negotiated armistice but a complete defeat. The strike lasted for a year and was broken by the gradual return to work of miners who realized their union had lost. Within two years, 120 out of 179 mines had closed. After the closures of the 1990s, only seven major deep mines are left in England and Wales. On the twenty-fifth anniversary of the strike, Scargill was again heard to blame other miners' unions, the working miners, the Labour Party, the Trades Union Congress and, of course, the Conservative government for the agony of the strike.

The failure of the strike seemed to show that the only way to defeat a modern government or remove a sitting Prime Minister was at the ballot box. The era of the industrial rebel seemed to have gone the way of the barons, pretenders, Roundheads and suffrage agitators, enveloped by the indifferent embrace of democracy. But English rebellion's remarkable capacity for reinvention could wound even the vanquisher of Arthur Scargill.

1381 and all that

No one would have predicted after the miners' strike that five years later an outpouring of extra-parliamentary rage would be instrumental in toppling Margaret Thatcher. One of the first policies that Thatcher's new government considered in 1979 was an alternative to the domestic rates system. This was presented as an issue about fairness. A tax on everyone who appeared on the electoral roll 'would counter a criticism of the rates that in one house one person has to pay the rates, while next door there might be several wage earners in one family'. It was not until 1985 that the issue was taken up again, and by then the potential *un*-fairness of the levy, which the government proposed to call a 'community charge', but which had already been christened by an older name in the press, was widely publicized. Although there were official proposals to reduce the charge for those on benefits, the idea that 'a dustman pays the same as a duke' stuck. Articles began to appear in the press about the population 'shrinking' if a tax was based on the electoral roll. The connection to the last attempt to raise a poll tax in England was also made, along with the similar 'shrinkage' that had occurred in the 1370s. It is harder to prove the contention that 'poll taxes as a means of raising revenue by the state have been unpopular for at least 1,500 years', but people got the message.

Undaunted, the Conservatives put plans for a community charge in their electoral manifesto, which did nothing to prevent their third election victory in a row in 1987. The tax was introduced first in Scotland in 1989, and then in England and Wales. An 'All-Britain Anti-Poll Tax Federation' was formed, and in March 1990 a demonstration under its auspices was organized in London. The demonstrators met at Kennington Park, the same place, then known as Kennington Common, where the great Chartist rally of 1848 had gathered. In 1990, about 140,000 protestors (perhaps 10,000 less than the Chartists had mustered) gathered to march to Whitehall.

The march proceeded peacefully, with a reasonably orderly sit-in outside Downing Street, before the demonstrators were moved on by police towards Trafalgar Square. It was there that a confrontation between mounted police and demonstrators turned violent. There is still disagreement about how the violence started, with some protestors alleging that police horses charged peaceful demonstrators unprovoked, while the police claimed that they had been attacked by 'militant' elements in the crowd. The response certainly seemed indiscriminate. One woman protestor thought that the 'police were going mad. When they charged towards me, everyone ran back. I was grabbed by one and thrown to the floor. I curled in a ball but one hit me with a truncheon across the head and some kicked me.' After the battles of the miners' strike, the Thatcher years had been blighted by riots in Brixton, Toxteth and Tottenham. Tactics used controversially against pickets, and honed against rioters out to cause deliberate damage and attack police were now employed against a 'mixed' crowd of mostly peaceful demonstrators. All sides admit that some marchers were intent on violence, but the police seemed unable to distinguish between trouble-makers and the law-abiding majority. At the end of 31 March, 400 protestors and 374 police were injured, and property damage ran into the millions.

The Poll Tax riot, combined with the ongoing campaign to refuse payment (by August of that year, it was reported that a fifth of the population still hadn't paid), convinced many in the Conservative Party that Thatcher could not win another election. She wasn't ousted for another eight months, but the reaction to the Poll Tax played a large part in her downfall. It seems unlikely that many who marched to Trafalgar Square in March 1990 thought they were following in the footsteps of the Chartists, let alone the Peasants' Revolt. It is still extraordinary to contemplate that the reason they were marching not against the 'community charge' but against the 'Poll Tax' was because a poll tax had become a byword for injustice more than 600 years before. The English rebel tradition has not always been a conscious one, but it has proved astonishingly long-lived.

Rebel futures

Low election turn-outs and reports of political 'apathy', especially among the young, might suggest that rebellion is a dying tradition. But there are still English rebels. One source of rebellion that has tapped into much of what has gone before is environmental protest. Those who set up camps against road or airport expansions are retiring to the 'greenwood' like rebels from the *silvatici* of the eleventh century to the 'camping tyme' of the sixteenth. Arguments between 'fluffies' and 'spikies' are the (linguistically infantilized) twenty-first-century versions of 'moral' and 'physical' force, militants versus law-abiders. Nor does the political left maintain a monopoly on rebellion: those rural activists who deliberately flout hunting laws are asserting rights that were disputed as long ago as the time of Magna Carta and its lesser-known little brother, the Charter of the Forest. There are more sinister home-grown rebels, too. The imported jihadism of suicide bombers may be more deadly than the situationist posturing of the Angry Brigade, but Robert Catesby's Gunpowder terrorists might recognize their fellow fanatics, inspired by a creed that recognizes no borders.

If there is such a thing as an English 'national character', it might seem self-evident (particularly, I hope, after reading this book), that rebelliousness is a part of it. To those who doubt the existence of such things as national character, we can say that the English are no different from any other nation in having so frequently known rebellion. Yet, so often, observers of the English have seen the opposite, portraying a patient people whose lot has been improved gradually, and from the top downwards. Even those who are content to caricature this view, that 'there is in the Englishman a combination of qualities, a modesty, an independence, a responsibility, a repose, combined with an absence of everything calculated to call a blush into the cheek of a young person', portray its more aggressive side as something closer to a natural phenomenon than a potentially political one.

One reason why the unrebellious myth has stuck fast is the fact that England avoided revolutions when Continental Europe had theirs, in the eighteenth and nineteenth centuries. This ignores the obvious point that England's revolutions came earlier, and that for centuries before that rebels were fighting in ways that still affect us today. It also confuses rebels and revolutionaries. The real tradition of English rebellion is not one of revolution, but the older one of targeted violence – against property as well as people. Some rebels want to overthrow the system, but more want to change it. The targets vary, but the sense that something may be gained by attacking in a limited way remains. The lesson has been assimilated that, for all its longevity, the English state and its governors can be made to bow to extraordinary pressure. Frequently, rebels have been wrong in that assumption. But this often unarticulated conviction explains how rebelliousness can cross political and social divisions, as well as temporal ones – how rituals of protest can resurface over hundreds of years. It cannot be emphasized enough that this tendency is often anything but progressive. Especially to contemporaries, English rebels have seemed misguided, fanatical, plain wrong. Some continue to appear so in the long term. Nonetheless, the English rebel explains something of the way England's history has played out: unpredictably, violently, and not necessarily as our masters have wished. Above all, English rebellion isn't exceptional. It is what has happened in this country for at least a thousand years, and we can safely predict that it will carry on happening.

Further Reading and Notes

As this book attempts a (skewed) view of the whole of post-Conquest English history, a detailed bibliography would run to thousands of titles. What I offer below instead is some suggestions for further reading, arranged by chapter, including a few of the works that have been most helpful to me in thinking about the subjects covered here. They include some 'classic' works, not because I have ignored the findings and arguments of more recent scholars, but because I am conscious that many of the terms of discussion in English historiography were established long before more 'scientific' methods prevailed. The notes contain detailed references to direct quotations from primary sources and historical discussion. For a more comprehensive guide to books on English history, rebellious in theme or not, the Royal Historical Society's online bibliography (www.rhs.ac.uk) is unsurpassed. My bibliographical constellation has had three guiding stars: the volumes of the *Oxford History of England*, both the old, pale-blue-jacketed familiars and, where available, the contributions to the more thematic new version (though the Pelican/ Penguin series is hardly less authoritative, and was often equally useful); the *New Oxford Dictionary of National Biography*, online as well as between hard covers; and the mighty *English Historical Documents* (1955–77, in twelve volumes running up to 1914, under the general editorship of David Douglas). The best way to follow the marches, retreats, musterings and final stands of rebels across the country is with *The Penguin Atlas of British and Irish History*, edited by Barry Cunliffe et al. (2001).

Introduction

The 'whig' views of English history evinced by Edmund Burke or (in spite of himself) G. K. Chesterton are most plainly on view in the classic historical works of the nineteenth century and some of the twentieth.

The most eloquent statement of this approach is Lord Macaulay's, in his *History of England from the Accession of James II* (1849–55), but it is there too in Macaulay's great-nephew G. M. Trevelyan's progressive view of England's past (in his 'sequel' to Macaulay's *History*, *England under Queen Anne* (1930–34), as well as his own earlier (1920) one-volume *History of England*). Whig history wasn't the province of a single bloodline, of course, and another very different incarnation is on show in J. R. Green's great hymn to a perennial fight for English liberty, his *Short History of the English People* (1874). The historian who diagnosed this tendency in his forerunners (and fellows) was Herbert Butterfield, whose *Whig Interpretation of History* was published in 1931. A book such as Geoffrey Elton's *The English* (1992), for all its dry wit and mandarin confidence, betrays signs that the habit has not been entirely eradicated. English individualism was most memorably discussed in a very different context by Alan Macfarlane, *The Origins of English Individualism: The Family, Property and Social Transition* (1978).

xv **'consigned to destruction . . .'**: *The Westminster Chronicle*, quoted in Alastair Dunn, *The Great Rising of 1381* (2002), p. 83.

xvi **'simplicity of our national character . . .'**: Edmund Burke, *Reflections on the Revolution in France* (1790).

xvi **'straightforward, tolerant . . .'**: Wyndham Lewis, quoted by Peter Mandler, *The English National Character* (2006), p. 168.

xvii **'continuity in the institutions . . .'**: James Campbell, in Campbell (ed.), *The Anglo-Saxons* (1982), p. 240.

xvii **'Treason doth never prosper . . .'**: Sir John Harington, 'Of Treason', *The Letters and Epigrams of Sir John Harington . . .*, ed. Norman E. McClure (1977), Book 4, epigram 5, p. 255. The complete edition of his epigrams was first published in 1618.

xviii **'Whig Interpretation'**: see Herbert Butterfield, *The Whig Interpretation of History* (1930) ('the tendency . . . to produce a story which is the ratification if not the glorification of the present').

1. Resistance

There is as yet no equivalent *New Oxford* volume to Sir Frank Stenton's *Anglo-Saxon England c.550–1087* (3rd edn, 1971), although new histories of the Norman Conquest and studies of the battles of 1066 multiply. N. J. Higham's *The Norman Conquest*, and Frank J. McLynn's *1066: The Year of Three Battles*, both published in 1998, are good recent examples; Hugh M. Thomas's more academic *The Norman Conquest: England after William the Conqueror* (2008) came too late for me to use, but assimilates the latest scholarship. The same author's *The English and the Normans: Ethnic Hostility, Assimilation, and Identity 1066–c.1220* (2003) takes a long view of the encounter. Eric John's chapter 'The End of Anglo-Saxon England' in James Campbell (ed.), *The Anglo-Saxons* (1982), is a good starting-point from one side; R. Allen Brown in his *The Normans* (1984) from the other. The tipping of general historical opinion towards a less 'triumphalist' view of the conquest is on show not only in Christopher Hill's essay on 'The Norman Yoke', in *Puritanism and Revolution: Studies in Interpretation of the English Revolution of the 17th Century* (1958), but also in Michael Wood's essay of the same title in his *In Search of England* (1999), as well as Peter Rex's *The English Resistance* (2004). Rex is also the author of a biography, *Hereward: The Last Englishman* (2005).

1 **'bloodstained battleground . . .'**: William of Poitiers, *The Gesta Guillelmi of William of Poitiers*, ed. and trans. R. H. C. Davis and Marjorie Chibnall (1998).

1 **'doomed themselves and their country . . .'**: William of Malmesbury, *Gesta Regum Anglorum* (quoted in David C. Douglas and George W. Greenaway (eds.), *English Historical Documents. Vol. II: 1042–1189*, p. 315).

1 **The English, too, had suffered . . .**: 'Anglo-Saxon' is more or less a historian's term, useful for distinguishing the pre-Conquest inhabitants both from the Britons in whose land they had settled, beginning in the fifth century, and from the mixture of peoples that eventually resulted after the Norman settlement. But the country

William invaded was England, and it is not anachronistic to call its people 'English'.

3 **'made himself my vassal . . .'**: *Gesta Guillelmi*, p. 12.

3 **'held by all peoples . . .'**: ibid., II, 32, p. 157.

4 **'To the greenwood gone . . .'**: Charles Kingsley, *Hereward the Wake*, Ch. XXXIV.

5 **'still barbarous . . .'**: Marjorie Chibnall (ed. and trans.), *The Ecclesiastical History of Orderic Vitalis* (1969), Bk IV, Ch. II.

5 **Their champion was Edgar . . .**: see Nicholas Hooper, 'Edgar the Aetheling: Anglo-Saxon Prince, Rebel and Crusader', *Anglo-Saxon England*, 14 (1985), pp. 197–214.

5 **'the citizens of London . . .'**: *Anglo-Saxon Chronicle* 'D' ('Worcester Chronicle'), in *EHD II*, p. 148.

5 **'At that time, indeed . . .'**: *Gesta Guillelmi*, II, 28, p. 147.

6 **'it was a piece of great folly . . .'**: *Anglo Saxon Chronicle* 'D', in *EHD II*, p. 149.

6 **'The fire spread rapidly . . .'**: *Orderic Vitalis*, Bk III, Ch. XIV.

8 **'It was because they hated the Normans . . .'**: *Gesta Guillelmi*, II, 47, p. 183.

8 **William's initial occupation has been compared . . .**: see Peter Rex, *The English Resistance: The Underground War against the Normans* (2004), p. 8.

9 **'envoys to other cities . . .'**: *Orderic Vitalis*, Bk IV, Ch. II.

9 **'unremitting attacks . . .'**: ibid., Bk IV, Ch. IV.

9 **'his brother and . . .'**: ibid., Bk IV, Ch. II.

10 **'seething with discontent'**: ibid.

10 **'Fealty, oaths, and the safety . . .'**: ibid.

11 **'Swift was the king's coming . . .'**: ibid., Bk IV, Ch. V.

11 **'Storms of war . . .'**: ibid., Bk IV, Ch. II.

11 **'She secretly gathered . . .'**: ibid., Bk IV, Ch. V.

12 **'fearing the conqueror . . .'**: ibid., Bk IV, Ch. II.

12 **'the men of Devon . . .' (and following)**: ibid.

13 **'Nowhere else had William . . .'**: *Orderic Vitalis*, Bk IV, Ch. II.

13 **'so great a famine . . .'**: Simeon of Durham, *A History of the Kings of England*, trans. J. Stevenson (1858; reprinted 1987), p. 137.

13 **'more than 100,000 . . .'**: *Orderic Vitalis*, Bk IV, Ch. II.

13 **certainly an exaggeration . . .:** see Sally Harvey, 'Domesday England', in H. E. Hallam (ed.), *The Agrarian History of England and Wales. Vol. II: 1042–1350* (1988), pp. 46–9; quoted in D. M. Palliser, 'The "Harrying of the North"', in *Northern History*, 29, 1993.

14 **'with great honour . . .':** *Anglo-Saxon Chronicle*, 1074.

16 **'One of us shall be king . . .':** Orderic Vitalis, Bk IV, Ch. XIV.

17 **'Then the severed head . . .':** ibid., Bk IV, Ch. XV.

17 **'No good song . . .':** ibid., Bk IV, Ch. II.

18 **'his men all over England . . .':** *Anglo-Saxon Chronicle*, 1085.

19 **'now subject to the rule of foreigners . . .':** quoted in John Hayward, 'Hereward the Outlaw', *Journal of Medieval History*, 14 (1988), pp. 293–304.

21 **'But meanwhile the English were groaning . . .':** Orderic Vitalis, Bk IV, Ch. II.

21 **'yoke of perpetual slavery . . .':** quoted in Richard Barber, 'The Norman Conquest and the Media', *Anglo-Norman Studies*, XXVI (2003), p. 4.

2. A Kingdom Divided

The *New Oxford* histories start with Robert Bartlett's *England under the Norman and Angevin Kings, 1075–1225* (2000), which includes a discussion of the phenomenon of Anglo-Norman rebellion. Odo and Ranulf's colourful exploits are best seen in the primary sources referred to in the notes. For the reigns they disrupted, Frank Barlow's *William Rufus* (1983) and Judith A. Green's *Henry I: King of England and Duke of Normandy* (2006) are excellent guides. Matthew Strickland's essay 'Against the Lord's Anointed: Aspects of Warfare and Baronial Rebellion in England and Normandy, 1075–1265' is the most directly relevant in a consistently fascinating collection, George Garnett and John Hudson (eds.), *Law and Government in Mediaeval England and Normandy: Essays in Honour of Sir James Holt* (1994). For the 'anarchy' of Stephen's reign, R. H. C. Davis's biography, *King Stephen, 1135–1154* (1967), has been expanded on by David Crouch, in *The Reign of King Stephen, 1135–1154* (2000). J. H. Round's *Geoffrey de Mandeville: A Study of the Anarchy* (1892) gives the maximum interpretation of what Stephen was up against. The essays in E. King (ed.), *The Anarchy of King Stephen's Reign* (1994), give a more recent historiographical picture.

23 **'You are ill-advised to free . . .'**: Marjorie Chibnall (ed. and trans.), *The Ecclesiastical History of Orderic Vitalis* (1969), Bk VII, Ch. XVI.

24 **'each of them went . . .'**: *Anglo-Saxon Chronicle*, 1088.

24 **'Halters, bring halters . . .'**: *Orderic Vitalis*, Bk VIII, Ch. II.

25 **'We will fight for you . . .'**: ibid., Bk VIII, Ch. II.

25 **Actually, another chronicler . . .**: *The Chronicle of Florence of Worcester*, trans., notes and illustrations Thomas Forester (1854), p. 189.

25 **they called him Godric . . .**: William of Malmesbury, *Gesta Regum Anglorum*, ed. and trans. R. A. B. Mynors, completed by R. M. Thomson and M. Winterbottom, Vol. I, p. 716 (1998); quoted in Judith A. Green, *Henry I*, p. 61.

26 **Whether by chance . . .**: Actually, hunting in the New Forest seems to have been a dangerous business. Rufus and Henry's elder brother Richard had been killed there before 1074, and their nephew, another Richard, also died, possibly as another victim of 'friendly fire'.

26 **'special care of England . . .'**: *Gesta Regum Anglorum*, Vol. I, p. 745.

26 **'above all the magnates of the realm'**: *Orderic Vitalis*, Bk X, Ch. IV.

27 **'torn to the bone'**: ibid.

27 **'presumed to enter . . .' (and following)**: ibid.

29 **'the calm of this brilliant . . .'**: *Gesta Regum Anglorum*, quoted in David C. Douglas and George W. Greenaway (eds.), *English Historical Documents. Vol. II: 1042–1189*, p. 322.

32 **In earlier reigns, rebels did not automatically . . .**: R. H. C. Davis, *King Stephen* (1967), p. 27.

34 **'occupy the moral high ground . . .'**: David Crouch, *The Reign of King Stephen 1135–1154* (2000), p. 77.

35 **'it was their own right . . .'**: K. R. Potter (ed. and trans.) and R. H. C. Davis (new introduction and notes), *Gesta Stephani* (1976), p. 7.

36 **'with the bells ringing everywhere . . .':** ibid., p. 125.

37 **the proposal left no place . . .:** see *Gesta Regum Anglorum* and *Gesta Stephani* for contrasting accounts of post-Winchester negotiations.

38 **'everywhere in the kingdom . . .':** *Gesta Stephani*, p. 161.

39 **Geoffrey cropped up as a local folk tale . . .:** see Jennifer Westwood and Jacqueline Simpson, *The Lore of the Land: A Guide to England's Legends, from Spring-Heeled Jack to the Witches of Warboys* (2005), p. 273.

41 **'disinherited should be restored':** *Gesta Stephani*, p. 158.

3. Rebels with a Cause

For Henry II and his nemesis, William Warren's *Henry II* (1973) and Frank Barlow's *Thomas Becket* (1986) are exhaustive. J. C. Holt puts Robin Hood into historical and legendary perspective in his classic study (1982). John Gillingham's biography of *Richard the Lionheart* (1989) gives the background to William fitz Osbert's rising, which is discussed in some detail in G. W. S. Barrow's article for *History Today*, 'The Bearded Revolutionary' (1969). The historiography of Magna Carta is vast, but the works of J. C. Holt (especially *The Northerners* (1961) and *Magna Carta* (2nd edn, 1992) are indispensable. W. L. Warren's *King John* (1990) is a cool re-examination of a much mythologized king. Claire Valente's *The Theory and Practice of Revolt in Medieval England* (2003), which begins with the Magna Carta barons and runs up to 1415, is a rare example of an attempt to look at ways of 'containing' the monarch over a long period.

43 **'more truly a king than his master':** William of Newburgh, quoted in W. L. Warren, *Henry II* (1973), p. 60.

46 **'what miserable drones . . .':** Edward Grim, quoted by Frank Barlow, in *Thomas Becket* (1986), p. 235.

47 **'really a rebel . . .':** quoted in J. D. Mackie, *The Earlier Tudors 1485–1558* (1952), p. 396.

48 **'the father, with a view . . .':** Ralph Diceto, quoted in W. L. Warren, *King John* (1990), p. 175.

49 **In 1826, a mound . . .:** see T. E. Tomlins (ed.), *Monastic and Social*

Life in the Twelfth Century, Exemplified in the Chronicle of Jocelin of Brakelond (1844), notes, p. 41.

50 **an impressive £400 a year . . .:** See May McKisack, *The Fourteenth Century 1307–1399* (1959), p. 173.

50 **'fight against God and the Church . . .':** C. R. Cheney and W. H. Semple (eds.), *Selected Letters of Pope Innocent III Concerning England, 1198–1216* (1953), quoted in Christopher Holdsworth, 'Langton, Stephen (*c.*1150–1228)', *Oxford Dictionary of National Biography* (2004); for Langton and Becket, see P. B. Roberts, 'Archbishop Stephen Langton and His Preaching on Thomas Becket', in T. L. Amos, E. Green and B. M. Kienzle (eds.), *De ore Domini: Preacher and Word in the Middle Ages* (1989), pp. 75–92.

52 **died of fright . . .:** see A. L. Poole, *From Domesday Book to Magna Carta 1087–1216* (1951), p. 368.

53 **'four generations had not sufficed . . .':** Sir Walter Scott, *Ivanhoe* (1819), Chapter One.

54 **52,000 citizens to his cause . . .:** William of Newburgh, *The History of English Affairs*, eds. with commentary P. G. Walsh and M. J. Kennedy (1988).

55 **Most disapproved of his attempt . . .:** see William of Newburgh (against) and Matthew Paris, *English History: From the Year 1235 to 1273*, trans. from the Latin by the Rev. J. A. Giles (1852–4) (more sympathetic).

56 **'the Northerners', a description . . .:** see J. C. Holt, *The Northerners* (1961, revised 1992), p. xv.

63 **talking up the 'Britishness' . . .:** see Gordon Brown's speech on liberty (25 October 2007) at the University of Westminster, http://www.number10.gov.uk/Page13630.

64 **'barons, knights and . . .':** in letters patent of the Chancery of King John, see J. C. Holt, *Magna Carta* (revised 1992), p. 292.

65 **'All these barons . . .':** from a memorandum listing the number of knights mustered at London, printed in Holt, *Magna Carta*, pp. 478–80.

65 **'agreement which is not only . . .' (and following):** letter to the English, 24 August 1215; quoted in Harry Rothwell (ed.), *English Historical Documents. Vol. III: 1189–1327*, p. 326.

4. The False Dawn of Reform

J. R. Maddicott's *Simon de Montfort* (1994) is a comprehensive reappraisal, while D. A. Carpenter's engagement with the long reign of Henry III covers resistance to him in all its forms (*The Minority of Henry III* (1990) and his 1996 collection of essays, *Henry III*). Montfort is one of those rare figures in English history who seems to be recast with each passing fashion. But the Victorian view of him, as evidenced in Oliver H. Richardson's *National Movement in the Reign of Henry III* (1897), was still discernible in the works of R. F. Treharne (*Baronial Plan of Reform, 1258–1263* (1932) and the collection edited posthumously (1986) by E. B. Fryde, *Simon de Montfort and Baronial Reform: Thirteenth-Century Essays*). An excellent discussion of the idea of the 'community of the realm' is to be found in M. T. Clanchy, *England and Its Rulers 1066–1272: Foreign Lordship and National Identity* (1983). For Edward I, as for his two successor namesakes, the first port of call is Michael Prestwich, author not only of the *New Oxford* volume for the period, *Plantagenet England 1225–1360* (2005), but also of *Edward I* (1988), *The Three Edwards: War and State in England, 1272–1377* (1980), and a handy compendium on the only (half-) rebellion of the first Edward's reign, *Documents Illustrating the Crisis of 1297–8 in England* (1980).

67 **'. . . in tears was made the song . . .':** 'Lament for Simon de Montfort', in Harry Rothwell (ed.), *English Historical Documents. Vol. III: 1189–1327*, p. 916.

68 **'Dressed in royal robes . . .' (and following), promised to carry the boy king . . .:** see the *History of William the Marshal*, cited in *EHD III*, pp. 81–4.

70 **'hives of Christ . . .':** 'The Taking of Lincoln', in Thomas Wright (ed.), *Political Songs of England* (1884), p. 38.

70 **'England hath grasped . . .':** ibid., p. 35.

71 **Magna Carta was reissued . . .:** see the catalogue by Nicholas Vincent for the Sotheby's sale in 2007 of a copy of Magna Carta reissued in 1297, available online at http://www.sothebys.com/liveauctions/event/No8461MagnaCarta.pdf.

73 **'ridiculous that this alien . . .':** Gilbert de Clare in 1265, in Rish-anger's Chronicle, quoted in J. R. Maddicott, *Simon de Montfort* (1994), p. 362.

73 **'What is it you fear? . . .':** Matthew Paris, quoted in *EHD III*, p. 129.

74 **'you seduced my sister . . .':** Matthew Paris, quoted in Maddicott, p. 25.

75 **'Who can believe . . .' (and following):** ibid., p. 87.

76 **around £4.7 billion today:** based on conversion rate for earliest available date (1270) at www.nationalarchives.gov.uk/currency/results.aspmid.

76 **'Many of the nobles . . .' (and following):** Paris, quoted in *EHD III*, p. 130.

77 **'reform the state . . .' (and following):** Royal letters, 2 May 1258, in R. F. Treharne and I. J. Sanders (eds.), *Documents of the Baronial Movement of Reform and Rebellion, 1258–1267* (1973), pp. 73–6.

78 **'knot to bind their Proteus':** Paris, quoted in *EHD III*, p. 119.

78 **'advise the king . . .':** Provisions of Oxford, in Treharne and Sanders, p. 111.

80 **'. . . numberless dead bodies . . .':** Paris, quoted in *EHD III*, p. 126.

80 **'if we cannot accomplish this [reform] as fast . . .':** Treharne and Sanders, pp. 120–21.

81 **'from this moment . . .':** ibid., p. 241.

82 **'will in good faith . . .':** Mise of Amiens, 23 January 1264, in ibid., p. 283.

83 **'we quash and invalidate . . .':** ibid., p. 287.

86 **'acting against the utility . . .':** quoted in Claire Valente, *The Theory and Practice of Revolt in Medieval England* (2003), p. 47.

86 **These numbers do not include . . .:** ibid., pp. 90–105.

86 **playing at a game of Simon and the Lord Edward . . .:** ibid., p. 47, footnote.

87 **'one of the largest armies . . .':** Maddicott, p. 290.

88 **'has been provided by . . .':** quoted in F. M. Powicke, *The Thirteenth Century 1216–1307* (2nd edn, 1962), p. 217.

88 **Songs of praise and lament . . .:** 'Song of the Barons' and 'Lament for Simon de Montfort', *EHD III*, pp. 915–16.

89 **the head, gruesomely adorned . . .:** Chronicles of the Mayors and Sheriffs, 1259–66, *English Historical Documents III*, p. 183.

89 **'But if he [the king] have sought . . .':** 'Song of Lewes', *EHD III*, p. 899.

89 **'In all things his predecessor's opposite':** J. R. Maddicott, Edward I and the Lessons of Baronial Reform', in Peter R. Cass and Simon Lloyd (eds), *Thirteenth-Century England: I* (1986), p. 1.

90 **'By God, O earl, either you go or hang . . .':** *The Chronicle of Walter Guisborough*, quoted in Michael Prestwich, *The Three Edwards: War and State in England 1272–1377* (1980), p. 28.

91 **'of which the king . . .':** Royal Proclamation, 12 August 1297, in *EHD III*, p. 479.

91 **'community of the land':** Articles of Grievance (*Monstraunces*), 1297, in ibid., p. 469.

91 **'those standing about in his chamber':** Matthew Paris, quoted in Prestwich, *The Three Edwards*, p. 29.

5. Revenge

Edward II's two great opponents have received differing treatments. Thomas of Lancaster is the subject of academic scrutiny in J. R. Maddicott's wide-ranging biography, subtitled *A Study in the Reign of Edward II* (1970), while Roger Mortimer's life has only recently been written up in more 'popular', though no less well-researched, style by his namesake (no relation), Ian Mortimer, in *The Greatest Traitor* (2003). Prestwich's *Three Edwards* covers the whole reign, while Natalie Fryde's *The Tyranny and Fall of Edward II 1321–1326* (1979) picks up where Maddicott leaves off, at the bloody denouement.

95 **'who rejected the counsel of the elders . . .':** Wendy R. Childs (ed. and trans., based on N. Denholm-Young), *Vita Edwardi Secundi* (2005), p. 33.

96 **'the things that are still being done . . .':** quoted (in original French) in J. R. Maddicott, *Thomas of Lancaster 1307–1322: A Study in the Reign of Edward II* (1970), p. 73.

97 **'unswerving love':** ibid., p. 9.

97 **'There is not one that pitieth my case . . .':** ibid., p. 59.

98 **'[I]t was thought most certain . . .':** ibid., p. 11.

98 **'there would be no other judges than royal judges . . .' (and following):** Harry Rothwell (ed.), *English Historical Documents. Vol. III: 1189–1327*, pp. 525–6.

99 **'I fear that if they [the poor] had a leader . . .':** quoted in Maddicott, p. 107.

100 **the two men did small favours . . .:** ibid., p. 6.

101 **The Ordinances now specified . . .:** *EHD III*, p. 533.

103 **'Lift him up, lift him up . . .':** Childs, p. 49.

103 **'being of higher birth . . .' (and following):** ibid., p. 51.

107 **'Office of St Thomas of Lancaster':** Thomas Wright, *Political Songs of England* (1839), pp. 268–72.

107 **it had come by a tainted route . . .:** see Gerald Harriss, *Shaping the Nation: England 1360–1461* (2005), pp. 483–4.

112 **'An unwise king destroyeth his people':** Ecclesiasticus, 10:3.

6. A Rebel People

R. B. Dobson's *The Peasants' Revolt of 1381* (1970) is not only an invaluable collection and translation of the most vital primary sources for the rising, but in its introduction and editorial matter provides a comprehensive overview. The historian who transformed the study of the English medieval peasantry is R. H. Hilton, whose work on 1381 itself includes *Bond Men Made Free: Medieval Peasant Movements and the English Rising of 1381* (1973); and a more popular book, co-authored by Hyman Fagan, *The English Rising of 1381* (1950). Hilton also co-edited a selection of essays on *The English Rising of 1381* with T. H. Aston (1984), and published his Ford Lectures, as *The English Peasantry in the Later Middle Ages* (1973). The most accessible modern narrative account of the Rising is, however, *The Great Rising of 1381: The Peasants' Revolt and England's Failed Revolution* by Alastair Dunn (2002).

116 **'this impatient nettle . . .':** from R. B. Dobson (ed.), *The Peasants' Revolt of 1381* (1970), p. 381.

117 **'great and unexpected calamity . . .':** Thomas Walsingham, in ibid., p. 131.

117 **'in the sky of India . . .':** Charles Canning, speech to the East India Company, 1855, quoted in Thomas R. Metcalf, 'Canning, Charles John, Earl Canning (1812–1862)', *Oxford Dictionary of National Biography* (2004).

118 **'each person of the kingdom . . .':** Dobson, p. 105.

118 **'all men in the realm of England . . .':** Henry Knighton, in ibid., p. 183.

120 **'hoped to subject all things . . .':** Walsingham, in ibid., p. 132.

121 **'threaten[ed] the prior and his household . . .':** *Calendar of the Patent Rolls 1272–81*, 16 June 1278, p. 290.

123 **'counsellors, procurers . . .' (and following):** Dobson, pp. 76–8.

123 **'ordain that no one . . .':** *Anonimalle Chronicle*, in ibid., pp. 126–7.

124 **'gathered to the number . . .':** ibid., pp. 124–5.

124 **'so called because of his trade . . .':** Knighton, in Dobson., p. 136.

124–5 **'fled towards London . . .':** *Anonimalle Chronicle*, in ibid., pp. 124–5.

125 **'where there's no treachery . . .':** 'The Outlaw's Song of Trailbaston', in Thomas H. Ohlgren (ed.), *Medieval Outlaws: Ten Tales in Modern English*, 1998, p. 103.

125 **'from town to town . . .':** *Anonimalle Chronicle*, in Dobson, p. 124.

125 **'fifty thousand of the commons gathered . . .':** ibid., p. 125.

125 **'The commons sent several letters . . .':** ibid., pp. 125–6.

125 **'full of obscurities' (and following):** Walsingham, in Dobson, p. 380.

126 **'a sum which would have ruined . . .' (and following):** *Anonimalle Chronicle*, in ibid., pp. 126–7.

126 'so that once the memory of ancient customs . . .' : Walsingham, in Dobson, pp. 133–4.

126 'to maintain and advise them . . .': *Anonimalle Chronicle*, in ibid., p. 127.

127 'arrived on the other side . . .': ibid., p. 129.

127 'With whom hold you?': *Anonimalle Chronicle*, in A. R. Myers (ed.), *English Historical Documents. Vol. IV: 1327–1485*, p. 131.

129 'of [the rebels'] accord': Froissart in Dobson, p. 188.

129 'favoured the rustics': Walsingham, in ibid., p. 168.

129 'for fear of their lives': *Anonimalle Chronicle*, in ibid., p. 156.

129 'no harm or injury': ibid.

129 'eighteen persons were beheaded . . .': ibid., p. 158.

130 'none of them . . .': ibid., p. 159.

130 'their throats sounded . . .': Walsingham, in Dobson, p. 173.

131 'required that henceforward no man . . .': *Anonimalle Chronicle*, in Dobson., p. 161.

131 Up to 160 people suffered . . .: ibid., p. 162.

132 'kept throwing . . . from hand to hand . . .': Knighton, in Dobson, p. 186.

132 'Sir king, seest thou . . .': Froissart, in ibid., pp. 194–5.

132 'by the hand, shaking his arm . . .': *Anonimalle Chronicle,* in ibid., p. 164.

132 'with his head covered . . .': The 'monk of Westminster', in Ranulf Higden's *Polychronicon*, in Dobson, p. 203.

132 'There should be no law but the law of Winchester' (and following): *Anonimalle Chronicle*, in Dobson, pp. 164–5.

133 'With marvellous presence of mind . . .': Walsingham, in Dobson, p. 179.

134 'quashed, annulled and judged worthless . . .': Knighton, in ibid., p. 183.

134 'disinheritance of themselves . . .': Parliament Rolls 98–103, in ibid., p. 329.

134 'found in an old house hidden . . .': Froissart, in ibid., p. 198.

134 'Straw's 'confession': survives . . .': Walsingham, in ibid., p. 365.

135 'You wretched men, detestable . . .': ibid., p. 310.

135 Five hundred rebels were killed . . .: ibid., p. 311.

136 **'We are not an organisation created out of special conditions . . .':** speech to 28th Labour Conference, quoted in Clare V. J. Griffiths, *Labour and the Countryside: The Politics of Rural Britain between the Wars* (Oxford, 2007).

137 **'all bond men be made free':** Kett's demands being in rebellion in Anthony Fletcher and Diarmaid MacCulloch, *Tudor Rebellions* (5th edn, 2008) p. 157.

137 **'Such a manumission . . .':** Parliament Rolls 98–103, in Dobson, p. 329.

139 **'very much in the nature . . .':** Nicholas Ridley, *My Style of Government* (1991), p. 67.

7. Challenging the Realm

Nigel Saul's biography of Richard II (1997) shows how a king who tried to expand the idea of kingship ended up losing his throne. Gerald Harriss's *New Oxford* volume, *Shaping the Nation: England 1360–1461* (2005) is magisterial in all respects, but particularly elucidating on the rise of Bolingbroke. The doyen of historians of the period is still (Harriss's former doctoral supervisor) K. B. McFarlane, whose lapidary style made up for his glacial approach to publication. His *Lancastrian Kings and Lollard Knights* (1972) and lectures and essays (*The Nobility of Later Medieval England* (1973) and *England in the Fifteenth Century* (1981)) are elegantly essential. Ian Mortimer's *The Fears of Henry IV* (2007) is an admirable attempt to reconstruct the psyche of the rebel who became a king, without straying too far into speculation. C. T. Allmand's *Life of Henry V* (1992) goes easy on the hagiography. For a discussion of Oldcastle and Falstaff, see Alice-Lyle Scoufos, *Shakespeare's Typological Satire: A Study of the Falstaff–Oldcastle Problem* (1979).

141 **talked about as a potential saint . . .:** see Michael Bennett, 'Henry of Bolingbroke and the Revolution of 1399', in Gwilym Dodd and Douglas Biggs (eds.), *Henry IV: The Establishment of the Regime* (2003) – referring to Simon Walker, in *The McFarlane Legacy* (1995), and J. S. Edwards, 'The Cult of 'St' Thomas of Lancaster

and its Iconography', *Yorkshire Archaeological Journal*, 64 (1992), pp. 103–22.

142 **'you shall have such mercy . . .':** continuation of the *Eulogian Historiarum*, in Chris Given-Wilson (ed.), *Chronicles of the Revolution 1397–1400* (1993), p. 65.

143 **'. . . We are on the point of being undone . . .' (and following):** Rolls of Parliament, 29–30 January 1398, in ibid., p. 86.

147 **'when the Welshmen . . .':** Jean Creton, in ibid., p. 139.

147 **'came to an agreement . . .':** Monk of Evesham, in ibid., p. 127.

148 **'blessed is he . . .':** Philip Repingdon to Henry IV, 4 May 1401, in George Williams (ed.), *The Official Correspondence of Thomas Bekynton* (1872), Vol. I, p. 152.

148 **'to reclaim, with your royal permission . . .':** Monk of Evesham, in Given-Wilson (ed.), p. 130.

148 **'My Lord, I have come sooner . . .':** Jean Creton, in ibid., p. 150.

148 **'and recommended their city . . .':** Adam of Usk, in ibid., p. 159.

149 **'the matter of setting aside' (and following):** ibid., pp. 160–61.

149 **'I, Henry of Lancaster' (and following):** ibid., p. 186.

151 **'of his own':** see Gerald Harriss, *Shaping the Nation: England 1360–1461* (2005), p. 499.

152 **'one of the wyrste bataylys . . .':** Gregory's Chronicle, quoted in J. H. Wylie, *History of England under Henry IV* (four vols., 1884–98), Vol. 1, p. 362.

155 **'the greatest man that ever ruled . . .':** K. B. Macfarlane, *Lancastrian Kings and Lollard Knights* (1972), p. 133.

158 **'crowds of people flocking . . .':** David Prest (trans.), James G. Clark (ed.), *The Chronica Maiora of Thomas Walsingham 1376–1422* (2005), p. 394.

159 **'still alive in the kingdom of Scotland . . .':** ibid., p. 428.

8. *Wars of the Roses*

The Wars of the Roses are almost as vigorously fought over by historians as by Yorkists and Lancastrians. Two excellent discussions are John Gillingham, *The Wars of the Roses* (1983), which concentrates more on the military strategy than does Christine Carpenter's identically titled book, subtitled *Politics and the Constitution in England, c.1437–1509* (1997). I. M. W. Harvey's study of *Jack Cade's Rebellion of 1450* (1991) provides the missing link between popular politics and aristocratic. For the Pastons, Colin Richmond's extended scholarly engagement, in the three volumes of *The Paston Family in the Fifteenth Century* (1990, 1996 and 2000), has been complemented by the more digestible *Blood and Roses: The Paston Family in the Fifteenth Century* of Helen Castor (2004). Warwick the Kingmaker has been steadily reclaimed from Shakespeare, first by Charles Oman in 1891, and more recently by M. A. Hicks (1998) and A. J. Pollard (2007). Perkin Warbeck's little-documented life has been afforded lavish and poetic (as well as imaginative) treatment in Ann Wroe's *Perkin: A Story of Deception* (2003).

161 **'wars of the White and Red Roses':** Walter Scott, *Anne of Geierstein* (1829; Edinburgh edn, ed. J. H. Alexander, 2000), p. 66.

163 **'a power struggle between Plantagenets':** A. A. Gill, 'Towton, the bloodbath that changed the course of our history', *Sunday Times*, 24 August 2008.

164 **'the said enemies been so bold . . .':** Norman Davis (ed.), *The Paston Letters* (1963), 12 March 1450.

168 **'other men . . . have the revenues . . .' (and following):** 'The Bills of Complaint of 1450', in I. M. W. Harvey, *Jack Cade's Rebellion of 1450* (1991), p. 187.

172 **'my lord has put a bill . . .':** William Wayte to John Paston, I, 6 October 1450.

173 **'the king is well amended . . .':** Edmund Clere to John Paston, I, 9 January 1455.

180 **'bisecting the face and cranial vault . . .':** 'The Towton Mass Grave Project', at www.brad.ac.uk/acad/archsci/depart/resgrp/towton/.

9. The People's Wars of Religion

The best guide to the risings that take the shine off the Tudor image is Anthony Fletcher and Diarmaid MacCulloch's *Tudor Rebellions* (5th edn, 2008), which contains some of the most important of the rebels' texts. The essays assembled in *Order and Disorder in Early Modern England* (1985), edited by Fletcher and John Stevenson, and in the *Past and Present* collection edited by Paul Slack, *Rebellion, Popular Protest and Social Order in Early Modern England* (1984), put the risings in social as well as political context. For individual rebellions, R. W. Hoyle's scholarly *The Pilgrimage of Grace and the Politics of the 1530s* (2001) is more thorough, if less vivid, than Geoffrey Moorhouse's *The Pilgrimage of Grace: The Rebellion That Shook Henry VIII's Throne* (2002). For 1549, Andy Wood's *The 1549 Rebellions and the Making of Early Modern England* (2007) is unusual in considering the western and eastern risings side by side. Eamon Duffy's *The Voices of Morebath: Reformation and Rebellion in an English village* (2001) shows what involvement in the Western Rebellion could mean on the ground. Chris Skidmore's biography of *Edward VI: The Lost King of England* (2007) is the source of the speculation on Kett and the court factions behind the young King.

192 **the largest popular revolt in English history . . .:** see C. S. L. Davies, 'Popular Religion and the Pilgrimage of Grace', in A. Fletcher and J. Stevenson (eds.), *Order and Disorder in Early Modern England* (1985).

193 **'spriede . . . sedicious, false . . .':** Quoted in Adam Fox, 'Rumour, News and Popular Political Opinion in Elizabethan and Early Stuart England', *The Historical Journal*, Vol. 40, No. 3 (Sept. 1997), pp. 597–620.

194 **'now the profits of the abbeys suppressed . . .':** Anthony Fletcher and Diarmaid MacCulloch, *Tudor Rebellions*, (5th edn, 2008), p. 132.

195 **'the chief occasion of this business . . .':** R. W. Hoyle, *The Pilgrimage of Grace and the Politics of the 1530s* (2001), pp. 108–9.

196 **'the place where they . . .':** 'Article 10 of the Ten Articles, 1536',

in David Cressy and Lori Anne Ferrell (eds.), *Religion and Society in Early Modern England: A Sourcebook* (2005), p. 25.

198 **'What whoresones were we . . .':** Fletcher and MacCulloch, p. 25.

198 **'having a black coat . . .' (and following):** from 'The Maner of the Taking of Robert Aske in Lincolnshire . . .', in Mary Bateson, 'The Pilgrimage of Grace', *English Historical Review*, Vol. 5, No. 18. (April 1890), p. 330.

199 **'for the love that ye do bear . . .':** 'The Oath of the Honourable Men, 1536', in Fletcher and MacCulloch, p. 143.

201 **'We will all wear no badge . . .':** 'The Maner of the Taking of Robert Aske', quoted in Fletcher and MacCulloch, p. 37.

201 **'In every man's mouth . . .':** Hoyle, p. 304.

201 **'a loss to this realm . . .':** Aske's prison deposition, in ibid., p. 297.

203 **'made the English Reformation possible . . .':** Hoyle, p. 453.

204 **'comocyon tyme':** see Eamon Duffy, *The Voices of Morebath: Reformation and Rebellion in an English Village* (2001), p. 130, for a discussion of the different conventions for naming the uprisings of 1549.

205 **'knoweth no other lord ther . . .':** Andy Wood, *The 1549 Rebellions and the Making of Early Modern England* (2007), p. 162.

206 **'altogether bent to overrun . . .':** John Hooker, in Fletcher and MacCulloch, p. 54.

206 **'Had you rather be like [mag]pies . . .':** ibid., p. 60.

206 **'we the Cornyshe men . . .':** ibid., p. 152.

209 **'in order to have a fayre shew . . .' (and following):** quoted in Duffy, p. 130.

211 **Kett's articles have even been interpreted . . .:** Diarmaid MacCulloch, 'Kett's Rebellion in Context', in Paul Slack (ed.), *Rebellion, Popular Protest and Social Order in Early Modern England* (1984), pp. 54–5.

211 **'brychles and bear arssyde':** Fletcher and MacCulloch, p. 88.

211 **'amici ac delegati':** warrant quoted in F. W. Russell, *Kett's Rebellion in Norfolk* (1859), p. 47.

214 **'levytie . . . softnes':** William Paget to Protector Somerset, in Fletcher and MacCulloch, p. 160.

10. Queens and Their Rebels

Mary's coup is discussed in detail by Anna Whitelock and Diarmaid MacCulloch in 'Princess Mary's Household and the Succession Crisis, July 1553' (*Historical Journal*, 50:2, 2007). David M. Loades is the author of a biography of Mary that concentrates on primary sources, *Mary Tudor: The Tragical History of the First Queen of England* (2006), as well as a pamphlet on *The Wyatt Rebellion* (2000). The Rebellion of the Northern Earls is discussed by Fletcher and MacCulloch, and has recently been the subject of a scholarly monograph by Krista J. Kesselring, *The Northern Rebellion of 1569: Faith, Politics, and Protest in Elizabethan England* (2007). Steer's conspiracy is anatomized in 'A "Rising of the People"? The Oxfordshire Rising of 1596' by John Walter (*Past and Present*, No. 107, 1985, and collected in Slack (ed.), *Rebellion, Popular Protest and Social Order*). Lytton Strachey's *Elizabeth and Essex* (1928) may still be the raciest treatment of the ageing Queen's tragic dalliance. P. E. J. Hammer's *The Polarisation of Elizabethan Politics: The Political Career of Robert Devereux, Second Earl of Essex, 1585–1597* (1999) is an extremely solid counterweight to Strachey's flightiness. For a discussion of the origins of the 'monstrous' mob in Elizabethan discourse, see *The Many-Headed Hydra: The Hidden History of the Revolutionary Atlantic* (2000) by Peter Linebaugh and Marcus Rediker.

216 **as a 'coup d'état' . . .:** see e.g. J. D. Mackie, *The Earlier Tudors 1485–1558* (1952) p. 526.

217 **'You know, the realm . . .':** quoted in Chris Skidmore, *Edward VI: The Lost King of England* (2007), p. 266.

217 **'All the forces in the country . . .':** ibid., p. 265.

219 **'innumerable companies of the common folk':** *The Chronicle of Queen Jane and Two Years of Queen Mary*, quoted in Mackie, p. 528.

220 **'everie strett full of bon-fyres':** diary of Henry Machyn, quoted in Ann Weikel, 'Mary I (1516–1558)', *Oxford Dictionary of National Biography* (2004).

220 **Mary and her household may have prepared . . .:** Anna Whitelock and Diarmaid MacCulloch, 'Princess Mary's House-

hold and the Succession Crisis, July 1553', *Historical Journal*, 50:2 (2007).

220 **a petition rediscovered only recently . . .:** see R. Hoyle, 'Agrarian Agitation in Mid-Sixteenth-Century Norfolk: A Petition of 1553', *Historical Journal*, 44 (2001).

223 **'You may not so much as name religion . . .':** from John Procter, *The Historie of Wyates Rebellion*, quoted in Ian W. Archer, 'Wyatt, Sir Thomas', *Oxford Dictionary of National Biography* (2004).

223 **'lo, now even at hand . . .' (and following):** Anthony Fletcher and Diarmaid MacCulloch, *Tudor Rebellions*, (5th edn, 2008), pp. 95–6.

225 **'without eny whit saying to them' (and following):** *The Tower Chronicle*, 1554, quoted in ibid., p. 149.

228 **'disobedience to the prince . . .':** quoted in Richard L. Greaves, 'Concepts of Political Obedience in Late Tudor England: Conflicting Perspectives', *Journal of British Studies*, Vol. 22, No. 1 (Autumn 1982), p. 27.

229 **'hazard myself for the marriage':** 'The Examination of the Earl of Northumberland, 1572', in Fletcher and MacCulloch, p. 165.

230 **'better not to stir':** ibid.

230 **'the common people are ignorant . . .':** Sir Ralph Sadler to Sir William Cecil, 1569, in Fletcher and MacCulloch, p. 163.

230 **'trewe and catholicke religion' (and following):** 'The Proclamation of the Earls, 1569', in Fletcher and MacCulloch, p. 163.

231 **'Hys wyfe beyng the stower . . .':** Lord Hunsdon to Sir William Cecil, in Fletcher and MacCulloch, p. 111.

232 **'Our first object . . .':** 'The Examination of the Earl of Northumberland, 1572', in Fletcher and MacCulloch, p. 165.

237 **It has been argued that *As You Like It* . . .:** see Richard Wilson , '"Like the Old Robin Hood": *As You Like It* and the Enclosure Riots', *Shakespeare Quarterly*, Vol. 43, No. 1 (Spring 1992), pp. 1–19.

11. Republicans and Revolutionaries

The Gunpowder Plot never exhausts its students. Two very readable recent historians of Catesby and his fellows are James Sharpe, *Remember, Remember the Fifth of November* (2005), and Antonia Fraser, *The Gunpowder Plot: Terror and Faith in 1605* (1996). But the English Civil Wars make the Fifth of November look neglected by comparison. The Earl of Clarendon started the ball rolling with his *History of the Rebellion and Civil Wars in England*, first printed in 1702 and available in numerous editions (and selections, most recently by Paul Seaward, 2009). S. R. Gardiner brought Victorian indefatigability to the subject, and his vast treatment, *The History of the Great Civil War* (5 vols., republished most recently in paperback in 2002) set the benchmark for all followers. These have included G. M. Trevelyan (*England under the Stuarts* (1904)), Veronica (C. V.) Wedgwood (including *The King's War, 1641–1647* (1959)) and Hugh Trevor-Roper from various angles (in essay form, on the gentry during the period, and on Archbishop Laud). There was a major flowering in the 1980s and '90s, when Roger Lockyer (*The Early Stuarts: A Political History of England 1603–1642* (1989)), Conrad Russell (*The Fall of the British Monarchies 1637–1642* (1991)), Mark Kishlansky (*Monarchy Transformed: Britain 1603–1714* (1996)) and Derek Hirst (*England in Conflict 1603–1660* (1999)) all produced reworkings of the period. Austin Woolrych's *Britain in Revolution 1625–1660* (2002), notwithstanding its scale and erudition, is also a pleasure to read, and is the first work to assimilate all that new study. Diane Purkiss's equally entertaining *The English Civil War: A People's History* (2006) looks at the period from the ground up; and the titles keep coming, from Ian Gentles's *The English Revolution and the Wars in the Three Kingdoms 1638–1652* (2007) to M. J. Braddick's *God's Fury, England's Fire* (2008).

Books on Cromwell are only slightly thinner on the ground. Barry Coward's biographical study (1991) is the handiest, Christopher Hill's *God's Englishman: Oliver Cromwell and the English Revolution* (1970) the most impressive. For the rebellions within the rebellion, Hill is vital, including *The World Turned Upside Down* (1972), *Puritanism and Revolution* (1958) and *Liberty against the Law* (1996). Hill edited and introduced a volume of Gerrard Winstanley's works, *The Law of Freedom, and Other Writings* (1983). The Levellers' own words are heard in G. E. Aylmer's *The Levellers in the English Revolution* (1975). Fifth Monarchists are explained in Bernard Capp's *Fifth Monarchy Men* (1972), while the Ranters (and their alleged non-existence) have been tracked in the pages of *Past and Present* by G. E. Aylmer (1987), J. C. Davis (1990) and J. F. McGregor et al. (1993).

239 **'incessant peals of muskets . . .':** from the 'Narration of the Siege and taking of . . . Leicester', 6, quoted in Barbara Donagan, *War in England 1642–1649* (2008), p. 89, n. 71.

239 **'there was no tumult . . .':** John Manningham's diary, quoted by Leanda de Lisle in *After Elizabeth* (2005).

240 **Records of fines for 'recusants': . . .:** figures in Jenny Wormald, 'Gunpowder, Treason, and Scots', *Journal of British Studies*, Vol. 24, No. 2 (April 1985), pp. 141–68.

243 **'most horrible':** *Records of the English Province of the Society of Jesus*, quoted in Thomas M. McCoog, 'Garnett, Henry (1555–1606)', *Oxford Dictionary of National Biography* (2004).

244 **'loved [him] above any worldly man':** *Cobbett's Complete Collection of State Trials* (1809–28), Vol. II, p. 186.

244 **'very fair Hungarian horseman's coat . . .':** Mark Nicholls, 'Rookwood, Ambrose', *Oxford Dictionary of National Biography* (2004).

245 **'booted and spurred':** Francis Edwards (ed. and trans.), *The Gunpowder Plot: The Narrative of Oswald Tesimond Alias Greenway*, quoted in James Sharpe, *Remember, Remember the Fifth of November: Guy Fawkes and the Gunpowder Plot* (2005), p. 5.

247 **'one has to call it something':** Hugh Trevor-Roper, 'The Continuity of the English Revolution', in *From Counter-Reformation to Glorious Revolution* (1992), p. 214.

248 **'the truth is . . .':** Edward Hyde, Earl of Clarendon, *The History of the Rebellion: A New Selection*, ed. Paul Seaward (2009), p. 31.

248 **'Our blessed Predecessor . . .' (and following):** 'The King's Answer to the Nineteen Propositions of Parliament', in Joyce Lee Malcolm (ed.), *The Struggle for Sovereignty: Seventeenth-Century English Political Tracts* (2 vols.), Vol. 1 (1999), pp. 23–5.

248 **'vast power itselfe . . .'**: 'Henry Parker, the Case of Shipmoney', in ibid., p. 92.

250 **'I must say that . . .'**: Charles to Prince Rupert, in Austin Woolrych, *Britain in Revolution 1625–1660* (2002), p. 320.

251 **'the soul of the commonwealth . . .'**: quoted in ibid., p. 134.

251 **half a million deaths . . .**: estimation in Ian Gentles, *The English Revolution and the Wars in the Three Kingdoms 1638–1652* (2007), discussion on pp. 433–9.

253 **'greatest liberty of the kingdom . . .' (and following)**: Pym's speech on grievances, 17 April 1640, in J. P. Kenyon, *The Stuart Constitution, 1603–1688: Documents and Commentary* (1986), pp. 183–9.

256 **'upon the word of a king . . .'**: quoted in Woolrych, p. 178.

256 **'reprieve him until Saturday'**: quoted in S. R. Gardiner, *History of England from the Accession of James I to the Outbreak of the Civil War: 1603–1642* (1884), p. 368.

256 **Their outlook has been compared . . .**: Conrad Russell, 'Pym, John (1584–1643)', *Oxford Dictionary of National Biography* (2004).

257 **'those evils under which we have . . .'**: 'The Grand Remonstrance, with the Petition Accompanying It', in S. R. Gardiner (ed.), *The Constitutional Documents of the Puritan Revolution, 1625–1660* (1906) , pp. 202–32.

259 **more reminiscent of the rebel calls to arms . . .**: See D. H. Pennington, 'The Rebels of 1642', in R. H. Parry (ed.), *The English Civil War and after, 1642–1658* (1970).

259 **'could not be fixed again . . .'**: Clarendon, p. 142.

261 **'The king cares not how oft he fights . . .'**: quoted in Woolrych, p. 291.

264 **'that the failings of former kings . . .'**: in Andrew Sharp (ed.), *The English Levellers* (1998), p. 34.

266 **'long and rambling'**: Andrew Sharp (ed.), *The English Levellers* (1998), p. x.

266 **'at how high a rate . . .'**: *An Agreement of the People for a Firm and Present Peace upon Grounds of Common Right and Freedom*, in ibid., pp. 92–101.

267 **'For really I think . . .' (and following)**: in ibid., p. 103.

270 **'such strength of heart . . .'**: 'A Defence of the People of Eng-

land, 24 February, 1651', in D. M. Wolfe (ed.), *Complete Prose Works of John Milton. Vol. 6: 1650–1655, Part I* (1966), p. 535.

271 **'the earth should be made . . .':** see Christopher Hill (ed.), *Winstanley: 'The Law of Freedom' and Other Writings* (1983; 2006), p. 24.

271 **'turned upside down':** *The World Turned Upside Down* was the title of a pamphlet published in 1647 and adopted as the title of Christopher Hill's *The World Turned Upside Down: Radical Ideas during the English Revolution* (1972).

12. Good and Glorious

Ronald Hutton's *The Restoration: A Political and Religious History of England and Wales, 1658–1667* is the best introduction to Charles II's reign, John Miller an excellent historical biographer of both Charles (1991) and his ill-starred brother (*James II* (1978)). Among Stuart rebels, Thomas Venner and Henry Danvers appear in Capp's *Fifth Monarchy Men* and in R. L. Greaves, *Deliver Us from Evil: The Radical Underground in Britain, 1660–1663* (1986). There is an excellent article by Alan Marshall on the Rye House Plotters in the *Oxford Dictionary of National Biography* online (www.oxforddnb.com/vicw/theme/93794). For Monmouth's rebellion, as for the Glorious Revolution, Lord Macaulay's matchless treatment in the *History of England* can never be superseded for style, even if its confident judgements have always been in need of seasoning. Peter Earle's *Monmouth's Rebels: The Road to Sedgemoor, 1685* (1977) has been joined by Robin Clifton's *The Last Popular Rebellion: The Western Rising of 1685* (1984). For 1688, John Miller's *Seeds of Liberty* (1988) is a clear introduction, while Patrick Dillon's *The Last Revolution* (2006) connects political events to a wider sense of cultural turmoil. Jonathan Israel's edited collection *The Anglo-Dutch Moment: Essays on the Glorious Revolution and Its World Impact* (1991) puts the Continental context back, as does Jonathan Scott on a longer timescale in *England's Troubles: Seventeenth-Century English Political Instability in European Context* (2000).

275 **'the reign of King Charles . . .':** Gilbert Burnet, *History of My Own Time* (1724–34), Book III, p. 1.

276 **'differences of opinion . . .'**: Declaration of Breda, in Andrew Browning (ed.), *English Historical Documents. Vol. VI: 1660–1714*, pp. 57–8.

276 **'couching with this motto round it . . .'**: Thomas Venner's journal, in Champlin Burrage, 'The Fifth Monarchy Insurrections', *English Historical Review*, Vol. 25, No. 100 (1910), p. 726.

276 **'Fanatiques . . . should dare and do so much mischief . . .'**: *Diary of Samuel Pepys*, entries for 10 and 19 January 1661.

278 **'much struck . . .'**: Mahatma Gandhi, 'Did Ram Shed Blood?', in *Collected Works*, Vol. XLI, p. 278.

283 **'seditions, tumults and wars . . .'**: J. Robertson (ed.), *Sydney on Government: The Works of Algernon Sydney* (1772), p. 188.

284 **'never be out of a plot . . .'**: *State Trials* 9.409, in Melinda Zook, 'Ferguson, Robert (d. 1714)', *Oxford Dictionary of National Biography* (2004).

285 **'he had certainly cut . . .'**: Daniel Defoe, *Tour through the Whole Island of Great Britain* (1724–6), Letter 4, Part 2, Somerset and Wiltshire.

286 **after the first stroke, the Duke 'lookt up . . .'**: Edmund Verney, quoted in Tim Wales, 'Ketch , John', *ODNB* (2004).

287 **'that circuit of which the memory . . .'**: Thomas Babington Macaulay, *The History of England from the Accession of James the Second* (1848), p. 217.

287 **'in his glories . . .'**: ballad quoted in Macaulay, p. 584.

287 **'last popular rebellion'**: see Robin Clifton, *The Last Popular Rebellion: The Western Risings in 1685* (1986).

288 **'neither glorious, nor a revolution'**: see e.g. Lisa Jardine, *Going Dutch: How England Plundered Holland's Glory* (2008); Google gives more than a hundred others.

288 **'The Glorious Revolution is a term . . .'**: see http://www.parliament.uk/documents/upload/G04.pdf .

288 **'Immortal Seven'**: the Tories Thomas Osborne, Earl of Danby; Charles Talbot, Earl of Shrewsbury; William Cavendish, Duke of Devonshire; and Bishop Compton; and the Whigs Lord Lumley, Edward Russell and Henry Sidney.

289 **'standard of rebellion'**: Burnet, Book IV, p. 471.

290 **'the people are so generally dissatisfied . . .':** letter of invitation to William of Orange, 30 June 1688, in *EHD VI*, p. 120.

291 **'caprices of the English . . .':** Gregorio Leti, *Monarchie universelle*, quoted in Patrick Dillon, *The Last Revolution: 1688 and the Creation of the Modern World* (2006), p. 140.

292 **'I for my own part . . .':** Dillon, p. 165.

293 **'a suppositious child':** Dillon, p. 173.

13. *Returners and Rioters*

Jacobites tend (understandably) to be treated as a Scottish subject, but Daniel Szechi's *The Jacobites* (1994) deals with the English followers of the King over the water. Ian Gilmour, *Riot, Risings and Revolution: Governance and Violence in Eighteenth-Century England* (1992) is an assured guide to the rebels of the eighteenth century, while Adrian Randall, *Riotous Assemblies: Popular Protest in Hanoverian England* (2006) is a comprehensive study of the century's characteristic form of tumult. The Sacheverell riots are discussed in Geoffrey Holmes's essay, published in the serially useful Paul Slack collection, *Rebellion, Popular Protest and Social Order*. Another useful collection which begins at the end of the eighteenth century and runs up to the twentieth is *Popular Protest and Public Order: Six Studies in British History*, edited by Roland Quinault and John Stevenson (1974). Stevenson's own *Popular Disturbances in England, 1700–1870* (1979) brilliantly connects the turbulent eighteenth century to the supposedly more genteel nineteenth. E. P. Thompson's *The Making of the English Working Class* (1963) recast English social history for this period, and his essays, for example in *Customs in Common* (1991), are equally pathbreaking.

295 **'bought and sold for English gold':** Robert Burns, 'Such a parcel of rogues in a nation' (1792).

297 **'If the king should require of thee . . .':** Hugh Latimer, sermon preached at Stamford, 9 November 1550, in George Elwes Corrie, *Sermons by Hugh Latimer* (1844), p. 300.

302 **'grand Corrupter . . .':** William Bulkley's Diary, 18 February

1742, quoted in Paul Langford, *A Polite and Commercial People: England 1727–1783* (1998), p. 185.

302 **'Such were the men and women . . .':** W. H. Chaloner (ed.), *The Autobiography of Samuel Bamford. Vol. One: The Early Days*, 1967, p. 22.

304 **'The beginnings of the second Richard's reign . . .':** 'To the Reader', in *Idols of the Clownes* (1654), quoted in Michael A. Seidel, 'The Restoration Mob: Drones and Dregs', *Studies in English Literature, 1500–1900*, Vol. 12, No. 3, *Restoration and Eighteenth Century* (Summer 1972), pp. 429–43.

305 **'more afraid of the mob . . .':** Strahan writing to John Hall, letter quoted in Arthur H. Cash, *John Wilkes: The Scandalous Father of Civil Liberty* (2006), p. 428, n. 52.

305 **'hang out the bloody flag . . .':** in Geoffrey Holmes, *The Trial of Doctor Sacheverell* (1973), p. 17.

310 **'the bad example of suffering . . .':** Adrian Randall, *Riotous Assemblies: Popular Protest in Hanoverian England* (2006), p. 169.

310 **'a great hardship upon the country . . .':** Nicholas Rogers, *Crowds, Culture, and Politics in Georgian Britain* (1998), p. 78.

310 **'moral economy . . .':** E. P. Thompson , 'The Moral Economy of the English Crowd in the Eighteenth Century', *Past and Present*, No. 50 (Feb. 1971), pp. 76–136.

14. Agitators

The background is provided by the books referred to for the previous chapter (as well as the usual general sources). For Wilkes, Arthur H. Cash's biography, *John Wilkes: The Scandalous Father of Civil Liberty* (2006), is excellent, while John Sainsbury's *John Wilkes: The Lives of a Libertine*, published in the same year, takes a less traditional approach. Lord George Gordon hasn't had a biography since 1795, but his 'cause' appears in Colin Haydon's *Anti-Catholicism in Eighteenth-Century England, c.1714–80: A Political and Social Study* (1993). The Spithead and Nore mutinies are covered by Stevenson, *Popular Disturbances in England, 1700–1870* (1979), Richard Woodman, *A Brief History of Mutiny* (2005) and

N. A. M. Rodger, *The Command of the Ocean: A Naval History of Britain 1649–1815* (2004).

313 **'This is not the clamour of a rabble . . .':** quoted in Arthur H. Cash, *John Wilkes: The Scandalous Father of Civil Liberty* (2006), p. 113.

316 **'If ministers can once usurp . . .':** Wilkes to his constituents in 1769, quoted in Ian Gilmour, *Riot, Risings and Revolution: Governance and Violence in Eighteenth-Century England* (1992), p. 319.

316 **'When the spirit of the nation . . .':** quoted in Peter D. G. Thomas, 'The Beginning of Parliamentary Reporting in Newspapers, 1768–1774', *English Historical Review*, Vol. 74, No. 293 (Oct. 1959), pp. 623–36.

317 **'the meanest mechanic, the poorest peasant . . .':** quoted in Cash, p. 349.

318 **'Wilkes and liberty . . .':** Peter D. G. Thomas, 'Wilkes, John (1725–1797)', *Oxford Dictionary of National Biography* (2004).

319 **'for the diabolical purpose of arming the Papists . . .':** quoted in Robert Kent Donovan, 'The Military Origins of the Roman Catholic Relief Programme of 1778', *Historical Journal*, Vol. 28, No. 1 (March 1985), p. 101.

320 **'until they pulled down . . .':** Ian Gilmour, *Riot, Risings and Revolution: Governance and Violence in Eighteenth-Century England* (1992), p. 363.

320 **'the wisest that had ever been created':** ibid., p. 351.

322 **'had got a twist in his head':** Charles Turner, MP, quoted in Colin Haydon, 'Gordon, Lord George (1751–1793)', *ODNB* (2004).

325 **'well-dressed men haranguing the populace . . .':** James Bland Burges, in John Stevenson, *Popular Disturbances in England, 1700–1870* (1979), p. 172.

15. Revolutionaries and Reformers

Colonel Despard has been the subject of two biographies this century, *Colonel Despard: The Life and Times of an Anglo-Irish Rebel* by Clifford D. Conner (2000), and Mike Jay's *The Unfortunate Colonel Despard* (2004).

On the other hand, a rebel with a longer, if less lurid, track record, Sir Francis Burdett, hasn't been written up since 1932, though the two volumes of M. W. Patterson, *Sir Francis Burdett and His Times (1770–1844)* are enough to be getting on with. The Luddites have long excited popular interest. Both M. I. Thomis's clear-eyed account, *The Luddites: Machine-Breaking in Regency England* (1970), and Brian Bailey's *The Luddite Rebellion* (1998) are helpful. For the Spenceans, *The Political Works of Thomas Spence* have been published in a collection edited by H. T. Dickinson (1982), and there is a biography of Spence by P. M. Ashraf, *The Life and Times of Thomas Spence* (1983). The Spa Fields insurrection hasn't been treated at book length, but the Cato Street Conspiracy has, in V. S. Anand and F. A. Ridley's account (1977). Anniversaries have produced several studies of the Peterloo massacre, by Donald Read (1959), Robert Walmsley and Joyce Marlow (both 1969), and Robert Reid (1989). Henry Hunt is studied in context in John Belchem's '*Orator*' *Hunt: Henry Hunt and English Working-Class Radicalism* (1985). For Parliamentary Reform more generally, the best single-volume work is still John Cannon, *Parliamentary Reform, 1640–1832* (1973). The Swing disturbances are the subject of a classic of social history, Eric Hobsbawm and George Rudé's *Captain Swing* (1969). Chartism's first historian, Thomas Carlyle, published while the movement was still going (*Chartism* (1840)). Asa Briggs's edited collection *Chartist Studies* (1959) began the modern study of the movement, while Dorothy Thompson's *Early Chartists* (1971) traced it to its origins. An excellent recent general history is Malcolm Chase's *Chartism: A New History* (2007). Chartists produced a vast amount of literature themselves. The six-volume edition of Chartist writings *The Chartist Movement in Britain, 1838–1850* (2001), edited by Gregory Claeys, is invaluable. Ernest Jones and Feargus O'Connor are the most studied Chartists: see *Ernest Jones, Chartism, and the Romance of Politics, 1819–1869* (2003) by Miles Taylor; and *The Lion of Freedom: Feargus O'Connor and the Chartist Movement, 1832–1842* (1982) by James Epstein.

330 **'blow the mob to the devil':** quoted in John Stevenson, *Popular Disturbances in England 1700–1870* (1979), p. 216.

330 **'an equalization of Civil, Political, and Religious Rights':**

Malcolm Chase, 'Despard, Edward Marcus (1751–1803)', *Oxford Dictionary of National Biography* (2004).

332 **'promise effectual resistance':** Stevenson, p. 187.

332 **'cause of a single accident . . .':** ibid., p. 189.

332 **'in the distracted kingdom . . .':** Thomas Paine, *Common Sense* (1776).

332 **'It is vain and ridiculous to tell us . . .':** J. Baxter, *Resistance to Oppression* (1795), in Gregory Claeys (ed.), *Political Writings of the 1790s. Vol. IV: Radicalism and Reform 1793–1800* (1995).

333 **'weight of taxes . . .':** Edward Smith, *William Cobbett: A Biography* (1879), p. 162.

334 **'Distressed Manufacturers, Mariners, Artisans . . .':** John Belchem, *'Orator' Hunt: Henry Hunt and English Working-Class Radicalism* (1985), p. 56.

334 **'a person mounted a coal-waggon . . .' (and following):** *The Times*, Tuesday, 3 December 1816, p. 3, 'Spafields Meeting'.

335 **'large and repeated potations . . .':** *The Times*, Thursday, 21 November 1816, p. 3, 'Death of Mr Henry Hunt the Orator from Bristol'.

336 **'Why not go forth as the Barons of old . . .':** John Gast, quoted in J. C. Belchem, 'Henry Hunt and the Evolution of the Mass Platform', *English Historical Review*, Vol. 93, No. 369 (Oct. 1978), pp. 739–73.

337 **'with *no other weapon* . . .':** Belchem, *'Orator' Hunt*, p. 106.

337 **'the delusion which had led them . . .':** *The Times*, Thursday, 19 August 1819, p. 2, 'Dispersal of the reform-meeting at Manchester by a military force'.

337 **'the dreadful fact . . .':** *The Times*, Thursday, 19 August 1819, Editorial.

337 **'the triumph of calumniated reform':** Belchem, *'Orator' Hunt*, p. 122.

338 **'arousing hatred and contempt . . .':** Stevenson, p. 216.

340 **'The real name of King Ludd was Swing':** E. J. Hobsbawm and George Rudé, *Captain Swing* (1969), p. 298.

341 **'we were within a moment of general rebellion':** Stevenson, p. 226.

343 **'fill up the vacancy . . .'**: Malcolm Chase, *Chartism: A New History* (2007), p. 13.

343 **'embracing the principles . . .'**: 'The People's Charter', in Edward Royle, *Chartism* (1980) p. 94.

344 **At Hartshead Moor, Yorkshire . . .**: Hanson and Stephens quoted in Chase, *Chartism*, p. 30.

345 **'It would be a great mistake . . .'**: *Some Social and Political Pioneers of the Nineteenth Century*, quoted in Royle, *Chartism* (2nd edn, 1986), p. 133.

346 **'to meet all acts of oppression . . .'**: Cornelius Bentley and Thos. Moore to William Lovett, in Royle, *Chartism*, p. 97.

347 **'tall working man . . .'**: Chase, p. 110.

348 **'employment on any terms . . .'**: Stevenson, p. 262.

350 **A wave of repression followed . . .**: Figures from Chase, p. 326, and Paul Foot, *The Vote: How It was Won and How It was Undermined* (2005), p. 113.

350 **'outward and visible form . . .'**: *Friend of the People*, 19 April 1851, in Chase, p. 336.

350 **conservative publications . . .**: *Quarterly Review*, October 1867, pp. 555–6, referred to in Carl F. Brand, 'The Conversion of the British Trade-Unions to Political Action', *American Historical Review*, Vol. 30, No. 2 (Jan. 1925), pp. 251–70.

351 **more than a tenth of the adult male population . . .**: figures from D. G. Wright, *Democracy and Reform 1815–1885* (1970; 1991), p. 105.

16. Women and Workers

The best history of the campaign for female suffrage is Martin Pugh's *The March of the Women: A Revisionist Analysis of the Campaign for Women's Suffrage, 1866–1914* (2000). Harold L. Smith's *The British Women's Suffrage Campaign, 1866–1928* (2nd edn, 2007) discusses the most recent interpretations of the militant and non-militant aspects, and includes a selection of documents. Pugh's family biography *The Pankhursts* (2001) is sympathetic but level-headed. Emmeline, Christabel and Sylvia all published their side of the story (*The Suffragette: The History of the Women's Militant*

Suffrage Movement, 1905–1910, by Sylvia Pankhurst (1911); *My Own Story*, by Emmeline Pankhurst (1914); *Unshackled: The Story of How We Won the Vote*, by Christabel Pankhurst (1959)). June Purvis's biography of Emmeline (2002) rescues her subject both from Sylvia's hostility and more recent 'demeaning', 'masculinist' perspectives; the collection of essays Purvis edited with Sandra Stanley Holton, *Votes for Women* (2000), gives an idea of the shades of historical opinion on the movement more generally.

Annie Besant's role in the match-girls' strike is discussed in Anne Taylor's biography (1992). Of histories of the General Strike, Patrick Renshaw's *The General Strike* (1975) and G. A. Phillips's *The General Strike: The Politics of Industrial Conflict* (1976) put the events of 1926 in a longer context than most other studies, which tend to offer a vivid but isolated 'day-by-day' approach. The hunger marchers are discussed in *Voice of Protest: A History of Civil Unrest in Great Britain* (1968) by Harold Priestley.

352 **'I incite this meeting to rebellion' (and following):** quotations in Harold L. Smith, *The British Women's Suffrage Campaign, 1866–1928* (1998; 2007), pp. 126–7.

353 **In 1908, an anonymous female correspondent . . .:** *The Times*, Tuesday, 18 February 1908, p. 11.

357 **'twenty years of peaceful propaganda . . .':** Hannah Mitchell, quoted in Martin Pugh, *The Pankhursts: The History of One Radical Family* (2001), p. 129.

357 **'We are here, not because we are law-breakers . . .':** quoted in ibid., p. 185.

358 **'mob [which] played a sort of Rugby football . . .':** Mitchell; and citation from a memorandum sent to the Home Office in February 1911, both quoted in Smith, pp. 122, 124.

358 **'the sensation is most painful . . .':** Mary Leigh, quoted in Pugh, p. 195; and Mary R. Richardson, quoted in Smith, p. 126.

359 **'Mr Asquith himself will have shown . . .':** quoted in Pugh, p. 216.

359 **'Property to them [governments] is far dearer . . .':** Albert Hall speech, 17 October 1912, quoted in Smith, p. 127.

360 **'Perhaps the women born in happier days . . .':** from the preface to E. Sylvia Pankhurst, *The Suffragette* (1911).

361 **'the abominable conduct . . .':** General Sir Dighton Probyn to Herbert Jones, in John Hislop and David Swannell (eds.), *The Faber Book of the Turf* (1990), p. 228.

361 **'injured innocence . . .':** Teresa Billington-Craig, quoted in Smith, pp. 120–21.

363 **'our Votes for Women victory . . .':** Christabel Pankhurst, *Unshackled: The Story of How We Won the Vote* (1959), p. 294.

364 **'above all extraordinarily silly':** Millicent Fawcett to Lady Francis Balfour, 28 November 1910, in Smith, p. 125.

365 **'one, who appears to be . . .':** *The Link*, No. 21, Saturday, 23 June 1888.

366 **'eight young women':** *The Times*, Wednesday, 18 July 1888; p. 12, 'End of the match girls' strike'.

370 **'Not a penny off the pay':** Cook's speech at York, 3 April 1926, reported in *The Times* ('The old rank and file . . . persisted in their slogan . . .'), 5 April 1926.

370 **'we are at your mercy':** Patrick Renshaw, *The General Strike* (1975), p. 171.

370 **'the moral basis of the Government . . .':** ibid., p. 129.

371 **'public ownership of coal . . .':** ibid., p. 140.

373 **'spontaneous generosity . . .':** A. J. P. Taylor, *English History 1914–1945* (1965), p. 244.

373 **'we have committed suicide':** Renshaw, p. 225.

373 **'This was not a strike against the state . . .':** ibid., p. 249.

17. Outsiders

For Oswald Mosley, Robert Skidelsky's biography (1975), published during Mosley's lifetime, has unfairly been characterized as overly sympathetic to its subject. Stephen Dorril's *Blackshirt: Sir Oswald Mosley and British Fascism* is vastly detailed, leaving one in no doubt of the repugnancy of Mosley's project, and the vaingloriousness of the man behind it. For the contested story of Cable Street, see *Remembering Cable Street: Fascism and Anti-Fascism in British Society*, edited by Tony Kushner and Nadia Valman (2000). Two excellent recent histories of the movement are *Fascism in Britain: A History, 1918–1985*, by Richard Thurlow (1987), and Martin Pugh's '*Hurrah for the Blackshirts!': Fascists and Fascism in Britain between the Wars* (2005). For nuclear disarmament, see *Against the Bomb: The British Peace Movement, 1958–1965*, by Richard Taylor (1988). *Common Ground: The Story of Greenham*, by David Fairhall (2006), tells the story of the movement's highest-profile action. Gordon Carr's history of *The Angry Brigade: The Cause and Its Case* (1975) tries to make sense of an often baffling group. The miners' strike received partisan treatment before the dust had settled, from Ian McGregor (*The Enemies Within: The Story of the Miners' Strike 1984–5*), and a more even-handed account (though more sympathetic towards the miners' side) from Martin Adeney and John Lloyd, in *The Miners' Strike, 1984–5: Loss without limit* (both published in 1986). Paul Routledge's unauthorized biography *Scargill* (1993) takes a balanced approach to its unique subject. The Poll Tax protestors are discussed in Peter Joyce's *The Politics of Protest: Extra-Parliamentary Politics in Britain since 1970* (2002), and a lively account of the events of 31 March 1990 is to be found in Ian Hernon's *Riot!: Civil Insurrection from Peterloo to the Present Day* (2006). For the newest English rebels, see *DiY Culture: Party & Protest in Nineties Britain*, edited by George McKay (1998).

376 **'an explosion against intolerable . . .':** quoted in D. S. Lewis, *Illusions of Grandeur: Mosley, Fascism and British Society 1931–81* (1987), p. 5.

377 **'discipline, effort and sacrifice':** in ibid., p. 26.

378 **'new leader of genius':** *Daily Mail*, 2 May 1934.

378 **'gross brutality . . .':** W. J. Anstruther-Gray, quoted in Ian Hernon, *Riot: Civil Insurrection from Peterloo to the Present Day* (2006), p. 165.

378 **London's Jewish population . . .:** see p. 83 (of course, London didn't have a visible Jewish population between the Jews' expulsion by Edward I in 1290 and their readmittance by Oliver Cromwell in 1656).

380 **'polite thanks for his offers of support':** quoted in Stephen Dorril, *Blackshirt: Sir Oswald Mosley and British Fascism* (2006), p. 406.

380 **'in the highest degree odious':** quoted in A. W. Brian Simpson,

In the Highest Degree Odious: Detention without Trial in Wartime Britain (1992), epigraph.

381 **'Celts, Reds and Conchies':** Angus Calder, *The Myth of the Blitz* (1991), chapter title.

382 **'prejudicing Britain's relations with its ally':** see Ray Monk, 'Russell, Bertrand Arthur William, third Earl Russell (1872–1970)', *Oxford Dictionary of National Biography* (2004).

384 **'we're beaten if we ever do it that way . . .':** Sarah Hipperson in an interview with the Imperial War Museum (http://www.iwm .org.uk/upload/package/22/greenham/Hipperson1.htm).

385 **'this pre-dated all of the socialist classics':** Tariq Ali, *Street Fighting Years* (1987; 2005), p. 201.

385 **'I told them it was a terrible idea . . .':** quoted in Martin Bright, 'Look Back in Anger', *Observer*, Sunday, 3 February 2002.

386 **'The Labour Party, the Unions and their minions . . .':** quoted in Gordon Carr, *The Angry Brigade: The Cause and the Case* (1975), p. 114.

386 **'thought he was the reincarnation of A. J. Cook':** Jimmy Reid, in Paul Routledge, *Scargill* (1983), p. 256.

387 **'the greatest day of my life . . .':** quoted in Hernon, p. 220.

387 **'Arthur Scargill drew the lesson that brute militant force . . .':** quoted in Routledge, p. 129.

389 **'was always on about . . .':** John Walsh in ibid., p. 43.

390 **On the twenty-fifth anniversary . . .:** Arthur Scargill, 'We could surrender – or stand and fight', *Guardian*, Saturday, 7 March 2009, pp. 26–7.

390 **'would counter a criticism of the rates . . .':** Christopher Warman, 'Poll tax one of five options studied as rates replacement', *The Times*, Tuesday, 20 November 1979, p. 13.

391 **'poll taxes as a means of raising revenue . . .':** Hugh Clayton, 'Poll tax could "shrink" population', *The Times*, Wednesday, 3 April 1985, p. 2.

391 **'police were going mad . . .':** Anna Goodhind, quoted in Hernon, p. 243.

393 **'there is in the Englishman a combination of qualities . . .':** Mr Podsnap in Charles Dickens, *Our Mutual Friend* (1865).

Index